REMAKING THE CHINESE LEVIATHAN

REMAKING THE CHINESE LEVIATHAN

MARKET TRANSITION *and the* POLITICS *of* GOVERNANCE *in* CHINA

Dali L. Yang

STANFORD UNIVERSITY PRESS

Stanford University Press
Stanford, California

Printed in the United States of America
on acid-free, archival-quality paper

Library of Congress Cataloging-in-Publication Data

Yang, Dali L.
    Remaking the Chinese leviathan : market transition and the politics
of governance in China / Dali L. Yang.
        p.   cm.
    Includes bibliographical references and index.
    ISBN 0-8047-5493-4 (paperback : alk. paper)
    1. China—Economic conditions—2000–   2. China—Economic
policy—2000–   I. Title.
HC427.95.Y36   2004
330.951—DC22

                                                    2003027754

Original Printing 2004

Last figure below indicates year of this printing:

13 12 11 10 09 08 07 06

For Ethel, Claudia, and Edward

ACKNOWLEDGMENTS

In writing this book I have incurred many institutional and personal debts. First and foremost my thanks and appreciation go to my wife Ling, without whom this and much else would have been impossible. At the University of Chicago, I have received financial support from the Council of Advanced Studies in Peace and International Cooperation (CASPIC), the David Greenstone Memorial Research Fund, the Committee on Chinese Studies, the Social Sciences Divisional Research Fund, and the Center for International Business Education. More importantly, the university has served as my intellectual home; a number of chapters were first presented and discussed at the University of Chicago Workshop on East Asia and the Workshop on Organizations and State Building.

A fellowship from the National Program for Advanced Research in China of the American Council of Learned Studies provided the funding for my fieldwork in 1996–97. While I have privileged written sources, these sources are supplemented by interviews on research visits I have made over a decade to Beijing, Chongqing, Guangdong, Hainan, Jiangsu, Jiangxi, Shaanxi, Shandong, Shanghai, Tianjin, and Zhejiang. I wish to express my deep gratitude to the many people who have given generously of their time and insights but, given the protocol of "human subject research," must remain anonymous. The Institute of Industrial Economics of the Chinese Academy of Social Sciences and the Department of Sociology of Qinghua University offered me a hospitable institutional environment during two different time periods.

I am enormously grateful to David Bachman, Thomas Bernstein, Marc Blecher, Dorothy Solinger, and anonymous readers for the press for reading earlier versions of the entire manuscript and offering guidance on revisions. I would also like to give my special thanks to John Brehm, Mel Gurtov, John Mark Hansen, the late D. Gale Johnson, Kenneth Lieberthal, Justin Yifu Lin, John Mearsheimer, Kevin O'Brien, John Padgett, Robert Pape, Bernard Silberman, Alfred Stepan, and Dingxin Zhao for comments and other forms of support. Over a number of years, Sam Wilkin, Ying Yu, Jieun Yoo, Daniel Young, and especially Hugo Lui provided capable and efficient research support for this project.

I am much indebted to Muriel Bell at Stanford University Press for supporting this project from inception to publication. Tim Roberts managed the publication process with care and sensitivity. Richard Steins copyedited the manuscript. I am deeply indebted to the late Professor Tang Tsou and to Dr. Yi-chuang Lu for their encouragement and friendship. Li Qiang, Barry Naughton, William Parish, Susan Shirk, Lynn White III, and Zhu Guanglei stand out for their generosity and professionalism. Sustaining me in myriad ways were a group of other friends including but certainly not limited to Cheng Tongshun, Ian Johnson, Guo Kesha, Frank Langfitt, Li Dun, Qin Hai, Shi Xiaomin, Wei Houkai, Zhang Weiying, and Zhou Xiaozheng. Yuan Bai, Mike Chu, Yanzhong Huang, Cheng Li, Fubing Su, and Xu Wang were wonderful fellow travelers.

At the University of Chicago, Dean and now Provost Richard Saller helped arrange the leave time that made it possible for me to finally wrap up this project. I wish to thank Associate Deans John MacAloon and Lois Stein for their support as I oversaw the Committee on International Relations. A number of incredible professionals have helped keep me out of trouble over the years; they are Kathy Anderson, Heidi Parker, and Mimi Walsh in the Department of Political Science, Diane New, Diana Gray and Meyosha Smiley at the Committee on International Relations, Ted Foss in the Center for East Asian Studies, and Fione Dukes and Matt Lagen at the Social Sciences Local Business Center.

Writing a book on a country in the throes of great and rapid change presents special challenges. As my project evolved and metamorphosed, I have spoken to audiences at the University of California, Berkeley, the University of Michigan, and Yale University and at Beijing, Nankai, Qinghua, Suzhou, and Xi'an Jiaotong universities in China. I wish to express my gratitude to my hosts and interlocutors for their hospitality, questions, and constructive comments. I have also presented or tested some of my arguments at the following conferences or workshops and would like to thank the organizers, discussants, and participants for stimulating discussions and insightful comments: the Workshop on Personnel Monitoring and Policy Implementation, University of California, San Diego, June 1998; the Conference on Central-Local Relations in China, Meridian International House, Department of the State, February 1999; the International Conference on PRC Reforms at Twenty, Grand Hotel, Taipei, April 1999; the International Conference on Center-Periphery Relations in China, the Chinese University of Hong Kong, March 2000; the Conference on Financial Sector Reform in China, Harvard University Kennedy School of Government, September 2001; the Conference on Modern State Structures in the Chinese World, London School of Economics and Political Science, May 2002; as well as the annual meetings of the American Political Science Association and of the Association of Asian Studies. An earlier version of Chapter 3 appeared in Barry Naughton and Dali Yang, eds., *Holding China Together: Diversity and National Integration in Post-Deng China* (Cambridge University Press, 2004).

Because of the economics of academic publishing, the length of the final manuscript is one quarter shorter than the full version. This has entailed the elimination of two chapters, one on the transformation of state-business relations and the other dealing with government reforms in the 1980s and early 1990s. Also cut are certain sections in the remaining chapters, as well as various cases and examples. In certain places I have indicated the excisions, but oftentimes I have not. Moreover, shortened forms of notes and dates are used to save space. As a result of this late "surgery," the chapters have been rearranged to provide, I hope, a sharper focus on institutional development.

CONTENTS

*A Note on Translation, Transliteration,
    Names, and Currency Exchange Rates*   *xiii*
Abbreviations   *xv*
Map of the People's Republic of China   *xvi*

1 Economic Transition and the Problem
   of Governance in China   1

2 Market Transition and the Remaking
   of the Administrative State   25

3 Institutional Development and the Quest
   for Fiscal Prowess and Market Order   65

4 The Smuggling Crisis and the Leveling
   of the Economic Playing Field   110

5 Administrative Rationalization and the Reorientation
   of Government Behavior   150

6 Market Incentives and the Disciplining
   of Government Discretion   186

7 Institutional Reforms and the Struggle
   against Corruption   217

8 Institutions of Horizontal Accountability
   and Good Governance: Legislative Oversight
   and Government Audit   259

9 Conclusions   290

Appendix: The Composition of the State Council,
    1992 and 2003   315
Abbreviations Used in Notes and Bibliography   319
Notes   323
Selected Bibliography   371
Index   395

A NOTE ON TRANSLATION, TRANSLITERATION, NAMES, AND CURRENCY EXCHANGE RATES

All translations are by the author unless otherwise noted. *Pinyin* is used for the transliteration of Chinese names and terms. With the exception of Chinese writers who published in English and presented their names in Western fashion, Chinese names appear in Chinese form, with surname preceding given name. For example, Jiang, not Zemin, is the surname of Jiang Zemin; Zhu, not Rongji, is the surname of Zhu Rongji.

For 1996–2004, one U.S. dollar was worth about 8.28 Chinese yuan (RMB).

ABBREVIATIONS

CCP	Chinese Communist Party
CDIC	Central Discipline Inspection Commission
CIRC	China Insurance Regulatory Commission
CPPCC	Chinese People's Political Consultative Conference
CSRC	China Securities Regulatory Commission
MOF	Ministry of Finance
MOFTEC	Ministry of Foreign Trade and Economic Cooperation
MPC	Municipal People's Congress
NAO	National Audit Office
NPC	National People's Congress
PBOC	People's Bank of China
PLA	People's Liberation Army
PPC	Provincial People's Congress
SARS	Severe Acute Respiratory Syndrome
SDPC	State Development Planning Commission
SDRC	State Development and Reform Commission
SETC	State Economic and Trade Commission
SOEs	State Owned Enterprises
SPC	State Planning Commission
WTO	World Trade Organization

REMAKING THE CHINESE LEVIATHAN

chapter one

ECONOMIC TRANSITION AND THE PROBLEM OF GOVERNANCE IN CHINA

[F]ree markets could never have come into being merely by allowing things to take their course. . . . *laissez-faire* itself was enforced by the state.
—Karl Polanyi

Since 1989, China's leaders have lived in the age of trial. Confronted with one crisis after another, including the Tiananmen incident of 1989, the fall of communism in Eastern Europe and the former Soviet Union in the early 1990s, the domestic economic turmoil of 1993–1994, the Asian financial and economic crisis of the late 1990s, and the SARS (Severe Acute Respiratory Syndrome) crisis of 2003, China has nonetheless persevered on the path of liberal economic reforms and enjoyed rapid economic growth. Yet the official commitment to economic liberalization has been accompanied by major uncertainties in governance. Simultaneously having to deal with the strains and disruptions of industrialization, marketization, urbanization, and globalization, the Chinese leadership has been in a marathon quest for institutional development, rationalizing existing institutions and building new ones to cope with the unruliness of markets and bring about a regulative economic order.

Contrary to prevailing predictions, China has made substantial progress in improving the institutional framework for economic governance. To anyone concerned about the welfare of the Chinese people or about the rise of China for regional and world affairs, the significance of such institutional development is obvious. A sound institutional infrastructure is vitally important for sustained economic development.[1] Moreover, a small number of political scientists have also emphasized the importance of a well-functioning administrative state for the consolidation of democracy.[2] As Joseph Schumpeter noted in his classic *Capitalism, Socialism, and Democracy*, a competent bureaucracy "is not an obstacle to democracy but an inevitable complement to it."[3] Therefore, though they are concentrated in the area of economic governance, China's governance reforms not only bear on economic growth but will also have major implications for political development.

In this study, my first task is to document the changes in Chinese governance, including the rationalization of the administrative state, the strengthening of the fiscal sinews for the central state, the enhancement of the regulatory apparatuses, the divestiture of businesses operated by the armed forces and other state institutions, the reforms of the administrative approval system and the improvement of transparency and governmental service, the ascendance of institutions for horizontal accountability, and the introduction of myriad institutional mechanisms to cut down on waste, improve financial supervision, and curb corrupt practices. To be sure, as the Chinese leadership's initial mishandling of the SARS crisis highlighted, in many respects China still falls far short of the standards of good governance demanded of democratic polities.[4] Yet I submit that, in light of the circumstances and of the conventional wisdom, the magnitude and scope of China's multifaceted governance reforms, particularly in economic governance, are quite significant and worthy of serious intellectual attention.

Second, although the Chinese leadership articulated the general goal of building a market economy as national policy in the early 1990s, many of the specific institutional reform measures for achieving that goal did not get implemented until the late 1990s and beyond. How and why did the reformist ideas get converted into policies for implementation with such a time lag? In the analytical framework adopted in this volume, I submit that the interplay of three major factors, namely changing economic conditions, internal politics/political leadership, and crises (real or perceived), have been the most important elements catalyzing the stream of policy choices to be described and analyzed.[5]

Third, this study suggests that the significance of the governance reforms as a whole may be larger than the sum of the parts. The individual reforms are generally designed to achieve certain specific goals, such as to attract more investment, to save the government money, to close loopholes in government financial management, or to cut down on smuggling. Yet together they also alter the landscape for the struggle against corruption and the exercise of governmental authority in general.

In the rest of the introductory chapter, I first present the historical setting for the study, namely the immediate efforts by the post-Tiananmen Chinese leadership to strengthen the political machinery while renewing the commitment to economic reforms. Then I note that China's partial reforms undertaken until then had forged a strong nexus between state and enterprise and survey the contrasting scholarly perspectives on that nexus. Next I draw on the general literature on the politics of reforms to see how that literature would assess the difficulties China would face to move beyond the partial reforms and build a modern market economy. Much of this literature would counsel pessimism regarding the prospects for institutional rejuvenation and transformation in China. Yet, in spite of what the literature would predict, China has undertaken myriad governance reforms to be discussed in the rest of this book. The last section provides an overview of the book's analytical framework and offers a preview of the chapters.

The Historical Context

Nineteen eighty-nine will forever be remembered as one of the bleakest years in the history of Chinese political development. A decade into the post-Mao reform era, China saw a dramatic confrontation between state and society end in bloodshed in Beijing. In a matter of hours, the worldwide exhilaration over the power of the people—built up for weeks with the aid of global television—was turned into profound disillusionment and despair by images of violence and bloodshed. The *Financial Times* of London reported that "the outlook both for economic reform and the economy are not bright." Indeed, according to the journalist, "economic reform [in China] is likely to unravel" under pressure from the hardliners in the leadership.[6] Writing for the *New York Times*, veteran journalist Fox Butterfield noted that an ad hoc coalition of conservative Communist Party elders led by Deng Xiaoping had prevailed over more liberal leaders such as General Secretary Zhao Ziyang. According to Butterfield, the purge of Zhao and others not only revealed the heavily autocratic nature of Chinese politics but also put in jeopardy the economic reforms that had given China a growth rate of 9 percent per year.[7] Soon China scholars were publishing volumes on why the Tiananmen crackdown was but a new page in China's long book of autocracy.[8]

For those who lived within China after the 1989 crackdown, it was an understatement to say that the political atmosphere was chilling. To be sure, immediately following the crackdown paramount leader Deng Xiaoping emphasized again and again that China should stay on the course of reform and opening up. Yet, as Ling Zhijun, a senior reporter for the Communist Party's *People's Daily*, noted in his diary, then Premier Li Peng and others were pursuing policies of economic stabilization (*zhili zhengdun*) at the expense of reform and opening up.[9] Deeply worried that the vicious attacks on deposed party General Secretary Zhao Ziyang might turn into an assault on the first decade of China's reforms, Ling reported that, amid the official criticism of bourgeois liberalization, many private businessmen, managers who had contracted for state-owned enterprises, as well as farmers had fears about being accused of pursuing capitalism and were concerned about becoming victims of political account settling at the top.[10] Indeed, incoming party General Secretary Jiang Zemin quickly announced that private businessmen would not be permitted to join the Communist Party. For reformers, these were the days of doom and gloom.

Strengthening Political and Military Control

Even before students went to Tiananmen Square en masse, Deng Xiaoping had harped on the overriding importance of maintaining stability and warned against the dangers of chaos. During a meeting with visiting U.S. president George Bush on February 26, 1989, Deng argued that China, in the absence of a stable environment, would not be able to achieve anything and might even lose what had been accomplished.[11] To help maintain stability and prevent chaos, Deng repeatedly called for strengthening central authority. The jitters from Tiananmen, international sanctions, and the spillover effects of the Soviet breakup further prompted China's leadership to take measures to shore up the center.

Key to the Chinese Communist Party's longevity has been its power over personnel appointments. The post-Tiananmen leadership has clung tightly to the Leninist nomenklatura system, the organizational sinew of the Communist Party. In moves reminiscent of the 1970s transition from Mao, the central leadership has used its appointive power to reshuffle provincial leaders, armed police commanders, and PLA (the People's Liberation Army) regional commanders to ensure that these officials follow the wishes of the central leadership and not become centrifugal forces.[12]

Unlike the ad hoc maneuvers of the 1970s, however, regular cadre rotations and exchanges have become institutionalized as a key ingredient of the Chinese personnel management system since the 1990s.[13] The regulations on cadre exchanges include detailed rules of avoidance and stipulate that the exchanges are targeted at cadres with promotion prospects so that they may broaden their experience.[14] Those who have worked in the same locality or department for ten years must change positions with their counterparts in other localities. Such rotations can help curb localism, strengthen central control, as well as inculcate professionalism among the elite and reduce nepotism and corruption. The results of the cadre exchange and avoidance policy are widely recognized. Between 1991 and 1999, there were 691 exchanges of cadres at the level of the provincial department deputy chief and above.[15] In 1999, for example, 21 (67.7 percent) of the party secretaries in 31 provincial units were not serving in their hometown provinces.[16] By 2002, the percentage had risen further to 82 percent even with provincial governors included.[17] In the year before and after the sixteenth National Party Congress (November 2002), the reshuffling and rotations of provincial and ministerial leaders were widely publicized.

Such periodic reshuffles and rotations clearly mark local officials as subordinates in a giant hierarchical organization, in effect, a "China Incorporated." Whereas in Russia the Communist nomenklatura system disintegrated and power fell into the hands of elected regional governors not beholden to the Kremlin, the Chinese central leadership has been able to pull the levers of the nomenklatura system to enhance hierarchical discipline and curb localist tendencies that had become prominent with the decentralizing reforms of the 1980s.[18] Such discipline has been crucial for the execution of a diverse range of major policy initiatives to be discussed in this volume, ranging from tax and fiscal reforms to the divestiture of businesses operated by the PLA, the armed police, and other state institutions.

No modern state can go without a coercive apparatus. Yet the mobilization of the regular army (the PLA) against students and other civilians in 1989 was an indication of the failure of the internal security apparatus. The use of military violence against peaceful demonstrators underscored the legitimacy crisis facing the ruling elite, hurt China's image badly, and resulted in a severe downturn in China's international relations. It also raised serious issues concerning the proper role of the armed forces in domestic politics as well as fears of military insubordination. Most foreign countries typically use the police or special antiriot police units in situations of domestic unrest. To avoid a repeat of the Tiananmen debacle of using the regular army to quell domestic unrest, the Chinese leadership quickly began to reconstitute the instrument of state surveillance and violence. It has steadily enlarged and strengthened the armed police (to more than a million troops) as well as the antiriot units of the ordinary police and expanded the domestic functions of the Ministry of State Security. In 2000, the armed police commander was formally appointed a member of the Central Comprehensive Governance and Control Committee (Zhongyang Zonghe Zhili Weiyuanhui), the oversight group in charge of crime fighting and social stability.[19]

Finally, the central leadership has used efforts to curb corruption as a powerful whip to wield above the heads of officials. Chen Xitong, the powerful party boss of Beijing, for example, was put in jail for corruption. Since 1998, the national-level anticorruption bureau, the Ministry of Supervision, and the Party Central Committee's Central Discipline Inspection Commission have been actively involved in detaining "big tigers" in the provinces.[20] In Chapter 7 I shall return to the issue of organizational control in anticorruption.

Renewing the Commitment to Economic Reforms: Changing the Paradigm

Sadly, the Tiananmen confrontation derailed serious initiatives to reform the political system from above.[21] Nevertheless, the efforts by the post-Tiananmen Chinese leadership to beef up organizational discipline and fortify its means of coercion went hand in hand with renewed commitment to economic reforms. For Deng Xiaoping, political stability, particularly the continuity of Communist Party leadership, was a necessary condition for further economic reforms. Deng clearly recognized that the promotion of economic development through further economic reforms would be essential if the ruling elite were to regain the sort of performance legitimacy it had acquired in the 1980s. In many ways, Deng followed in the footsteps of his East Asian authoritarian predecessors in South Korea, Taiwan, and even Singapore and hoped that authoritarianism coupled with reform and development would provide the recipe for keeping the Communist Party in power.

Thus even as Deng led the patriarchs to oust the liberal-minded party General Secretary Zhao Ziyang and crack down on the student demonstrators, he was careful to reiterate his commitment to economic reforms.[22] When reforms appeared to stall under Jiang Zemin, Deng made a celebrated tour to southern China in early 1992 to stoke the fires of bold reforms and innovation. In his remarks on the tour, Deng stated that the criterion for judging reforms should go beyond capitalism and socialism. Whether foreign investment or the market in general should be protected in China depended on whether these and other institutions or organizations are conducive to the development of productive forces, the enhancement of national strength, and the improvement of people's living standards. For Deng, socialism, like capitalism, can have both plan and market.[23]

Prompted and emboldened by Deng, Jiang Zemin and his colleagues put reform back on the agenda and contemplated the construction of a new economic order.[24] Speaking at the Central Party School in spring 1992, Jiang noted that the limited introduction of the market had enlivened and energized the Chinese economy. For Jiang, while the state would continue to play an important role in the economy, market competition would provide the incentives for firms to improve their performance, and a well-functioning market mechanism would be indispensable to the development of the socialist economy. While Jiang said that there was no rush to end the raging debate on the proper role of the market in a socialist economy, he nevertheless stated that more and more people in socialist countries had come to recognize and appreciate the virtues of the market.[25] He argued further that "it is baseless and incorrect for some people to worry that a larger role for the market would mean going capitalist." The thirteenth Party Congress, held in 1987, had called for China to build a "socialist planned commodity economy (*shehui zhuyi jihua shangpin jingji*)," a self-contradictory phrasing that caused much headache for those who had to explain the term to ordinary people and foreign visitors. Jiang now proposed the term "socialist market economy (*shehui zhuyi shichang jingji*)."[26] The change in terminology was duly endorsed at the fourteenth Party Congress in October 1992. Though seemingly innocuous, this terminological shift to "market economy" with "socialist" as the adjective was profound; it marked the first time in history a ruling Communist Party in a socialist state had decided to embrace the market.[27]

The comprehensive economic reform platform Jiang outlined in 1992 marked China's move away from Hayekian experimentalism to Polanyian programmatic reform. For much of the 1980s Chinese reforms proceeded in an ad hoc manner under the nonstrategy of "groping for stones to cross the river."[28] For both ideological and other reasons, China's leaders were neither sure about how deep and treacherous the river was nor clear about where they wanted to land on the other side. Now Jiang and his colleagues clearly saw themselves as playing the leading role in recasting China's economic institutions. Specifically, Jiang's Central Party School speech outlined key aspects of China's market transition. The government would transform its functions such that it would desist from micromanaging firms and focus on providing macroeconomic control through economic levers. The state would "vigorously nurture and develop the market and build a unified and complete socialist market." This called for the state to improve and enforce regulations for a well-functioning market while promoting trade in products as well as stocks, bonds, technology, labor, information, and real estate. Major efforts should be made to improve the infrastructure, including both hardware (telecommunications, computer networks, banks, transportation) and software (accounting, auditing, statistics, taxation), in order to ensure economic order.[29] Rather than continuing to serve as administrative appendages of the government bureaucracy, state enterprises would become market-oriented.

Partial Reforms and the State-Enterprise Nexus

Jiang's proposal for a "socialist" market economy was overdue. After more than a decade of reforms, the supply of most farm and consumer products had become plentiful. As a result, as the next chapter will note, planners were able to remove price controls on most products and allow the formation of product markets without engendering the sort of hyperinflation that characterized the shock therapy administered to most former planned economies. Nevertheless, from the perspective of reform history, the formation of product markets was only the beginning of the long march to a market economy.

Historically, the development of modern market economies in different countries has pushed states to "develop rules about property rights, governance structures, rules of exchange, and conceptions of control in order to stabilize markets."[30] In the United States, the historian Robert H. Wiebe famously noted, the march of nationalization, industrialization, mechanization, and urbanization exerted enormous strains on the ethos and institutions of small-town America and prompted a search for order.[31]

The state that was forged in the Civil War became inadequate to the push and pull of industrialism, and "a qualitatively different kind of state" was built in the late nineteenth and early twentieth centuries during what is now known as the Progressive Era.[32] Civil service reforms were introduced to curb the corrupt localism and particularism of patronage politics; a managerial and regulatory state arose to tackle problems ranging from poor public health to monopolies. Echoes of the Progressive Era political struggles and negotiations over the shape of this regulatory state continue to be heard in today's United States, often magnified in episodes such as the collapse of Enron and Worldcom.[33]

In contrast to the "leisurely" pace of development that the early industrializers enjoyed, many underdeveloped countries with per capita income levels similar to China's suffer from the lack of a state capable of the basic tasks of governance, and some of these countries remain afflicted by civil war or are otherwise known as failed states.[34] In China, the post-Mao reformers inherited a modernizing state that was wrought on the anvil of the Chinese civil war and the purgatory of Maoist rule. It was this state that had, under Mao's leadership, ruthlessly pursued land reform, collectivization, and forced-draft industrialization while suppressing popular demands for consumption, thus lending support to theories of late development that gave center place to the role of a strong state.[35] Even though ruinous Maoist policies such as the Great Leap Forward and the Cultural Revolution did much to weaken the bureaucracy, post-Mao China inherited a substantial Leninist state apparatus bent on modernization. In Huntingtonian terms, the post-Mao Chinese state started with plenty of organizational resources and mobilization capacity.

Yet the reformation of socialist economies led by Leninist parties presents special challenges. In these economies the state, partly through the central planning apparatus, became omnipresent and largely abolished market-based exchanges.[36] Rather than building state capacity to take care of the markets, the daunting task of market reforms in socialist economies not only involves the introduction of markets but also the rebuilding of the state into one that is qualitatively different and suited to markets. Simply put, market reforms cannot succeed without the reconfiguration of the socialist state. It is necessary to get the omnipresent state to retreat in some areas of the economy, to change its behavior in others, and yet to build and rebuild the institutions and capacity to govern markets and provide various forms of public goods. The making of markets must go hand in hand with the remaking of the state. Whereas previously liberal international institutions such as the World Bank were strong advocates for the downsizing of government and of generally reducing the role of the state, even these institutions have come to appreciate the importance of building effective states by the late 1990s.[37]

Though China has enjoyed rapid economic growth, until the late 1990s the Chinese leadership had far less success in transforming the functions of government and the nature of the Chinese state in general. As is well known in studies of China and discussed in the following chapter, it was the government at different levels and in various guises that eagerly pursued investment opportunities in the 1980s and sought to protect their investment interests. The dual-track reforms not only entailed the continuation (albeit gradual shrinkage as a percentage of total economic activities) of the plan but also meant the persistence of bargaining relationships between state (as well as collective) enterprises and their bureaucratic superiors. These relationships were ones of mutual dependence.[38] The enterprises counted on their superior government agencies for supply of energy and raw materials at subsidized prices, assistance with access to capital (bank credit and grants), protection from encroachment (including encroachment by other state agencies), favorable treatment in regulatory enforcement (environment, quality, and so on), and various forms of preferential treatment (such as tax and interest exemptions or steering projects their way). In return, the enterprises furnished their bureaucratic superiors with revenue (both in-budget and extra-budget as well as other forms of income), employment (which often served as a patronage benefit), and products for the plan. As a result, economic reform and administrative reform were caught in a classic chicken-and-egg situation. As long as the government supplanted the market, state enterprises would do well to seek a bureaucratic umbrella.[39] Yet the remaking of the administrative state stalled, because the webs of relationships engendered demands for administrative protection, coordination, and decision.[40] The bilateral interdependence amid partial reforms provided fertile soil for government expansion during an era of rapid economic growth. Between 1978 and 1995, Chinese state revenue grew by 5.1 times while administrative expenses in state expenditure expanded by 17.8 fold.[41] Most ominously, government administrative expenditure as a percentage of total government expenditure rose from only about 5 percent in the mid-1970s to nearly 15 percent by the mid-1990s.

Contrasting Perspectives on the
State-Business Nexus

There have been two opposite views of the growing state-business
nexus in reformist China. One account, which I shall call the "developmental school," sees the strong state involvement in China as a crucial ingredient of economic success. On this account, the Chinese state has become developmental, just like its counterparts in China's neighboring
economies (at least prior to the Asian financial crisis). Under the decentralizing reforms, local governments in China ranging from villages to
provinces to central government ministries have taken the mantra of development to heart and become deeply engaged in bureaucratic, government, or state entrepreneurship. They have not only forged alliances with
business but have frequently been the investors themselves.[42] The bonds
between government and business thus lead China to a sort of corporatist
arrangement that some have called socialist corporatism and, in the case of
local governments, local state corporatism.[43] The high growth rates became
the justification for existing institutional practices. Some economists developed theories to prove that local government ownership in China
helped curb state predation, increase local public goods provision, and reduce costly revenue hiding.[44] Others even suggested that the rapid growth
of the collectivist township and village enterprises (TVEs) challenged standard property rights theory. Li, for example, argued that in China's imma-
ture market environment, the ambiguous property rights of the TVEs are
often more efficient than unambiguously defined private property rights.[45]

While the developmental school has generally emphasized the positive role of state, particularly local state, involvement in the economy and
downplayed the predatory aspects of state entrepreneurship, the alternative
account, here to be known as the "distorted market school," has tended to
look beyond the temporary benefits of state involvement and highlight the
market-distorting aspects of state entrepreneurship and the obstacles it
poses to further market-oriented reforms.[46]At the turn of the 1990s, the
World Bank noted that China's post-Mao reforms were caught between
plan and market.[47] Various other studies pointed to the problematic nature
of the rampant government involvement in the economy. In the words of
Susan Shirk, "while local officials draped themselves in the mantle of market reform, what they meant by reform was, in fact, the perpetuation of the
hybrid, partially reformed system, not a genuine market economy. They

preferred to maintain their quasi-ownership rights over local factories and to exploit these rights to collect rents for themselves rather than playing only the role of referee in market competition."[48] In the absence of adequate mechanisms for fostering and policing the internal common market, "many local governments have focused on trade barriers and aggressive anti-market policies within their jurisdiction."[49] The result, some commentators pointed out, was the worst of both worlds: local protectionism such as regional blockades, market segmentation,[50] and "continuing bureaucratic management of industry."[51] Simply put, "bureaucratic entrepreneurialism in China has become the main obstacle to the market economy the nation wants to build."[52]

A number of economists/commentators based in China, notably He Qinglian and Yang Fan, have been especially outspoken about the dangers of state agents combining with businesses and even organized crime at a time of sharply rising income inequalities.[53] The union between officialdom (*guan*) and business (*shang*), they argue, has not only become the hotbed of corruption and self-aggrandizement but also provided a powerful rent-seeking block against reforms.[54] In an article published in *China Reform News,* Zhong Guoxing wrote apocalyptically that the combination of markets and corruption would lead to economic retardation, distortions, bubbles, and social unrest.[55] Against the background of the Asian financial crisis and the fall of corrupt leaders such as Indonesia's Suharto, scholars based in the West have become especially sensitive to the predatory aspects of China's "developmental state." For example, Xiaobo Lü notes that China has evolved into a sort of "booty socialism" in which "[b]ureaucratic discipline is low, while policy implementation and rule enforcement remain problematic."[56] The articulation of such an undisciplined state apparatus has made it more difficult to promote fair competition within China and make the Chinese economy truly competitive in the world.

Indeed, as will be discussed later, for the 1980s and much of the 1990s it was not just government departments that engaged in business dealings. The military, the police, and the courts, indeed, just about any party and state agency that could convert its power, assets, and privileges into lucre, were running business operations and aggrandizing themselves. Not only did efforts to streamline the government stall, but the flouting of political power and privilege also easily translated into the flouting of the rules. Local governments competed to offer preferential treatment to attract overseas investors and strong-armed state banks to make loans to indigenous firms. Officials in state agencies racked their brains to collect fees and levies. Judges, accountants, and others were at the beck and call of the rich and powerful. Corruption became rampant. Some major government agencies, notably the Customs Administration, became captured by organized crime in some localities. Some local governments, including the major cities of Shenyang and Xiamen, also came under the sway of criminal elements.

To be sure, the Chinese economy has enjoyed rapid growth rates. Some scholars have even suggested that corruption helped to soften cadre resistance to market reforms, serving "the function of delaying political while permitting economic reform."[57] Yet the capture and appropriation of the state by the diverse agency interests could well settle into some sort of equilibrium state. This means, if we follow Max Weber, that further rationalization of the state structure away from this state of capture would be extraordinarily difficult.[58] It is thus by no means clear that the world's most populous country could navigate itself out of the turbulent shoals of corruption and unfair competition. In field interviews, many interviewees expressed indignation at the corruption that was eating away the moral fiber of the Chinese state and society and asked whether China was becoming just like the kleptocracies commonly found among countries with China's level of economic development. Some scholars have come to similar conclusions. At the beginning of the 1990s, Hilton Root suggested that corruption in China was becoming systemic.[59] By the late 1990s, scholars placed China right in the league of countries such as the Philippines and Indonesia. According to X. Lü, the entrenchment of bureaucrats as moneymakers makes it likely that "the Chinese bureaucracy will remain neotraditional, nurtured by a 'booty capitalism'—a fragmented but administratively managed market economy—similar to what exists in India today."[60] All in all, whether in making investments themselves or in regulating businesses, the conventional wisdom is that agents of the Chinese state tend to exercise power arbitrarily, often in search of rents individually or institutionally. Harking back to Vivienne Shue's *The Reach of the State*, Lü asserted that "the cellularization and feudalization that existed even before the reform have been exacerbated."[61]

Comparative Politics and the Challenge
of State Remaking

For all the achievements China has made in introducing the market, has Chinese governance, as the studies by Root, Lü, and many others suggest, become stuck in a sort of undesirable institutional equilibrium that includes heavy doses of corruption, patrimonialism, and the arbitrary exercise of power? We might gain some perspective on this question by looking at the historical experiences of economic reforms in Eastern Europe and the former Soviet Union. Here, however, even a cursory review does not inspire confidence in the prospects for completing China's partial reforms and transforming the Chinese state.

It is well known that these countries stayed on the treadmill of reforms for long periods before the political collapse of the ruling regimes. The "big bang" reforms unleashed in these countries in the 1990s seemed to promise more shock than therapy.[62] Indeed, with plummeting economic outputs and declining social indicators, the big bang reforms launched with fanfare appeared to be stuck in the middle, caught between the certainties of central planning and the dynamism of capitalist markets but unable to offer either.

For Stephen Holmes, Russia's problems of governability stemmed from the debility of the state.[63] Yeltsin's policy choices further aggravated rather than alleviated the problems of market reforms. Others have paid special attention to the interaction between state and social groups. For Aslund, the economic transition in the countries of the former Soviet bloc was about the struggle between radical reformers and rent-seekers. Market reforms and democracy cannot thrive where the monstrosity of state apparatuses lived on corruption and was not tamed.[64] Indeed, the reforms have often produced interests that become obstacles to further reforms. In his study of reforms in Eastern Europe, for instance, Hellman found that the strongest opposition to further reform came not from the temporary victims of reforms but from the early winners.[65] Groups that benefit from the early distortions of a partially reformed economy seek to maintain the partial reforms at the expense of the public good. The completion of the reform programs thus required the restraining of the early winners rather than the marginalization of the losers. In consequence, Hellman concludes, political systems that are more inclusive of the losers have been able to adopt and sustain more comprehensive economic reforms than states insulated from popular pressures.

Though Aslund, Hellman, Holmes, and others focused on Eastern Europe and Russia, their studies complement the findings of Root, Lü, and other China analysts. These comparative studies are again suggestive of the daunting political challenges for China's leaders to sustain the reform momentum. On the one hand, compared with the ruling regimes in Eastern Europe and Russia, the nondemocratic Chinese government was easily the most insulated from popular pressures. Yet the crackdown of 1989 was hardly an indicator of the Chinese ruling elite's political strength. Partly triggered by discontent with inflation and corruption, especially corruption in the form of official profiteering made possible by reformist policies such as dual pricing, the dramatic state-society confrontation in 1989 was a clear sign of a legitimacy crisis. The resort to violence contributed to the further loss of legitimacy and persuaded many commentators ranging from dissidents such as Liu Binyan to academic scholars such as Jack Goldstone to predict regime collapse and China's disintegration.[66] Efforts by the Chinese leadership to downsize and streamline the administrative state in the 1980s had produced mixed results at best. The Chinese state at the start of the 1990s was still far from the sort that would be deemed to be suited to a modern market economy. Indeed, the very fiscal foundations of the Chinese state were considered to be on shaky ground; scholars such as Wang Shaoguang and Hu Angang warned in the early 1990s that failure to boost revenue extraction would doom the Chinese state.[67]

From the perspective of the politics of promoting market reforms, Jiang Zemin was catapulted to the top posts at an especially ominous moment in history. For the first decade or so of China's reforms, the Chinese leadership under Deng Xiaoping took care to placate and compensate potential losers in introducing virtually every major reform policy.[68] At the same time, Chinese officials in all levels of government eagerly participated in industrial and commercial development by making new investments and building firms ranging from central government conglomerates such as CITIC (China International Trust and Investment Corporation) to township and village enterprises. The massive investments not only helped prop up China's economic growth rates but also created powerful interests that profited from incomplete markets, faulty regulations, and political discretion. Indeed, as the referees and guardians also turned game players, corruption became rife. The existence of powerful entrenched interests in the economy, many of which, such as the armed forces and the judicial institutions, enjoyed special privileges that violated the rules of fairness, makes it evident that a fair and competitive market environment will not emerge spontaneously in China. Besides invoking claims that the conditions are not yet ripe for further reforms, these interests tend to be well organized and can marshal enormous financial and political resources to protect themselves. "[F]ree markets," as Karl Polanyi noted with respect to Europe, "could never have come into being merely by allowing things to take their course."[69]

Anyone who hopes for China to tame corruption and improve governance must therefore begin with questions such as these. How can the Chinese government become a modern regulator if its departments simultaneously own many of the businesses subject to their own regulation? How can we expect the Chinese state to regulate, adjudicate, and police the markets fairly if the government regulators cannot discipline businesses operated by the military, the armed police, and other agents of the state? Can we reasonably expect China's one-party rule to effectively discipline the state, reshape the ethos of government, and offer a level playing field for economic development if the party itself and other institutions are busy with the business of business? Simply put, can the Chinese state remake itself into a regulatory state, offering sound laws and regulations and enforcing them in a reasonably impartial manner?

Seen from the vantage point of the early 1990s, it was not simply the existing distribution of institutional interests that appeared to be arrayed against continuing reforms. At the same time, leaders such as Jiang were handpicked by the elders and lacked mandates of their own that would help them overcome the vested interests. Indeed, Jiang Zemin was then almost universally seen as a transitional and even transitory figure. To say the least, every Chinese leader at the turn of the 1990s must have remembered well that two Communist Party general secretaries had lost their posts in the latter half of the 1980s for pursuing relatively more liberal policies.[70] In this context, it was no surprise that, for more than two years after he went to Beijing, Jiang plotted his moves carefully and avoided making bold and hasty policy splashes.[71] Even after announcing the goal of building a market economy at the prompting of Deng, Jiang and his colleagues would for several years to come continue to placate existing interest groups and tolerate the business operations of the military, the armed police, and other government and party institutions. Meanwhile, Deng Xiaoping's failing health meant that his celebrated southern tour to reignite reforms in 1992 was his swan song (though Deng had the wisdom to bring Zhu Rongji into the State Council to manage the economy in the previous year).

All in all, Jiang's 1992 call for building a socialist market economy in China and later pronouncements by China's leaders indicate that the leaders clearly saw the need to remake the Chinese state and the nature of economic governance, level the economic playing field, and reshape the relationship between state and business. Yet it was one thing to present a goal for reform; it was quite another to achieve it. Given the existence of powerful vested interests in favor of the status quo, the relatively weak leadership, and in light of international experiences as well as a hostile international environment, there was much to argue for a repeat of the pessimistic scenario in Chinese history that is captured in a common refrain: Those who reform will come to no good end.

Toward an Analytical Framework: Economic Transition and the Politics of Governance Reforms

Based on an analysis of a vast amount of published materials from China as well as extensive field interviews, this volume suggests, however, that the pessimistic scenario has so far turned out to be untrue.[72] Instead, the Chinese leadership has by the beginning of the new century achieved remarkable progress in streamlining and downsizing the government, divesting the state institutions of their business operations, and generally remaking the relations between state and business and leveling the economic playing field. Alongside these changes, the Chinese leadership has also strengthened the fiscal and regulatory sinews of economic governance as well as introduced major public management reforms designed to discipline the behavior of bureaucrats, create a fairer and more transparent economic environment, and curb corruption. At the same time, a variety of institutions of horizontal accountability has either grown in importance or been created, helping to impose certain restraints on government, lock in reforms that have occurred, and provide incentives for further institutional refinements. To be sure, in various respects the institutional innovations and renovations still reflect the fact that China is a developing country with a nominal per capita GDP of around $1,000 (as of 2003). Yet, though much remains to be done, there has been a tectonic shift in the way the Chinese government conducts itself, signified by the transparency requirements that China's membership in the World Trade Organization demands. Taken together, the evidence suggests that, against conventional prognostications and allowing for substantial—both good and bad—regional variations, China has made real progress toward making the Chinese state into a regulatory state suited to a functioning market economy.

How and why did these changes happen? Take the case of the government reforms: why did they stall in the 1980s and early 1990s and pick up speed in the late 1990s? Likewise, Chinese leaders had earlier called for the army and other state institutions to refrain from engaging in businesses, yet why did the divestiture not happen until the end of the 1990s? Similarly, why did governments at different levels eagerly take up businesses in the 1980s and yet give them up in the late 1990s? What accounts for the change in anticorruption strategies and the introduction of sweeping public management reforms beginning in the late 1990s? These and other contrasts present interesting theoretical puzzles that are also of much political importance.

To facilitate our understanding of the political dynamics of reform making, the many reforms documented in this volume are presented and discussed in an analytical framework stressing three major factors: the changing economic conditions; the importance of leadership and the rhythm of domestic politics; and the role of crises as catalyzing events for politicians to adopt certain reforms.

China's reforms have partaken of a global trend toward liberalized markets. Yet China's course of development, responding to both domestic and international stimuli, has not been a linear one. The dynamics of China's economic reforms at first provided incentives for government authorities to strengthen their ties to existing enterprises and to make new investments. But the progression of market competition then ushered in such transformations in economic conditions—notably growing state-sector losses—that the strong bonds between state institutions and enterprises began to weaken, making it easier for political entrepreneurs to reshape the state-business relationship, get state institutions out of the business of doing business, and restructure government institutions. The sorry condition of the state sector has also increased demands for social outlays such as unemployment benefits, dented the government's fiscal health, and offered fertile soil for public discontent. In response, the central government has sought to increase revenue by strengthening its tax collection apparatus and cracking down on smuggling and other forms of tax evasion and by auctioning off land-use rights. It has also provided incentives for the introduction of institutional mechanisms for saving money, reducing waste, and enhancing financial supervision (government procurement reforms, project bidding and tendering, budget and management reforms). In short, the progression of market reforms created both the demand for new institutions to sustain the emerging markets and the environmental conditions that made it easier for national leaders, often borrowing from the practices found in developed market economies including the United States and Japan, to adopt initiatives for institutional restructuring and state rebuilding.

The changing conditions of the economy have helped provide a more hospitable environment for the reforms, but political action is needed to demolish, reshape, and build or refurbish institutions. Yet the degree of the Chinese leadership's political commitment to reforms has varied with time and circumstance. For the period covered in this volume (1989– 2003), a small number of people from the same age cohort were in charge of national policies. Jiang Zemin served as Communist Party general secretary until November 2002, though for the first few years of his job he was under the shadow of Deng Xiaoping (who passed away in early 1997) and focused on consolidating his political position. Li Peng was premier of the State Council until March 1998 (acting premier, November 1987; first term 1988–1993; second term 1993–1998) and then moved on to become chairman of the National People's Congress. He was succeeded as premier by Zhu Rongji (1998–2003), who was first made a vice premier in the spring of 1991 with Deng Xiaoping's strong backing. In late 2002 and early 2003, Hu Jintao succeeded Jiang as general secretary and state president. Wen Jiabo took over the premiership.

Scholars of China have long observed certain cycles in Chinese politics and economy.[73] For the period covered in this volume, major administrative and economic reforms were launched at the start of a new State Council administration following on the heels of a national congress of the Communist Party: 1993, the start of Li Peng's second term; 1998, the start of Zhu Rongji's term; and 2003, the start of Wen Jiabao's term. Zhu, as is well known, is by leaps and bounds the more hard-charging reformer compared with Li. In 1993, for example, Vice Premier Zhu, with the backing of Jiang, pushed hard to implement important tax and fiscal reforms while Li pulled his punches in streamlining the central government bureaucracy. When Zhu finally became premier in 1998, he quickly wielded his heavy axe to cut the size of the bureaucracy. Though the SARS crisis is likely to speed up reforms in certain areas, the 2003 administrative rationalization program is very much a continuation and refinement of the 1998 program.

Politicians do not make policy choices in a vacuum, however. Implementation of practically every one of the major reform initiatives documented in the volume requires that substantial vested interests are overcome or neutralized. Retention of the Leninist organizational structure has given China's leaders much leverage, but they still must work with a finite amount of political capital, economic resources, and personal energy and must therefore focus on those reforms that are feasible or those that demand immediate and urgent attention. In this aspect, both domestic and international crises, real or imagined, have served as key events to grab the attention of China's leadership.

There has been a long-standing scholarly concern about how crisis has affected political development.[74] Higgs, in particular, has emphasized that the American government grew in response to real or imagined national emergencies.[75] More generally, social scientists from a variety of disciplines have paid attention to the role of crises in focusing attention, altering existing balances of power, and reshaping institutions.[76] Internally, the Tiananmen crisis initially led to the stalling and even regression of certain reforms while the post-Tiananmen leadership, centered on the newly installed Jiang, concentrated their attention on political control and economic stabilization. Fear of the political repercussions from Deng's death provided impetus for Jiang and his colleagues to put the house in order. Inflation and fiscal weaknesses helped convince the central leadership to shore up the fiscal foundations for the central state and undertake important financial reforms. Meanwhile, external factors have had significant and even decisive influence on the making of reform policies. The collapse of Communism and the disintegration of the former Soviet Union were another major factor behind the Chinese leadership's aggressive pursuit of fiscal reforms, the ideas for which had already existed prior to the Tiananmen crisis. Similarly, the ferocity of the Asian financial crisis and the fall of governments from Indonesia to South Korea were striking negative examples that stimulated the Chinese leadership to restructure the central banking system and the financial system in general, strengthen other governance mechanisms, and seek to curb corruption through institutional reforms. At the same time, the currency realignments during the Asian financial crisis severely exacerbated China's smuggling problem and caused the Chinese leadership to take drastic measures and led to the long-awaited divestiture of businesses operated by the armed forces and other state institutions as well as major reforms of the Customs Administration.

In short, while Jiang articulated a vision for a market economy in 1992, the construction of the institutions for a market economy has not followed a carefully scripted blueprint. Instead, pieces of the construction were put into place through political struggles for order. There were palpable and indeed severe tensions, whether in reforming the fiscal and tax system or getting state institutions, particularly the People's Liberation Army, to divest their commercial operations. These were not times for muddling through or "crossing the river by feeling the stones" but moments for leadership, creativity, and decisive political action, spiced as they were with Machiavellian machinations. *Within an authoritarian political framework and amid changing economic conditions, it has required political leadership, often responding to crises, real or perceived, to remake the Chinese state.* Once the basic building blocks of the institutional infrastructure for the market economy are in place, the age of tinkering has arrived.

Preview

The rest of this volume is organized as follows. Chapter 2 begins with the puzzle that, in spite of the early commitment by Deng Xiaoping to government downsizing, it was not until well into the 1990s that significant progress was made in cutting the size of government and reorienting government functions. While leadership was important, I contend that that the crucial variable for understanding the vicissitudes of government reforms is the one that was already alluded to in the discussion on state-enterprise relations. Partial reforms did not just beget strong state-enterprise ties but also big government. In contrast, the arrival of buyer's markets eroded state enterprise profits and provided incentives for governments to reduce their liability in the state sector and remake the government in line with changing economic circumstances. The rest of the chapter examines the 1998 and 2003 government restructuring programs; the main focus is on the implementation of the 1998 government downsizing program at the

State Council and in the localities, with special attention to the reform of the *shiye danwei* (see below).

The downsizing is merely one aspect of any program to reform the government. Of perhaps more importance is the need to build new institutions more suited to the markets. As the venerable Herbert Simon reminded us: "The introduction of markets without the coincident introduction of socially enforced rules of the game for their operation and the simultaneous creation of viable and effectively managed organizations cannot create a productive economic system."[77] More specifically, modern economies rely on the state to supply various public goods, including sound monetary policy and law enforcement. The first decade of China's post-Mao reforms was characterized by decentralization in many spheres of government affairs. In the 1990s, the pendulum began to swing back, not toward central planning, but toward a sort of strong central authority as the post-Tiananmen leadership sought to balance local initiative with central authority.

Chapter 3 provides an organizational perspective on this turn toward central control through vertical integration of different aspects of state organization. Among the institutional restructuring efforts are fiscal and taxation reforms, the reconfiguration of the regulatory systems for banks, securities markets, and insurance, as well as the revamping of regulatory agencies concerning environmental protection, food and drug production and distribution, quality and technical supervision, coal mine and maritime safety, and others. Taken together, these reforms represent major steps to strengthen the central government's fiscal prowess and provide the foundations for a modern regulatory state.

Several crises have provided major impetus for political leaders to bite the bullets and accelerate long-desired reform measures. This is clear in the events discussed in Chapter 4, namely the smuggling crisis of 1998 and the subsequent divestiture of businesses operated by the military, the armed police, judicial institutions, as well as party and government offices. While the chapter focuses its attention on the smuggling crisis as the precipitating cause of the divestiture, it also pays attention to longer-term economic factors that provided the incentives for state institutions to accept the final divestiture decision. The success of the divestiture is crucial to the goal of promoting a level economic playing field for all economic actors. In fact the divestiture contributed to the effort to establish an arm's-length regulatory framework for businesses and has been followed by an important program to rationalize the professions.

The divestiture is a major development that speaks to the delimitation of governmental behavior. In fact, with the passage of time and with the impetus provided by China's entry into the WTO, reformers have put together a relatively coherent program to curb bureaucratic excesses. In Chapter 5, we discuss initiatives to reform the administrative approval program, improve government transparency, and make government agencies more service-oriented. Chapter 5 also offers an overall assessment of the effectiveness of the government reforms.

The fight against smuggling, the divestiture, as well as the government reforms all contribute to the struggle against corruption. Despite these measures and the fact that China easily leads the world in the number of corrupt officials executed and jailed, it is conventional wisdom that China is plagued by rampant corruption. Yet, it can be said that all talk of improving governance would be empty if no progress is made in fighting graft. Chapters 6 and 7 tackle the issue of corruption head-on. Chapter 6 documents the institutional reforms in several areas noted for rampant corruption, including government procurement, the management of government-funded construction projects, the allocation of land-use rights, and the process for listing securities on stock markets. The introduction of relatively standardized processes for competitive tendering and bidding, auctions, as well as the abolition of stock listing quotas appears to have helped improve the transparency and fairness of the bureaucratic processes and, if properly enforced, should help rein in corruption in these areas.

Chapter 7 takes a broader look at the evolution of China's anticorruption strategies. We find that, in line with the recommendations in the literature on anticorruption, the Chinese leadership has since the latter half of the 1990s increasingly turned to the adoption of institutional mechanisms to prevent corruption from occurring in the first place. Some of these mechanisms are documented in Chapter 6, and earlier chapters also included initiatives—for example, the reform of the administrative approval system—that bear a direct relationship to corruption. Chapter 7 describes a variety of others, including initiatives to strengthen official accountability and reshape the incentives for official behavior, the introduction of financial reforms such as the use of real names for bank accounts and the imposition of financial audits on officials, as well as comprehensive reforms of government accounting, budgeting, and financial management practices. Taking into consideration these reforms as well as those discussed earlier, this chapter assesses whether China has constructed an institutional framework for disciplining the behavior of officials and civil servants in areas of economic governance. It also draws on the results from various surveys to offer an interim assessment of the impact of these institutional reforms on corruption fighting.

In Chapter 8, we move to the issue of horizontal accountability by looking at the role of people's congresses, particularly the National People's Congress, and of the National Audit Office. The ascendance of these institutions, together with reforms within the bureaucracies, promises to help to lock in the improvements in governance.

Finally, the concluding chapter provides a quick retrospective view of some of the major themes covered and draws on the historical experiences of the United States and contemporary Russia to shed light on China's political development. Moreover, by pulling the multifaceted institutional reforms together, the chapter points to the thickening web of constraints on governmental power at a time when the Chinese press as well as various political leaders have paid more than lip service to the concept of "limited government."[78] It ends with some reflections on the real and potential implications of China's governance reforms.

chapter two

MARKET TRANSITION AND THE REMAKING
OF THE ADMINISTRATIVE STATE

Ever since the post-Mao reforms started in the late 1970s, the Chinese reform discourse has included persistent criticism of excessive government interference in enterprise management and demands for government streamlining and downsizing. Yet even a cursory review of China's reform trajectory reveals that, some local successes notwithstanding, the reforms of state enterprises and of the government had been disappointing well over a decade into the reform era. Instead, during the first decade or so of China's reforms, the state-business nexus became stronger in many respects, and the size of government steadily expanded. Repeated efforts to streamline and downsize the government have failed to reduce government payroll.

In the late 1990s, however, the pace of government reforms, measured in terms of downsizing and change in government functions, picked up noticeably. In spring 1998, the incoming Zhu Rongji administration began a major program of government rationalization. By mid-2002, this rationalization program had trimmed authorized staff size in all party, government, and government-sponsored mass organizations by 1.15 million (including 890,000 at the municipal, county, and township levels). In addition, local government at the municipal, county, and township levels also laid off 430,000 employees not on the authorized staff list (*chaobian renyuan*).[1] As Zhu retired from the premiership in spring 2003, his successor, Wen Jiabao, followed up with another government rationalization program. As a consequence of these reforms, the bureaucratic lineup, as far as the institutions for economic governance are concerned, has undergone a major metamorphosis (see Appendix on the composition of the State Council).

Why did the attempted government reforms produce few results in the 1980s but proceed rapidly since the late 1990s? How have the reforms in the late 1990s been carried out? How has the nature of the Chinese government changed with these programs to downsize and streamline? This chapter first examines the causes for the acceleration of government reforms in the late 1990s. This is followed by a description and analysis of the 1998 government restructuring and how this reform program was implemented at the central government level. Next we look at the reforms in the provinces and also pay attention to the reform of the *shiye danwei*, the myriad government-funded, not-for-profit organizations and institutions, before assessing the costs and benefits of the 1998 reform program as a whole. Finally we go over the government reorganization program of 2003.

Economic Incentives, Political Leadership, and Government Restructuring

Before we examine the details of the government reforms, it is useful to briefly discuss how the major shifts in China's market revolution paved the way for the rationalization of government and affected the pace of government reforms. I suggest that the logic behind the evolution and transformation of state-enterprise relations also helps illuminate the vicissitudes of government reforms over time.

Partial Reforms and the Rationalizing Treadmill

Space limitations do not permit me to elaborate on the dynamics of state-enterprise relations during the first decade of the reforms. Studies of China's reforms have rightfully pointed to the political and economic significance of decentralization from the central to local governments and state-owned enterprises. While local governments were the administrative units of the central government in the command economy, fiscal decentralization coupled with the gradual introduction of market mechanisms increasingly made local governments and enterprises masters of their own will. Even without taking account of the growing amount of extra-budgetary revenue, the terms of the fiscal contracting arrangements between central and provincial governments gave sub-national governments strong incentives to promote local economic growth in order to generate new revenue. As Jean Oi pointed out, fiscal reform "assigned local governments property rights over increased income and created strong incentives for local officials to pursue local economic development."[2]

Yet the fiscal incentives, which have been carefully analyzed by Oi (1992), Walder (1995), Wong (1992), and others, were necessary but not sufficient for explaining the evolving patterns of state-enterprise relations. We also need to take cognizance of the characteristics of China's transitional economy. These transitional characteristics, including high pent-up demand, high prices for consumer products as well as dual-track pricing, and cheap capital, were strong inducements for local governments to invest in sectors ranging from bicycles to television assembly. From the perspective of the 1980s, there was little risk in getting involved in industrial investments, particularly because government officials used their regulatory power to limit entry by private businesses. The combination of the fiscal incentives effect and the transitional characteristics powerfully pushed local governments and enterprises together as the former saw the latter as cash cows while the latter received various forms of assistance from the former in a dense web of bargaining relationships.[3] Thus, even though the central government's program for urban reforms, first promulgated in October 1984, called for reducing direct government interference in enterprise management and making enterprises pure economic entities,[4] the factors described here helped forge closer bonds between state and enterprise through the 1980s. Likewise, even though General Secretary Jiang Zemin stated that government departments at all levels must not set up enterprises and that existing enterprises should sever their ties with the government departments in the early 1990s, this injunction had only a brief restraining effect.[5] In fact, provided with meager budgets, bureaucratic departments and other state institutions had to generate revenue to supplement inadequate government funding. Such institutionalized incentives for revenue generation turned into incentives for rent-seeking. As is well known, virtually all elements of the Chinese state, from the military, the armed police, to judiciary departments and the party propaganda department, established and owned businesses to supplement their budgets amid the free-wheeling economic atmosphere of the early and mid-1990s (see esp. Chapter 4). This business fever of the state had a deleterious effect on government ethos, fair competition, and state-society relations.

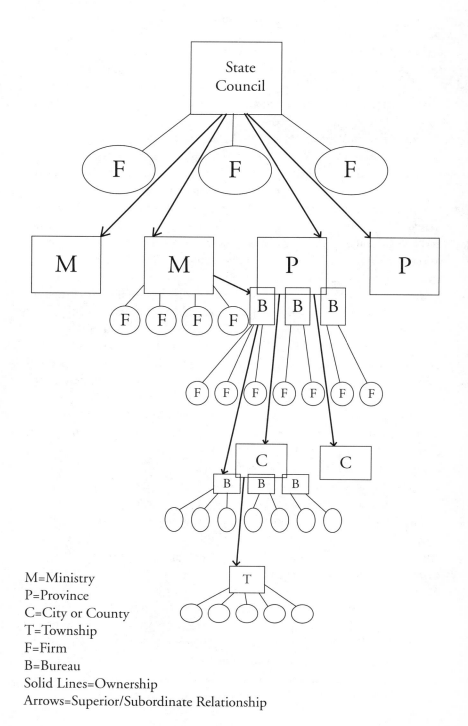

M=Ministry
P=Province
C=City or County
T=Township
F=Firm
B=Bureau
Solid Lines=Ownership
Arrows=Superior/Subordinate Relationship

The tenacity of this system of mutual embeddedness of political and economic actors, as depicted in the accompanying figure (Figure 2.1), was revealed when supervision of large state enterprises was delegated to local governments. The local authorities often had a hard time ensuring that the delegated enterprises had adequate supply of raw materials and energy and an outlet for their products, which were controlled through the now-defunct Ministry of Materials Supply. In consequence, local officials sometimes begged central ministries to take these enterprises back.[6] In the command economy, an enterprise that lacked a super-ordinate government bureau was an orphan, while a government agency that controlled no enterprises was a mere shell. Without alternatives to government allocation of resources, an enterprise that cut its ties to its controlling government bureau was like a ship that lacked moorings. In such a system, the growth of social and intermediate organizations was severely retarded. The politicization of the economy begot more political intervention.

Yet the pathologies of the system were also obvious. As long as the bureaucracies played significant roles in providing for and protecting the enterprises under their jurisdiction in a partially reformed economy, efforts to rationalize the bureaucracy and state-business relations would meet with much resistance as they would touch on vested interests. Meanwhile, the growth of market-based activities alongside the plan demanded the creation of new institutions to coordinate, govern, and regulate. Because Chinese decision making emphasized consensus, the proliferation of bureaucratic agencies and organizations required ever more time and effort for coordination. In consequence, numerous ad hoc offices, such as for aircraft manufacturing, nuclear power, or electronics, were set up within the central government to act as coordinators and facilitators, only to engender conflicts with existing ministries and commissions.

The expansion and proliferation of formal and informal bureaucratic organizations resulted in an exponential growth of decisions that were referred to higher levels for final decisions, while the growth of social and intermediate organizations was retarded.[7] In consequence, Chinese decision making tends to be plagued by delays and inefficiency while the agenda of top leaders is overloaded with what would have been trivial in a market economy. In the early 1980s, the city of Beijing had to seek the permission of the Communist Party's Political Bureau just to increase the price of a box of matches from two cents to three cents.[8]

All in all, the bilateral interdependence between political and eco-

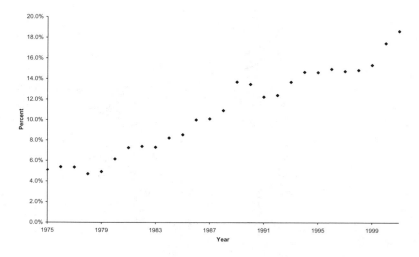

Figure 2.2. Administrative Expenditure as a Percentage of Total Government Expenditure (1975–2001). Sources: ZGTJNJ 2001–2002. Based on budgetary expenditure data broken down by function.

nomic actors amid partial reforms provided fertile soil for government expansion during an era of rapid economic growth. As was mentioned in Chapter 1, from 1978 to 1995, Chinese state revenue grew by 5.1 times while administrative expenses in state expenditure grew by 17.8 times.[9] Most ominously, government administrative expenditure as a percentage of total government expenditure rose from about 5 percent in the mid-1970s to nearly 15 percent by the mid-1990s.

As I have discussed elsewhere, there were several waves of government reforms from the early 1980s through the early 1990s.[10] Various local governments such as Shenzhen, Shanghai, and Hainan also experimented with important initiatives and generated valuable experience for government reforms. Nonetheless, the local experiments in government reforms also served to highlight the difficulties of government reform from below.[11] For local governments, there is huge organizational pressure to have a government setup that corresponds with those at upper levels. Without such organizational correspondence, local officials may not receive central documents and invitations to policy conferences and thus risk falling out of the policy loop. When the city of Changzhou in Jiangsu province abolished various industrial bureaus in 1988, city officials became so frustrated with the result that they restored the old setup three years later.[12] Similarly, authorities in Shaanxi's Huanglong county resurrected a number of government offices and affiliated organizations they had abolished earlier so as to be better in the bureaucratic loop.[13] In another case, Fujian's Shishi municipality set up a government with only 14 departments and a staff of 600 at the turn of the 1990s. The Economic Bureau alone dealt with 34 superordinate agencies or organizations. A decade later, however, the number of government departments in Shishi had risen to 25, and staff size had more than doubled, to over 1,300.[14] Partly to cope with the pressure for organizational correspondence, local governments that abolished bureaus often retained remnants of the former bureaus in the form of offices in order to remain a part of the official policy and benefits loop. For the same reason, local governments would allow one office or bureau to simultaneously be known under different guises.

Market Competition, Government-Business Relations, and Government Reforms

While in the 1980s and early 1990s partial reforms temporarily strengthened the bonds between government and state-owned enterprises (SOEs) and generated revenue for government expansion, the transition to a buyer's market has produced the opposite effect. The logic behind the turn was simple. Growing competition steadily turned ownership of state firms into liability. By the mid-1990s, most prices were set by supply and demand; only a small percentage of prices continued to be subject to government control. The transitional dual-price system had largely become history. Producers in most industrial sectors, ranging from textiles to household appliances, were confronted with a buyer's market, the first most Chinese had ever experienced in their lifetime.[15] In 1990, the State Statistical Bureau reported that, for state-owned industrial enterprises with independent accounting status, the money losers lost a total of 34.9 billion yuan while the profitable enterprises had after-tax profits of 38.8 billion yuan in 1990. A similar set of figures (36.7 and 40.2) was reported for 1991.[16] When we take into consideration government subsidies and creative accounting practices that made the accounts look better than they should be, these enterprises most likely had no real after-tax profits in those years.

Not all firms were money losers, however. Aggregate data from the 1995 industrial census, seen in Table 2.1, show the skewed distribution of state industrial enterprise profits by different levels of ownership. The cen-

Table 2.1
Financial Indicators of State-owned
Industrial Enterprises (1995)

	Number	Gross Output (billions)	Money-Losing (percent)	Debts (billion yuan)	Pretax Profits (billion yuan)	Net Profits (billion yuan)
Subtotal	87,905	2,589.0	33.8	3124.2	287.4	36.1
CG-owned	4,738	900.0	32.5	996.7	163.5	33.1
LG-owned	83,167	1,688.9	33.8	2127.5	123.9	3.0
Large	4,685	1,590.7	28.2	1,863.8	227.6	48.4
Medium	10,983	530.2	34.9	678.8	38.5	-5.5
Small	72,237	468.0	33.9	581.6	21.2	-6.8

CG is central government, LG is local government. All enterprises have independent accounting status. Source: Third Industrial Census.

tral government's 4,738 firms generated 33 billion yuan in net profits, compared with a mere 3 billion for the 83,167 state firms owned by the various local governments. Moreover, the local firms were more than twice as heavily indebted as the central government firms. Simply put, as of the mid-1990s most local governments had their investments in relatively small firms and in sectors with excessive competition and low capacity utilization rates. Thus it was no surprise that local government officials and managers felt keenly that it had become exceedingly difficult to find new products and new projects with good prospects of making a profit. Already heavily in debt, the local SOEs also found their credit lines were increasingly tightened as state banks with growing deposits became reluctant to lend.[17]

The economic and political cost to alter the prevailing institutional arrangements declined as the returns on government investment in industry plummeted. From this brief discussion of the patterns of state sector profits and losses, it is expected that the governments would rationalize their ownership in state firms on the basis of firm size. Since local governments had most of the money-losing state enterprises and felt more fiscal pressures for change than the central government, it is not surprising that cash-strapped local governments would lead the most far-reaching reforms in the state sector. By 1995, a conscious strategy had been formulated under the rubric of *zhuada fangxiao,* which means literally "grasping the large, releasing the small." By the end of the 1990s, various state actors, especially provincial and sub-provincial governments, had become so eager to sell off state enterprises that some reporters called it "Big Bang, Chinese-style." The number of court-processed bankruptcy cases rose from a mere 32 cases in 1990 to 4,527 in 1997.[18] By the end of June 2000, 76 percent of the small state enterprises nationwide had undergone some form of corporate reforms (*gaizhi*), including reorganization, sale, joint venture, and leasing.[19] With the retrenchment in state ownership, as measured in the number of state-owned or state-controlled industrial enterprises, state-sector employment also declined (Figure 2.3).

While unprofitable SOEs, mostly small and medium-sized ones, have been privatized or otherwise off-loaded, the state—particularly central, provincial, and major municipal governments—has devoted enormous energy and resources to the reorganization and governance of the largest and most profitable state firms. While monitoring and supervision have been enhanced, the biggest SOEs have also received special government backing, including priority in listing on stock markets and access to bank credit. The firms controlled by the central government have become especially dominant. For 2001, the 64 industrial firms owned or controlled by the central government, such as PetroChina and China Telecom, generated 110.4 billion yuan in profits, or 47 percent of the total profits produced by industrial firms owned or controlled by the state.[20]

The rationalization of the government's involvement in the economy has had major implications for government reforms. First, the trend toward divestiture and de facto privatization has reduced the need to expand the government to take care of the SOEs. Instead, just as it became easier to merge and reorganize state firms that belonged to different bureaucratic umbrellas, it should also become easier to reorganize government operations because there are simply fewer "interests" for different government departments to fight over. In reality, as government bureaus ceded ownership as well as direct control over state enterprises, staff in these bureaus have keenly felt their loss of power and realized that the bureaus are looking more and more like shells.[21] In response, some officials of the bureaus and ministries have become eager to jump ship and land in the major companies rather than become irrelevant. The case of the minister of Electric Power becoming the chairman of the State Power Corporation was one of the most prominent cases.

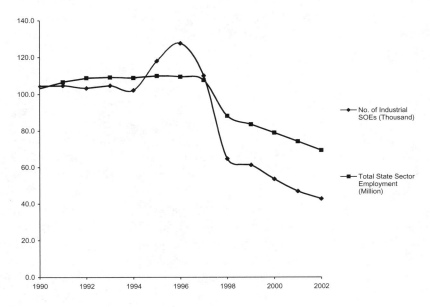

Figure 2.3. Number of Industrial SOEs and Total State-Sector Employment. Note: The number of industrial SOEs includes both state-owned and state-majority-controlled industrial enterprises. For 1990–1995, the figures are for state-owned enterprises (SOEs) only. Sources: ZGTJNJ 1995–2002; ZGTJZY 2003.

Second, with the relative decline of the state sector, local governments have faced strong fiscal pressures to fulfill their growing social obligations (pension liabilities, unemployment payments, and so on) and thus have incentives to restrain the growth of administrative outlays. As time elapsed, local government officials frustrated by the double whammy of soaring administrative expenses and declining state-enterprise performance realized that there would be no quick relief in sight, making government downsizing an important option. These concerns were compounded by the tax and fiscal reforms of 1993–1994 that strengthened the central government's control over the revenue stream vis-à-vis provincial authorities and prohibited local authorities from incurring budget deficits (see Chapter 3).

Thirdly, the expansion of the Chinese state did not just produce a proliferation of fees, levies, and surcharges that became burdens on businesses and citizens. Businesses associated with various state agencies were also rigging the regulatory landscape and engendering corruption just as some of the collapsed economies in Southeast Asia had become afflicted with "crony capitalism." Such organizational corruption threatened to undermine not only the basis for sustained economic growth but also the legitimacy of the Chinese leadership and of the reforms. For China's leaders concerned about the long-term viability of the regime, it was urgent to undertake rationalizing reforms (see especially chapters on divestiture and corruption).

Finally, by the mid-1990s, the experiences of rationalizing reforms in the special economic zones as well as in Shanghai, Shunde, and other places were becoming widely known in both internal and popular publications.[22] These reports and discussions implied endorsement of the local experiences and served to widen the realm of the possible and open up new vistas for officials elsewhere to emulate at a time when the pressures or incentives for reform had become stronger. In certain cases, well-connected officials promoted pioneering reforms in the hope of gaining greater political visibility. For example, Liaoning's Haicheng (where Li Tieying, a state councilor and then the minister of the State Commission for Restructuring the Economic System, started his political career) promulgated a twenty-article program for comprehensive economic system reforms in mid-1995. The program centered on reforming government ownership of enterprises through asset sales. It resulted in the abolition of various industrial bureaus and a significant reduction of direct government involvement in the economy.[23]

By 1997, on the eve of the fifteenth National Congress of the Communist Party, some major cities, including Hubei's Wuhan and Guangxi's Nanning, had chosen to follow in the steps of Shanghai and others. In March 1997, the Wuhan municipal government announced that it would promote industrial adjustment by breaking through old administrative boundaries. It abolished five municipal industrial bureaus (Machinery, Electronics, Textiles, First Light Industry, and Second Light Industry) as well as the Chemicals State Asset Management Corporation and adjusted the functions of other bureaus. The companies overseen by these bureaus as well as the industrial companies in instruments, non-ferrous metals, automotive, construction materials, and packaging, and three conglomerates (Changjiang Dongli, Wuhan Guolu, and Gehua) were reorganized and rationalized by industry and put into three state asset holding companies in machinery and electronics, light industry, and textiles. As in Shanghai, the reorganization allowed the holding companies to become asset management companies empowered to make decisions such as equity sales and joint ventures. Each of the holding corporations controlled between 40 to 80 enterprises with total assets valued at 8 to 9 billion yuan. In the meantime, a supervisory office assumed the functions of overseeing the industries.[24]

The initiatives in Wuhan and other cities offer evidence that, by 1997 and early 1998, the incentives and pressures for government rationalization had increased as had the range of politically acceptable reforms, many of which anticipated central government reforms by several years' time. In fact, in response to the nonstop expansion in the overall size of the government, there were growing domestic demands for comprehensive government reforms. During the National People's Congress (NPC) annual meeting in spring 1997, delegates complained that the government had failed to deliver on its promise for state enterprise reforms. One major concern was the regulatory "disorder" that resulted from a proliferation of government agencies.[25] As noted by Zhang Zhijian, a vice minister and deputy director of the Central Commission on Organizations and Staff Size, China had a dozen government ministries and commissions that oversaw the economy, compared with just a few in developed countries.[26] Reformers worried that failure to reform the government might leave China stuck between plan and market forever and permanently condemn the country to the fate of corruption and underdevelopment. As a former party secretary of Hangzhou noted, "without solving the issue of administrative reforms, China has no hope, and it will be very difficult to form a framework for the market economic system."[27]

Yet, ultimately, as was the case with the rationalization of the state in various other countries, the decision to pursue major governmental reforms is a political one.[28] While the factors mentioned so far helped prepare the ground for administrative rationalization, it was the onset of the Asian financial crisis that gave the final push for a major rationalization drive launched on Premier Zhu Rongji's watch. Concerned about the contagious effect of the Asian financial crisis, China's leaders took measures to stabilize the banking and financial system (Chapter 3). Meanwhile they put comprehensive reform of the government organization and of public finance high on the agenda. In addition, crisis conditions in the economy also prompted the Chinese leadership to move up the decision to divest the military and other state institutions of their business operations (Chapter 4) and gave urgency to a host of other institutional reforms in public management (Chapters 6–7). As this book goes to press, the SARS crisis has elicited much-needed government initiatives to tackle long-standing problems in China's public health system.

In his report to the fifteenth National Congress of the Communist Party, held in fall 1997, General Secretary Jiang Zemin reiterated the need for a new round of administrative reform. As justification for the reform, he stated that "unwieldy organization, bloated personnel, failure to separate functions of government from those of enterprises, and serious bureaucratism directly hamper the deepening of reform and the development of the economy and affect the relationship between the party and the masses."[29] The following March, the National People's Congress approved a sweeping plan by incoming premier Zhu Rongji to streamline the bureaucracy and reduce the staff size of the central government by as much as one-half. According to Personnel Minister Song Defu, the contradictions between the government setup and the market economy had become sharper day by day. Lack of further government reforms would "obstruct the development of society's productivity, affect the relations between the Party and the masses, and create a heavy burden on the state and the people."[30] In spite of press speculations of bureaucratic resistance, the plan was approved by the NPC with 97 percent of the votes cast, an overwhelming endorsement by the increasingly assertive legislature.

The 1998 Government Restructuring Program

The 1998 government restructuring program reduced the number of central government ministries from 40 to 29, with staff size trimmed by nearly half.[31] Party organizations also underwent downsizing, albeit by a smaller percentage. In addition 21 "mass organizations" overseen by the Central Commission on Organizations and Staff Size (Zhongyang Jigou Bianzhi Weiyuanhui), including the All China Federation of Trade Unions (ACFTU), the Chinese Communist Youth League, and the All China Women's Federation cut their staffing size by 25 percent in 2001.[32]

The heaviest axe of the government restructuring fell on the industrial ministries that had been the bulwarks of the central planning system. The Ministry of Electric Power surrendered its regulatory powers to the State Development Planning Commission and became the State Power Corporation. The Ministries of Coal Industry, Machine-Building, Metallurgical Industry, Internal Trade, and Forestry, as well as the national councils of Light Industry and Textile Industry were streamlined and downgraded to become state administrations (*guojia ju*) under the supervision of the State Economic and Trade Commission (SETC) in 1998. In addition, the State Administration of Petroleum and Chemical Industry, also put under the SETC, was established by merging the administrative functions of the Ministry of Chemical Industry, the China Petroleum and Natural Gas Corporation, and the China Petroleum and Chemical Industry Corporation. By early 2001, eight of these state administrations under the SETC had been abolished, with their functions absorbed into the SETC.[33]

The major exception to this trend of subsuming industrial regulation under the SETC was the creation of the Ministry of Information Industry (MII). In an apparent attempt to break down administrative barriers and streamline regulatory functions, the MII was created out of a merger of the Ministry of Posts and Telecommunications and the Ministry of Electronics Industry to oversee the industrial sectors playing a key role in China's information revolution. The MII also assumed certain government functions for information and network management that previously resided in the Ministry of Broadcast, Film, and Television, the China Aerospace Industry Corporation, and the China Aviation Industry Corporation. This consolidation of regulatory power in the MII has been used not to monopolize but to promote competition through a breakup of China Telecom and the entry of new players.

Streamlining and downsizing also occurred within the remaining ministries, and the number of departments (*si* or *ju*) in ministries decreased by more than 200.[34] Much of the streamlining and reintegration was aimed at promoting the unity of administrative authority and curbing the sort of bureaucratic fragmentation that China scholars have long noted.[35] Some of the streamlining and reorganization happened immediately while others were undertaken as reformers applied the same logic to other and often more complex policy areas. For example, the regulation of fishing was previously divided into three separate law enforcement units dealing respectively with fishing administration (*yuzheng*), supervision over ports and harbors (*yugang jiandu*), and fishing boat inspection (*yuchuan jianyan*). Such fragmentation of administrative authority served to weaken the unity of law enforcement. Moreover, some administrative units regulating fishing relied on fees and fines to finance their daily operations, and the over-zealous collection of fees and fines added to the burdens of fishermen. In August 1999, the Ministry of Agriculture merged the three disparate units into one administration for the implementation of the Law on Fisheries. The merger resulted in streamlined operations and staff reductions. Moreover, incomes from fees and fines were separated from expenditure to promote clean and honest law enforcement (see also Chapter 7).[36]

A similar reorganization occurred in China's border management. As part of the drive to improve the foreign investment climate, the State Council reorganized and centralized the exit-entry administration under the Customs Administration in 1998–1999. Prior to the reorganization, there were separate institutions for health quarantine, animal and plant quarantine, and commodity inspection. Each also belonged to a different government agency (Ministry of Health, Ministry of Agriculture, and the Ministry of Foreign Trade and Economic Cooperation). The reorganized exit-entry administration merged all three under the roof of the State Administration of Exit-entry Inspection and Quarantine (also known as China Inspection and Quarantine, or CIQ).[37] Leaders of CIQ were empowered to directly supervise 35 local offices nationwide and unify inspection and visa procedures, standards for forms, certificates, statistics, and computer applications, as well as the fee schedule.[38] While importers and exporters previously had to deal with three different sets of gatekeepers that collected fees for service, the consolidation of CIQ has made it possible for an importer or exporter to go through CIQ for sampling, inspection, or quarantine just once.[39] With the reduction in operational overlap and in a move designed to improve China's investment environment, the reorganized CIQ reduced its service charges by an average of one-third (totaling 420 million yuan from May to December 1999) while improving the quality of its service.[40] The CIQ reorganization, together with reforms of the Customs Administration, laid the foundation for comprehensive port management reforms that have steadily reduced the average customs passage time. As China neared entry into the WTO and as part of the drive in 2001 to rectify and regulate the order of market competition (see Chapter 3), the Chinese leadership further merged CIQ with the State Administration of Quality and Technical Supervision into one ministerial-ranked general administration (*zongju*) called the State (General) Administration of Quality Supervision, Inspection, and Quarantine.[41]

Still another important area concerns the regulation of water use and disposal. With the encouragement of the Ministry of Water Works, several provincial units, including Shanghai, Guangdong, and Inner Mongolia, introduced reforms to integrate fragmented authority over water into one single agency.[42] In Shanghai, for example, water was previously managed and regulated by at least five different government agencies (Construction

Committee, Public Utilities Bureau, Municipal Works, Water Works, and Environmental Bureau), and coordination was often a challenge. In May 2000, Shanghai integrated all government functions concerned with water into a single Bureau of Water Affairs (*Shuiwu ju*) to provide unified management and oversight for one of the most ubiquitous yet increasingly precious resources. The experiences in Shanghai and elsewhere provided models for other cities to emulate. By November 2001, 804 cities and counties (44 percent of the total) had integrated government functions related to water into one agency.[43] The principle of integrating regulatory authority over water resources was enacted into the amended PRC Law on Water in 2002.

As most industrial ministries lost their separate institutional identities, the bureaucratic lineup of the Chinese government became much like those found in other East Asian economies. The State Planning Commission, renamed the State Development Planning Commission (SDPC), retained its functions in heavily regulated areas such as power and grain but shifted its main duty to that of forecasting medium- and long-range growth targets. Much of the day-to-day macroeconomic steering, including industrial policy implementation and regulation of investments in technical renovation projects, was housed in the powerful State Economic and Trade Commission. The SETC and SDPC were joined by the Ministry of Finance and the People's Bank of China as the central institutions of economic governance. These macroeconomic agencies were complemented by a list of newly organized ministries including Science and Technology, Education, Labor and Social Security,[44] Personnel, Land and Resources, as well as the Commission of Science, Technology, and Industry for National Defense. Moreover, administrative and regulatory agencies in charge of the environment, industry and commerce, intellectual property rights, and quality standards were upgraded to ministerial status and augmented administratively (see Chapter 3). The Ministries of Railways, Communications (transportation), Construction, Agriculture, Water Resources, Foreign Trade, and Economic Cooperation were retained. Other agencies that were spared include the State Family Planning Commission, the State Ethnic Affairs Commission, and the Ministries of Foreign Affairs, National Defense, Supervision, Culture, Health, Justice, Public Security, State Security, Civil Affairs, as well as the National Audit Office.

The shakeup in the bureaucratic lineup in 1998 was matched by the transformation in economic philosophy that State Councilor Luo Gan enunciated in his report to the National People's Congress. For Luo, the main duties of government agencies such as the State Economic and Trade Commission, the State Development Planning Commission, and the People's Bank of China should be focused on maintaining an overall economic balance, curbing inflation, and optimizing economic structure. To American readers familiar with the talk from the chairman of the Federal Reserve or the treasury secretary, the Chinese stance sounds remarkably familiar.

The government statement on state-enterprise relations is particularly important. The industry administrations under the SETC were still charged with the formulation and implementation of sectoral policies and regulations and the maintenance of market order. However, they lost the right to directly supervise and intervene in enterprises and institutions such as universities and research institutes, most of which were divested in subsequent months.[45] According to Luo, the economic departments "should all practice the separation of administration from business operations, effectively change their functions, and no longer directly administer enterprises." Generally speaking, the government would supervise state enterprises, including the evaluation and appointment of management, only as far as its owner's equity permits it. Even so, these enterprises, like their nonstate competitors, should manage enterprise operations on their own with a view toward enhancing shareholder's asset value, take responsibility for their own profits and losses, and pay tax according to law.[46]

Implementation of the Central Government Reforms

The strong legislative mandate notwithstanding, the bold government-restructuring plan was greeted by mixed feelings. Enthusiasts believe the restructuring would mark the final stage of China's market-oriented reforms. Once this restructuring is complete, the Chinese bureaucracy will finally have been transformed from an apparatus for old-style planning to a regulatory state. Skeptics, however, point out that the history of Chinese bureaucratic reforms is littered with aborted reform plans. Huang Zhong, an NPC deputy from Shaanxi, worried that though the former industrial ministries would be downgraded to administrations within the SETC, they might still retain much power to intervene in enterprises. Indeed, a Guangdong deputy commented that the industrial administrations might become even more ferocious. Others were concerned that the downsizing at the central government level would not be followed by equally substantial reforms in the localities.[47] They thus expected little chance of success for the effort at bureaucratic rationalization.[48] After all, the Chinese leadership already had enough socioeconomic challenges on hand and would probably hesitate to alienate a large number of government employees.

In fact, while causing some short-term uncertainty, the streamlining of the central government confounded skeptics and proceeded quickly, indeed ahead of schedule, through the aggressive use of early retirement, allowances for graduate studies, and job placement in affiliated organizations. Altogether half of the State Council staff, or over 16,000 government employees, including about 600 senior administrators at the level of department director (*sizhang* and *juzhang*) or above, were let go (*fenliu*). Over 3,000 of the 16,000 were enrolled in graduate professional programs at leading universities.[49] The State Council General Office set an example by cutting its staff size from 435 down to 217.[50] The State Development and Planning Commission downsized from 1,119 to 590; the Ministry of Finance and the headquarters of the People's Bank of China went from 1,144 and 948 to 610 and 500, respectively.[51] The government ministries and administrations I visited in August–September 1998 had already decided on a slimmed-down staff and were operating with reduced staff levels. For example, the State Administration of Textile Industry, which was put under the supervision of the SETC, retained a staff of just 70 people in Beijing, down from 280. Other sectoral administrations also trimmed their staff size from more than 200–400 to less than 100. In the case of the Bureau of Internal Trade, staff size was cut from 842 to 160.[52] Staff members I interviewed recognized then that this arrangement would be temporary. Indeed, in 2001 these administrations and their functions were absorbed into the SETC, with most staffers of the industrial administrations being diverted to various industry associations. Local officials also noted that even with the downsizing of 1998, the government setup was still not fully developed for a market economy and needed to be further transformed.[53]

All agencies did not go through downsizing. While the Ministry of Electric Power had an authorized staff size of 280, the State Power Corporation that the ministry metamorphosed into was permitted to employ 460 at its headquarters. In some other ministries such as the Ministry of Electronics, those who were downsized tended to possess technical skills and were reassigned to institutions and companies under the purview of the MII.[54] Nevertheless, as would have been the case anywhere else, some of those who lost their official positions found it hard to accept their fate. Wang Zhongyu, head of the State Council General Office, reportedly saw some departing cadres as many as five times to persuade and counsel them.[55]

Overall, the downsizing was eased by the adoption of quasi-democratic mechanisms (see also discussion on civil service reforms in Chapter 5). The heads of bureaus and divisions were first elected by staff before they were formally appointed. The elected bureaucratic officials then chose the staff staying on. Staff members at several government agencies that I talked to all agreed that the process of choosing who got to stay was generally fair and acceptable. Following the downsizing, the average age of central government staff was reduced, and the percentage of staff with a college degree or above rose from 69.7 percent to 77.4 percent.[56]

Sub-national Government Downsizing

Compared with the reorganization of the State Council (central government), the downsizing of lower levels of government was both far more significant and more arduous to implement. While the size of the central government staff numbered in the tens of thousands only, the staff size for local administrations was 5.2 million, and actual payroll was about 5.5 million.[57] Even the smallest township boasts a full complement of state organs—Party, government, people's congress, people's political consultative conference—as well as government-supported organizations including schools and hospitals. The growth in sub-national government staff size increased payroll and administrative costs, which have been a major cause of state-society tensions. In Fujian province, for instance, payroll and administrative expenses in 1997 amounted to 15 billion yuan while the provincial government's fiscal revenue was only 25.1 billion yuan. According to a provincial estimate, if the provincial government staff size was cut by half of 200,000, the savings would amount to 3 billion yuan per year.[58] Leaving these fiscal concerns aside, it is local officials who interact with businesses and citizens on a daily basis. Only when local governments are reformed can there be genuine easing of the state-society relations that have often been frayed by bureaucratic rent-seeking. Yet, whereas central government staff tend to have university degrees, technical skills, and other forms of social capital that make them easier to place outside the government bureaucracy, the far larger number of local staff to be made redundant tend to possess less human capital on average and will thus face more difficulty in securing alternative employment, especially in a time of growing unemployment.

Provincial-Level Reforms

In mid-1999 the central government began to formally promote provincial government reforms that sought to match the extent of staff cuts at the central government. The reform plan called for reducing the number of government bureaus/departments and agencies in most provincial-level governments from around 53 to about 40 (around 30 in underdeveloped and less populous provinces or autonomous regions). For centrally administered municipalities (Beijing, Shanghai, Tianjin, and Chongqing), the number of bureaus and agencies would be set at about 45, down from 61. In other cases, large cities would have about 40 bureaus or agencies, down from 55, whereas medium-sized cities would be allowed 30 and small ones only 22, down from 37 and 30, respectively. For counties (and county-ranked cities), large ones would cut the number of departments and agencies from 30 to 22; medium-sized and small counties would have between 14 and 18, down from an average of 24.[59]

The time lag between central and provincial government reforms gave provincial and sub-provincial government officials and staff time to become better prepared mentally for the tough decisions ahead. In principle most government employees were in favor of government reforms and believed that bureaucratic restructuring was essential for economic development. A survey of 747 government staff in 13 cities and counties of Hubei found that 70 percent of the respondents had considered the possibility of themselves being downsized.[60] Even in underdeveloped Gansu, 77 percent of the government staff surveyed by the Gansu Administrative Management Association supported the objectives of government reforms.[61]

Yet when it came to implementing the reform, few wanted to be the ones downsized. Since the second wind of reforms came amid deepening domestic economic downturn (and the Asian financial crisis), however, it engendered much complaint as well as foot-dragging among provincial officials. Local officials told central officials sent on fact-finding trips that they feared that the massive government restructuring might trigger conflicts and strong reactions in light of the slowing economic growth and tensions in state-society relations. While originally administrative reforms in provincial and prefectural governments were to be basically completed by the end of 1999, the target date was pushed back. Provincial authorities in interior provinces were particularly deliberate in initiating the downsizing. Indeed, more than 1,900 at the department level and above in Sichuan province allegedly sent a petition letter to central leaders to resist the downsizing initiative.[62]

Central leaders recognized the political difficulties of government downsizing in a perilous economic environment, but they persisted. Central leaders including Jiang Zemin, Zhu Rongji, and Hu Jintao invoked party and organizational discipline to browbeat sub-national officials. In the aftermath of the major tax and fiscal reforms in the first half of the 1990s (see Chapter 3), provincial-level leaders were fully aware of their relatively weak positions vis-à-vis the central authorities and were in no mood to fight the center's wishes. By May 2000, when China's economic prospects had become significantly brighter than a year earlier, all 31 provincial units had received the central government's approval for their administrative reform plans.

The provincial plans followed the central guidelines, with much of the administrative streamlining done to correspond to the central government setup. The industrial and commercial bureaus were downsized and absorbed into the provincial-level economic committees, as had already been done in a number of pilot cities.[63] In the meantime, various regulatory agencies were upgraded. The Patent Bureaus, for example, were carved out of the Science and Technology Commissions to become Intellectual Property Bureaus that directly report to the provincial-level leadership.

Authorized staff size (*bianzhi*) for provincial governments was decreased by 47 percent, or 74,000 people nationwide (excluding the police and judicial organs or *zhengfa bumen*).[64] In Guangdong province, for instance, the government staff size was cut by 49.3 percent.[65] The number of provincial government departments and institutions (*jigou*) was reduced from 57 to 47, including 27 institutions that are counterparts of those in the central government.[66] In Hainan province, staff size for the party establishment was cut by 20 percent, and that of the government by about 50 percent. The number of departments in the provincial party establishment dropped from 12 to 9 (including the Discipline Inspection Committee [same as the Supervision Bureau], general office, organization, publicity, united front departments, and politics and law committee). The number of provincial government departments was reduced from 38 to 32, including the general office, 21 bureaus, and 10 organizations that report to the provincial leadership (*zhishu jigou*).[67] Even in Guangxi, an ethnic region that received more lenient treatment from the central authorities, the cut in staff size reached 47.5 percent.[68]

Sub-Provincial Restructuring

Even before the centrally mandated administrative restructuring for county and township governments began in earnest in 2001, local authorities in some fiscally strapped areas had already adopted a variety of creative schemes to provide work for redundant local government staffers, reduce administrative expenses, and alleviate the burden on society (particularly farmers faced with various levies). One controversial scheme, found in provinces as diverse as coastal Shandong and poverty-stricken Guizhou as well as middle-income provinces such as Sichuan and Hubei, was to allow government employees to go on leave with basic pay in the hope that these employees would engage in business and perhaps not even want to return to government service after the leave ended. Another initiative is known as *lungang*, or taking turns to serve in government posts. Employed in a variety of localities in Shandong, Henan, Jiangxi, and other provinces, this mechanism of rotations requires between one-third and one-half of local government staff members to stay away from government work on base pay or less. Those who are off duty are encouraged to engage in businesses. The *lungang* system reduces government administrative expenses and helps instill a sense of responsibility among government staff.

For the sake of space, I shall not dwell on the details of these programs. It is obvious that the leaves and rotations were stopgap measures that did not immediately reduce the number of people on government payroll but merely postponed the day of reckoning. Moreover, the business dealings of government employees on leave also raised serious concerns about conflicts of interest and public ethics.[69] Nonetheless, these initiatives served to inculcate a sense of urgency about the need for government reforms and thus helped prepare the ground for the reforms being discussed here.[70]

Meanwhile, the reorganization of rural government, particularly the merger of smaller townships and villages into larger ones, has assumed far more significance and would greatly contribute to the eventual fulfillment of the targets for county and township government reforms. Between 1989 and 1999, the number of towns (*zhen*) and townships (*xiang*) in China decreased from 55,800 to 44,500.[71] The merger of township governments not only helped reduce the size of government staff but also promoted the con-solidation of schools and other public facilities. It is estimated that the re-duction of one township government resulted in fiscal savings of one to three million yuan per year in Shandong and Jiangsu provinces.[72] A num-ber of coastal provinces, including Jiangsu, Shandong, and Zhejiang, led the country in rural government mergers and staff reductions. In economic powerhouse Jiangsu, the legacy of TVE development had left many villages with a dozen officials and in some cases as many as 20–30 people on the payroll, making for a substantial financial burden on residents. Provincial leaders decided to decrease the number of township and village adminis-trations as well as the number of rural cadres because the conversion of township and village enterprises into shareholding and private firms re-duced the need for rural officials to oversee enterprise management. Under provincial guidelines adopted in 1999, the number of village cadres was limited to a maximum of five in villages with fewer than 1,000 residents, with one additional official for each additional 500 residents.[73]

By the time provincial authorities had put together and received cen-tral government approval for their plans for reforming governments and state institutions at the county and township levels in fall 2001, most local government employees knew very well that the reforms were coming. Ac-cording to the provincial plans, county, and township-level governments and institutions would see a cut in staff size of 19.3 percent, slightly below the 20 percent target. Government agencies (see especially Chapter 3) un-der the rubric of vertical administrations, including the tax administra-tions, would downsize similarly. However, in an indication of the central leadership's preoccupation with law and order, political and judicial insti-tutions (including the police, procuratorates, and courts) were put in a sep-arate category and only had to cut their staff size by 10 percent.[74]

Because most local government administrations had also taken on staff not counted in the authorized staff size, the downsizing was deeper than the plan numbers indicated. Take Hubei, a province with a popula-tion of about 60 million in 2000. Its sub-provincial governments and state institutions were staffed with 156,800 people as well as 36,083 (or 23 per-cent) people who were not on the formal payroll. Separately, the police and judicial institutions employed 86,903 people plus 17,473 (or 20 percent) unauthorized personnel.[75] As noted at the start of this chapter, the sub-provincial reforms had by mid-2002 reduced the number of state employees by 890,000 and cleaned out 430,000 unauthorized hires.[76] These numbers suggest that the unauthorized hires were the first to be let go.

A major component of the sub-provincial reform was the acceleration of the trend toward mergers and reorganization of township governments. In 2000 the State Council's reform office and the Ministries of Agriculture and Civil Affairs urged sub-national governments to systematically decrease the number of towns and townships through mergers and closures as part of the centrally mandated local government reforms to reduce local government staff size. Provinces issued guidelines on the optimal size of townships.[77] Yet the township government reforms were slower than expected at first because a related reform to rationalize rural taxes and fees became stalled in 2001. In 2002, however, the rural tax and fee reforms were reenergized and spread to about 20 provincial units after the central government came up with additional funds to support rural education in underdeveloped areas.[78] By curbing levies and rationalizing the structure of rural extraction, the central authorities estimated that the fiscal burdens on rural residents were reduced by around 30 percent and more than 30 billion yuan per year in 2002.[79] By 2003 these reforms had spread throughout the country.

Since most income from the levies on rural residents is used for administrative expenses as well as funding for various public projects and schools, the rationalization of rural extraction reinforced the trend toward mergers of villages and townships and of related public services such as schools. Indeed, in areas that experimented with the fee-for-tax reforms, the limitation on local fees and levies forced local officials to not only cut government payroll but also accelerate the merger of rural governments. For example, Jiangsu province reduced the number of towns and townships by more than 600 (from 1,974 to 1,351) from 2001 to spring 2002 as it promoted rural fee and tax reforms. In contrast, in the two years of 1998 and 1999 the decrease in the number of townships was less than 600.[80] By the end of March 2002, 15 provincial units including Beijing, Jiangsu, and Anhui had basically completed reforms of the town and township governing institutions.[81] Nationwide, between 2000 and 2002, the total number of towns and townships decreased by 4,681 or 10.7 percent while the number of villages was cut by 40,200 or 5.5 percent.[82]

The Reform of *Shiye Danwei*

A major weakness of pre-1998 government downsizing was the failure to reduce payroll numbers. Bureaucrats eased out of their bureaucratic posts were most often moved to other not-for-profit government-funded organizations or institutions known as *shiye danwei*.[83] These include major regulatory institutions such as the China Securities Regulatory Commission and the China Insurance Regulatory Commission. They also include industry associations, research institutes, geological survey and engineering institutions, educational institutions (including universities and schools), hospitals, media organizations, publishing houses, and social service organizations such as agricultural service stations and youth centers. The annual expenditures for the *shiye danwei* accounted for 17 percent of central government spending in 1998.[84] As a result of the lateral transfers from bureaucratic posts to government-affiliated organizations, there was little effective reduction in government payroll size; once a person got on the government payroll, he or she could expect to continue to "eat government grain" for the rest of his or her career, indeed for life.[85]

The history of such lateral transfers made it sensible to regard any initiative to downsize the government with deep skepticism. In fact, the 1998 reforms proceeded quickly in trimming the authorized government staff size in the central and provincial governments partly by transferring some government functions and personnel to government-affiliated *shiye* units. Most prominently, the central government industrial ministries that were absorbed into the SETC in most cases spun off personnel and functions into industry associations. Similar developments were also reported in the localities.[86] As of 2002, there were more than 1.3 million government-affiliated *shiye danwei* institutions. Together they employed just under 30 million (29.97 million) people, of whom 1.73 million were in units affiliated with the central government and 28.25 million worked in provincial and subprovincial government-affiliated institutions. Of the total, 48.6 percent were in education (11.56 million) and health care (3.02 million).[87]

Yet, in an important departure from the past, the 1998 reforms included a comprehensive program to wean most *shiye danwei* from government budgetary support over a number of years.[88] Even institutions such as the State Information Center must generate significant revenue to maintain existing levels of personnel and operations. To understand the pattern of *shiye danwei* reforms, it is useful to work with a simple classification of the *shiye* units. In terms of functions, the *shiye* units may be roughly divided into four categories. In the first category are institutions that carry out regulatory and law enforcement functions such as the securities and insurance regulatory commissions and others such as testing centers affiliated with the State Administration of Quality Supervision, Inspection, and Quarantine. While in other countries such organizations are often based in the private sector, in China it is the government that has played the dominant role in supplying regulatory authority. Each city also boasts urban management brigades (*chengguan dadui*) to enforce laws and regulations despite the gray legal status of such brigades. With the exception of the urban management brigades, which are being converted into part of the civil service, the institutions in this category will for the foreseeable future continue to be funded by the government and operate much like government agencies or their affiliates. Meanwhile, a variety of industry associations will also likely continue to receive limited government budgetary allocations, though a growing number can support themselves with membership fees. In general, units in this category have been going through streamlining and some downsizing but are maintained as handmaidens of the state.

The second category consists of units that provide important public services such as education, health care, and research and development. The educational institutions have continued to receive government support. Major universities have in fact gotten increased government funding though most of them behave much like American public universities in that they also derive income from tuition, affiliated businesses, and private donations. Meanwhile, local public schools, as noted above, have been subjected to streamlining in tandem with the mergers of towns and townships. For example, the Shanxi provincial government announced in 2003 that it would reduce the number of elementary- and middle-school teachers by 50,000, or about 15 percent of the total staff in elementary and middle schools. Since schoolteachers and staff account for about one-third of the total *shiye danwei* employment, this move alone would reduce *shiye danwei* employment in Shanxi by 5 percent.[89] In the hospital sector, under reforms promoted by the Ministry of Health, some hospitals will become for-profit institutions, but most hospitals continue to be not-for-profit and receive some public funding; the level of public funding has been limited, however, and most hospitals must generate substantial revenue to support themselves. Major media operations, under the watchful eyes of the Party Propaganda Department, have also become holding corporations that have little need for government largesse as they generate rising income from advertising and subscriptions. A new initiative launched in 2003 would purportedly close most publications that require government or party subsidy.[90]

The major reforms have occurred with government-supported research institutions. According to Science and Technology Minister Xu Guanhua, half of the research institutes are engaged in applied research and should be turned into business firms. The other half, those that focus on basic research or public services, are to be retained as not-for-profit institutions, but their staff size is to be reduced by 70 percent so as to enable increased funding per person (the Chinese Academy of Sciences announced a plan to cut its permanent staff from 60,000 to 20,000 by 2005).[91] In May 1999, the SETC and the Ministry of Science and Technology formally asked 242 institutes previously under the jurisdiction of industrial ministries to become companies or be merged into other related enterprises. With various forms of government support, including tax incentives, most of the 242 research institutions had been converted into companies or technology intermediaries by 2000, thus removing large numbers of personnel off the government's back.[92] As corporatization reforms at the 242 institutes were concluded, the central government also instructed more than 4,000 research institutions belonging to both the central and local governments to pursue similar reforms. In the central government, the Ministry of Science and Technology took its axe to another 270 research institutions affiliated with the Ministries of Construction, Land Resources, Water Resources, Agriculture, as well as the State Forestry Administration, the State Seismological Bureau, China Meteorological Administration, the State Bureau of Surveying and Mapping, and other governmental departments.[93] Provincial and sub-provincial governments oversaw 4,000 of China's 5,000 research institutions. About half of the 4,000 were applied research institutions. The Ministry of Science and Technology asked that the 2,000 applied research institutions be corporatized.[94] Of its 69 provincial S&T organizations, the Guangdong provincial government decided to phase out fiscal allocations for 39 technology organizations over a three-year period and reduce allocations to another 18 technical consultancies by 70 percent. The money thus saved would be used for major research programs.[95] In Shandong, the provincial government even permitted researchers to buy out smaller government-funded research institutes.[96] As the corporatization of research institutions became official policy, the research institutes saw the writing on the wall and began to restructure internally. In Jilin, a survey of four leading research institutes found that they had cut staff by 14 percent (157 out of 1,119) by the summer of 2000.[97]

The third category of *shiye* units are ones offering intermediary services, mostly the professions engaged in accounting and auditing, law, and myriad other specialized services. Under a comprehensive program to divest and rationalize the professions, the government-affiliated services have been turned into partnerships and limited liability companies (see Chapter 4). The final category consists mostly of government-owned hotels and service and training centers. Even with the divestiture of businesses owned by the military, the armed police, and other state institutions (see Chapter 4), the central and local governments as well as various government-funded institutions still owned a host of these services for their own convenience. However, a trend has begun to consolidate these services into more market-oriented operations and move the employees off the government payroll so as to save money, improve service, and curb corruption. In Jiangsu province, for example, the Zhongshan Hotel Group was formed in 2001, incorporating hotels, a gas station, a vehicle fleet, and a vehicle service center that had been part of the provincial government rear services.[98] With the formation of the Zhongshan business group, the Jiangsu provincial government's rear services were effectively divested out of the government administrative lineup. Some sub-provincial governments have undertaken similar reforms. The city of Jiangyin in Jiangsu was noted for introducing private businesses to provide catering and conference facilities as well as day-to-day typing services. The move allowed the government to enjoy better services while substantially reducing payroll and costs.[99]

In general there has been a broad trend toward the marketization of nonessential service operations. Government-funded universities that used to provide all services such as housing and cafeterias for faculty, staff, and students have increasingly turned to the market for the provision of such services. This reform has allowed higher-education institutions to reduce spending on infrastructure, cut services-staff payroll, and focus on their core missions of teaching and research.[100] In the meantime, state enterprises are divesting their interests from affiliated schools, hospitals, and other social functions to become firms focused on economic returns. Remarkably, even the armed forces have started to offload various rear services such as hospitals, transportation, supplies, and housing. In fall 2002, the State Council and the Central Military Commission directed local governments at all levels to include provision of rear services for the military in their development planning programs so that the military would use facilities available locally and reduce the amount of its investment on rear services.[101]

In conclusion, though the reforms of the *shiye* units generally lagged behind those of state enterprises, they have by the end of the 1990s become a natural extension of the broader public sector reforms. In the context of the massive reorganization and downsizing of giant state firms including banks as well as oil and petrochemical firms, the reforms of the *shiye* units have proceeded with little buzz, though some government policy researchers have criticized the reform of research institutions as too drastic.[102] According to then Personnel Minister Song Defu, the *shiye danwei* directly under the State Council had by mid-2000 cut staff size by one million, including more than 600,000 in units that converted into companies.[103] By 2002, the *shiye danwei* reforms had reached towns and townships as part of the government reforms. Provincial authorities ranging from Jiangsu to Sichuan directed town/township governments to cut the staff of their *shiye* units by 20–30 percent and promote the consolidation of existing services into services centers for agriculture, culture, as well as construction, environment, and health.[104] It thus appears that, unlike in previous government reforms, painful and far-reaching reforms have indeed reached the *shiye danwei*.

Discussion: The Pains of Transition and the Benefits of Reform

Skeptics may question the extent to which the Chinese government's declared positions on government reforms have been realized. In one respect, that of reducing payroll expenses, the reforms have yielded few dividends so far. As in the past, some of the government employees were moved to not-for-profit organizations affiliated with the government and thus remained on government support (though the trend toward *shiye danwei* reforms should help over time). And various forms of inducements (salary boosts, one-time subsidies, and paid leaves) were offered to some employees so that they would retire early or would otherwise vacate their government posts. Even lowly township officials were often eased out of their positions without a corresponding reduction in salary.[105] Indeed, while the government staff size was reduced, Premier Zhu Rongji doubled the base salaries for government employees as well as retirees between 1998 and 2002.[106] A special allowance of 10 billion yuan was made available to interior provincial units when these places started their downsizing program.[107] The salary boost helped make government employment more attractive and improved the morale of government employees, but it has also raised the costs of keeping and reducing government personnel. Indeed, administrative expenditure as a percentage of total government expenditure rose from less than 15 percent in 1998 to 18.6 percent in 2001 (Figure 2.2). Only when major headway is made in the reforms of *shiye danwei*, which appear to be under way, will genuine payroll savings be realized.

To be sure, the combination of civil service reforms with downsizing appears to have helped improve the competence and efficiency of the bureaucracy as a whole (see Chapter 5). Yet the downsizing at the central and provincial levels, by making one size fit all, was so drastic that various departments in the central government and provincial administrations had to "borrow" personnel from subordinate units or institutions in order to get their work done.[108] This was partly because the cuts in personnel preceded the transformation of government functions, a problem later reforms, particularly the reform of the administrative approval system (see Chapter 5), have helped to alleviate to some extent. In some sense, the drastic cuts in personnel helped give impetus to the reform of the administrative approval system; various government departments seeking to fulfill their mission with fewer hands are expected to be more willing to get rid of nonessential bureaucratic requirements.

Every government reform initiative has tended to create some short-term uncertainty and confusion, particularly for the departments and agencies directly affected by the reforms. The 1998 reforms, given their scale, were no exception. Moreover the government reforms also produced a temporary regulatory vacuum in a number of areas. For example, the regulation of workplace safety was to be transferred from labor bureaus to the economic and trade committees in the provinces. Yet the transfer took time. In Shenzhen, home to tens of thousands of foreign-invested manufacturing businesses, the Shenzhen Bureau for Production Safety was not transferred from the Labor Bureau to the Municipal Economic and Trade Bureau until the end of 2001. While awaiting the transfer, the labor bureau was not giving safety regulation the priority it deserved. Thus the uncertainties associated with government reorganization contributed to the weakening of the enforcement of safety regulations.[109] It took a major wave of safety accidents across the country, ranging from mine explosions to capsized boats, to galvanize the State Economic and Trade Commission into action and establish the State Administration of Coal Mine Safety Supervision, which doubles as the State Administration for Workplace Safety Supervision, with greatly augmented regulatory muscle (see Chapter 3).

In the case of pharmaceutical regulation, the State Drug Administration was established in 1998, and provincial administrations soon followed. Yet monitoring and enforcement of pharmaceutical laws and regulations depend crucially on having a strong network of sub-provincial offices at the municipal and county levels. Originally the State Council set September 2001 as the target date for the establishment of these field offices. Yet by the end of August 2001, only 17 of 31 provincial administrations had produced concrete plans for establishing the local offices, and only 84 local offices had been set up. At the same time, some local administrations still maintained official links with pharmaceutical companies, with some regulatory officers doubling as company executives.[110] Such arrangements compromised the integrity of the regulatory system.

The uncertainties and contentions over resources were also ever present in the consolidations of town/township governments and of villages. Generally, the mergers were rarely of equals, and those localities that were in essence taken over were rarely happy. In townships that are taken over, residents often need to travel farther to reach the township government. The mergers of schools and clinics have caused inconvenience to those who have to use facilities at another location farther away.[111] In some localities, the "reforms" became victories for one locality over another and touched off firestorms over control and disposal of town/township assets. Some local interests sought redress by making petitions to higher levels of authority, causing political unease for elites obsessed with stability. In response to these developments, the Ministry of Civil Affairs and six other government ministries and offices issued a set of seven guidelines in August 2001 directing local authorities to make better preparations in merging and consolidating towns, townships, and villages.[112]

On balance, in spite of the transition problems, which have generally been eased or resolved over time, the downsizing and streamlining of government agencies, coupled with the program to reform the system of administrative approvals, should help boost administrative efficiency and enhance service. In Chapter 5, we shall discuss in detail some of the initiatives to improve transparency and service. Here it is useful to note the following points.

To begin with, the Chinese bureaucracy is known for its grinding consensual decision-making process, which has generally provided equally ranked agencies veto power over policy proposals made by their peers.[113] For this reason, the Ministry of Posts and Telecommunications could never get its version of a proposed draft Telecommunications Law approved at the State Council owing to objections from the Ministry of Electronics Industry and others. There is a saying that while one-third of the bureaucrats seek to push forward, another one-third are actually pulling backward. It appears the pursuit of a more coherent and efficient bureaucracy was a major reason behind the central leadership's decision to streamline government staff and yet continue to pay the downsized staff for an extended time period.[114] While some overlaps, notably between the SETC and the SDPC (see below about the 2003 reforms, however), continued to exist, overall the 1998 government reorganization and streamlining helped reduce overlapping functions that induce infighting and gridlock. For example, once telecommunications regulation was put under the umbrella of the Ministry of Information Industry, the turf wars became muted and telecom regulation more even-handed. Gradually the Chinese government engendered competition by breaking up existing telecom service providers (China Telecom became China Telecom, China Netcom, and China Mobile) and introducing new ones (China Unicom, China Railcom). Moreover, as will be noted shortly, the reforms made it easier for the Chinese leadership to negotiate the terms of China's WTO membership.

Secondly, the earlier expansion of government and the proliferation of government agencies were a major driving force behind the proliferation of levies and fees on enterprises and citizens. Even when top government leaders intended to free enterprises from the constraints imposed by the myriad agencies, they found it hard to do so without paying a price. Indeed, the leadership in one city decided to allocate 15 million yuan to 14 government departments (*zhuguan ju*) in exchange for these departments to give autonomy to the enterprises they oversaw.[115] For this reason alone, managers of state enterprises, who are at the receiving end of bureaucratic intervention more than any other group, were the most enthusiastic supporters of the government-downsizing plan.[116] In the words of Wang Hongming, chairman of Shenyang-based Liming Group, "it's impossible for [state] enterprises to innovate if their super-ordinate [administrative agencies] do not."[117] Likewise, private firms often feared visits from regulators even while they sought assistance from officials with much discretionary power.[118] Like the daughters-in-law in traditional Chinese house-holds, enterprises of all stripes have welcomed reforms that reduce the scope and power of mothers-in-law.[119] With government reforms, there are now fewer government ministries and departments and a smaller staff to trouble firms with inspections and various levies and fees, which the central government has also sought to rein in by other means, including a major overhaul of the enforcement apparatus in cities.

Thirdly, as the government has begun to focus its energies on a smaller number of major functions, especially the provision of public goods and infrastructure, there is also more room for nongovernment organizations ranging from neighborhood committees to industrial associations and professional organizations even though the Chinese state still acts vigilantly to crack down on organized political dissidence. In fact, as industry associations lose their quasi-governmental functions, get less from government budget allocations, and rely more on membership dues, they have become more aggressive in pleading the interests of their members and lobbying government departments for policy action.[120]

Reorganization, Bureaucratic Coherence, and WTO Negotiations

The government reorganization also became a major factor in China's international economic policy making. By abolishing most industrial ministries, the government reorganization severely curtailed the policy influence of the manufacturing industries ranging from autos, chemicals, to steel, all of which had been dragging their feet on China's negotiations to join the World Trade Organization (WTO). Whereas previously the ministers of each of the industrial ministries were directly represented at the State Council and its executive meeting, the reorganization made the State Economic and Trade Commission and the State Development Planning Commission the aggregators of sometimes competing industrial interests. In the absence of most industrial ministries, the internationalist Ministry of Foreign Trade and Economic Cooperation became more prominent than ever. By curbing parochial interests, the government reorganization made it easier for Chinese negotiators to strike trade deals that require sacrifices in some sectors that had previously possessed much bureaucratic clout.

It was thus no coincidence that China's WTO negotiations proceeded quickly, with major concessions by China, following the initiation of the central government reorganization. While the commitment of the Chinese leadership, notably Jiang Zemin and Zhu Rongji, was crucial to the breakthrough deal with the United States, it was nevertheless striking that the sub-ministerial industrial administrations, still reeling from their recent downgrading and expected disappearance, had practically no organized opposition to the making of the WTO deal. Instead, reports of vigorous resistance to the opening up centered on interests representing agriculture and telecommunications.[121] The telecom interests, represented by the Ministry of Information Industry, were able to persuade Chinese negotiators to reduce the percentage of foreign ownership to under 50 percent compared to the original offer of April 1999. In the case of agriculture, unlike its counterparts in many other countries, the Chinese Agriculture Ministry oversees production in rural areas and leaves agricultural trade to the Ministry of Foreign Trade and the State Development Planning Commission.[122] Nevertheless, traditionally the party leadership has always made rural affairs a major issue—this is all the more so as farm prices became depressed worldwide in the late 1990s and early 2000s. Top-level concerns about rural instability and public perceptions prompted Chinese negotiators to bargain hard over the permitted level of agricultural subsidies to the very end of the negotiations.[123]

The 2003 Government Restructuring Program

Almost as soon as the 1998 reforms were launched, there was already recognition that another round of reforms would be needed to iron out lingering problems of bureaucratic fragmentation (such as over trade regulation) and to deal with newly emerging problems. One major issue, made all the more prominent by the abolition of the industrial administrations and the divestitures, was how to promote the trend toward a relatively neutral regulatory state and yet maintain proper and efficient supervision over the multitude of state enterprises. After all, though the relative size of the state sector in the overall economy and society has declined significantly over time, the state continues to hold vast business assets and remains the dominant player in a number of sectors ranging from airlines to power to telecommunications.

By the early 2000s, the following mechanisms had been put in place to oversee the major state enterprises. In this largely ad hoc institutional framework, the largest firms that the central leadership believed to be important for its ability to guide and control the economy were put under the Central (Committee) Enterprise Work Committee. Through this committee, the party retained the power to appoint the leaders of the key state firms which are subject to the regulation of government ministries and commissions. Meanwhile, the Ministry of Finance had the right to register state assets and approve asset transactions.

As of the end of 2000, the Central Enterprise Work Committee oversaw 180 firms with tens of thousands of subsidiary corporations. Some of these firms were handed over during the AJPG divestiture (see Chapter 4), such as the Poly Group. Others emerged from the clutches of government ministries (including those that were disbanded). For example, in late 2000, assets worth 90.5 billion yuan under the Ministry of Railways were reorganized into five companies and handed over to the Central Enterprise Work Committee.[124] Major reforms in the airline, power, and telecom sectors also put some distance between government owners and regulators. The same philosophy of relative regulatory neutrality has also reached the Ministry of Health and the State Administration of Industry and Commerce (SAIC). The former has advocated that health bureaus should focus on the supervision and regulation of hospitals not on actually operating them, though the health bureaus have yet to fully disengage themselves. In the case of the SAIC, Premier Zhu Rongji in 2001 directed its leaders to take a principled stand on severing the ties between administration and business. The SAIC followed up with a strict deadline. At the end of 2001, most provincial industry and commerce bureaus had divested their assets in various markets (*shichang*) so that they would devote themselves to their regulatory role.

The Central Enterprise Work Committee also had the power to dispatch supervisory boards to major state corporations.[125] While the supervisory boards represent the State Council in monitoring the performance of state enterprises, they are not authorized to intervene in day-to-day operations.[126] In principle, these large state firms are limited liability companies that are to operate, distribute profits, and pay taxes in accordance with the law. The managers of these key state enterprises or enterprise groups are authorized to manage state assets on behalf of the government on a fiduciary basis (*shouquan jingying*).[127] Nevertheless, in light of the overlapping controls instituted by the party and the government, some top managers in these leading firms have complained that the reins on them have become tighter even as the Chinese economy continues to liberalize.[128]

For local authorities, oftentimes the state firms are overseen or managed by state asset management corporations or state asset operating companies.[129] For instance, the State Asset Committee of Shenzhen uses three asset management corporations, the Shenzhen Investment Management Corporation, the Shenzhen Construction Investment Holdings Company, and the Shenzhen Trade and Commerce Investment Company, to oversee the state firms on behalf of the municipal government. This arrangement clarifies property rights, separates government regulators from business operations, and yet enables the government to strengthen external monitoring of its assets. At the end of 1998, Shenzhen's state firms had gross assets of 176.1 billion yuan, net assets of 63.5 billion yuan, and a profit of 4.2 billion yuan.[130] Provincial authorities in other areas have also turned to this model.[131]

The profusion of formal and ad hoc institutions overseeing the major state enterprises elicited demands for simplification so as to make the life of a SOE manager easier. In spring 2003, the State Council, with Wen Jiabao succeeding Zhu Rongji as premier, announced a new round of administrative reforms, which were duly approved by the National People's Congress on March 10, 2003. Again the bulk of the changes are about economic institutions. Building on the 1998 reform plan and the reforms that had been undertaken from 1998 to 2002, the 2003 plan is more about rationalizing and fine tuning than about downsizing.[132] The central focus of the 2003 plan is to reduce institutional conflicts of interests, minimize institutionalized turf battles, and improve bureaucratic coherence. Meanwhile, the regulatory apparatuses in banking, food and drug administration, power, and workplace safety are elevated to higher or independent status (this aspect of the 2003 reforms will be discussed in Chapter 3).

The most prominent part of the 2003 plan is the dismemberment of the once powerful State Economic and Trade Commission, which for a decade was arguably China's most prominent institution for economic governance within the State Council. The SETC's bureaus on state enterprises went into a newly created State-owned Assets Supervision and Administration Commission (SASAC). The SASAC is a ministerial-ranked agency, but it is not part of the lineup of ministries and commissions whose ministers must receive NPC approval. On paper the SASAC is placed in the category of bureaus and administrations directly under the

State Council (*Guowuyuan zhishu jigou*), but it is really in a category of its own, a somewhat ad hoc but massive institutional device to oversee the largest state enterprises. Also merged into the SASAC are a part of the Ministry of Finance that acted as de facto equity owner and had power to register and approve equity transactions such as mergers as well as the former Central Enterprise Work Committee, which oversaw appointment of top managers and supervisory boards in large state enterprises owned by the central government. The Central Enterprise Work Committee oversaw 195 large and medium-sized SOEs with an estimated 12,000 subsidiary corporations.[133] Li Rongrong, the former head of the SETC, was appointed head of the SASAC; his deputy is Li Yizhong, former chairman and president of China Petroleum and Chemical Corporation.

According to the State Council's explanation, the SASAC would help promote the strategic restructuring of state enterprises (with the exception of state-owned financial firms such as banks) and further separate government ownership, enterprise, and management. The SASAC is authorized to draft laws and regulations regarding the management of state assets and provide guidance and supervision of the SASAC's local equivalents, which look after the state enterprises owned or controlled by local authorities. Altogether the SASAC and its local counterparts oversee assets worth more than 10 trillion yuan, with the central SASAC looking after a little less than half of that amount. In line with the political report of the sixteenth Party Congress, a major goal of this institutional reform is to sort out who owns what between central and local authorities (which has consequences in terms of tax payment).

By gathering together the previously dispersed powers to supervise the central government's state enterprises and armed with a newly devised set of regulations on state assets, the SASAC is empowered by the State Council to act much like owners or controlling shareholders of state corporations. In line with the structure of corporate governance, it will dispatch boards of supervisors to some of the largest SOEs, evaluate and reward as well as appoint and remove the chief officers of these SOEs in accordance with the Company Law, and conduct inspections and audits on the value of state assets. Nonetheless, the SASAC is enjoined to give management autonomy to operate and manage on a daily basis. While the Chinese government has indicated that it would retain stakes in certain sectors of strategic importance, the SASAC is expected to force SOEs to improve economic performance and to whittle down the size of the state sector by reducing ownership in nonstrategic sectors. In the first few months of its existence, the SASAC had already forced the merger of several firms and is known to aim for more.

While most of SETC became the SASAC, the SETC's important policy and regulatory functions on industry (industrial planning and policy, economic operations and control, supervision of investment in technical renovation, macroeconomic policy guidance on enterprises of all ownership types, promotion of small and medium-sized enterprises, and planning for import and export of raw materials) were given back to the State Development Planning Commission, rechristened the State Development and Reform Commission (SDRC). Meanwhile, the remnant of the former State Economic System Reform Commission, which had in 1998 been downgraded to a modest office under the State Council, was merged into the SDRC, making "reform" an integral part of macroeconomic policy making and implementation.[134]

The disappearance of the SETC and the takeover of the Reform Office leave the SDRC as the key institution for macroeconomic planning and implementation, much like Japan's MITI (now METI), and should promote the coherence of development policy making and implementation. With the SASAC looking after key state firms, the State Development and Reform Commission is to become more even-handed in its policy making and regulatory functions and formulate policies and strategies with the entire economy on its "mind." The removal of the word "planning" from its name affirms the trend toward using market-oriented mechanisms to manage the economy rather than reliance on approvals, permits, and microeconomic interventions.

Another area of regulatory fragmentation was in China's trade apparatus. Following the 1998 government restructuring, internal trade became the responsibility of the SETC; foreign trade was mainly the responsibility of the Ministry of Foreign Trade and Economic Cooperation (MOFTEC), while the SETC and SDPC were involved in the import of key commodities and products (for example, oil, automobiles, and airplanes). These agencies also shared regulatory functions in light of their authority over different types of investment: importing equipment for technical renovation required approval from SETC, and imports for major projects needed the nod of the SDPC.[135] This institutional setup made it exceedingly cumbersome and difficult for companies to secure approvals and presented serious problems following China's entry into the WTO. For example, cases for antidumping and antisubsidies must first be launched at the MOFTEC before they are transferred to the SETC for investigations into whether harm has been done to Chinese industry. After the SETC makes its investigations and determination, it is the MOFTEC that announces the results of the investigations.[136] To overcome the various forms of regulatory fragmentation that attended China's trade apparatus, the 2003 reform merged the Ministry of Foreign Trade and certain bureaus of the SETC and the SDPC (domestic commerce regulation, plan implementation for the import and export of certain key commodities and products, including agricultural products) into a new Ministry of Commerce to offer a more unified approach to trade regulation and to facilitate China's compliance with the terms of China's WTO membership.

Conclusions

In China as elsewhere, government reforms have not occurred simply because someone had good plans for such reforms. In the early 1980s as well as in 1997, strong political commitment helped produce more sweeping cuts than in the late 1980s and early 1990s. The importance of politics and even an element of contingency have been apparent in the push for government reform since 1997. It was the perceived crisis of the state against the background of the Asian financial crisis, manifested in dramatic revenue shortfalls and rampant corruption of state agents that finally galvanized the Chinese leadership to implement a massive restructuring of the government. Aspects of the government reforms were further cemented by the need to comply with the terms of China's WTO membership.

While the rationalization of government administration is a political act, politicians need the right soil for their ideas to germinate into new formation. This is particularly the case for the transformation of the socialist state. The mutual dependence between bureaucratic agency and state enterprise has proven to be especially tenacious. Such mutual dependence, as Chinese leaders correctly noted, also implied a strong interrelationship between government reforms and economic reforms. Whereas the administrative reforms of the early 1980s quickly petered out, the growth and steady expansion of market competition since then have provided a nourishing environment for the rationalization of the state since the late 1990s. As an official from Liaoning's Haicheng put it, "it was the market that liberated the government" and enabled the latter to truly reform itself.[137] The transformation in government has in turn made it easier to preserve the fruits of market reforms and promote further reforms of state enterprises, social security, and the financial system.

Unlike the reforms of the 1980s, there has been much deliberateness in the Chinese government reforms since the late 1990s. The process of local experimentation, summing up, and national adoption was not only important in finding out whether certain types of reforms were feasible but also helped guide public opinion to become more tolerant of such reforms.[138] Much momentum was gained when the central government restructuring plan won overwhelming support at the national legislature in spring 1998. As the 1998 reforms were carried out, it almost seemed natural to continue with another round of reforms and to iron out some major glitches in the administrative system with the 2003 reform plan. And, as the 2003 plan is implemented, there is already talk of further need to rationalize the regulatory structures for energy and transportation, as well as to clarify the relationship between the newly established Electricity Regulatory Commission and the State Development Reform Commission. For many Chinese, reform is not merely practice but has become an attitude.

Despite an earlier emphasis on cost savings, the downsizing of government has produced little savings in payroll expenses because of the way the downsizing was carried out and because of significant increases in civil servant salaries since 1998. Yet it seems fair to conclude that the 1998–2003 government reforms have reshaped the structure of government, symbolized by the abolition of industrial ministries that once served as the core of the planned economy and the rise of the regulatory agencies (to be further discussed in Chapter 3). The adjustment of the government structure and its associated functions, together with the evolution of the relationship between government and state enterprises and the reforms of the *shiye danwei*, should help delimit the role of government in the economy. In Chapters 5 and 6, we go beyond the structure of government to examine the changes in how the government, in its many manifestations, is changing the way it interacts with businesses and citizens.

chapter three

INSTITUTIONAL DEVELOPMENT AND THE QUEST
FOR FISCAL PROWESS AND MARKET ORDER

For China's leaders, the downsizing and rationalization of the governmental structure were by no means intended to weaken the power of the state and their own control over that power. Quite the opposite. In fact, the government reforms have been a key aspect of the Chinese leadership's efforts to enhance the efficiency and legitimacy of the state apparatuses and augment the central leadership's capacity to project power nationally in an era of socioeconomic liberalization.

For the first 15 years or so of the post-Mao reform era, the expansion of government went hand in hand with the decentralization of resources and diffusion of power in the Chinese political system. While the post-Tiananmen leadership carried on the program to reform government administration that was initiated in the Zhao Ziyang era, they also saw the era of Hu Yaobang and Zhao Ziyang as one of excessive decentralization. In the aftermath of the Tiananmen crisis of 1989 and the collapse of the Soviet Union, and amid macroeconomic difficulties, Jiang Zemin, Premier Li Peng, and other central leaders feared losing their grip over the ponderous organizational setup. In response, they worked tirelessly to reconstitute the sinews of governance, especially the levers of central control, even as the government steadily extricated itself from direct intervention in the operations of state firms and other economic entities.

The introductory chapter has already briefly reviewed Jiang's efforts to strengthen control over military support as well as political appointment. In contrast to Yeltsin's Russia, where the regional governors acquired their own power bases independent of the center and could veto federal policies via the Federation Council, the Chinese central leadership's ability to appoint provincial and other officials has been a fundamental factor in China's successful economic stabilization and economic reforms in the 1990s.[1] It is conventional knowledge that both Jiang Zemin and Hu Jintao have carefully placed their own followers and supporters in key positions throughout the country.[2] The case of Guangdong provides a striking illustration of this argument. During the Asian financial crisis of 1997–1999, it was widely noted that the central leaders relied on party Secretary Li Changchun (transferred from Henan) and Executive Vice Governor Wang Qishan (from the central government), both outsiders who were closely associated with Jiang Zemin and Zhu Rongji, respectively, to steer the course of financial stabilization and cleanup in Guangdong.[3]

Yet governance is not simply about brute power or Machiavellian control. It is also about having the capacity to implement policies that bear on the interests and welfare of the population. Such capacity, often in short supply in developing countries, may be measured in the availability of personnel and institutions to generate financial resources and to enforce laws and regulations. In this chapter, I shall focus on the restructuring of the taxation, fiscal, banking, and financial systems as well as the empowerment of regulatory agencies to reveal the extent to which central state capacity has been refined and augmented through the adoption of "vertical administration." In contrast to commentators who have suggested that the recentralization of the 1990s would have been approved by Mao and could go as far as to choke off growth,[4] I suggest that China's leaders appear to have found a middle ground for reorganizing the framework for state action.

Economic Turmoil and the Demand for Institutional Building[5]

Besides strengthening control over areas that the Communist Party had traditionally emphasized, including military power, personnel appointments, and the propaganda apparatus, the crisis in the economy at the turn of the 1990s prompted the central leadership to seek to reassert economic control. In groping for levers to stabilize the economy, however, the Chinese leadership quickly found existing economic institutions inadequate for fine-tuning an economy in transition.

One may date the start of the economic crisis of the 1990s to Deng's southern tour in 1992. Dissatisfied with the slowdown in economic growth and reforms that followed on the heels of the Tiananmen crackdown, Deng Xiaoping went on a highly symbolic tour to promote faster economic growth and set the agenda for the fourteenth Party Congress in the fall of 1992. In Deng's view, while the economic adjustment of 1988–1991 was necessary, it served only the goal of stability and did not adequately promote growth. While on the tour Deng encouraged the localities that had been chafing at the central government's strictures to leap ahead, calling on Guangdong, Shanghai, and Jiangsu in particular to grow faster than the national average. He stated that whoever obstructed the reform campaign ought to be removed. In praising those provinces that had grown faster than the national average during the austerity program, Deng implied that it was all right for local leaders not to pay careful attention to central policies as long as they generated superior economic growth.

Following the southern tour, central leaders, including both Jiang Zemin and Li Peng, shed their cautious stance to jump on the Deng bandwagon by introducing a variety of reformist policies. By wielding his enormous prestige, Deng tipped the balance in favor of the localities and unleashed a wave of reform euphoria. On the one hand, provincial authorities could now invoke Deng to justify expansionary policies, thereby precipitating a round of emulation and competition among the localities in adopting "innovative" policies. On the other hand, as central leaders jumped on the bandwagon of bolder reforms one after another, there was no longer any serious effort to prevent economic overheating from occurring, given Deng's injunction on those who dared to block reform.[6] As every locality sought to do better than average, macroeconomic stability became the casualty of uncoordinated local actions. Local governments rushed to set up development zones, with preferential policies to attract investment from overseas. There was a massive increase in the number and scale of government-sponsored construction projects. For the 1991–1995 period, state sector fixed asset investment increased by 32.6 percent per year, compared with 15.8 percent for 1986–1990 and 12.2 percent for 1981–1985. In 1992–1993, the increases were 48.1 and 44.1 percent, respectively.[7] China hadn't seen such heady growth since the disastrous Great Leap Forward.

A bubble was in the making. For the first half of 1993, the Chinese economy grew by nearly 14 percent. Industrial production jumped by 25.1 percent (and 30.2 percent for June) compared with the same period of 1992. Measured on a year-to-year basis, inflation accelerated to 21.6 percent in large cities in June after averaging 17.4 percent through the first half.[8] The massive rise in investment, including much land and real estate speculation, was supported largely with bank credit. As inflation accelerated, however, the growth of bank deposits slowed to a standstill and then went into the negative in spring 1993, putting banks into a precarious situation. In mid-1993, the normally ebullient State Statistical Bureau concluded that the Chinese economy had entered the "red light" danger zone.[9] With the jitters from 1989 still fresh in many people's minds, there was much concern about the social and political consequences of economic instability.

The economic turmoil of 1993 was followed by an extended economic stabilization program engineered by Vice Premier Zhu Rongji. Broad money-supply growth rate was reduced from 37 percent in 1993 to 25 percent in 1996. The growth rate of fixed asset investment was reduced from 61.8 percent in 1993 to 18 percent in 1996. The deceleration of demand was reflected in the inflation rate. While the annual inflation rate in 1994 was 21.7 percent, the highest recorded in the history of the PRC, it was brought down to 6.1 percent by 1996, allowing the People's Bank to begin a series of interest rate cuts. In the meantime, economic growth averaged 12 percent per year from 1992 to 1996. The widely hailed soft landing helped make the death of Deng Xiaoping in February 1997 an uneventful political juncture.[10] It also propelled Zhu Rongji to the post of State Council premier in 1998.

When the economic stabilization program was initiated with Document no. 6 in 1993, Zhu Rongji stated in June 1993 that he would rely primarily on economic and legislative means and use "necessary administrative means" only as a supplement.[11] Nevertheless, while the various stabilization efforts—currency intervention, interest rate hikes, the promotion of treasury bond sales—suggest the adoption of market-conforming measures, nearly all these measures had to be accompanied by strong-arm tactics to be made effective. The interest rate changes were backed up by bank lending quotas that were a relic of the central planning system (the lending quotas were finally phased out in 1999). While the People's Bank poured dollars into the swap centers to stabilize the dollar-yuan exchange rate in the summer of 1993, the government also had to increase administrative control in currency transactions. The promotion of state bond sales was similarly subjected to atavistic practices for the moment. As rising inflation diminished the attractiveness of state treasury bonds, the Ministry of Finance twice adjusted bond yields upward in conjunction with interest rate rises on bank deposits, finally pegging bond yields to inflation in order to make the bonds more attractive to buyers. But the Finance Ministry had to resort to far more than simple yield hikes to attract buyers. In a circular issued by the State Council in June 1993, the central government asked local authorities to adopt all possible measures to improve bond sales. Local governments were prohibited from issuing stocks and corporate bonds before they had sold their allocated quota of state bonds. It was also stipulated that corporate bond yields could not exceed those of state treasury bonds. More egregiously, millions of workers found their June salaries summarily docked for bond purchases.[12]

Besides these economic strong-arm tactics, President Jiang Zemin used his party portfolio to enhance party discipline and tighten ideological control. Complementing the central policy on macroeconomic control was a circular issued, also in late June 1993, by the CCP's Central Commission for Discipline Inspection and the Ministry of Supervision. The circular pointedly stated that some localities and departments had not taken effective action to implement the various party and government documents and regulations designed to deal with problems in the economy, and demanded that all localities strictly abide by the principles of discipline outlined by the party and the government.[13] President Jiang personally chaired regional economic conferences to convince provincial leaders to support the central government's endeavor to regain macroeconomic control.

In general, central-local relations during the economic stabilization conformed to earlier patterns.[14] With central leaders united behind a policy platform, the locals largely complied with the center's decisions on unauthorized loans, tax reductions, and exemptions. While not all unauthorized loans were withdrawn, enough were recalled to puncture the bubbles in the stock and real estate markets. Nonetheless, as they grappled with economic turmoil, China's leaders realized that the Chinese economic system was not conducive to the sort of fine-tuning they had in mind. Frustrated by the difficulties of maneuvering a makeshift economic system and afraid that they might not be able to get the house in order before Deng died,[15] the Chinese leadership began to push for sweeping rationalizing reforms of the economic system, a project that was originally adumbrated in 1992. The first order of business was to shore up the fiscal foundations of the central government.

Restructuring the Fiscal System and
Tax Administration

As is well known, the introduction of the fiscal contracting schemes in the 1980s served to bring about a steady decline in the ratio of government revenue to GNP. Tax revenue as a percentage of GNP fell from 23 to 12.6 percent between 1985 and 1993.[16] Moreover, the adoption of fiscal contracting between the central government and the provincial governments limited the central government's revenue intake. As a result, central government revenue as a share of economic activities such as GNP declined over time, making it difficult for the center to secure a stable macroeconomic environment and undertake redistributive policies.[17] Indeed, China's fiscal system in the late 1980s exhibited features common to most developing countries where "budget deficits have been financed to an excessive extent by money creation and borrowing abroad with consequent inflation and foreign debt problems."[18]

Analytically, Chinese economists and policy advisers recognized the potential pitfalls of the fiscal contracting system soon after it was launched.[19] For example, Xue Muqiao, China's senior economic statesman, was also was one of the most respected and high-profile advocates for fiscal reforms from 1989–1993. Xue concluded that the fiscal contracting system had become a major source of the macroeconomic problems and argued for adopting a tax assignment system to strengthen the central government's macroeconomic capacity.

Premier Li Peng and Vice Premier Yao Yilin made an attempt to rationalize the fiscal system in 1990. This attempt faltered, however, for two major reasons. First, China's central leaders were timid about making major reforms amid the atmosphere of political crisis both in China and abroad. Secondly, the economic slowdown that resulted from the austerity programs of 1988–1990 not only dampened people's expectations but also sharply decreased government revenue growth. In consequence, local efforts to fight for the fiscal status quo were much more determined than would have been the case had the economy been booming; and it was therefore politically difficult for central leaders to negotiate with local interests for a greater share of the revenue stream.[20]

Yet the delay in revamping the fiscal system and the continuing increase in central government budget deficit fueled a lively debate over China's fiscal difficulties, providing the intellectual impetus for fiscal ra-

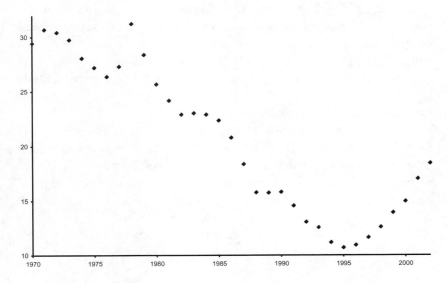

Figure 3.1. Government Revenues as a Percentage of GDP. Note: Government revenues excludes debt. Sources: ZGTJNJ 2000–2001; ZGTJZY 2003.

tionalization.[21] There was widespread recognition that with the declining ratio of central government revenue to national income, the central government faced major fiscal difficulties and something had to be done. Chen Yuan, then a deputy governor of the People's Bank of China and the son of conservative patriarch Chen Yun, warned publicly that the decline of central revenue as a share of national income might lead to "the further loss of economic control and [even] economic disintegration."[22] This rhetoric of fiscal crisis would reach a crescendo in 1993 as the central government once again pushed for rationalization in anticipation of the Third Plenum of the fourteenth Central Committee.[23]

The near unanimity with which analysts both in China and abroad dissected China's fiscal situation helped Chinese leaders to focus on promoting fiscal reforms. In contrast to only two years earlier, the psychology of the political actors had changed considerably by 1992. First, the central leaders had largely steadied their nerves after the Tiananmen crisis and the collapse of the Soviet Union and Eastern Europe. Second, an unintended but nonetheless striking effect of the 1988–1990 economic austerity was to further expose the weak fiscal foundations and foster the perception of fiscal crisis and thus a sort of consensus about fiscal reforms among the top elite. Third, the disintegration of the Soviet Union underscored the importance of keeping the central government strong; needless to say, fiscal prowess was considered a major pillar of central government strength. Finally, China in the aftermath of Deng's southern tour was enveloped in an economic euphoria. With expectations of economic prospects running high, local officials would likely be more willing to strike a bargain with the central government over fiscal reforms.

Against this background, Deng Xiaoping's ever-advancing age and feeble health imparted a special sense of urgency for shoring up the central government's fiscal foundations. Besides the succession factor, the macroeconomic difficulties of 1992 and the limited success the leadership had with reining in economic overheating in 1993 also reminded central leaders that they should make certain fundamental institutional reforms. In 1993, the central government's intake of the budgetary revenue was only 22 percent of the total. The fiscal enervation of the central government relative to the localities made central leaders feel that they were piloting an aircraft carrier using the tools for a small boat. As then Finance Minister Liu Zhongli put it baldly, "when the [central] government does not have money, its words no longer count."[24] Thus the central leadership, particularly Jiang Zemin and Zhu Rongji, chose to bite the bullet and push for revamping the taxation and fiscal systems in 1993. They invoked alarmist visions and the authority of Deng to gain leverage over provincial authorities. In driving the bargain, they promised that the provinces would not see a reduction in their current level of fiscal income. Afraid that provincial leaders would present a united front in collective bargaining, the central leadership marshaled its organizational and other resources and adopted a divide-and-rule strategy vis-à-vis local officials.[25] A special working group, made up of 60-plus people, including central leaders Vice Premier Zhu Rongji and officials from the Ministry of Finance and other government departments, traveled to 17 provinces one by one to hammer out the base revenue figures for each province and readjust the fiscal relations between the central government and the provinces.

From Fiscal Particularism to Tax Assignment

By the end of 1993, a sweeping reform of the taxation and fiscal systems had been put together for implementation starting in 1994. In contrast to the fiscal contracting system that had given the central government

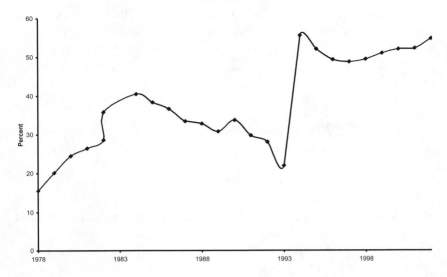

Figure 3.2. The Central Government's Share of Total Budgetary Revenue. Source: ZGTJZY 2003.

only a set amount of revenue, the new fiscal and tax assignment system, much like the federalist system used in many Western countries, designated different categories of taxes to the central and local governments, respectively.[26] The new system also standardized the taxation system and simplified tax categories and tax rates (particularly through the replacement of complex product taxes with a uniform value-added tax). Most importantly, the new system was designed to help the central government benefit from the marginal growth in the economy and in revenue generation.[27]

The fiscal reforms were put into place without much difficulty—partly because provincial authorities were guaranteed a base revenue no less than the 1993 revenue figure—and had an immediate impact on the division of revenue between the central government and the provinces.[28] In 1994, the central government's share of budgetary revenue (versus the provinces) rose to 56 percent, an increase of 33.7 percentage points from a year earlier. It remained at just below 55 percent in 2002 (Figure 3.2). At the same time, total government budgetary revenue as a percentage of GDP has also recovered substantially, rising from a low of 10.7 percent in 1995 to 18.5 percent in 2002 (Figure 3.1).[29] While the central government returns most of the increased central revenue to the provinces as rebates and transfer payments, its effective control over the revenue stream has recovered substantially and is expected to grow over the long run. In the meantime, local authorities now collect their own taxes and thus have far less interest in hiding wealth from the central government than before. In consequence, local tax revenue has also grown far more rapidly than before the fiscal reforms.

The Institutional Underpinnings of the
Tax Assignment System

Prior to the 1994 reforms, the central government relied on locals to collect taxes for remission to the central treasury. Local governments used their discretionary power to negotiate tax payments with enterprises and offered tax exemptions to overseas investors to attract investments. There were multiple tax arrangements for different enterprises, enterprises of different ownership, and different industries. The delegation of tax authority to the local level was therefore not conducive to the creation of a level playing field. In contrast, the change from contracting to tax sharing between central and provincial authorities dramatically increased the central government's desire to monitor tax administration effort, where previously it had simply waited for the delivery of the contracted amount from local authorities. What better way to strengthen its monitoring than to set up its own tax collection apparatus! Thus a key element of the tax reforms was the establishment of separate central (national) and provincial (local) tax administrations.[30] In short, the 1994 reforms not only demarcated the taxation powers between the central government and the provinces but also led to the establishment of separate state and local taxation bureaus in the provinces.

In terms of organizational hierarchy, the State Administration of Taxation (SAT) directly oversees the provincial state taxation bureaus (*guoshuiju*) in what is known as *chuizhi guanli* or vertical administration. Within this vertical administration structure, each level supervises the next level in matters of organization, staffing, budgets, and leader duties.[31] This organizational strategy signaled a retreat from the emphasis on decentralization that had prevailed for more than a decade and was evidently a key element of the new focus on strengthening central control of the organizational hierarchy. The establishment of the state tax (*guoshui*) administration means that the central government is no longer dependent on the goodwill of the local authorities. In 1999, the SAT further directed provincial tax bureaus to align their organizational structure with headquarters to facilitate communication and guidance. Local tax bureaus (*dishuiju*) at the prefecture, city, and county levels were also urged to streamline organization to focus on tax collection.[32] Meanwhile, as the state tax bureaus are built up, the Customs Administration, the collector of customs tariffs for the central government, was upgraded to ministerial status and reconstituted. The reform placed 41 customs offices directly under the supervision of the central administration and made the Customs Administration one of the most vertically integrated agencies.[33]

Because the state taxation bureaus are largely staffed with people recruited from the localities in which they are based, the Ministry of Finance is concerned about local influences on the behavior of these bureaus. While such concern is to some extent mitigated by the fact that the local authorities share in some of the major taxes collected by the state tax bureaus, interviews suggest that local government officials, including deputy governors, sometimes ask the state tax bureaus to show lenience in collecting taxes for the central government. To improve compliance with central government policies, the Ministry of Finance has established special representative officials in provincial units as well as large cities with independent planning status (*jihua danlie shi*) in conjunction with the tax and fiscal reforms. The representative office in Shandong, for example, has a staff of more than 40 (compared with over 30,000 employees in the State Taxation Bureau). The rep office has two major functions: the supervision of centrally disbursed expenditures to ensure compliance with central government spending targets and the supervision of the State Taxation Bureau to ensure the collection of taxes due to the central government.[34]

In spite of the adoption of vertical administration and the establishment of the supervisory rep offices, it became more difficult for the central government to collect taxes proportionate to its share of ownership in various enterprises owing to the growing diversification and complexity of ownership. When bureaus of industry and commerce register firms by capital structure, they do not differentiate between central and local ownership (both are under the rubric of state ownership), thus making it difficult for central state taxation personnel to keep track of central-government-owned shares. As a result, the rep offices proposed that the corporate income tax be changed into a tax shared proportionately between central and local governments. This proposal became official policy in 2002 (see below). Moreover, in an effort to boost the central government's effective control over tax administration, the state tax bureaus have also been given the responsibility of collecting the corporate income tax for firms formed in 2002 and after.[35]

Supervision of the provincial local taxation bureaus is shared between the SAT and provincial governments under dual leadership, but the provincial governments supply the funds and personnel and are the dominant partner. In most provinces, the director of the provincial finance department doubles as director of the provincial local taxation bureau. While the state and local tax bureaus collect different taxes, they also coordinate and collaborate with each other. This is most obvious in tax registration. The state taxation bureau is responsible for registering taxpayers liable for the value-added tax, while the local taxation bureau registers those who pay the business tax and other local taxes. The two bureaus are to share their registration lists for reference and to conduct verification of the list jointly.[36] Within the provinces, provincial authorities have adopted vertical administration in the local taxation bureaus to better monitor and control sub-provincial tax administration.

Through institutional reforms and persistent efforts to crack down on various forms of tax evasion and fraud (especially since August 2000), the Chinese government has in recent years been able to boost tax revenue growth well above the rate of economic growth. Much remains to be done to make the tax system more coherent and less convoluted and to improve the quota-oriented tax administration. By the turn of the 2000s, the central government had launched three major initiatives to strengthen the enforcement of tax laws.

First, in an effort to plug the holes in existing legislation on tax collection, the PRC Tax Collection and Administration Law was amended and put into effect on May 1, 2001. While it offers greater details about the rights and obligations of taxpayers and stipulates that tax collectors must follow the law in tax administration, the amended Tax Collection and Administration Law is clearly intended to legally empower the tax authorities. It stipulates that the industry and commerce administrations are legally obligated to supply the tax administration with information. It also requires banks and other financial institutions to cooperate with tax authorities in seeking to collect taxes and specifies penalties for financial institutions and individuals that fail to provide such assistance.

Second, the tax administrations have set up direct monitoring relationships with major business taxpayers. By spring 2003, the number of firms included in this program had risen to 21,768 (compared with 1,500 in

2000), accounting for about 43 percent of the domestic tax revenue.[37] Meanwhile, a tax police (*shuijing dadui*) was set up and put under the direct command of the Ministry of Public Security. While so far the tax collectors have little law enforcement authority and needed to work jointly with the police, the tax police, with an initial staff of 67,000 in late 2000 and eventual target size of 300,000, may make the Tax Administration the one institution that taxpayers love to hate.[38] In 2002–2003, the tax authorities tackled a variety of high-profile tax fraud cases and clearly put China's new rich on notice about tax compliance.

Last but certainly not least, technology has become a vital element in reforms of the tax administration and the handmaiden of enhanced central control. For example, the nationwide adoption of computer-based receipts for value-added tax, as part of the Golden Tax Project, has helped to cut down fake receipts as well as boost transparency.[39] Various cities including Beijing, Shanghai, and Suzhou have introduced computer-generated "lotteries" for receipts from restaurants and other businesses to encourage customers to demand receipts and thus force these businesses to pay taxes. With the aid of new technologies, the State Administration of Taxation began in 2001 to experiment with major reforms of the tax administration in Shandong, Zhejiang, Henan, and Shenzhen and extended the reforms to Beijing, Tianjin, Chongqing, Hubei, Hunan, as well as 20 other major cities the following year.[40] Prior to the reforms, the tax administration was organized according to the types of firms, with separate sub-bureaus (*fenju*) dedicated respectively to central-government- and provincial-government-owned firms, local firms, and overseas-invested firms. Where they are implemented, the reforms have done away with the sub-bureaus oriented to firms of different types of ownership; instead each city or county tax administration is empowered to collect taxes from all types of firms. The collection of taxes from major corporations, including multinationals, is centralized in municipal or even provincial-level tax bureaus. In Shandong, the removal of a layer of tax bureaucracy helped reduce the number of administrative personnel by 30 percent.

The prereform sub-bureaus targeted at firms of different ownership types enjoyed much discretion. Frontline tax collectors would collect less than required from some businesses in response to bribery and personal relationships. The reorganization, by reducing administrative personnel and flattening the tax administration, is partly intended to reduce the discretion of these offices. With massive investments in the State Tax Administration Information System as part of the Golden Tax Project, corporations can file and pay taxes electronically. Accounting by tax administrators is centralized into county/city tax bureaus, and statistical aggregations are accomplished at prefecture-ranked cities as well as provincial tax bureaus. At the same time, the processes of tax administration can be more easily monitored and supervised by superior offices in real time. For example, the data center of the Guangdong State Tax Bureau polled the data for 1.2 million taxpayers into one central database in early 2003. All 17,800 tax collectors/processors must process tax payments on software linked to shared prefectural and municipal tax databases, making it less likely for tax collection professionals to process tax payments in violation of standard operating procedures.[41] Indeed, eventually the Beijing headquarters will likely be able to directly monitor county-level tax bureaus on a daily basis.

Fiscal Reforms and the Limits of
Local Autonomy

While the 1994 fiscal and taxation reforms introduced elements of fiscal federalism, they were nevertheless intended to strengthen the central government's control over the revenue stream. Since then, the emphasis on central control has predominated. Not only has the trend toward uniformity and transparency in taxation been accompanied by policies to limit local autonomy, but subsequent fiscal reforms, notably the reapportionment of corporate and personal income taxes in 2002, have further enhanced the central government's dominance.

To begin with, fearing rampant debt defaults and excessive overseas debt exposure, the central leadership prohibited local governments from incurring budget deficits or issuing bonds without Beijing's approval. This stipulation, not always followed to the letter, was later enshrined in the Budget Implementation Law enacted in 1994, making China a typical transition economy in terms of controlling sub-national borrowing.[42] The fiscal discipline was evident in 1998–1999 when the central government, with approval from the National People's Congress, issued special treasury bonds of 160 billion yuan. Part of this intake was borrowed for local governments that are legally prohibited from incurring budget deficits.

Moreover, there has been a major initiative to crack down on discretionary tax reduction and remission, practices that local authorities had used widely to compete for investments.[43] Curbing rampant tax reductions and exemptions authorized by local authorities was one of the first policy goals adopted by Zhu Rongji in 1993 when the macroeconomic stabilization program was launched. With the 1994 reforms, the State Administration of Taxation ruled that it was illegal for local governments to offer tax breaks and exemptions for investors. In an effort to boost the attractiveness of the local investment environment, some local governments skirted this ruling by first collecting the local taxes from investors and then refunding them with funds from local government budgets. The SAT believed this behavior was illegal as well but at first decided that such refunds were "not a matter of tax policy" and thus "beyond the reach of tax offices."[44] At the turn of 2000, the State Council clarified this issue by issuing a directive on rectifying the local practice of rebating taxes. Authority to grant tax rebates is centralized in the State Council; local authorities are only permitted to manage the slaughter, banquet, and animal husbandry taxes.[45] At the same time, the various preferential tax policies for special zones and other areas have also been whittled down. For example, products produced and consumed in the special economic zones used to be exempt from the value-added tax. By 2003, all special economic zones had phased out this tax privilege.[46]

Furthermore, efforts are under way to convert some levies and fees into formal taxes (see also Chapter 7). As a result of the conversion, the tax administrations will take over the collection from other government departments and agencies. For example, in 2001 the central government began to collect a vehicle purchase tax to replace the vehicle purchase surcharge previously collected by the transportation (communications) bureaus. At the end of 2002 the vehicle purchase tax collectors based in the communication bureaus were formally moved to the tax administration.[47] The rationalization of fees and levies not only promises to boost the transparency of state extraction and curb arbitrariness, but also helps centralize the state financial power in the Tax Administration and the Ministry of Finance.

Finally, the continuing realignment of the fiscal relations between central and local governments in favor of the central government has underscored the central authorities' dominance of these relationships. Besides the 1994 reforms, the central government has also taken control of the stamp tax on stock trading. All these changes suggest that the central government is in control and China is far from being federalist.[48]

Nowhere is the power of the central government more evident than in the reapportionment of the personal and corporate income taxes. The 1994 fiscal reforms assigned all personal income tax revenue to local authorities. This decision made sense at the time because the personal income tax is hard to collect and local authorities with local information are better positioned to collect this tax than the central government. Yet developed countries have tended to rely on the personal income tax for government revenue as globe-trotting corporations find various ways to reduce their tax burden. Within China, the personal income tax revenue has been the fastest growing revenue category in the reform era. It grew by an average of 47.5 percent between 1993 and 2001, jumping from 4.7 billion yuan in 1993 to 99.6 billion yuan in 2001 on the back of rapid economic growth.[49] There was widespread anticipation that the local authorities, particularly the richest provincial units, should not be allowed to keep this increasingly important tax source all to themselves.

Meanwhile, the 1994 fiscal reforms also left corporate income taxation in a sort of tangle: central-government-owned SOEs paid corporate income tax to the state tax bureau while local-government-owned SOEs paid their corporate income tax to the local tax bureau. By the late 1990s, however, corporate income taxation had become more and more complex as corporate reforms had obscured the boundaries of ownership over time. Moreover, the central-local corporate taxation division by ownership became an obstacle to mergers and acquisitions among firms owned by different governments (different regions; and central versus local).

In 2001, the central government went back to the drawing board and made both the corporate and personal income taxes shared taxes between central and provincial governments, beginning in 2002. As in the reforms negotiated in 1993, local authorities are guaranteed a base amount, which is pegged to the localities' corporate and personal income tax revenues for 2001.[50] Corporate and personal income tax revenue above the base amount is split between central and local governments. The ratio was set at 50:50 for 2002 and 60 percent for the central government in 2003.

Over time the 2002 reforms are expected to dramatically expand the central government's fiscal prowess, just as the expansion of the personal income tax in the United States greatly facilitated the expansion of the federal government. The Chinese central leadership has justified this fundamental change by saying that it will use the additional revenue to boost transfer payments to the interior regions, thus binding the less developed areas more tightly to the central government's largesse.[51] Likewise, transfer payments within the provinces have also helped augment the power of the provincial governments vis-à-vis the sub-provincial governments, a trend that is also enhanced by the fee-for-tax reforms in rural areas.

Central Bank Restructuring and the Pursuit of Financial Stability

While the central government has solidified its fiscal foundations, it has also put reform of the financial system, particularly the banking sector, on the agenda. Nevertheless, it was not until the Asian financial crisis that China's leaders finally pursued the reform of the banking system aggressively. Key to the banking reforms was the restructuring of the central banking system and the enhancement of banking supervision.

Until the late 1990s, branches of the People's Bank of China (PBOC), officially the central bank since only 1984, were not only based in provincial capitals and larger cities but were also subject to the dual leadership of provincial and local governments. Provincial party officials were key players in choosing heads of the PBOC's provincial branches; they also had much influence on the choice of branch officers of the major state banks. Consequently, as Lardy noted, until 1993 "the provincial branches of the central bank responded primarily to provincial level political leaders rather than central bank headquarters in Beijing."[52]

While fiscal decentralization increased the need for macroeconomic coordination and control, the decentralization of the banking system, by making central bank branches (as well as branches of the major state banks) beholden to local authorities, compounded that need. Local government officials seeking high growth rates—on which basis they tended to be evaluated—eagerly exerted pressures on state banks to make loans to local enterprises. For them, macroeconomic stability is a public good best supplied by others. As a World Bank study put it: "the decentralized financial network was overly generous (under political prodding) in responding to the demands for credit from enterprises. . . . Unless the intense investment hunger can be blunted and provinces induced to adhere to common development goals, the demand for credit will remain strong as will the political pressure on banks to grant credit even if it means violating [credit] ceilings."[53]

As a result of the intermarriage between political and financial power, the Chinese state banks through the first half of the 1990s became overextended in capital investment and real estate development, often through bank-affiliated investment and trust companies. Some of the bank funds were also funneled into speculative investments, including the nascent stock market. During the financial turmoil of 1993–1994, state bank branches often had little cash to pay farmers or lend to factories for operating funds and wage payments. According to veteran banking analyst Yang Peixin, banks usually set aside as much as six yuan in cash reserves for each 100 yuan in deposits, but in May 1993, the average was reduced to only about one yuan.[54] China was on the brink of financial chaos in 1993.

Much of the lending from Chinese banks was made to state enterprises; a high percentage of the loans have ended up as nonperforming loans that continue to plague the banking system.[55] Until bankruptcy of state enterprises became a real possibility in the late 1990s, it was rational for bank officials to follow the instructions of government officials and lend to state enterprises. Moreover, because domestic real interest rates were until recently consistently negative, credit demand far outstripped supply and bank lending was generally based on bureaucratic rationing through lending quotas rather than careful assessment of creditworthiness. The intermarriage of politics and finance thus provided officials in both local governments and banks plenty of opportunities for patronage and corruption.

Clearly, improvement in the regulation of the banking system was sorely needed in China. The problem was not that the People's Bank of China, the central bank, was not independent, though central bank independence is increasingly believed to contribute to stable macroeconomic performance.[56] Rather, the People's Bank of China was until recently so beholden to local interests that it was often hardly acting like a central bank at all. By 1988, the People's Bank of China had 29 provincial branches, 529 city branches, and 1,760 county branches and more than 130,000 employees—several times the number of employees in the U.S. Federal Reserve.[57] The more branches the bank boasted, the more access points were opened up to political influence from local elites. Local officials not only had much influence on lending decisions but also interfered in efforts by the central government to improve banking regulation and deal with financial irregularities.

To be fair, the Chinese leadership had shown much concern about the central banking system, beginning with the formal designation of the People's Bank of China as the central bank. There was also early recognition of the harmful effect of local influence over central bank branches. In

1988 the head office of the People's Bank of China was empowered to appoint managers of branch offices.[58] Yet this order had only limited impact on local interference. Leaders of central bank branches continued to succumb to pressure from powerful local officials; the bankers needed the local governments' assistance in their work and their personal interests, including welfare for family members and postbanking jobs for themselves, also benefited from rapport with local officials.[59] Moreover, the large number of local bank offices diluted the ability of the central bank headquarters to micromanage appointments. In fact, by the end of 1996, the number of PBOC employees had risen to some 180,000.[60]

As the central government worked hard to tame inflation and shore up the fiscal sinews of the state in 1993, it was again proposed that the central banking system be revamped to make it more independent of local interests.[61] The third plenum of the fourteenth CCP Central Committee held in November 1993, called for actively creating the conditions for setting up central bank branches that span provincial boundaries so as to insulate the branches from local meddling.[62] The banking laws, promulgated in 1995, also stipulate that the People's Bank of China conducts an independent monetary policy under the leadership of the State Council and that the PBOC's operations shall be free from interference from local governments, government departments, social organizations, and individuals.[63]

In spite of these pronouncements, the banking reform plan did not get off the ground immediately. This was partly because central leaders focused their attention on tax and fiscal reforms. The negotiations over these reforms required the expenditure of significant political resources by central leaders. Another reason was the fear that the proposed cure might make the disease even worse. Not wanting to fight political battles on all fronts, the central leaders put central bank restructuring aside for the time being. Instead, they combined monetary policy with political discipline, highlighted by the appointment of Vice Premier Zhu Rongji as governor of the People's Bank of China, to control credit and bring about the soft landing mentioned earlier.

The Asian Financial Crisis and Central Bank Restructuring

The onset of the Asian financial crisis in the summer of 1997, however, sent a jolt to the Chinese leadership. To be sure, compared to Thailand, Indonesia, South Korea, and other countries, China fared quite well during the crisis; this was partly because China had accumulated a large foreign exchange reserve in the aftermath of the 1993–1994 macroeconomic crisis and partly because the Chinese currency was not freely convertible for the capital account. Nevertheless, like most other Asian countries, China was also afflicted with the problems of an unsound legal system, corruption, a banking system that would be insolvent by Western standards, weak financial supervision, cozy relations between government and business, and other symptoms that were found to have contributed to the financial meltdown in Thailand, South Korea, and Indonesia. Moreover, China's status as one of the world's major traders and leading destinations for foreign direct investment also implied vulnerability to external shocks. The political fallout from the Asian crisis, as evidenced in elite turnovers in several countries and the dramatic fall of the Suharto regime in Indonesia, highlighted the potentially enormous political costs of financial meltdown for Chinese leaders. There was sufficient concern within China that a massive bank failure would not only cripple the Chinese economy but could bring to an end the Communist Party's rule.[64]

To cope with the effect of the Asian financial crisis and prevent a financial meltdown, the Party Central Committee and the State Council convened a national financial work conference in November 1997. By then, the death of patriarch Deng Xiaoping had passed uneventfully, and it was clear that the post-Deng leadership, which centered on Jiang Zemin, was in control. At the conference, the leaders decided to launch a three-year comprehensive restructuring of China's financial system, especially of the central bank. As part of this initiative, the China Securities Regulatory Commission (CSRC), the China Insurance Regulatory Commission (CIRC), and the Central Financial Work Commission would come into being.

The need for financial reform was highlighted by the failure of Guangdong International Trust and Investment Corporation (GITIC) in October 1998 when GITIC defaulted on debt of more than U.S.$2 billion. The failure of GITIC and other local government investment and trust vehicles, known as Itics, drove home the message that local authorities could not be relied on to enforce financial discipline as prudence demanded. This prompted the central leadership to accelerate financial reforms, including preparing the ground for overhauling the spatial structure of the PBOC. In particular, PBOC governor Dai Xianglong lamented the webs of local connections that enmeshed the PBOC's local branches. For Dai, intervention from local government officials was a major source of risky loans and financial irregularities. Dai noted that countries including the United States, Great Britain, Japan, Mexico, India, and many others all have central bank branches covering whole regions rather than single states or provinces.[65] It was argued that the PBOC should abolish its provincial branches in favor of super-provincial branches so as to make the central bank independent from local interests in exercising its supervisory role.

Branch	Coverage Area
Tianjin	Tianjin, Hebei, Inner Mongolia, and Shanxi
Shenyang	Liaoning, Jilin, and Heilongjiang
Shanghai	Shanghai, Zhejiang, and Fujian
Nanjing	Jiangsu
Jinan	Shandong and Henan
Wuhan	Hubei, Hunan, and Jiangxi
Guangzhou	Guangdong, Guangxi, and Hainan
Chengdu	Sichuan, Guizhou, Tibet, and Yunnan
Xian	Shaanxi, Gansu, Ningxia, Qinghai, and Xinjiang

In November 1998, the central government announced its plan for restructuring the PBOC. Under the plan, the 32 provincial-level branches were abolished and replaced with nine regional branches. The PBOC would directly appoint (and rotate) the heads of these regional branches and has taken care not to place appointees in their native provinces. By consolidating authority into regional branches not beholden to provincial authorities, this reorganization has strengthened the institutional integrity of the PBOC and improved monetary policy implementation.

In tandem with the restructuring, the PBOC has increasingly behaved like a central bank in a market economy. Among its new initiatives are the resumption in 1998 of open-market operations in the treasury bond market, the use of treasury bills as a monetary instrument in 2003, and a major program to encourage the development of credit appraisal and information systems. In 2002, the PBOC showed an unusual degree of independence by using its open-market operations to influence interest rates and to warn banks and other financial institutions of the risks associated with government debt securities issued by the Ministry of Finance. The move led to a sell-off in government bonds and resulted in some government debt issue being unsubscribed.[66]

The Mixed Record of Banking Sector Reforms

Yet the biggest challenge facing China has been how to tackle the extraordinarily high rate of nonperforming loans (NPLs) that have accumulated throughout the banking system—from the gigantic state-owned commercial banks, to trust and investment companies and the rural credit institutions. Simply put, the problem of bad loans in Chinese banks is so severe that it would have resulted in systemic financial crisis in most other countries.[67]

Limitations of space have led me to focus on broader institutional reforms in China's financial regulation and eliminate much of the detailed discussion of developments within the banking sector. In brief, to cope with the massive bad-loan problem afflicting the banking system, the Chinese leadership has undertaken a spectrum of major initiatives since the late 1990s. First, the entire trust and investment sector has been consolidated on the heels of the GITIC bankruptcy. Through mergers and closures, the number of trust and investment companies was reduced from 329 in 1999 to 50-plus in 2002.[68] A new law on trusts came into effect on October 1, 2001. Second, numerous banking fraud cases have been uncovered. On the long list of bankers punished for corruption and fraud are Wang Xuebing, former president of the Bank of China (BOC) and then of the China Construction Bank as well as an alternate member of the CCP Central Committee, and Zhu Xiaohua, the chairman of state-owned China Everbright (Group) and formerly a vice governor of the People's Bank of China. Third, as the central regulators have pursued investigations and promoted discipline and managerial reforms in the commercial banks, the major wave of banking reforms that started in 1998 has picked up significantly. These reforms have centered on controlling risk, reducing operating costs, as well as improving the portfolio of loans to include the consumer sector (mortgages, autos, and so forth).

For the sake of space, I will provide only a brief summary of the cost-cutting measures as indication of the scope and depth of reforms.[69] Generally speaking, the state-owned commercial banks have increasingly turned their attention from maximizing market share to making profits. Notably, all big four state-owned commercial banks have launched major programs to close and consolidate unprofitable local branches and reduce the number of employees to save on costs. The Bank of China cut its branch institutions by 2,284 or 15 percent between 1998 and March 2000. In 2001, the BOC's revenue grew by only 1.1 percent but its costs decreased by 7.6 percent, allowing the bank to increase profits.[70] The restructuring of the Industrial and Commercial Bank of China (ICBC), the largest of the big four, has been especially impressive. Between 1997 and 2001, ICBC trimmed its payroll by 25 percent (from 570,000 down to 429,000) and closed a third of its branches (from 42,300 to 29,200). In a striking indication of the urgency of reforms since the highly publicized BOC scandals, ICBC made most of its cuts, 8,700 branches and 115,159 employees, in 2000–2001.[71] The Agricultural Bank of China, the worst performing of the big four, had the most branch closures. Over 2000–2002, it cut the number of branches by 17,000 to about 40,000 at the end of 2002 and laid off 137,000 employees.[72] The scale of the restructuring at the big four would have been big news in other parts of the world, but it has received little attention in China or the West.

In spite of these reforms, China's banking reforms are still in a race against time.[73] At the end of 1998, the official NPL ratio for the big four stood at a whopping 41 percent. The transfer of 1.4 trillion yuan in bad debts from the big four to asset management companies (AMCs) brought the NPL ratio of the big four down by about 10 percentage points. At the end of 2000, the NPL ratio of the big four was still at around 28 percent based on the relatively generous four-category classification scheme.[74] Most of these nonperforming loans were incurred in the heady 1990s.[75] This was scant consolation to regulators. Indeed, the big four continued to pile on nonperforming loans after the establishment of the AMCs.

By 2003 it appeared that the reforms by the commercial banks had finally started to improve the viability of the banking system as measured in terms of the quality of the loan portfolio and balance sheets. With the aggressive restructuring in the post–Wang Xuebing years and favorable policy treatment (including reduction of the business tax), the NPL ratio in the Chinese banking sector has shown substantial improvement.[76] During 2001, the NPL ratio in the banking system (*yinhangye jinrong jigou*) decreased by 3.81 percentage points, marking "the first reduction recorded since bank reform efforts began in 1995."[77] In 2002, according to the four-class classification scheme, the NPL ratio declined by 4.5 percent to 19.8 percent and, rather than relying on growing deposits to bring the NPL ratio down, the absolute balance of NPLs was whittled down by 95.1 billion yuan.[78] At the end of 2003, the NPL ratio stood at 15.2 percent and the amount of NPLs was a whopping 2.4 trillion yuan or 20.6 percent of GDP.[79]

To be sure, the remaining NPL ratios remain very high by international standards. Nonetheless, the pace of improvements decidedly picked up over 2001–2003. These developments were paced by the big four. Based on a reading of publicly available information, it appears that the reduction in the NPL ratios was achieved even while accounting standards were tightened. In fact the banks were able to increase NPL write-offs, boost their asset bases, and increase provisions for bad debts.[80] The numbers are believed to be reliable to the extent that the banks have improved their management and strengthened reporting requirements and to the extent that the financial reports are audited by internationally reputable accounting firms in the post-Enron era. Building on these improvements, the Bank of China and the China Construction Bank, the two best-performing banks among the big four, were given foreign exchange injections and allowed to issue subordinated debts in preparation for listing their stocks. All in all, these changes suggest, with perhaps the exception of the Agricultural Bank of China, the possibility of a managed turnaround of the Chinese banking sector over a reasonable time frame.

The Restructuring of the Banking Regulatory Apparatus

The sense of urgency in banking reform is made acute by the Chinese government's WTO commitment to allow foreign banks unrestricted access to its domestic market by 2005. With domestic banks being weak and international competition getting ever more intense, the discovery of massive fraud cases greatly worried China's leaders and pointed to the possibility of systemic crisis. The combination of these factors suggested that it had been premature to express optimism about China's banking system following the restructuring of the PBOC in 1998.[81]

In fact, despite the restructuring of the PBOC along regional lines, significant reforms by commercial banks, and continual refinement of financial laws and regulations, Chinese analysts pointed to the numerous banking fraud cases to argue that the PBOC had not been effective in regulating the banking sector. More specifically, experts at the State Council Development Research Center noted that the PBOC, in having to manage monetary policy and the enforcement of banking regulation at the same time, had tended to make bank supervision an adjunct to monetary policy. For example, when the PBOC relaxed monetary policy in 1992, it also relaxed regulatory enforcement; in contrast, it tightened monetary policy and banking supervision at the same time in 1993. To overcome the inconsistency in banking regulation, it was argued that the PBOC should focus on monetary policy and be divested of its banking regulation and enforcement functions. Instead, as in the case of securities and insurance regulation, a Banking Supervisory Commission should be dedicated to regulating banking institutions only. Still others called for setting up a super-regulatory institution to oversee banks, securities, and insurance all together, particularly because the Glass-Stegall style separation among these different sectors was being eroded. The PBOC was against the sweeping reforms that would strip it of much regulatory power. It also dismissed a proposal for central bank independence as being ill suited to China's national conditions. Instead it favored an incremental move to set up a dedicated bank supervisory bureau within the PBOC.[82] This debate became so intense that it apparently delayed the second national conference on financial work by several months (the first was held in late 1997).

When this second conference was finally convened in February 2002, the PBOC position was adopted for the moment. Amid the bruising debate on its role and emboldened by the powerful precedent set by the investigation into the Bank of China, the PBOC quickened its push for banking reforms and stepped up its monitoring and enforcement efforts on top of those already adopted prior to 2002. On January 1, 2002, the PBOC began to implement a five-tier loan classification system (normal, require attention, second-rate, suspicious, and lost), which some banks including the Bank of China had adopted somewhat earlier.[83] In the second half of 2001, the PBOC's nationwide investigation of postal savings institutions resulted in the closure of 1,585 law-breaking branches and the dismissal of 1,110 unqualified staff members.[84] In 2002, the PBOC brought the rectification of city commercial banks to a temporary closure. The rectification, first initiated in 1998, gave about a hundred city commercial banks the green light to continue operations and expand their capital base. Initial efforts were also launched to restructure the troubled rural credit cooperatives sector, and in a number of localities the cooperatives were given permission to experiment with a wider band for deposit and lending rates.[85] Most importantly, to show that it was serious about enforcement, the PBOC announced in May 2002 that it had punished 114 banking officers and staff for malpractice following a special inspection of the big four that uncovered 57.3 billion yuan in nonperforming loans. Fifteen of the 114 were sent to procurators for criminal prosecution and 13 were expelled from the banking industry.[86]

These announcements, partly designed to influence the top leadership right before the sixteenth Party Congress, failed to persuade incoming General Secretary Hu Jintao and Premier Wen Jiabao (Wen had served as secretary of the Central Financial Work Commission from 1998 to 2002). Almost immediately following the Party Congress, the party leadership set up a Central Financial Security Leading Small Group with Wen as its chair.[87] The following month, PBOC governor Dai Xianglong was removed and transferred to become Tianjin mayor, an apparent letdown that signaled the central leadership's dissatisfaction with the pace of banking reforms.[88] Shortly thereafter, the new Wen administration started its tenure with the 2003 government reform plan. As part of the plan, a ministerial-ranked China Banking Regulatory Commission (CBRC) was established. Separate from the PBOC, the CBRC was based on a merger of the Central Financial Work Commission and five regulatory bureaus from the PBOC. Troubleshooter Liu Mingkang was appointed the CBRC's first chairman.

The establishment of the CBRC complements the existing regulatory apparatuses for the insurance and securities industries (see below). Interestingly, the (super-provincial) regional branch structure of the PBOC is not replicated at the CBRC. While the regional structure helped the original PBOC to reduce provincial influences on monetary-policy implementation, it was also recognized that the regional setup was less effective than expected and, indeed, was "not successful", as far as regulatory enforcement was concerned.[89] While the regional setup reduced local influence, regulators also found it more difficult to secure the cooperation and support of local authorities in enforcement action. In recognition of this issue, the Banking Regulatory Commission has established centrally controlled branches (*fenju*) in every province in line with the existing territorial administrations, with sub-branches (*zhiju*) in prefectures and cities.[90]

Since the PBOC remains the lender of last resort to commercial banks being regulated by the CBRC, the two, given their different institutional roles, will likely come into conflict from time to time. Yet the two institutions will also need to share information and coordinate their actions.[91] The passage of the PRC Law on the Supervision and Management of the Banking Industry and amendments to the Banking Law and the Commercial Banking Law have legally empowered the CBRC and helped demarcate the respective functions of the PBOC and the CBRC.[92] For its part, the CBRC has quickly shown its mettle. While continuing to prioritize reforms of the state-owned commercial banks and the rural credit cooperatives, the CBRC used its first directive to order the big four to account for their nonloan assets, a little-noted category that could be a potential black hole beside the NPLs. In 2003, the CBRC penalized 1,243 financial institutions and 3,251 individuals for illegal and irregular operations.[93]

Restructuring the Institutional Apparatus for Securities Markets Regulation

The regulation of China's young securities industry has also been remade in the latter half of the 1990s, much like the restructuring of the central bank and its regulatory functions.[94] Simply put the securities regulatory reforms have been driven by the growing importance of the securities markets and the politicians' fear of popular discontent. For the sake of space and coherence, I focus on the reforms of the regulatory apparatus here, particularly the assertion of centralized regulatory authority, with only tangential discussion of the specifics of regulation.[95]

Even before the Asian financial crisis swept onto Chinese shores, the Chinese leadership, having become keenly aware of the growing economic and political significance of the stock markets, began to launch some serious efforts at curbing rampant speculation and manipulation in stock trading. Regulators imposed stiff penalties on a number of bank branches and brokerages that engaged in illegal activities and adopted a variety of measures to dampen speculation in 1996–1997.

The market gyrations and rampant speculation also prompted the central authorities to rethink the regulatory apparatus for the securities industry. In August 1996, the State Council Securities Committee promulgated the Regulations on Managing the Stock Exchanges. In a significant departure from past practice, the regulations empowered the CSRC to directly oversee and manage the stock exchanges, including the authority to nominate, with the concurrence of the local governments, the chairman and vice chairman of the boards of the exchanges as well as the general manager and deputy general manager of the exchanges. While previously the exchanges were controlled by the local authorities, the balance of regulatory authority now clearly tilted toward the center.[96]

The onset of the Asian financial crisis accelerated the efforts by the central authorities to gain direct oversight over the stock markets. Advocates for centralization noted that most developed economies regulate their securities exchanges under one nationwide unified authority rather than parceling out regulatory authority to local governments. In August 1997, just before the fifteenth Party Congress, the State Council empowered the China Securities Regulatory Commission to directly oversee the Shanghai and Shenzhen stock markets rather than leave them to the dual leadership of the municipal governments and CSRC. With this regulatory change, the CSRC promptly appointed its own choices for the general manager and deputy general managers of the stock exchanges.[97] In the meantime, the amended Criminal Law included provisions for prosecuting securities-related crimes including illegal issuance of stocks, insider trading, the spread of false information, and other forms of stock manipulation. Most importantly, the financial crisis in the rest of Asia prompted central leaders, notably President Jiang Zemin, to push for the enactment of the Securities Law.

The central government did not just take over the regulatory authority over the stock markets. With little fanfare, it also asserted its right to the stamp tax on securities transactions. Rather than letting local authorities collect the bulk of the growing stamp tax revenue, the central government chose to take 88 percent, leaving 12 percent to local authorities in the future. In October 2000, the State Council further decreed that the central government's take would be 91 percent beginning in October 2000, rising to 94 percent in 2001, 97 percent in 2002, and 98 percent in 2003.[98] The stamp tax revenue became a major tax category when the Chinese stock markets came back to life in 1999–2000.

The 1997 National Conference on Financial Work also decided to reform the administrative organization for securities regulation. While thus far companies and government agencies largely used the stock markets to collect money from the public to bail out under-performing state firms, the growing size of the stock markets and rapidly expanding scope of public involvement suggested that these markets had become an important economic institution. In fall 1998, in a move that paralleled the restructuring of the People's Bank of China, the central leadership decided that the system of securities and futures regulation was to be transformed from one of local fiefdoms into one under the direct and unified leadership of the China Securities Regulatory Commission, which was now given ministerial rank. Adopting the system of vertical administration (*chuizhi guanli*), the central commission oversaw the staffing size, party organization, and cadre management at local offices. Local regulatory authorities thus became branch offices representing the CSRC. The CSRC promptly required the local offices to place their emphasis on the protection of investors through regulation, standards, and discipline rather than on raising the most funds for local companies. With the formal implementation of the Securities Law on July 1, 1999, the CSRC's branches became operational nationwide, thus forming a centralized and unified network of securities supervisors. Shortly thereafter, Zhou Xiaochuan, a former PBOC vice governor with a Qinghua doctorate, was made CSRC chairman, unleashing the era of tougher supervision and enforcement.

The assertion of central regulatory authority, coupled with the installation of more decisive leadership, has sped up the adoption and enforcement of unified and transparent rules for the securities markets. In conjunction with the implementation of the Securities Law on July 1, 1999, the CSRC screened and standardized more than 250 existing laws and regulations and put securities regulation within a unified legal framework.[99] Armed with the Securities Law and a centralized administration, the CSRC has reformed the IPO process and strengthened supervision over share underwriting, corporate governance and disclosure, insider trading, mutual funds, and so on.[100] The CSRC has also delisted chronic loss-makers and given green lights to shareholders to bring lawsuits against fraudulent firms.

In launching these regulatory initiatives, the CSRC has had the cooperation of the Ministry of Finance (the accounting industry regulator) and the Supreme People's Court. The Ministry of Finance has steadily strengthened accounting standards and enforcement (Chapter 4) while the Supreme People's Court grudgingly permitted shareholders to launch civil lawsuits, including class action suits (*gongtong susong*), against companies and corporate officers for false and misleading information. Formal criminal proceedings were launched in 2002 against companies and individuals, notably China Venture Capital and Zhengzhou Baiwen, for false accounting and share manipulation.

Though still very young, the Chinese securities and futures exchanges have not only adopted cutting-edge technologies but have also been put under a single regulator for the securities and futures exchanges, a goal that has to date eluded the U.S. Securities and Exchange Commission.[101] By the time Zhou Xiaochuan, the CSRC chairman, was transferred to become PBOC governor at the end of 2002, the CSRC had even moved ahead of its counterparts in Hong Kong and other developed markets in certain respects, notably requirements on independent directors and corporate disclosures. Beginning in 2003, listed companies in China are required to report quarterly results while Hong Kong requires only semiannual reports. The CSRC also demands that at least one-third of the company board members be independent members.[102]

The Quest for Market Order and the Remaking of the Regulatory Institutions

The structural reconfiguration of the tax collection and financial regulatory apparatuses is but one facet of a broader change in China's political economy. As Karl Polanyi would have predicted, the expansion of markets, intermediated by politicians, has grown side by side with the remaking of the regulatory state in China.[103] Indeed, market competition in China has been accompanied by myriad types of criminal activities ranging from financial fraud to the counterfeiting of goods. In response, the Chinese government has had to devise a variety of institutional mechanisms to help maintain market order, complemented by a flurry of legislative activities to produce laws governing economic activities. This chapter has already discussed the reconstitution of the tax and fiscal systems that help pay for the upkeep of the state as well as the reconstitution of the apparatuses for financial regulation. These institutions, together with the National Audit Office and the Customs Administration, are designed to collect revenue for the state machinery and to keep the financial house in order.[104] Also important are a variety of other state administrations. The State Statistics Bureau (also known as the National Bureau of Statistics), for example, plays a crucial role by collecting and disseminating information that is indispensable for sound decision making.

In this section, I would like to discuss the building and restructuring of several other regulatory and enforcement agencies that play vital roles in ensuring market order and fair competition and in promoting sustained economic development. These agencies were mostly established in the reform era and include the State Environmental Protection Administration, the State Administration of Industry and Commerce, the State Administration of Quality Supervision, Inspection, and Quarantine (formerly the State Administration of Technical and Quality Supervision prior to its merger with China Inspection and Quarantine), the State Intellectual Property Office (formerly the State Patent Bureau), the State Administration of Press and Publications (National Copyright Administration), the State Drug Administration (renamed the State Food and Drug Administration in 2003), and the State Administration of Workplace Safety.

While ministries and commissions are constituent departments of the State Council, all the administrations listed here, as well as various others (including the tax and customs administrations and the State-owned Assets Supervision and Administration Commission), are administrations or offices directly attached to (*zhishu jigou*) the State Council. The banking, securities, and insurance industry regulatory commissions are of similar status but are classified as not-for-profit institutions directly under the State Council to give them greater freedom in hiring professionals. While most of the administrations as well as all three financial regulatory commissions have been gradually upgraded to rank at the ministerial level, their lack of cabinet status also means that the leadership appointment to these institutions is not subject to the ratification of the National People's Congress and is thus less subject to legislative oversight. They are instead purely executive organizations reporting to the premier.

The major executive and regulatory administrations work alongside the powerful State Development and Reform Commission (and its predecessors). Complemented by nongovernmental organizations such as the Chinese Consumers' Association, the regulatory agencies are charged with the enforcement of state laws on patents, copyrights, trademarks and brand names, the environment, quality standards, food and drug safety, workplace safety, as well as for the general protection of consumer rights.[105] The ubiquitous State Administration of Industry and Commerce, for example, not only registers companies and oversees the regulation of various market fairs (*shichang*) but also devotes much of its manpower to cracking down on trademark infringements, illegal advertising, and other practices that impair fair trade and harm consumers (particularly in the wholesale and re-tail areas). It can impose fines and order businesses to suspend certain op-erations and revoke business licenses.

Local Interests and the Need for Unitary Regulatory Authority

While the growing prominence of these regulatory enforcement agencies is evidence of the Chinese leadership's commitment to protect and sustain markets and promote an environment for fair competition in the market, these agencies have also been plagued by problems of local protectionism. Take the case of quality standards. For years the Chinese press has aired complaints about products ranging from exploding beer bottles to water heaters that leak poisonous carbon monoxide. The prolif-eration of fake and shoddy products harms consumers, hurts the reputa-tion of high-quality producers, and detracts from China's efforts to build world-class manufacturing, a goal that the Chinese leadership has been keen to pursue. According to an investigation in Henan province, 63 per-cent of products sold on the market were without a certificate of inspec-tion.[106] The State Council Development Research Center estimated that the amount of tax revenue lost due to the proliferation of counterfeit prod-ucts was 24.6 billion yuan in 1998 and between 27.5 and 34.5 billion yuan in 2001.[107] In a written instruction to a National Conference on Quality Work, Premier Zhu Rongji stated that the Chinese economy would have no hope if fake and shoddy products were tolerated.[108]

Yet why has China been quite ineffective in combating fake and shoddy products in its markets? A major explanation is the divergence of interests between central and local authorities. Simply put, as one com-mentator wryly noted, a crackdown on fakes does not generate revenue.[109] Instead, rather than emphasizing compliance with government product standards, some local officials have tolerated local manufacturers of sub-standard or counterfeit products because these businesses yield profits for the producers as well as generate employment and government revenue that improve the career prospects of local officials. Some local enforcement personnel and government officials may take bribes from producers of fake and substandard products and get directly involved in protecting the pro-ducers. The incentives for local authorities to crack down on local produc-ers of fake and shoddy products are further reduced because the products tend to be sold beyond the local confines. Indeed, there is a tendency for local enforcement offices to focus their enforcement efforts on goods from the outside. For the same reason, there is little reason for local enforcement authorities to cooperate on inter-regional cases. The enforcement of national and industry standards is thus a public good that tended to be undersupplied by local enforcement authorities. Without adequate enforcement, shoddy and counterfeit products undermine the reputation of Chinese products and hurt legitimate producers.

Why would local enforcement agencies not be fully dedicated to their stated mission? This had much to do with the institutional locus of these agencies. Local quality and technical supervision departments were departments within local governments and had only a "guidance" relationship with the national quality administration. Moreover, some regulatory functions, as will be mentioned below, were split among different regulatory agencies and suffered from poor coordination. According to Vice Premier Wu Bangguo, "The current local administration system is hard to ensure independent, unified, strict, and impartial law enforcement, which is inevitably subject to the interference of regional protectionism; it is difficult to deal with cases or impose a fine, and law enforcement personnel are even subjected to persecution and retaliation."[110] In short, the local departments must please local government officials first. Faced with a fragmented regulatory authority, manufacturers of fake and shoddy products thus had little fear of punishment. Similar institutional setups also plagued various other regulatory agencies.

From Decentralization to Semi-vertical Administration

Just as Upton Sinclair and the muckraking journalists were able to capture the imagination of consumers and lawmakers in the United States decades earlier, the exploding beer bottles and dangerous water heaters also caught the attention of consumers and government leaders alike in China. In response to popular demands and national economic interests, the Chinese leadership made the promotion of unified, effective law enforcement departments an important theme of the government rationalization program introduced in 1998. For example, the State Administration of Quality and Technical Supervision (hereafter the Quality Administration), previously subordinate to the State Economic and Trade Commission, was upgraded to the status of government administration directly under the State Council and given ministerial rank. Moreover, its staff size in the Beijing headquarters was not cut but remained at 180. In addition, the number of staff at affiliated centers and organizations in Beijing numbered around 4,000. Altogether the quality and technical supervision "system" had about 100,000 employees, generating 2 billion yuan in fees per year. Its 200-plus technical centers make it one of the most technical government services.[111] In 1999, the Quality Administration conducted random tests of 8,905 products belonging to 218 categories.[112] The 1998 government reorganization also allowed the Quality Administration to expand its functions. Previously the industrial ministries and departments and the Ministry of Labor were primarily responsible for issuing quality licenses for products such as boilers and elevators, leaving enforcement to the Quality Administration. The reforms gradually put both functions under the Quality Administration. All in all, with its power to oversee quality management systems (such as the ISO 9000) certification and product quality certification and the authority to publicize the certification results, the Quality Administration has become one of the main arms of the regulatory state.

In addition to acquiring higher bureaucratic ranks and integrating regulatory functions, the regulatory agencies were also empowered to strengthen hierarchical control through vertical administration (*chuizhi guanli*). Unlike the emphasis on centralized regulatory authority that characterized the apparatuses of financial regulation, the trend toward vertical administration in the various administrations has not gone as far. In December 1998, lower-level Industry and Commerce offices beneath the provincial level were placed under the direct supervision of the provincial offices instead of local governments.[113] In spring 1999, the Party Central Committee and the State Council decided to adopt vertical administration in the quality and technical supervision system in the provinces. As Vice Premier Wu Bangguo noted at the National Working Conference on Reforming the Quality and Technical Supervision Administration in March 1999, while local quality and technical supervision bureaus, primarily those at the county level, were previously overseen by local (county) governments, the adoption of vertical administration would empower the provincial bureaus to directly supervise the offices in prefectures and counties. Moreover, quality and technical supervision bureaus were also empowered to oversee technical units affiliated with them. The State Administrative of Environmental Protection and the State Drug Administration also followed with similar organizational changes later on.

Since 2000 vertical administration has become a model of institutional design and spread to various other areas including the Ministry of Land and Resources, the administrations of coal-mine safety inspection, maritime safety, and aquatic safety as well as public health, anticorruption, and the management of central government grain reserves and the control of infectious diseases.[114] In virtually all these areas, vertical control was imposed following disasters or reports of gross mismanagement. In the aftermath of a major maritime disaster in Shandong, the Ministry of Communications concluded that local officials had not been effective and chose to set up 20 maritime safety administrations in 11 coastal provinces. These local administrations are directly answerable to the ministry so as to ensure the implementation of central government regulations governing shipping safety.[115] After the adoption of this organizational revamp, the central government oversees safety on all China's coasts, the Chang Jiang River, the Heilongjiang River, and other open territorial waters.[116] Likewise, the SARS crisis of 2003 elicited major government initiatives to build up a system of data gathering and emergency response answerable to the central government.

In the case of China's accident-prone coal mines, while ownership of mines devolved to local authorities, the State Administration of Coal Industry was transformed into the State Administration of Coal Mine Safety Supervision (also simultaneously known as the State Administration of Workplace Safety).[117] Previously, local coal industrial administrations supervised coal mine safety in the localities but did not always place safety at top priority because they were also concerned with output and other economic indicators. In contrast, the new safety administration was given a single focus on safety and would "operate as an independent entity . . . and not be easily affected by local interests."[118] Local coal mine bureaus were abolished and replaced with coal mine safety supervision bureaus. These provincial safety supervision bureaus, which in turn set up field offices in major mines, are charged with the mission of safety supervision and report to the central administration.[119]

The Politics of Vertical Administration

In promoting hierarchical control via vertical administration, the reformers are apparently seeking to enable the Quality Administration and other regulatory agencies to enhance the hierarchical administration of the functions such as quality supervision and more effectively enforce laws and regulations with relative autonomy from the influence of local authorities. In the case of the Quality Administration, the Beijing headquarters previously only "guided" local developments. The reorganization under the rubric of vertical administration has empowered the Beijing headquarters to direct the provincial bureaus. Beijing can now veto appointments of the provincial bureau chiefs.[120] In general, the headquarters have gained more control over cadre management, organizational structure, staff size, and funding. A particularly significant development is the consolidation of budgets. The Planning, Finance and Technology Bureau of Quality Administration coordinates with the Ministry of Finance on a unified budget for the system and allocates funds for technical labs, thereby giving it much leverage. Budgets for local quality offices are consolidated in provincial-level budgets. Moreover, quality bureaus at various levels and their subordinate technical units are required to promptly deliver all fines, proceeds from confiscated property and goods, and administrative fees to the central or provincial-level finance departments in full. There was also hope that the institutional reform would improve staff quality by making it more difficult for local authorities to transfer personnel into quality-supervision departments.[121] By gaining more organizational control, the central government is able to improve the implementation of laws and regulations and thus promote market order. A *People's Daily* commentary hailed the reorganization as "significant for the improvement of product, project, and service quality, for the maintenance of an orderly market, for the defense of the interests of the people and the masses, and for the promotion of the healthy development of our national economy."[122]

Nevertheless, it should be pointed out that the system of vertical administration adopted in 1998–1999 resulted from a compromise. Apart from the State Tax Bureaus and the Customs Administration, most agencies adopted vertical administration only within provincial administrations. Take the State Administration of Environmental Protection as an example. Originally there was a push for putting local agencies under the direct command of the central administration rather than making them dependent on local governments whose leaders tended to put growth above the environment. Indeed, some of the most vocal advocates for vertical control over the past decade were local environmental officials who were caught between the task of protecting the environment and the clout of local authorities who prioritized growth and had much leverage over their agencies. Yet in the final push for vertical administration, some of these local advocates modified their stand on the reorganization. One central official I interviewed attributed this change of heart to the personal interests of local officials. When these local officials first advocated placing local agencies under the direct command of the central agency, they were middle-aged bureaucrats with professional ambitions who would presumably benefit from a streamlined ladder of bureaucratic promotions. By 1998–1999, however, these advocates were getting closer to retirement age. If full vertical command were adopted, they faced the prospect of permanent retirement within a few years. In contrast, if they stayed within the local political establishment, they could expect to transfer to the local people's congresses or political consultative conferences upon their exit from government administration and thus retain not only perks and benefits associated with their ranks but also some measure of real political influence. As a result of such local resistance, when the reform was finalized for the environmental agency, it was agreed that provincial environmental officials would not be under the sole direction of the central agency but would be subject to the dual leadership of the agency and of the provincial leadership.[123] Interviews with local offices of the Industry and Commerce Administration also confirmed that directors of the field offices are still subject to the supervision of local party committees. The trend, however, is toward the enhancement of functional hierarchy. For example, in reforming the drug administration, the Jiangsu Drug Administration emphasized that, besides financial separation, personnel management at sub-provincial administrations should mainly follow the provincial administration, with assistance from the local party leadership.[124]

Legislative Empowerment

As the bureaucratic ranking and authority of the regulatory agencies were upgraded and the sinews of administration were strengthened, there was also a concerted effort, partly driven by demands from deputies in the National People's Congress, to provide the legal backing (as well as discipline) for the regulatory agencies.[125] Again take the case of the Quality Administration. In 1999, the NPC Standing Committee made inspection of the enforcement of product quality laws a key item on its agenda. The NPC's inspection group went to Zhejiang, Chongqing, Shandong, Guangdong, and Henan in June and concluded that the situation in product quality was still grim. NPC vice chairman Tian Jiyun noted that fake and shoddy products not only seriously endangered people's lives and property but also could strangle economic growth. He called on governments at all levels and law enforcement agencies to enforce the Product Quality Law more thoroughly and give impetus to law enforcement supervision. The inspection group concluded that the existing Product Quality Law was flawed. Specifically, the Product Quality Law stipulated inadequate punishment for violators and did not sufficiently empower law enforcement agencies. As a result, violators of product quality laws tended to be "dealt with perfunctorily and not stopped once and for all." In response, the NPC took up the amendment and improvement of the Product Quality Law and formally approved the proposed amendments in July 2000.

The amended Product Quality Law gives law enforcers more power to inspect and provides for stiffer penalties against violators. It includes articles targeted at the government itself. Article 25 forbids the Quality Administration and other government agencies from recommending products so that the Quality Administration would not compromise its administrative integrity. Article 65 stipulates penalties for government employees involved in shielding and abetting counterfeiters.[126] Meanwhile, armed with its higher administrative status and legal authority, the Quality Administration started to promote a unified system of exemptions for qualified products in 2000. In 2003, the Quality Administration introduced the China Compulsory Certification (CCC) system to promote the trade of qualified products on a national scale.

Legislative initiatives to further empower national regulatory authority have also reached other areas. Following the reorganization and enhancement of the State Drug Administration in 1998, agency leaders gave priority to amending the 1985 Pharmaceutical Administration Law (*Yaopin guanli fa*). The 1985 law authorized local authorities to establish local drug standards and to approve drugs. Unfortunately, this decentralization of regulatory authority led to lax standards and poor product quality. Provincial authorities preoccupied with local development tended to lower the bar for indigenous pharmaceutical companies. In February 2001, the national legislature approved the amended Pharmaceutical Administration Law. The amendments increased penalties (including criminal prosecution) for unauthorized pharmaceutical producers and counterfeiters. Moreover, in line with legislative amendments in other regulatory spheres, the amended law scrapped the power of local authorities to issue local standards and to approve the manufacture of products stipulated in the national standards.

Instead, the power to approve the manufacture and sale of medical products was centralized in the State Drug Administration. Armed with the new legislation, the State Drug Administration had by the end of 2002 established branches in 352 cities (prefectures) and 2,060 counties (and county-ranked cities) and consolidated all central and local standards on traditional Chinese medicine products into one uniform standard. All local standards not incorporated into the central regime were put into disuse; and pharmaceutical drugs based on them were ordered to be put out of circulation and use by July 1, 2003. As part of the reapplication for permits to manufacture and distribute pharmaceutical products, 4,694 distributors lost their sales permits and 779 firms lost their manufacturing permits. Meanwhile, the promotion of GMP standards resulted in the closure of 196 plants that manufactured blood products and other products for injection.[127] In 2003, the State Food and Drug Administration further emphasized that drug producers would be held responsible for the safety and effectiveness of their products.[128]

The extensive amendments to the Product Quality Law and the Pharmaceutical Administration Law were only two of many legislative enactments the Chinese legislature worked on to upgrade the legal framework for regulation and to get China ready for WTO membership. Other legislation the NPC passed between 2001 and the first half of 2002 alone included new and amended laws on copyright, trademarks, the inspection of import-export commodities, promotion of clean production, and production safety.

The Rectification of Market Order

Armed with more administrative muscle and stronger legislative mandates, the regulatory agencies have become more forceful in enforcement, conducting more searches and giving out stiffer penalties to violators. For example, during a three-month nationwide quality inspection drive conducted between March and May 1999, quality inspectors from the Quality Administration confiscated 13,000 tons of shoddy seeds, 173,000 tons of low-quality chemical fertilizers, and 11,264 tons of fodder. They closed down 823 factories producing shoddy products and penalized 22,000 shops for selling illegal or shoddy products. Quality inspectors also urged local Bureaus of Industry and Commerce to revoke the business licenses of 94 manufacturers and shops.[129] Various provincial units announced tough punishments, including dismissal, for managers of enterprises producing substandard goods. These efforts have largely been kept up and the Quality Administration frequently announces the results of product inspections and regularly makes the results of such inspections available to the print and broadcast media.

In spring 2001, the central leadership decided to pool the initiatives of the individual regulatory agencies into a unified national drive to rectify market economic order.[130] As was the case during the Progressive Era in the United States, this drive, launched in concert with a national "Strike Hard" anticrime campaign, was designed to alleviate widespread public concerns about product quality, safety, financial fraud, and similar issues and was timed to help prepare the Chinese economy for entry into the WTO. Since the launch of the market-rectification drive, the various regulatory agencies as well as the Ministries of Culture and of Construction have worked in concert with the police to fight counterfeits and substandard products, illegal advertising, financial fraud, pyramid selling, smuggling, and tax evasion. Tougher requirements and standards on pharmaceutical products, bidding, and the management of construction projects have been imposed. In 2001 authorities shut down half a million workshops producing fake products, and confiscated 158 million illegal publications and 4.2 million copies of pirated software.[131] In mid-2002, the Quality Administration began to demand producers of defective and substandard products to make costly recalls, reminding consumers that, under provisions of the Product Quality Law, they may sue producers for compensation for damages caused by the defective products.[132]

As progress is made in some areas, more attention is given to others, generally in response to high-profile events. In 2001–2002, for example, production safety became one of the most prominent policy arenas for regulatory change. Numerous coal mines operated without proper licenses and lacked proper safety measures, often with the connivance of local authorities that were under pressure to raise revenue and generate employment. Partly because of these factors, China has had one of the most atrocious coal mine safety records. Likewise, firecracker factories tended to be poorly regulated and managed. A spate of high-profile coal mine and firecracker workshop explosions drew attention to the vacuum in safety regulation caused by the government reforms. In response to the bad publicity, central and local authorities have worked hard at damage control. In the coal mine sector, authorities have focused on closing small coal mines that often operate in violations of safety regulations. By the end of 2001, authorities had closed 58,000 small coal mines (more than 10,944 in 2001 alone), or about 73 percent of all small coal mines.[133] The crackdown on small coal mines was helped by the reinforcement of the regulatory apparatus. Having already set up the State Administration of Workplace Safety earlier, the central authorities introduced a number of major policy initiatives in 2001–2002. On April 21, 2001, Premier Zhu Rongji promulgated the State Council Regulations Concerning Administrative Accountability for Major Safety Accidents. The regulations referred especially to fires, traffic accidents, safety accidents arising from poor construction quality, safety accidents in handling explosives and chemicals, mine explosions, furnaces, and so on.[134] A number of provincial leaders have received administrative reprimands and demotions. Mayors in a number of cities have lost their portfolios to take responsibility for major disasters in their jurisdictions. Numerous lesser officials and managers directly responsible for the accidents have been subject to criminal prosecution. In October 2001, the State Administration of Coal Mine Safety Supervision issued a unified set of Regulatory Rules for Coal Mine Safety. The rules went into effect on November 1 to empower coal mine safety supervisors looking for safety violations.[135] Meanwhile, a legislative proposal on production safety was drafted by the State Council and enacted into law by the National People's Congress. In response to central demands, local authorities have tended to react drastically to local disasters. Most prominently, the Jiangxi provincial government has sought to close down its fireworks industry after a highly publicized disaster in 2001. The Beijing municipal government suspended the operations of all "Internet cafés" for a period of time after a deadly fire at an Internet café killed 25 people in summer 2002. In response to this and other accidents, the central authorities tightened regulations on Internet café operations nationwide, closing more than 3,300 and suspending another 12,000 in the second half of 2002 (out of a total of about 45,000).[136] Amid the SARS crisis, a slew of regulations has appeared on public health issues.

Away from the high-profile events, the struggle for an orderly market environment and against unfair competition is fought on a daily basis. In the first half of 2002, the market regulators focused on market fairs, gas stations, and tax collection. In the process, inspectors evicted 63,594 unlicensed business operators from market fairs and closed down 36,424 stalls selling fake and substandard products. They were also able to make some progress in curbing the proliferation of gas stations with quality, measurement, safety, and tax problems. By the summer, the unruly tourism market and the problems of the Internet cafés, along with food and drug concerns, had been put on the priorities list.[137] At the same time, government ministries such as the Ministry of Construction have focused on problems in their spheres. Besides the economic regulatory agencies, some nonregulatory institutions, such as the party's Publicity Department and the Communist Youth League, have pitched in as well. Multinational corporations such as Microsoft and Unilever joined in by launching their own counterfeiting associations and by taking advantage of the amended Copyright Law.

By one key measure, namely the number and pattern of consumer complaints, the national drive for an orderly market environment, coupled with the effect of market competition, has shown some encouraging results. According to data from the China Consumer's Association (CCA), the CCA received 690,062 consumer complaints in 2002, down 4.3 percent from 2001.[138] This decrease, only the second—the first being in 2000—since such data became available in 1985 occurred in spite of the emergence of new complaints arising from China's evolving economy.

Yet the tasks for market regulation remain arduous. As more and more consumers purchase real estate, automobiles, and computers, there have been a growing number of complaints about such purchases. In other respects, the fight against counterfeits and piracy in general, particularly of software and movies, has had limited results, judging by the fact that one can still purchase pirated movies and music relatively easily in major cities.[139] Increased enforcement efforts notwithstanding, foreign governments and companies continue to grumble that only a tiny percentage of the counterfeiting cases reported are prosecuted and the penalties are insufficient to discourage repeat offenders.[140]

As the experiences of more developed economies suggest, the nurturing of competitive markets and the struggle against all sorts of scams takes more than one campaign or national drive. All in all, it is well to quote then Vice Premier Li Lanqing, who was head of the Leading Group in Charge of National Rectification and Standardization of Market Economic Order, that the work to rectify and standardize market economic order would be "protracted, difficult, and complex."[141] In upgrading and reinforcing the regulatory agencies, the Chinese leadership has set up the institutional foundations for the regulatory state and is ready for protracted struggle.

Conclusions

In the 1980s and through the early 1990s, the Chinese reforms parceled out resources and power to local interests. Most studies of China believe that the decentralization and the flattening out of the organization of the Chinese state contributed to the rapid growth of the Chinese economy.[142] Yet, while the decentralization provided incentives for local development, it also gave local authorities the wherewithal to engage in all manners of local protectionism. Such protectionism in turn served to undermine the formation of a national market. More broadly, the institutional designs that stimulated local protectionism contributed to the legitimacy crisis of the party-state that was evident at the turn of the 1990s.

Whereas in Great Britain the arrival in London of IMF loan monitors in 1976 marked a turning point in British history and led to the rise of Prime Minister Margaret Thatcher and the search for solutions that included the privatization of state assets as well as the "comprehensive nationalization of local government and intermediary institutions,"[143] the tragedy of Tiananmen in 1989, the specter of inflationary spiral in 1993–1994, and the impending succession to Deng Xiaoping provided the impetus for Beijing to rein in the local authorities and redefine central-local relations and by extension of the sinews of governance for the central state. These politically costly restructurings were undertaken because central-local relations were not embedded in a stable and widely accepted constitutional framework but were based on much ad hoc bargaining that progressively gave local governments more resources as well as obligations.[144] Fortunately for the Chinese leadership, they were able to leverage their political clout to fundamentally restructure the tax and fiscal relations as well as tax administration in favor of the central state. Subsequent fiscal reforms, notably the central government's unilateral decision to take the bulk of the stock stamp taxes and the corporate and personal income taxes, have again and again shown that, as far as fiscal revenue is concerned, the center holds. Though in recent years the Chinese government has had to rely on deficit financing, the central government's grasp on the revenue stream from the personal income tax, seen in the light of the history of developed economies, suggests growing fiscal prowess for the central state relative to the provinces. These developments also suggest that the concept of "market-preserving federalism" has limited applicability in the case of China.

In like manner, the Asian financial crisis provided strong impetus for the Chinese leadership to pursue the restructuring of the central banking system and to strengthen the regulation of banks, securities markets, and the insurance industry. At the same time, continuing the adaptation to the demands of modernization and liberalization, there has been a series of initiatives to upgrade, reinforce, and reshape a variety of other regulatory institutions that help promote an orderly economic environment and enforce standards on quality and safety. In all these arenas, the institutional reconstruction, under the rubric of vertical administration, emphasized giving the central regulators more hierarchical control so as to promote the uniform implementation of state laws and regulations in a country known for its variegated conditions. Moreover, the reforms of the regulatory and enforcement institutions remain a work in progress. The separation of the banking regulatory commission from the central bank indicates the need to adjust the institutional mechanisms for different policy objectives.

The reconstitution of the sinews of central governance promises not only to furnish the fiscal prowess for the central state but also to provide the foundations for a regulatory state. With strong administrative muscle that is less beholden to local authorities, central state power can potentially be used to offer fair administration such as uniform registration for companies, protection for consumers, and production safety. In this sense, the ruling regime is not simply doing something that is only for its own good but also potentially for the good of the public. The reconstitution of the central state is therefore not simply a rebuilding of the old state that had an iron fist but short and weak fingers. Instead, with the reconstitution, the central state may finally possess elaborately constructed arms, hands, as well as fingers that could play in coordination to produce good music. In this respect, Jiang Zemin, Li Peng, and Zhu Rongji have taken the essence of Margaret Thatcher's reforms to heart: "We are strong to do those things which government must do and only government can do."[145] As with Thatcher, China's reforms at government streamlining and de facto privatization have been accomplished not by the dismantling of state power, but by a program to reconstitute it.

Yet while vertical administration alleviates problems such as local protectionism, it also raises serious issues of monitoring and supervision of these administrations, which can be just as corrupt or capricious governed from the center as they were under local command. By drastically reducing horizontal supervision in the localities, vertical administration requires improved internal monitoring and discipline. Some of the administrations have made major efforts to improve internal governance, but others have lagged behind, raising doubts about the legitimacy and authority of the administrations.[146] Can China's new regulatory institutions play fair? How can they be kept not only efficient, but also clean and honest? These are questions that should not be asked only of the regulatory agencies, but of the Chinese state in general.

chapter four

THE SMUGGLING CRISIS AND THE LEVELING OF THE ECONOMIC PLAYING FIELD

While economic incentives helped remake state-business relations and the regulatory institutions have been reconstituted, these developments do not automatically lead to a fair and transparent regulatory environment. There is no hope for such an environment if the government acts as both referee and player in the economy and allows super-players (such as the military) that flaunt the rules of the game. For example, until the late 1990s the Customs Administration and the coast guard struggled to curb rampant smuggling because many smuggling operations implicated powerful state entities such as the military and the armed police. Similarly, judges and procurators can hardly be expected to be fair-minded when the courts and the procuracies have their own business operations and have to adjudge between their own business interests and those of others.

In this chapter, I describe the chain of major reforms that was prompted by the massive smuggling crisis during the Asian financial crisis. For China's top leaders, the smuggling crisis gravely threatened the Chinese economy and the fiscal foundations of the Chinese state. Because the business operations of the military, the armed police, the judicial departments, and other party and government agencies and institutions (hereafter AJPG businesses) were heavily implicated in smuggling and were often beyond the reach of regulators, the smuggling crisis prompted the Chinese leadership to finally take action to divest the military and other state agents of their business operations in order to curb smuggling and level the economic playing field. Fortunately, the intensification of competition in the economy, the variable that has helped us account for the evolution and transformation of government-business relations, also made it easier for carrying out the divestiture that had long been a desired goal of Jiang Zemin and other Chinese leaders. With the divestiture of the AJPG businesses, it became much easier to promote an arm's-length regulatory framework for businesses and the rationalization of professions including accounting and law. The successful divestiture of the AJPG businesses in 1998 and beyond not only helped reduce smuggling and corruption but was also a vital step in China's efforts to build a modern regulatory state.

Smuggling and the Crisis of the State

Even though China in the reform era has steadily lowered its tariff levels, tariffs on many products, together with distortions in the foreign exchange regime, have been sufficient to make smuggling lucrative. For example, while a pirated CD cost only 1.7 yuan to produce, once smuggled into China it sold for 10 or more yuan on the black market. Similarly, because tariffs on assembled automobiles are far higher than for parts, smugglers have strong incentives to report assembled vehicles as parts and can immediately make a tidy profit from the operation. Sometimes smugglers sawed vehicles in half in order to claim them as parts eligible for lower tariffs. An estimated 153,700 motor vehicles worth U.S.$6 billion were smuggled or illegally imported into China in 1997.[1]

For the sake of space I shall not elaborate on the cycles of smuggling in China. Suffice it to say that the Asian financial crisis of the late 1990s, during which China kept its currency stable, provided a golden opportunity for smugglers. According to Premier Zhu Rongji, smuggling activities reached unprecedented levels by 1998 and as much as 100 billion yuan worth of commodities was smuggled into China each year.[2] The Ministry of Foreign Trade and Economic Cooperation estimated that about half of the 10 million mobile telephones sold in China in 1998 were smuggled. In the same year, competition from cheap smuggled products forced domestic oil companies to close 3,000 oil wells.[3] Provinces along the coast, especially Guangdong and Fujian, thrived on such gray market activities.[4] Guangdong's Zhanjiang was found to have accounted for at least 30 billion yuan (about U.S.$3.6 billion) worth of smuggled automobiles, oil, and steel.[5]

Smuggling and State Institutions

Because customs revenue from regular trade goes to the central government while fines on smugglers and revenue from the underground trade stay in the local economy, local governments have far fewer incentives to crack down on smuggling than the central government. Since staff in local antismuggling offices were appointed by local governments and beholden to local government officials, it was frequently impossible for the antismuggling offices to secure strong local backing to go against smugglers.[6] In various cases, local government officials willingly connived in smuggling operations and saw smuggling as a quick way to boost local economic growth, a leading indicator for assessing the performance of local leaders. For these officials, smuggling was a by-product of reform and opening up and should be harnessed for local economic prosperity. Indeed, as a *People's Daily* commentary put it, some officials regarded "the gaining of vast profits from smuggling by their localities, departments, or units as benevolent rule."[7] In consequence, as in other areas of Chinese law enforcement, law enforcers tended to levy fines on smugglers instead of launching formal legal prosecutions.[8] In essence, in a symbiotic relationship, smugglers paid fines to local governments in exchange for permission to run a regular smuggling operation.[9] The local government received extra revenue, which was often used for bonuses and perks for employees, while smugglers received protection. An implicit pact between the local elite and smugglers thus existed.

Smuggling not only causes loss of customs duties and taxes but also corrodes the state machinery. Smugglers generally use a portion of their proceeds to bribe law enforcement officers and regulators, spreading corruption through the state apparatus, particularly the Customs Administration. Li Jizhou, a former vice minister of public security and deputy head of the National Anti-Smuggling Leading Group, was found to have offered protection for Fujian's Yuanhua Group in Xiamen in exchange for huge bribes between December 1994 and the first half of 1997.[10] Many other cases of lesser-ranked officials have also been reported. The former head of the anti-smuggling office in Guangdong's Dongguan, for instance, was found to have taken in at least 1 million yuan between 1996 and 1998.[11] The head of Zhanjiang Customs accepted 2.4 million yuan in bribes. Lured by such large payoffs, the Zhanjiang customs officials as well as local party and government leaders virtually turned on the green light for smugglers. Between

1996 and 1998, the smuggling ring in Zhanjiang was estimated to have evaded 400 million yuan in taxes by smuggling at least 248 cars and more than 3,600 car bodies as well as hundreds of thousands of tons of steel, diesel, and sugar.[12] Widespread corruption among customs and other law enforcement agencies thus facilitated many of the smuggling operations.[13]

Elements of the military and the armed police were also heavily implicated in smuggling operations. When General Ji Shengde served as the military's intelligence chief, many of Ji's associates reportedly engaged in smuggling, using the cover of military intelligence. Some of the officials involved in the massive Zhanjiang case used exit permits to Hong Kong granted by the military intelligence agency. Ji was later found to have been closely associated with Lai Changxing, the kingpin of the Xiamen smuggling operations.[14] Some armed police units rented their vehicles or loaned armed police vehicle licenses to smugglers and even used police vehicles to transport smuggled goods and allowed the use of armed police sites by smugglers.[15] For instance, Chen Youwu and Luo Yicheng, commander and political commissar, respectively, of the Guangdong Huilai County Armed Police Unit, repeatedly led their unit to "escort" certain smuggling operations and eventually attacked an antismuggling police unit.[16] In the Zhanjiang smuggling case, officers from the South China Sea fleet made military vessels available, for a fee, to help smugglers avoid customs inspection.[17]

More generally, companies affiliated with and set up by the military, the armed police, government agencies, and law enforcement departments became major smugglers even while—and indeed precisely because—some of these departments were charged with cracking down on smuggling. For the first half of 1997, 63 percent of the smuggling cases uncovered by the Customs Administration and 86 percent of the value seized were attributable to legal persons (*faren*).[18] These companies or "legal persons" either paid a set amount of management fees or remitted profits to their "supervising" state agencies. Their background and special privileges made it virtually impossible for law enforcers to genuinely crack down on them. For example, the Eastern Industrial Trading Company in Jiangsu was owned by the Public Security Bureau. With the cooperation of the directors of the Lianyungang Public Security Bureau (the police department), the company smuggled 70 cars through the port city of Lianyungang in 1993, which cost the government more than 22 million yuan in lost tariff revenue.[19] While this particular case ended with the death or imprisonment of the principals and the arrest of 32 other law officers from

Jiangsu province's Public Security Bureau, numerous other cases went unchecked. As two *People's Daily* commentators noted: "Legal entities are rampantly engaged in smuggling, with collusion between insiders and outsiders and protection of smuggling."[20] At the conference on antismuggling work in September 1998, Premier Zhu Rongji reportedly estimated that the military establishment alone was responsible for more than 60 percent of the smuggled goods.[21] This led the premier and other national leaders to conclude that the fight against smuggling would be hopeless if smuggling by legal entities, particularly those businesses run by the armed forces, was not curbed.[22]

Perhaps the most obvious sign of pervasive involvement by state institutions in smuggling is the presence of smuggled vehicles in China.[23] Many of the automobiles smuggled into China, including luxury brands as well as expensive Toyota Land Cruisers were purchased or used by local government officials, often as status symbols. Since automobiles must be registered through the police before they can be operated on the road, local police officials are heavily implicated in registering smuggled vehicles. Indeed, the vice minister of public security, Li Jizhou, reportedly used his position to issue more than 70,000 registration plates for smuggled vehicles.[24] With officials such Li in charge of the police and antismuggling, lower-ranked police officers had few qualms of their own. Sometimes local officials did not even bother to secure license plates for their own vehicles.[25]

All in all, the incentives in the Chinese system were conducive to smuggling rather than its crackdown. In a sense, the central leadership, obsessed with political succession and macroeconomic stabilization, appeared to have tolerated some smuggling by the "state" businesses for much of the 1990s. Smuggling in turn stimulated corruption as various officials condoned, permitted, and even engaged in smuggling themselves.

Smuggling and the Crisis of the State

The Asian economic crisis that started in 1997 upset the above balance. Fueled by lower prices beyond China's borders, smuggling into China escalated dramatically and threatened the fiscal and political foundations of the Chinese state. This in turn prompted the Chinese leadership to take decisive action to crack down on smuggling and introduce major institutional changes to reduce the incentives for smuggling.

As mentioned earlier, because China maintained the value of its currency vis-à-vis the U.S. dollar while currencies in the rest of Asia declined precipitously in 1997–1998, the incentives for smuggling goods into China grew sharply. Most ominously, the smuggled goods were flooding the Chinese market as the Chinese economy itself finally slowed down in response to the macroeconomic stabilization program initiated in 1993.[26] The combination of domestic slowdown and growing competition from legitimate and illegitimate imports subjected Chinese firms to the severest market competition ever encountered in decades and pushed the Chinese economy into deflation mode. More and more domestic enterprises, including those in heavily regulated industries such as petroleum and petrochemicals, sank into the red. The China Petrochemical Corporation (Sinopec), a major profit maker for the government for over 15 years, lost more than 2 billion yuan in January–May 1998 in what the Chinese press referred to as "a period of unprecedented losses." The petrochemical sector lost nearly 3 billion yuan in the first quarter of 1998 alone. Rampant smuggling, accounting for as much as 60 percent of the domestic market, also put most of China's domestic photographic film producers in the red. Smuggling was thus a major factor behind the Chinese government's willingness to agree to a landmark deal that allowed Kodak to acquire three Chinese film companies.[27]

This smuggling wave became a major threat to the state, particularly the central government. First, the central government has been dependent on revenue collections at the border for a significant percentage of its disposal income. In 1995, for example, the central government's budgetary revenue income was 325.7 billion yuan, and a substantial amount of this was transfer payments to local governments.[28] In the same year, the Customs Administration collected 70 billion yuan in tariffs plus value-added taxes on imports.[29] This entire amount went to the central government. Thus, more than 20 percent of the central government revenue was collected at the border. Increased smuggling meant a reduction in tariff collections. Second, the escalation of smuggling activities also threatened the domestic foundation of state revenue because the state, particularly the central government, relied heavily on state enterprises for tax revenue. Deteriorating corporate performance severely constrained government revenue growth even while the government had to spend beyond its means to support various social programs, prop up money-losing state enterprises, and provide demand stimulus. In the first five months of 1998, state expenditures climbed 12.8 percent. In contrast, industrial and commercial taxes grew by only 7.9 percent, far below the targeted 12 percent; value-added tax and consumption tax revenues increased by merely 1 percent, 9.1 percentage points lower than the target.[30]

Much as smuggling almost brought down the East India Company—then the world's largest trading corporation—and threatened the financial basis of the British state more than two centuries ago, the rampant smuggling in contemporary China represented a serious threat to the Chinese state.[31] The *People's Daily* commentary I have mentioned earlier paraphrased remarks made by President Jiang Zemin and captured these ramifications well:

Smuggling "is causing huge losses of tens of billions of yuan to the national economy and state revenue, thus wrecking the environment of fair competition, damaging the interests of enterprises which operate normally, hitting at domestic markets and national industries, and intensifying the difficulties of state-owned enterprises in reform and development. . . . The crime of smuggling has also poisoned the social atmosphere, promoted corruption, given rise to departmentalism and decentralism in certain units and localities, sabotaged the unity of central decrees, and damaged the reputation of the party and government among the people."[32]

While aggrieved domestic enterprises repeatedly appealed to the central government for redress, there was real fear that the state itself could collapse because state agents ranging from local governments to the AJPG businesses profited from the continuation of smuggling.[33] As Luo Gan, a State Councilor and Political Bureau member, put it bluntly: "Smuggling can wreck the economy, and destroy the Party, the military and maybe even the country."[34]

China was thus caught in a sort of tragedy of the commons. It was logical for each local government to not crack down on smuggling and even to connive in it, particularly because punishment against officials who condoned smuggling had been relatively light (often involving lateral transfers). Yet the collective outcome of such individual actions threatened the national economic order as well as the fiscal foundations of the central state. President Jiang Zemin was keenly aware of the divergence of interests between Beijing and the localities, but he highlighted the potential tragedy of the unconstrained pursuit of local interests. For him, both Beijing and the localities were ultimately in the same boat and needed to work together to cross the river. "If we are not of one heart and one mind and go separate ways, especially if we tolerate rampant smuggling and the growth of other corrupt phenomena," Jiang claimed, then "all will fall overboard if the boat capsizes."[35] Following Jiang, the Chinese media were saturated with discussions of the need for all officials to thoroughly understand the importance of the struggle against smuggling and correctly handle the relationship between parochial and national interests.

The War on Smuggling

For most of the 1990s the Jiang Zemin group had been busy consolidating its power and preparing for the succession to Deng Xiaoping and was thus unwilling to take on powerful political interests that helped shield smugglers. Instead, after cracking down on smuggling in Liaoning and Shandong in the first half of the 1990s, the central leadership left the southeastern provinces of Fujian and Guangdong largely untouched. Guangdong, in particular, was under the protection of the powerful Ye family, whose patriarch Ye Jianying had served as kingmaker after Mao's death.

Following the death of Deng Xiaoping, however, Jiang Zemin made several carefully calculated political maneuvers. To begin with, various princelings (children of old revolutionaries and senior officials) with freewheeling corporate fiefdoms were eased out of their influential positions through retirements (He Ping, Deng's son-in-law) or promotions to ceremonial posts (Ye Xuanning, a son of Ye Jianying). Both He and Ye held influential positions in the military-industrial-commercial nexus. He Ping was head of the General Staff Department's Equipment Office. Ye Xuanning was head of the General Political Department's Liaison Office as well as chairman and president of the shadowy Kaili Group.[36] Personnel changes such as these made it easier to curb the involvement of the military and other state agencies in smuggling operations. Equally important, through a series of complex moves, the central leadership in early 1998 replaced the top Guangdong officials with loyalists Li Changchun (a member of the Political Bureau and Guangdong provincial party secretary) and Wang Qishan (executive vice governor) and thus paved the way for fighting financial chaos, corruption, and smuggling in Guangdong.

With these personnel moves behind them, President Jiang Zemin and Premier Zhu Rongji launched a war on smuggling and foreign exchange fraud.[37] Amid a crisis atmosphere, the CCP Central Committee and the State Council in mid-July 1998 convened a national meeting against smuggling that was originally scheduled for fall. Signaling the importance the leadership attached to the fight against smuggling, both Jiang Zemin and Zhu Rongji delivered speeches denouncing the nefarious effects of large-scale smuggling on the economy and on the reputation of the party and government. Both Jiang and Zhu pointed to the participation by legal persons (corporations) in rampant smuggling and expressed alarm at the involvement of central and local party, government, army departments, and law enforcement or judicial institutions in smuggling activities. They explicitly linked antismuggling with the struggle against corruption and the enforcement of discipline in the party and government.[38] For Jiang, the future of China's reform, development, and stability was at stake. Without truly taming the scourge of smuggling, the foundations of the party and state power might falter. He vowed:

We should eliminate all interference and thoroughly investigate all cases no matter which units or persons are involved, and promptly and strictly mete out punishment according to law. No unit or person is allowed to act as behind-the-scenes backer of smuggling or to support, tolerate, and participate in it. Party, government, and military organs as well as law enforcement and judicial departments in all localities must strictly investigate and deal with the problems of smuggling and shielding smuggling discovered in the companies run by their subordinate units or their affiliated companies. They must also thoroughly separate themselves from these companies in personnel, financial, and material resources. Customs personnel, as law enforcement personnel, must also be strictly investigated and handled and resolutely dismissed if they have participated in or shielded smuggling.[39]

With military leaders present, Jiang Zemin, as chairman of the Central Military Commission, called on the PLA to "make a clear-cut stand, take the lead in the nation, and set examples for society" in the antismuggling drive.[40] Nine party and government departments, including the CCP United Front Department, the Ministries of Public Security, Water Resources, Railways, and Communications, and the State Administrations of Radio, Film and Television (SARFT), Metallurgical Industry, Petrochemical Industry, and Light Industry were criticized at the conference for involvement in smuggling activities.[41]

The high-profile meeting mobilized the entire political machinery. On 18 July, the Central Discipline Inspection Commission and the Ministry of Supervision issued a circular on antismuggling work. Three days later, the PLA's four general headquarters held a joint meeting in Beijing to plan on implementing the party center's decision to crack down on smuggling. On various occasions, PLA leaders vowed strong support for the antismuggling campaign.[42] The armed police as well as every provincial unit also held its own meeting on antismuggling work and promised to investigate and punish subordinate companies found to have been involved in smuggling.

The Crackdown and Its Immediate Results

Premier Zhu Rongji personally spearheaded the crusade against smuggling. He gave special attention to smuggling in the coastal areas of Guangdong and Guangxi and the smuggling of finished oil products, cars, cigarettes, and pirated CD-ROMs.[43] He also attended a wide range of activities on antismuggling. Most notably, Zhu in October 1998 led an 80-member investigation team, including State Councilor Wu Yi and officials from the customs, trade, border control, and discipline departments, to freewheeling Guangdong and Guangxi to reinforce the tough penalties on malfeasant local officials involved in smuggling and foreign exchange fraud.[44] Zhu emphasized investigating smuggling by legal persons with special backgrounds. Having already dispatched trusted leaders to take the reins in Guangdong, the Guangdong antismuggling work, as part of an overall program to restore economic order, proceeded rapidly. By fall 1998, Guangdong's efforts to clean up illegal economic activities and restore economic order were held as a model for other parts of the country to emulate.[45]

As part of the antismuggling drive, massive investigations of customs officials were undertaken. Leading customs officials in two dozen customs offices, including Shenzhen, Hangzhou, Huizhou, Xiamen, and Zhanjiang, were arrested. Eventually, Li Jizhou, vice minister of public security and deputy head of the national antismuggling office, and Wang Leyi, deputy head of the Customs Administration and head of the Customs Administration's antismuggling office, were also taken into custody and sentenced to lengthy jail terms. In a classic display of state power, the intense crackdown on smuggling was highlighted by the execution of various smugglers and the imprisonment of others.[46] In the Zhanjiang case, six customs officials, including the head of Zhanjiang customs and the director of the customs investigation department, were sentenced to death in May 1999 for taking bribes and assisting smugglers. Another 74 were sentenced to lengthy jail time, including the Zhanjiang party secretary, a vice mayor, and the director and political commissar of border control of Zhanjiang and the head of Maoming customs. Moreover, six military officers at the rank of regiment commander were disciplined.[47]

The Chinese media have also reported on numerous other smuggling cases.[48] Zhao Yucun, the director of Shenzhen Customs, was sentenced to life in jail and deprived of personal property for taking bribes of about 9 million yuan.[49] Also sentenced to jail were Zhao's two daughters as well as the chairman of the Shenzhen Chengjian Group. The most dramatic smuggling case and trials so far have been the massive Yuanhua Group case in Fujian's Xiamen.[50] Yuanhua, controlled by Lai Changxing, was officially reported to have smuggled refined oil, vegetable oil, cars, and cigarettes worth 53 billion yuan (U.S.$6.4 billion) and evaded customs duties of up to 30 billion yuan between 1996 and 1999. Aided and protected by Li Jizhou and numerous local officials Lai bribed, the Yuanhua Group did much of the smuggling by avoiding customs declaration and making fake customs reports.

Following lengthy investigations spearheaded by a special task force from the Central Discipline Inspection Commission, five local intermediate courts in Fujian put 85 people, the first of several groups, on trial in fall 2000 for 25 separate smuggling cases. In November 2000, the courts sentenced 14 people to death (including three with a two-year reprieve), another 12 to life imprisonment, and gave prison terms of various lengths to 58 others. Among those receiving the death penalty was Yang Qianxian, the head of Xiamen Customs Office. Yang, found to have accepted 1.4 million yuan and other benefits from Lai Changxing, gave the green light to smugglers and tipped Lai off when the Yuanhua Group came under investigation. Others sentenced to death included Zhuang Rushun, deputy director of the Fujian provincial police department and chief of the Fuzhou municipal police department; Lan Pu, vice mayor of Xiamen; Ye Jichen, director of the Xiamen branch of the Industrial and Commercial Bank of China; and Wu Yubo and Fang Kuanrong, staff members of the Xiamen Customs Office. In addition, Liu Feng, a deputy secretary of the Xiamen municipal party committee, received a life sentence for taking bribes and offering political cover for the Yuanhua Group. Also given the same penalty were Chen Guorong, the head of the Bank of China's Fujian branch; Zhang Yongding, the head of the second regiment of the Fujian provincial marine police headquarters, and Chen Yuqiang, a Xiamen customs official in charge of detecting smuggling activities.[51] In the trial of the second batch of 129 suspects, four were sentenced to death while Yang Shangjin, former deputy head of the Investigation Bureau of the Xiamen customs, and five others were jailed for life. The other 119 were sentenced to varying terms of imprisonment.[52] Most prominently, the vice minister of public security and deputy antismuggling chief, Li Jizhou, was in late 2001 sentenced to death with a two-year reprieve for taking bribes and dereliction, mostly in connection with the Yuanhua case.[53] Separately, Major

General Ji Shengde, the chief of military intelligence and the son of a former foreign minister, was sentenced to life imprisonment by a military tribunal for accepting bribes from Lai Changxing and for embezzlement.[54] Verdicts on a host of other Lai-related cases, such as that of Shi Zhaobin, a deputy party secretary of Fujian province, were announced in 2002. Lai Changxing, however, fled to Canada and is still fighting a request to extradite him back to China as of early 2004.

Spurred on by determined central leaders, local officials increased personnel and resources devoted to antismuggling and improved coordination among different departments in what is known as comprehensive management.[55] As the crackdown proceeded, state media reported massive seizures of smuggled goods. From January to October 1998, the Customs Administration cracked 20 percent more smuggling cases than in the same period in 1997 and seized 9.5 billion yuan worth of illegal goods, up 68 percent (5.1 billion yuan were made from mid-July, the start of the antismuggling campaign).[56] According to another statistical measure, customs, public security, industry and commerce, and other law enforcement agencies in the second half of 1998 uncovered 4,305 major and important smuggling cases with a value of 13.48 billion yuan.[57] For 1999, the Customs Administration, police, and the State Administration of Industry and Commerce cracked 21,117 smuggling cases, up 36 percent from 1998, and arrested thousands of smugglers. In an indication that the size of the average smuggling operations had declined in response to heightened state crackdown, the value of smuggled goods captured in 1999 was 12.7 billion yuan, down by 39 percent from 1998.[58]

To solidify government control on foreign currency and reduce the supply of foreign exchange to potential smugglers, efforts to crack down on foreign exchange fraud were also stepped up. Between mid-1988 and mid-1999, the Ministry of Foreign Trade and Economic Cooperation sanctioned 155 trading companies for smuggling or violations of foreign exchange rules. Thirty companies had their trading licenses and trading rights suspended for between three and six months, and another 122 were given warnings.[59] Various other companies were also punished for illicit foreign exchange activity.

By official accounts the crackdown on smuggling resulted in a significant reduction in smuggling, particularly large-scale activities, and helped stabilize the domestic economic order by fall 1998. Prices in sectors ranging from automobiles, cigarettes, computers, to film, newsprint, and oil and petrochemical products stopped their downward spiral. Domestic producers such as Sinopec were able to increase production and return to profitability.[60] As the "costs" of smuggling rise, imports through legal channels are expected to increase, leading to a rise in customs revenue. This was indeed the case. Starting from July 1998, China's customs revenue increased markedly; it set monthly records for a number of months and more than made up for shortfalls in the first half of 1998.[61] For the whole year, the central government treasury received a total of 87.9 billion yuan, an increase of 3 percent from 1997 and 9.9 billion yuan more than projected at the start of 1998.[62] In 1999, net customs revenue reached 159 billion yuan, 77 billion more than the target, up 81 percent from 1998. In Xiamen, where the Yuanhua case was uncovered, customs revenue rose by 138 percent in 1999—the year of the crackdown on smuggling.[63]

Institutional Reconstruction

These notable results notwithstanding, the Chinese leadership recognized that smuggling would not disappear. Confronted by the intense government crackdown, some smugglers have adapted by adopting new technologies and by exploiting legal loopholes.[64] The pervasive corruption in the Customs Administration was especially worrisome. To keep up the war on smuggling, Chinese leaders decided to revamp and strengthen antismuggling institutions. They increased funding for antismuggling equipment but also created a new and dedicated antismuggling force under the Smuggling Investigation Bureau of the General Administration of Customs. By the end of 1999 the Smuggling Investigation Bureau (*zousi fanzui zhencha ju*) had set up 42 branches nationwide.[65] The troop strength of the Guangdong antismuggling police alone reached 1,700 in early 2000, with an authorized size of around 3,000.[66]

To free it from local influence, the antismuggling police force is commanded by institutions under the direct leadership of the central government.[67] While the General Administration of Customs had only executive authority, the antismuggling police are given broad authority to search, detain, and arrest suspected smugglers.[68] Moreover, there is a built-in incentive for the antismuggling police to be aggressive and for local governments to cooperate; 35 percent of the proceeds from confiscated goods revert to the antismuggling force while the central and provincial governments share the rest.[69] Until the crackdown, the police were too busy with nonsmuggling cases and also tended to fine smugglers instead of having them indicted; following the crackdown, however, various Chinese reports suggested that the single-minded antismuggling police had been more effective in dealing with smugglers. Between 1999 and the end of 2002, the antismuggling police cracked 5,556 cases with a face value of 27.2 billion yuan and prosecuted 7,135 people on criminal charges.[70] Moreover, the amended Customs Law, which went into effect on January 1, 2001, further enhanced the authority of the antismuggling police. On January 1, 2003, the antismuggling police was renamed Antismuggling Bureau (*Jisi Ju*) and given authority to cover all smuggling-related cases, including those uncovered by other government agencies.

The institutional building is complemented by efforts to ferret out corruption and enhance discipline in customs, industry and commerce bureaus, police, and other antismuggling departments.[71] Between July 1998 and August 2000, the Customs Administration launched five drives to promote administration by law and ferret out corruption. By 2002, more than 400 corruption cases involving 800-plus customs officers had been uncovered in the Customs Administration, marking customs as one of the most corrupt government agencies.[72]

In tandem with the intense anticorruption drive, which culminated with the massive Yuanhua trials, the Customs Administration took a variety of measures to improve its institutional integrity. To facilitate monitoring and supervision and weed out those found to have been lax in combating smuggling, more than half of the second-tier (*er-ji*) customs offices (181 out of 331) had been eliminated by May 2001.[73] Senior customs officials, notably the customs chiefs reporting directly to the national Customs Administration, were rotated among different locales. Customs chiefs are now allowed to serve only a single term of four years and never more than seven years in one place. Audits are conducted on the customs chiefs whenever they leave their present posts (including promotions, transfers, and retirements).[74]

The Customs Administration also issued new regulations on the behavior of customs officers. In the past a number of practices compromised the integrity of the Customs Administration and invited collusion between customs officials and business firms at the expense of government revenue. Most prominently, the Customs Administration, to save on administrative costs, stipulated that customs employees going on government business must be provided with transportation and accommodation by the units or firms that received the employees. Moreover, employees of the Customs Administration "borrowed" vehicles and other valuable equipment from business firms. For example, customs offices in Guangdong had 339 loaner vehicles on the books. As the central government increased budgetary allocations for the Customs Administration, an effort was made to end these practices.[75] Furthermore, the Customs Administration also stipulated other behavioral norms governing employee behavior caught in conflict-of-interest situations.[76] Finally, the Customs Administration introduced formal ranks and badges for customs officers in 2003 to promote professionalism among officers.[77]

While efforts have been made to improve the transparency of customs work under what is known as *zhengwu gongkai,* or administrative transparency, special supervisors representing the Customs Administration (*jiandu tepaiyuan*) have been dispatched to some customs offices to provide on-site monitoring.[78] The antismuggling police set up 21 mutual supervision teams (*hucha xiaozu*) in May 2000 to strengthen internal discipline.[79] The Guangdong antismuggling police also invited members of the Guangdong People's Congress, the provincial government, and the press to serve as special supervisors (*teyao jianduyuan*) and help monitor the antismuggling police.[80] Finally, in 2002 the head office of the Customs Administration established special representative offices (*tepaiyuan banshichu*) in Tianjin and Shanghai to monitor administrative enforcement and official behavior in these two major customs offices.[81]

Technology has been a major weapon in the government's fight to combat foreign exchange and customs fraud and to improve the efficiency and transparency of customs inspections. In fall 2000, new computerized customs procedures under a new port management system were adopted in all customs offices to introduce internal checks and balances and improve the efficiency and transparency of customs inspections.[82]

These efforts at institutional improvement were complemented and prompted by amendments to the Customs Law. Originally the State Council's draft of the amended Customs Law stressed empowering customs agents against smugglers. Shocked by and disgusted with the repeated revelations of graft within the Customs Administration and collusion between customs officials and smugglers, lawmakers demanded more supervision of the Customs Administration so that the increased powers to customs agents would not lead to greater abuse. Specifically, they called for strengthening monitoring mechanisms within the Customs Administration as well as stronger legal supervision over customs offices and their directors.[83]

The AJPG Businesses, Smuggling, and the Decision to Divest

Transforming the institutional environment for smuggling was another major focus for the Chinese leadership. In his speech at the national meeting on antismuggling work, Premier Zhu Rongji dwelled on the "extremely negative impact" of smuggling by legal persons, particularly enterprises and institutions operated by or affiliated with party, government, military organs, law enforcement departments and judicial institutions. He called for making special efforts to crack down on smuggling by legal persons "with special backgrounds; severely punish organizers, planners, participants, and behind-the-scene supporters of smuggling by legal entities."[84] For Zhu, the success of the antismuggling drive depended critically on fighting smuggling by legal persons that were the hallmarks of "corporatism with Chinese characteristics."

Yet Zhu's call would be futile without empowering the Customs Administration and other civilian agencies over the AJPG businesses. It was here that Jiang and Zhu unveiled the biggest surprise. Calling for treating both the symptoms and causes of smuggling, they decided to ban the AJPG businesses. The crackdown on smuggling thus turned into a campaign to revamp the relations between state and business, rationalize the state, and level the economic playing field.

The AJPG Businesses and Unfair Competition

In a 1980 speech at the Central Military Commission, Deng Xiaoping noted that China's military expenditures were "rather high, to the detriment of national construction."[85] For Deng, economic development was then the paramount goal of the state, and the military should make its own contribution to economic development. Economic growth would in time provide the foundation of military prowess. Under Deng's leadership, China curbed defense spending in the 1980s to concentrate its limited resources on economic development.[86] It was in this context that the People's Liberation Army (PLA) and other state agencies were permitted and indeed encouraged to get into business operations. Speaking in a meeting of the Central Military Commission in November 1984, Deng Xiaoping explicitly urged the PLA to make its resources, including airports, ports, and industrial technology, for civilian use.[87] Though the PLA's involvement in production dated back to at least the Yan'an days, the reform era saw the

PLA engage in a much wider range of commercial activities to supplement its budget.

Some professional officers such as General Zhang Aiping questioned the wisdom of encouraging the military establishment to make profits.[88] Nonetheless, Deng's remarks provided the imprimatur for the military establishment's engagement in commercial businesses. Given the 1980s environment of partial reforms, profits came relatively easily, particularly because the military had "free" access to assets including land, vehicles, and other facilities that could be used to generate revenue. The number of PLA-affiliated businesses proliferated in the latter half of the 1980s and the freewheeling 1990s.[89] By 1988, the military businesses generated net profits of about 2 billion yuan per year.[90] It is widely known that these businesses reached every economic sector, from mining to manufacturing and services. In services, the investments included telecommunications and hotels as well as arms trading, massage parlors, and karaoke bars.[91] Some of the firms were high-profile names such as Poly Technologies, the Palace Hotel, and the 999 Group; but most tended to be lowly operations, including many that provided employment for spouses of career military officers. Still others were so-called briefcase companies that profited from China's incomplete reforms (such as dual prices).

By generating significant profits and creating employment, the PLA businesses played a major role in helping improve living conditions in the barracks in a time of budgetary stringency. To some extent, the businesses also helped enhance combat capabilities by making funds available for some equipment purchases. And at a time when the PLA steadily downsized and needed civilian jobs, the jobs created by the PLA businesses provided an important source of employment for soldiers and their dependents. Politically, as Cheung has suggested, a PLA that was itself involved in business was unlikely to resist the economic reforms.[92]

Nevertheless, as the PLA's business activities expanded, complaints about unfair competition also grew, and the AJPG businesses in general became obstacles to the further development of a well-functioning market economy. Within the military, there were substantial misgivings about the deleterious effects of business engagements.[93] In the late 1980s, the Central Military Commission issued various directives on the PLA's businesses in an effort to reduce corruption. Some of these orders called for military units below the army level to desist from running businesses, but they were not implemented.[94] Civilian policy makers were even more concerned about the military's growing business empire, even though they rarely aired their views in public. Speaking at a symposium on the military's business operations in spring 1989, the State Council policy adviser Wang Mengkui noted that the military businesses generated only modest profits but diverted from the PLA's mission. Not only did the military businesses engender corruption and corrode military morale, but they also undermined fair competition in the emerging market economy. If some of the soldiers engaged in business were trained and dispatched to help with tax collection, Wang argued, they would collect far more in additional tax revenue than the military businesses produced in profits. Wang called for finding a solution, such as complete divestiture of the military's business operations, to deal with the side effects of the PLA's business operations.[95]

In the aftermath of the 1989 Tiananmen crisis, the leadership undertook a modest cleanup of the military businesses. Before long, however, the cleanup was swept up in the 1990s mad rush by all government and state apparatuses, including the military, the armed police, and the judiciary departments, to engage in commercial businesses. Marked by Deng Xiaoping's southern tour in early 1992, these were the go-go years for China's growth; officials believed it was essential to generate additional income for bonuses and perks as well as to supplement the official budgets that were being eroded by inflation. While some of AJPG operations behaved like normal businesses, many relied on and flouted their official affiliations to turn power into gold, producing a type of "corporatism with Chinese characteristics." By the early 1990s, the number of such businesses had topped 20,000 and employed 600,000 civilians.[96]

Unlike Deng, however, General Secretary Jiang Zemin, concurrently chairman of the Central Military Commission, appeared to have fretted over the military's involvement in businesses. On the one hand, Jiang was careful not to alienate the military and indeed keenly cultivated the military's support in preparation for the transition to the post-Deng era. In January 1993, Jiang reportedly gave the PLA permission to continue its business pursuits. On the other hand, Jiang clearly indicated that he would prefer the PLA to stay out of business. "If somebody could find me 30 billion yuan," Jiang reportedly said, "I can stop the army from going into business."[97]

Amid the macroeconomic turmoil of 1993–1994, the Chinese leadership began to put the divestiture of military businesses on the policy agenda. Since various military-backed enterprises were involved in speculative activities that stoked the fires of inflation, it was natural for Vice Premier Zhu Rongji to think about getting the PLA and other state agencies out of commercial businesses. In this context, the Central Military Commission issued a decision on September 19, 1993, on rectifying and reforming army production and operations. The decision banned combat troops below the army level from engaging in commercial operations. In 1994 the PLA turned over its coal mines in Shanxi province to the local government for 1.3 billion yuan.[98] The buyout approach was of limited use, however; the deficit-plagued government could not raise all the funds needed to buy out all PLA enterprises. This explains the frustration President Jiang expressed in the quote above.

Without an imminent divestiture, Chinese leaders sought to rein in the wayward behavior of the AJPG businesses through regulation and supervision.[99] In early 1995, the PLA began to follow a set of "Auditing Regulations" that stipulated that all army units and departments that had economic activities must accept auditing supervision. According to official reports, the PLA's auditing departments audited the 1994 production and operation results of more than 1,100 finance, military supply, and production management departments and of over 9,000 enterprises. The audits revealed substantial hidden incomes, including 700 million yuan in net income and 150 million in profits due to upper-level authorities.[100] Other government agencies also sought to rein in the anticompetitive behavior of subordinate departments. In 1996, the Ministry of Public Security's Transportation Management Department directed all local transportation departments to stop the practice of forcing vehicles involved in accidents to go to repair shops designated by the police. Similarly the State Administration of Industry and Commerce issued a document directing local offices to sever ties with their own enterprises.[101] These directives were hailed as critical steps in the drive toward fairness in government behavior, but implementation fell short.

All in all, over 1993–1998 there was some serious effort to consolidate and regulate the military-business complex and promote professionalism, but the bulk of the military's business operations continued to operate, and every branch of the military establishment boasted its own enterprise group.[102] According to a 1999 report in the official *China Daily* newspaper, the total assets of the businesses operating under the PLA's umbrella were estimated to have reached roughly 50 billion yuan (U.S.$6.02 billion) by the end of the 1990s. They generated about 5 billion yuan (U.S.$602 million) in profits and taxes annually.[103] While such profits helped ease the PLA's budget constraint, they also meant that the PLA had become substantially addicted to its business operations.

While the military's business empire has received most of the attention, the range and scope of the AJPG businesses covered practically the entire spectrum of Chinese party and state institutions. Even the Supreme People's Court seconded some officials to head various businesses.[104] Lower levels of the court system had their own business operations as well as affiliated law firms. Even then, cash-strapped courts asked winners of court cases to pay for expenses associated with the enforcement of verdicts. The Supreme People's Procuratorate and local procuratorates had a total of 1,635 economic entities registered with the Administrations of Industry and Commerce as of 1998.[105] For example, the Sichuan Provincial People's Procuratorate owned the Tiandu Realty Company, while the provincial Procuratorial Organs Union, Veteran Cadres' Group, and Procuratorial Cadres' School each had a business operation.[106] All in all, the different parts of the Chinese state served as trellises on which affiliated or subordinate companies were attached.

Even without smuggling and other shady activities, the AJPG businesses were becoming a major headache for those seeking to transform the Chinese state into a modern regulatory state and the economy into a well-functioning market economy. First, the commercial operations of different branches of the state had a major corrupting influence on the behavior of cadres and officers and of the institutions they served. PLA business earnings tended to stay with the units for business and welfare rather than being turned over to the central administration for weapons procurement or R&D. A substantial share of the earnings was probably used for entertainment and other activities that had little to do with military prowess. Because military units along the coast had more commercial opportunities than units in the interior, soldiers in the interior felt left behind and resentful. Some military commanders noted that the business operations demanded much energy from commanders and organizations as well as produced much negative impact.[107] Not surprisingly, party and military leaders had repeatedly warned about the ill effects of the military's commercial involvement.[108] As General Wang Ke noted, "any army that seeks luxury and worldly pleasure is bound to suffer from a slack morale and weakened fighting will, leading to defeat eventually."[109] Similarly, Jiang Zemin pointed out that "if the leading cadres are sluggish, seek special privileges, or even waste public funds at will, they will not have any moral authority, and the masses will not show any respect for them."[110] Thus, as Chinese reforms progressed, there was growing concern that the AJPG businesses compromised the integrity of state institutions. When these institutions, including the military, are absorbed in making money, how can they be expected to devote themselves to their core missions?

Second, the AJPG businesses severely undermined the development of fair competition. Some of the military's commercial businesses, such as in transport and telecommunications, relied on privileged access to land, radio frequencies, and airports. Thanks to their special status, many of these businesses also enjoyed tax privileges and immunity from legal prosecution. These enabled many military firms to enter into unfair competition with normal businesses and made it difficult for the government to regulate the economy with fairness, causing friction between army units and civilian authorities. Because quite a number of the high-profile military firms were run by the princelings, they fed popular perceptions of widespread nepotism and corruption.[111] In certain areas, the AJPG businesses simply flouted established norms or laws. The customs administration and coast guard found it difficult to crack down on smuggling partly because the majority of the smuggling operations were conducted by legal entities affiliated with the state (including the military and the armed police) and possessing political clout. From time to time, the involvement of PLA businesses in arms trading and smuggling operations also strained China's foreign relations.

The AJPG businesses also had a pervasive influence on the behavior of the judicial and law enforcement establishment. Courts and procurators as well as the police running business operations are hardly expected to be fair-minded when they have to deal with disputes between their own business interests and those of others. Indeed, many such businesses relied on their regulatory power to make money. It was not unusual for the police departments to designate their own repair shops for repairing vehicles involved in accidents. Likewise a fire safety department might set up a store for firefighting equipment and inform buildings under the department's jurisdiction to buy the required firefighting equipment from its own store. Building managers that did not buy from the designated store soon found that they had trouble having their firefighting equipment approved by the police unit for compliance with safety codes.[112] Similar examples abound to undermine fair competition in the market, symbolized by the fact that vehicles owned by the military, the armed police, as well as other state agencies rarely pay tolls on the road. In the words of Vice President Hu Jintao, "the practice of engaging in business activities by [the state institutions] not only seriously interferes with their performance of duties and affects their impartial enforcement of laws, but it could also breed corrupt and unhealthy practices."[113]

All in all, the AJPG enterprises were endowed with privileges that they would be foolish not to make use of. As competition intensified and making money became harder or even impossible through fair competition, it was not surprising that some of the AJPG enterprises flouted their privileges and turned to smuggling and other dubious practices. They risked little in doing so.

The Smuggling Crisis and the Decision to Divest

The increasingly wayward behavior of the AJPG enterprises caused widespread public resentment. Members of the National People's Congress and the CPPCC submitted motions calling for the central leadership to disengage the military and other state institutions from businesses. Meanwhile, it became increasingly apparent to Jiang and other leaders that fundamental reforms of the AJPG establishment were necessary to complement reforms in other areas of the Chinese government and economy. They noted that the PLA's pursuit of business interests was detrimental to military professionalism and combat effectiveness. Likewise, the involvement by the armed police and public security department in businesses had undermined the enforcement of law. The AJPG businesses also disrupted the implementation of government policies on finance, trade, and taxation. They were a major source of corruption and public discontent.[114]

In late spring 1997, shortly after weathering the death of Deng Xiaoping, the Party Central Committee and the Central Military Commission (CMC) decided to deal with the issue of the PLA, public security, and armed police units running businesses. Liu Huaqing, then vice chairman of the Central Military Commission, noted that the policy of having these units running businesses had outlived its usefulness. The military leadership decided to strengthen monitoring over these businesses and eventually, perhaps over five to seven years, transfer them to civilian authorities so as to truly curb corruption in these units.[115] Speaking to the PLA delegation to the NPC in March 1998, Jiang Zemin called for stemming the spread of corruption at the source by strengthening rules and regulations and by intensifying supervision.[116] In short, the central leadership envisioned a gradual winding down of the AJPG businesses, particularly those of the PLA and the armed police.

The gradual approach toward the divestiture was confirmed by developments in early 1998, when the Central Military Commission reportedly asked PLA units to sever their ties with commercial enterprises.[117] We do not know much about this CMC order, but it certainly did not result in a significant change. In fact, on April 2, 1998, a government newspaper in Jilin reported that the Jilin provincial government had recently issued a set of 11 preferential policies, including priority access to land and certain types of loans, to support the development of army-run enterprises.[118]

Yet the political scales had tipped in favor of President Jiang Zemin. By spring 1998, a year had passed since Deng's death. With the uncertainty surrounding the succession to Deng Xiaoping behind him, Jiang, as the chairman of the Central Military Commission, was clearly in command. Following nearly a decade at the helm, Jiang had demonstrated his commitment to the armed forces as an institution by steadily increasing budgeted military expenditures, reversing the trend set by Deng in the 1980s. At the same time, Jiang had significantly reduced the military's representation in the party center. Only two out of 22 members of the Political Bureau Standing Committee were from the military, and none was a full member. In the Party Central Committee, the PLA's representation had dropped to 20 percent, down from 33 percent in 1992.[119] Moreover, Jiang had staffed the Central Military Commission with generals he could trust. Time and perseverance had made it possible for Jiang to anchor the ship of state much more firmly than when he was first catapulted to the top job in 1989. As Premier Zhu Rongji tirelessly pushed for sweeping reforms of government administration in 1998, Jiang promoted reform in the military establishment. At an enlarged meeting of the Central Military Commission in April 1998, he urged the PLA to speed up the restructuring of its establishment (including the General Armament Department) and cut the size of the army by half a million.[120] Jiang also called for the divestiture of PLA enterprises over three years, that is, by 2000.[121]

At this point, the smuggling crisis—amid the hurricane of the Asian financial crisis—intervened. As Jiang Zemin and Zhu Rongji came to realize the extent to which the AJPG businesses were involved in major smuggling cases as well as other forms of corruption and influence peddling, they were infuriated. It was clear that the supposed pillars of the state were actually undermining the very foundations of the state. The scourge of rampant smuggling could not be tamed without curbing the involvement of the AJPG businesses. Speaking at a Political Bureau meeting on July 20, 1998, Jiang Zemin concluded: "The military must no longer be in business. Otherwise, this tool of proletarian dictatorship will collapse, and the socialist state power will change color."[122] Thus, as the Chinese leadership launched the war on smuggling in July 1998, they also asked the military and the armed police to earnestly fight smuggling. Most importantly, they decided to rush the schedule of divestiture. According to Premier Zhu Rongji:

Various local party, government, and military organs, and law enforcement and judicial departments must resolutely screen their subordinate companies and affiliated companies, and must completely disconnect themselves in aspects including personnel, funds, and materials from these subordinate companies and affiliated companies within a specific time period. We have talked about these tasks for many years, but so far have yet to properly implement them. Party and government organs as well as military troops and armed police are funded by the state: They are absolutely forbidden to conduct commercial activities or operate companies. This time, we must be determined to expeditiously resolve the problems. If the problems are complex, they should at least disconnect themselves first, and then carry out rectification later.[123]

Thus in the summer of 1998 the CPC Central Committee and State Council ordered the military, the armed police, and the public security and judicial departments to sever their ties with commercial businesses in months rather than over several years.[124] As Vice President Hu Jintao bluntly stated in July 1998, the purpose of the divestiture "is to further improve the party's work style and promote clean government in military, PAP [People's armed police], judicial, procuratorial, and public security organs; to prevent and fight corruption once and for all; and to maintain the character and true qualities of organs of the people's democratic dictatorship and the People's Army, so that they will perform their duties better."[125] Invoking Deng Xiaoping and Jiang Zemin, Hu warned that the nature of the Party, the state, and the military might change and the socialist state might be ruined if corruption was not fundamentally tackled.[126] The military commanders dutifully echoed this refrain. In the words of Wang Ke, a member of the Central Military Commission and director of the PLA General Logistics Department, the antismuggling campaign and the divestiture were needed to ensure that "the country will never change color and the armed forces never degenerate."[127]

Implementing the Divestiture Order

In early October 1998, the Party Central Committee, the State Council, and the Central Military Commission formally announced the order for the PLA, the armed police, and the law enforcement and judicial organs to disengage from business activities. Unlike in the early 1990s, the divestiture decision was accompanied by a clear stipulation that the military, the armed police, the Supreme People's Court, the Supreme People's Procuratorate, and the Ministries of Public Security, State Security, and Justice would be "eating royal grain" for performing their designated functions.[128] There was a report, later corroborated by increased budget allocations to the military, that Premier Zhu Rongji, who had abhorred the military's participation in businesses ever since he became a vice premier, personally met with General Zhang Wannian and pledged that the state would set aside several billion yuan a year to make up for the military's business earnings.[129] Thus, even though some military interests grumbled that the divestiture order was imposed on them without much consultation, the compensation arrangement helped soothe the ruffled feathers.[130]

By doing one package deal rather than haggling over compensation for individual firms, it was clear that the order to divest was a political decision rather than a business transaction. Under Vice President Hu Jintao, the point man for implementing the divestiture, the principle for the divestiture was "transfer first, then sort out and clean up."[131] Simply put, China's leaders, fearing that delay might cause a loss of momentum and ruin the entire initiative, chose tactics that favored the swift implementation of the divestiture order. Politics thus took command, albeit for the sake of rationalization. The central leadership made the divestiture a political litmus test for officials and asked them to carry out the divestiture with a heightened sense of urgency and political responsibility.[132]

For their part, the generals quickly swung behind the divestiture program and pursued it like a military campaign. On July 21, CMC Vice Chairman Zhang Wannian convened an executive meeting of the Central Military Commission and set up a leadership group to oversee the divestiture. Under the direction of the leadership group, planning for the divestiture was mapped out. On July 24, Wang Ke, a member of the Central Military Commission and director of the General Logistics Department, stressed that the key to the divestiture would be "implementation, implementation, and implementation again."[133] Wang instructed the General Logistics Department, which oversaw most of the military's commercial operations, to come up as quickly as possible with a plan for disengaging the armed forces from commercial operations and act immediately and earnestly to screen all commercial companies operated by military units.[134] The military regions immediately dispatched special teams to compile information on their commercial enterprises. In October 1998, the Party Central Committee, the State Council, and the Central Military Commission jointly convened a meeting on the business disengagement for military, armed police, and law enforcement agencies. The four PLA general departments jointly vowed that they would resolutely implement the central decision on divestiture. Thus, by the time the divestiture order was formally announced in October 1998, the establishment had already been mobilized to carry it out.

The rollout in other departments was similar. Shortly after the central leadership issued its "Circular Concerning Military, People's Armed Police, Judicial, Procuratorial, and Public Security Organs Disengaging from Business Activities," the party's Central Discipline Inspection Commission and Central Politics and Law Commission convened a national video teleconference on July 28 to drum home the political significance of the divestiture and demand concrete plans. On the heels of the national conference, a highly orchestrated and organized program began to emerge. Ideologically, officials were asked to study Deng Xiaoping's and Jiang Zemin's speeches on the need to combat corruption and on the importance of safeguarding the interests of the party and state.[135] Organizationally, the central leadership set up a leading group to oversee the divestiture; various government ministries as well as provincial and municipal governments also formed their own leading groups. Leaders were given clear responsibilities and specific target dates to inventory assets, plan for the divestitures and finally complete the divestiture. The different agencies in turn assigned responsibility to lower levels. For example, the Ministry of Public Security (police) stipulated that the heads of institutions and those directly in charge of commercial operations would be held accountable for misrepresentation of facts and delays.[136] In fact, the PLA, armed police, and public security departments, as well as each of the provincial units' convened meetings to publicly avow their support for the decision to intensify anti-smuggling efforts nationwide and to cease all commercial activities.[137]

By October 1998, the divestiture process had entered the substantive stage. On October 6–7, the Party Central Committee, the State Council, and the Central Military Commission convened a working conference to specify the scope of the divestiture for the military and armed police and make detailed arrangements for the divestiture.[138] This was followed by another round of local and departmental meetings to implement the guidelines of central authorities on speeding up the divestiture process. Vice President Hu Jintao laid out detailed instructions on what needed to be done and what pitfalls to avoid (Five Do's, Six No's).[139] By now both central and local governments had set up special offices for taking over divested enterprises. In the central government, the Office for the Handover of Enterprises Run by the Military, Armed Police, and Political and Legal Organs (The National Receiving Office) operated under the State Economic and Trade Commission. The National Receiving Office was made up of members from 16 departments including the State Planning Commission and the State Commission for National Defense Science, Technology, and Industry. It became the central institution organizing and coordinating the handover of AJPG enterprises. Provincial governments and departments set up their own special offices.

Beginning in late November 1998, ceremonies for handing over enterprises were held in various localities. The enterprises were either transferred to the National Receiving Office or to local offices. Enterprises affiliated with the PLA headquarters, academies of military sciences, universities of national defense, and headquarters of the armed police went to the National Receiving Office while provincial, regional, and municipal offices in charge of the handover took charge of the locally based commercial enterprises operated by the PLA and the armed police.[140] The same pattern held for businesses from the judicial departments. The Supreme People's Court and the Supreme People's Procuratorate were the first to finish the divestiture by completing their disassociation from commercial businesses by November 30, 1998. By mid-December 1998, the PLA and armed police units (including the hydropower, gold, and traffic control departments under the Armed Police Force), the Forestry Police, and the Ministries of Public Security, State Security, and Justice had disassociated themselves from commercial operations.[141]

In spite of reports of resistance in the PLA, armed police, judicial and law enforcement departments, and much skepticism about the success of the divestiture,[142] the unity of the leadership and strong organizational work carried the day. By the end of 1998, in less than half a year's time, the

PLA, the armed police force, and the public security, procuratorial, and judicial organs had closed 19,241 enterprises, handed over 6,491 other firms to the receiving offices, and severed relations with another 5,557.[143] Accordingly Vice President Hu Jintao declared in spring 1999 that army, armed police, and various levels of judicial organs had completely separated from their business entities and stopped engaging in business activities by the end of 1998, thereby fulfilling the target set by the central government on schedule.[144] In essence, the military's involvement in the civilian economy had reverted to the prereform mode.

The Second Wind of the Divestiture

For a program of such magnitude and complexity, some problems are bound to arise. First, the PLA's withdrawal from business left much uncertainty as well as bitterness for partners of the formerly PLA-owned enterprises and debts that no one wanted to assume.[145] Second, while the military had to let go their commercial enterprises, they were allowed, for the time being, to operate service enterprises meeting their own needs, such as clothing factories, farms, military repair factories, and guesthouses.[146] Most of these businesses had existed before the military's commercial drive in the reform era. Nevertheless, since the PLA was allowed to choose what to keep, it was likely that it retained some significant businesses that bore little relationship to the military's needs.[147] Other state agencies also retained guesthouses and related businesses.[148]

While it could be argued that the military and other state institutions retained some firms legitimately, the most prominent issue was whether the military and other state institutions had truly complied with the divestiture order. In early 1999, it was announced that the PLA and the armed police had "completely gotten out of business operations" by transferring 2,937 enterprises and closing 3,928 others at the end of 1998.[149] The value of the assets, including those that were closed down, was estimated at 200 billion yuan.[150] Soon it turned out that Vice President Hu Jintao's declaration of complete divestiture was premature. Government officials estimated that the military had not properly accounted for about 10 percent of its commercial businesses.[151] Some of these businesses were well-known names such as the Palace Hotel, China United Airlines, and Great Wall Telecom. It was obvious that the military was dragging its feet in the hope of keeping these businesses.

The civilian leadership's resolve on the divestiture was put to test. They responded by asking the military and the armed police to transfer the remaining commercial enterprises by August 1999. Under the glare of international media, some of the high-profile firms with military backgrounds were quickly turned over. In late March 1999, for example, the PLA formally transferred its 60-percent stake in the Palace Hotel, one of the crown jewels of the PLA business holdings in the heart of Beijing, to the China Everbright Group, then headed by an associate of Premier Zhu Rongji.[152] In 1999, the military and the armed police turned over another 593 commercial firms to the receiving offices.[153]

Great Wall Telecom (GWT), a 50-50 joint venture between the PLA and China Telecom that was started in 1995, came to symbolize the difficulties of divestiture. For several years, GWT sought to skirt the divestiture order by expansion and some sort of leasing deal rather than being taken over by China Unicom. When asked about the PLA's involvement in Great Wall Telecom at a press conference in March 2000, Premier Zhu Rongji stated that the Central Military Commission had decided that the PLA would not be permitted to involve itself in any commercial activities or run any enterprises, thus presaging a final showdown over the fate of Great Wall Telecom. Nevertheless, in a gesture of goodwill toward the PLA, Zhu said that the government was trying to work out a way to allow continued cooperation between the PLA and commercial operators on the development of the CDMA system, and to meet the PLA's needs for mobile telecommunications.[154] Three months later, on June 18, the State Council finally issued a document (No. 40) that ordered the military to turn over Great Wall's networks to China Unicom. Even then, the military apparently still bargained hard for better terms and did not acquiesce to the deal until mid-July.[155] It was not until January 1, 2001, after several months of auditing and account settling, that the transfer of all existing businesses, including a subscribership that had risen to 550,000, was formally completed.[156] Great Wall's operations were absorbed into China Unicom in 2002.

In spite of these delays and related problems, the CCP Central Committee, the State Council, and the Central Military Commission convened a teleconference on May 25, 2000. This time Vice President Hu Jintao declared that the basic goals of the divestiture had been accomplished and warned that officials would be held accountable and subject to disciplinary action if the army, armed police, and judicial departments were found to have again engaged in commercial businesses.[157] In the meantime, the central leadership launched a second wind of military divestiture by asking the military to rid itself of firms it kept during the 1998 divestiture as well as most of those from the prereform era. This divestiture covered factories for munitions and uniforms, repair facilities, and certain medical facilities, as well as 588 farms that had been suffering from stagnant grain prices. By October 2001, this second wave of divestiture was well under way.[158] The major business operations the PLA still retained—arms trading, the dual-use China United Airlines—could plausibly be claimed to be for military purposes.

As a result of the divestiture, the PLA has truly become dependent on "royal grain." The 1999 government budget provided for a 12.7 percent increase in military expenditure over 1998, bringing China's official defense expenditure past the 100 billion yuan mark for the first time (a similar percentage rise was also made for 2000; the budgeted increases for 2001–2003 were 17.7, 17.6, and 9.6 percent respectively).[159] In light of official figures on PLA enterprise profits, rising government budget deficits, and low inflation, the increase in defense expenditure has been substantial and is at least partly designed to compensate for the divestiture. In 2000, for example, 5.6 billion of the 16 billion yuan increase in military expenditure was attributed to compensation for revenue losses arising from the divestiture.[160] Meanwhile, as part of an implicit pact, there was no mass punishment against the military for its involvement in smuggling-related activities.

Some commentators suggest that President Jiang Zemin "lost more than he gained" through the divestiture of military businesses.[161] This is quite unlikely. In fact, the divestiture of businesses operated by the military and other state institutions, launched in response to the smuggling crisis, was completed without precipitating a crisis in civil-military relations. Indeed, the divestiture turned out to be far more successful than critics had ever anticipated. With the handover, a special chapter of Chinese-style corporatism was effectively brought to a close. Although much remained to be done to sort out the enterprises that had been handed over, they were now in civilian hands, facing the contentious options of corporate reorganization, merger, and closure.[162] With the completion of the divestiture, some of the most dangerous roadblocks to the emergence of a regulatory state and the formation of fair market competition were removed. The divestiture is one of the most valuable legacies of the Jiang era.

Explaining the Divestiture

Why did earlier efforts at divesting flop and yet the 1998 divestiture get carried out so swiftly? While the political commitment of China's leaders was undoubtedly a major factor in the success of the 1998 divestiture, the military and other state apparatuses accepted the divestiture order without much resistance for both professional and economic reasons. Professionally, it was refreshing for the military to renew its core mission even while some departments or units that had profitable enterprises were probably unhappy. As Liu Jibin, head of the Commission on Science, Technology, and Industry for National Defense, pointed out, it was abnormal for the military to be involved in commercial activities. Such involvement resulted in "some very unhealthy manifestations." Instead, the army must rely on the country for its finances and concentrate on defending the country.[163] In fact, soon after the divestiture, the PLA for the first time launched a program to check and register the assets of all combat units in an effort to strengthen and improve logistical management.[164] It has since launched major initiatives to improve procurement (Chapter 6).

Economically, the central leadership's promise of a substantial monetary compensation for the divestiture certainly helped ease the feelings of the top brass. In this connection, the tax and fiscal reforms discussed in Chapter 3, which have strengthened the central government's financial prowess, can be said to have provided the indispensable financial wherewithal for the divestiture. Yet there were other fundamental economic incentives for the military to get out of the business of running businesses. As was the case for most state enterprises, increasing competition in the marketplace had made ownership of even the PLA firms less desirable over time. According to an estimate by Cheung, the contribution of the PLA businesses to military expenditures declined steadily in the 1990s. At their height, PLA business after-tax profits accounted for almost 12 percent of the defense expenditure in 1989 and averaged around 11 percent over 1990–1993. By 1996, however, this percentage had dropped to 7.4 percent.[165] While some of this decline could be attributed to the growing defense budget, the contributions from the PLA businesses failed to keep up with the budgetary growth because increased market competition had put most PLA-affiliated industrial firms into the red.

To be sure, some of the military-backed commercial enterprises such as the Sanjiu (999) Group and the Poly Group were significant profit makers. The Sanjiu Group, affiliated with the PLA's General Logistics Department, had by 1997 acquired ownership in 45 companies, ranging from pharmaceuticals to food processing, wine, agriculture, tourism, real estate development, and auto manufacturing. It had total assets of around 10 billion yuan.[166] Yet, high-profile and profitable firms such as the Sanjiu Group were the exception among the AJPG enterprises. Many AJPG firms, including some that were built during the Third Front Program, were not profit centers at all but uncompetitive money losers. Most of the PLA's industrial firms were relatively small and lost money. Others, such as discos, not to mention smuggling operations, made money but besmirched the reputation of the military and other state institutions. In an ironic twist, the growing involvement of AJPG firms in smuggling activities was itself an indication of the difficulty of making money by fair and legal means in the Chinese market. It thus appears that the PLA business establishment was relying more and more on services such as trading and even smuggling to generate revenue. In this sense, just like the local governments' divestiture of SOEs, the declining profitability of businesses in an exceedingly competitive business environment appears to have provided the single most important incentive for the military and other state institutions to give up their commercial operations that had quite often become a financial burden. If the state is willing to allocate more money from the budget, why go to the trouble of managing businesses and struggling for profits at the expense of professionalism and institutional integrity?

This emphasis on declining profitability as a major motivating factor for the divestiture of AJPG enterprises also helps to explain why previous injunctions on business disengagement had little impact and why the first major divestiture of military-run businesses occurred in the coal industry. First, little happened in 1991 and 1993 when the Chinese leadership also urged the military to divest their businesses. In these years it was still relatively easy to make money, and the military and other state institutions were understandably reluctant to give up assets that appeared to have great growth potential, especially since the top leadership could not come up with the funds to compensate for the divestiture.[167] Second, the first major divestiture occurred in the coal industry (mentioned earlier) because that industry had been one of the least profitable industries until the early 2000s.

The divestiture of AJPG enterprises has presented significant challenges to local governments taking over the firms because many profitable

AJPG enterprises made money only because of extralegal privileges such as low tax rates and exemption from road tolls for military vehicles. Some of them used military resources such as buildings and vehicles without having to bear the real costs of these resources.[168] Once these businesses were transferred to civilian hands, however, they would lose the privileges and likely cease to be profitable, leaving the recipient governments saddled with debts and welfare liabilities.[169] It was therefore understandable that government departments at both central and local levels groused about having to take over responsibility for the PLA's enterprises at a time of fiscal constraint.

These factors can be seen in Guangdong and Hebei, two provinces that had more enterprises affiliated with the PLA and armed police than most other provincial units.[170] In Guangdong, local governments received 420 AJPG enterprises at the end of 1998.[171] These enterprises were involved in hotel, restaurant, real estate, as well as manufacturing and transportation businesses. In 1998 they had profits of only 120 million yuan on revenue of 3.3 billion and generated 100 million yuan in taxes and fees for the government. These figures were probably overstated since 129 of the 420 enterprises either did not provide a financial statement or were set up only in 1998. The remaining 291 enterprises had assets valued at 11.93 billion yuan, but total debt on the books amounted to 9.3 billion yuan or 78 percent of assets. One hundred thirteen, or 39 percent, were in the red and lost a total of 220 million yuan.[172] The situation in Hebei was even worse. The PLA and armed police units in Hebei transferred 122 enterprises to the local government. These enterprises had 1.47 billion yuan in assets and 1.07 billion yuan of debts. Thus the amount of net assets—often inadequately depreciated—transferred was only 400 million yuan. Local government officials saw the handover as a headache. According to Qin Chaozheng, director of the Hebei Provincial Economic and Trade Committee, a majority of the enterprises being transferred were poorly managed.[173] They would cease to be profitable as soon as they began to operate like ordinary firms. The figures from Guangdong and Hebei thus suggest that local governments, which had themselves been working hard to divest existing state enterprises, had relatively little to gain by taking over the AJPG enterprises.

Expanding the Divestiture

The divestiture of the AJPG businesses occurred in the context of the government reforms discussed in Chapter 2. The government reforms then being launched forced the downgraded industrial ministries to give up direct supervision of state enterprises. By transferring the supervisory and regulatory role to macro as opposed to sectoral agencies, the reform was a major step toward transforming the role of government departments from being both owner and regulator to some sort of arm's-length regulator. In this context, the divestiture of the AJPG businesses was a crucial piece of the puzzle for making the Chinese state into a regulatory state and creating a fairer economic environment. The remarkably quick conclusion of the divestiture further emboldened the reformers. With the divestiture of the military enterprises, it was logical for the central leadership to seek to rationalize the relationship between other party and state agencies and business. At the end of 1998, the central leadership ordered departments under the Communist Party Central Committee, the National People's Congress, the Chinese People's Political Consultative Conference, most departments under the State Council, as well as the local counterparts of these institutions, to end their business activities.[174]

With the momentum gained from the initial divestiture, the business divestiture of the party, NPC, and so on proceeded rapidly under the direction of the central leadership. By the end of 1998, the group in charge of the divestiture of party and government businesses had produced a plan for implementation of the divestiture order and received approval from the Party Central Committee and the State Council. The plan was for "severing the central party and government organs from economic entities and enterprises run by them or under their control" so that the departments concerned would no longer exercise direct control over these enterprises. Instead, depending on their operating conditions, the enterprises were to be transferred to government departments in charge of enterprises, merged with others, or shuttered.[175] The People's Bank of China and State Economic and Trade Commission established two interdepartmental working groups and were able to basically complete the transfer in 1999.[176]

Local authorities undertook similar moves. In Guangdong, the provincial leadership was able to declare their delinking effort a success in October 1999. Guangdong had 35,899 enterprises (*jingji shiti*) operated by or under the direct supervision (*zhiguan*) of party and government agencies. These enterprises had total assets of 687 billion yuan and debts of 577.5 billion yuan. Of these enterprises or economic entities, 2,510 were transferred (*yijiao*), 4,356 were closed (*chexiao*), 17,723 had their administrative ties (*xingzheng lishu*) removed, and 8,828 ceased their affiliation with party or government agencies. The 20,293 firms that either were transferred or had their administrative ties cut were reorganized into about 200 asset management or fiduciary operating companies subject to government oversight and regulation.[177] At the provincial level, 1,546 firms previously with the military and some 50 state and government institutions and agencies were consolidated into four asset management companies and 18 enterprise groups.[178] Wang Yuanhua, secretary of the Provincial Discipline Inspection Commission in Guangdong, vowed that henceforth party and government agencies would no longer be permitted to operate enterprises, accept enterprise affiliations (*guakao*), or serve as guarantors for enterprises. Nor would party and government staff be permitted to hold concurrent positions in firms, collect funds or reimbursements from firms, or use firms' funds and goods for free.[179]

Following the separation from their administrative parents, the 500 or so large enterprises—subject to merger and reorganizations—were placed under the supervision of the Central Large Enterprise Work Committee, and their assets and capital were put under the oversight of the Ministry of Finance. Financial firms were temporarily put under the direct supervision of the Ministry of Finance and the central bank, while small enterprises were taken over by local industrial authorities. All together central party and government agencies severed direct supervisory relationships with 530 enterprises.[180] It should be kept in mind that central leaders continued to influence appointments of company executives via the Enterprise Work Committee as well as the Central Financial Work Committee. For example, Wang Xuebing, chief executive and party boss of China Construction Bank as well as an alternative member of the CCP Central Committee, was fired in early 2002 for his work at the Bank of China by the CCP Organization Department and the Central Financial Work Committee.[181] In the provinces, following the streamlining discussed in Chapter 2, the Enterprise Work Committees were part of the provincial party organization departments.[182] As part of the 2003 government reorganization, these firms have come under the State-owned Assets Supervision and Administration Commission and its local counterparts.

Rationalization of Professional Services

As the divestiture and delinking progressed, the State Council leadership also strove to rationalize the intermediary professions, including accountants, lawyers, notaries, appraisers, that play vital roles in ensuring the integrity of an economic system. The government's twin aims were to make the professions independent of government agencies and accountable to the law in order to better prepare these professions and the Chinese economy for the increased competition following China's entry into the WTO.

The main problem afflicting China's intermediary professions arose from the statist origins of these professions. Practices ranging from law offices to accounting firms to others were invariably set up by state agencies and put on government payroll. With economic reforms and rising costs, the state agencies eagerly set up such practices to generate incomes and provide employment for extra staff, sometimes with the same staff doubling as both government employees and professionals offering accounting, notary, and other services. Moreover, there was growing competition among state agencies fighting for regulatory power over the intermediary services, resulting in a convoluted and fragmented regulatory framework for the dozens of intermediary services.

As competition in the services markets grew, the state agencies conveniently used their power and influence to steer business the way of their affiliated intermediary services. Indeed, because of lax regulation and policing, a sort of Gresham's Law prevailed; firms had few ethical constraints and often lowered charges as well as professional standards in order to win businesses. By undermining the authenticity and quality of economic information, substandard intermediary services in turn undermined public trust, a situation similar to the Anderson-Enron cases in the United States. As Vice Minister of Finance Zhang Youcai noted in 1999 with respect to the accounting profession, China's accounting was characterized by fake statistics. It was not unusual for accountants to "dress up" firms for listing with the support of government departments. Zhang warned that the spread of fake numbers had "reached an unbearable situation. If not rectified, not only the entire accounting profession but the entire economy and society could be destroyed in no time."[183]

There had been some tentative attempts to rationalize the intermediary services before the divestiture of AJPG businesses.[184] Yet, as in the divestiture of AJPG businesses, government agencies were reluctant to sever their ties with the intermediary services that generated revenue and patronage opportunities.[185] Nevertheless the success of the AJPG divestiture underscored the central leadership's determination to cleanse the economic environment of unfair business practices and helped give momentum to the rationalization of the professions. In early 1999, the State Council began to tackle the rationalization of intermediary services in earnest. As in the case of the AJPG divestiture, the State Council set up an interagency office, State Council Leading Group on Improving and Rectifying Social Intermediary Organizations [that possessed powers of] Economic Certification, to oversee the rectification of the intermediary services. Finance Minister Xiang Huaicheng served as head of the leading group. Provincial-level authorities established their own leadership teams.

Though there were delays in the severance of ties between government agencies and the professional services firms, the strong central government commitment carried the day. By the end of 2001, the economic intermediary services, including certified public accountants, certified asset appraisers, certified tax consultants, property evaluators, land evaluators, cost engineers, township enterprise asset appraisers, rural collective assets appraisal organs, lawyers, notaries public, grassroots law services, patent agents, trademark agents, and specialized service agencies, had mostly severed their ties to government departments and organizations and were mostly converted into partnerships or limited liability companies. More specifically, the service professions had to sever their government ties in four respects (name, personnel, finances, and service).[186]

In the process of severing the professions' ties to the government, the Ministry of Finance and the State General Administration of Taxation also sought to promote the consolidation of the different certified professions to facilitate regulation and professional development. In 2000, these two government agencies ordered the merger of the accounting, asset appraisal, and tax service professions under one professional umbrella. After protracted bargaining, the merger was finally achieved in late 2002, albeit only on a limited basis: the asset appraisal association was completely merged into the accounting association (as the state asset management bureau had earlier been merged into the Ministry of Finance, the regulator of the accounting profession) while the tax service association became a group member of the accounting association but remained under the direct oversight of the Taxation Administration. There remain separate examination and certification requirements for accountants and tax professionals.[187] In the area of legal services, efforts were made to sort out the relationship between law firms, other legal services, and notaries public, and the bar exam was unified for lawyers and judges. The Ministry of Finance was also studying the various appraisal services (price appraisal, township enterprise evaluation, property evaluation, land evaluation, and project cost consultants) in the hope of consolidating these services.[188]

While rationalizing the structure of the professions, the Chinese government has also paid attention to the lessons from Enron and other cases and adopted measures to strengthen regulation and professional standards. Take the case of the accounting profession. In 2000, the Ministry of Finance stipulated that an accounting firm must have a minimum of 20 accountants qualified for securities business (up from eight) before the firm could be certified for securities industry practice. This minimum size was raised to 40 in 2002. These requirements have helped promote mergers among accounting firms. In the nine months after the minimum size was raised to 20 in 2000, there were more than 60 mergers, though in some cases the mergers were on paper only to satisfy the regulatory requirement.[189] Most importantly, armed with an amended Accounting Law, government agencies have imposed penalties on accounting firms for violating professional standards. In mid-2000, the China Securities Regulatory Commission admonished 11 companies, their securities underwriters, and accounting firms after the companies performed more than 20 percent below the forecasts made when they first listed in 1999.[190] In December 2000, the Ministry of Finance, in association with the People's Bank of China and the China Securities Regulatory Commission, began to certify accounting and law firms for auditing financial businesses and undertaking legal work for firms listing overseas. Such certification, to be renewed annually, may serve as a powerful incentive for the established professional firms to maintain professional standards in order to be eligible for some of the most lucrative assignments in their businesses.[191]

The year 2002 appears to have marked a watershed in the regulation of China's accounting profession. The Ministry of Finance launched another round of accounting inspections into the 2001 accounts of 192 major enterprises and their 91 accounting firms and uncovered serious misstatements to the tune of 11.5 billion yuan (of which the misstatement of profits amounted to 2.4 billion yuan).[192] Several prominent cases, in particular, attracted national attention. Because of its failure to uncover major accounting fraud at the publicly listed Yinchuan Guangxia Company, Zhongtianqin, one of the foremost accounting firms in China, lost its operating license as well as the right to conduct securities and futures related businesses in early 2002. Two of the lead accountants also lost their accounting licenses. Since then, regulators have revoked the licenses of a number of other accounting firms for poor practices.[193] In November 2002, the former chairman and president of Zhengzhou Baiwen were sentenced to suspended jail terms for falsifying accounting information in 1998 in one of China's high-profile corporate fraud cases.

As these measures were taken, professional firms began to change their behavior. In a clear recognition of their accountability and liability, accounting and law firms have started to purchase liability insurance. Faced with more vigorous regulatory attention, there is also indication that accounting firms in 2002 finally became more willing to issue reservations on corporate financial reports and squeeze out the froth in corporate accounting. According to a review of the accounting profession in Hunan, 31 accounting firms were able to ferret out a historic 4 billion yuan worth of accounting dishonesty in auditing the accounts at 223 state firms.[194] Meanwhile, drawing on the lessons of Enron (which resulted in the Sarbanes-Oxley Act in the United States), the China Certified Accountants Association, in accordance with the Accounting Law and the Law on Certified Accountants, transferred various regulatory functions back to three departments in the Ministry of Finance at the end of 2002.

Conclusions

In many ways, the justifications for rationalization were available well before the divestiture. Nevertheless, as was also true of a variety of institutional reforms discussed in this volume, the existence of the argument for rationalization and professionalism did not automatically lead to adoption of the argument. In the case of this chapter it was the smuggling crisis that provided Chinese leaders with the political impetus and determination for launching the sweeping divestiture and pushing it through in record time. While the ground for the divestiture had been prepared by the growing competition within the Chinese economy and thus the rising costs of owning business, it required extraordinary political commitment on the part of the Chinese leadership to launch the massive drive and carry it through to conclusion. The divestiture thus points again to the interplay of political and economic factors.

Though born of the smuggling crisis, the divestiture of myriad businesses run by or affiliated with China's party and state institutions, particularly the armed forces, was not a simple ad hoc move but part of the overall trend toward the rationalization of the state and of government-business relations. As Hu Jintao stressed, the divestiture had "great significance for maintaining the socialist market economic order, and for ensuring smooth progress in reform, opening up, and modernization as well as long-term national stability."[195] Put more plainly, the divestiture marked a milestone in the transformation of the state apparatus. The PLA, shorn of its commercial operations, has improved its status as a professional establishment. Likewise, divestiture of business operations combined with internal reforms have helped the police, the courts, the procurators' offices, and myriad other institutions to gain greater institutional integrity measured in terms of devotion to core missions.

While the divestiture was designed to help the Chinese government tame the scourge of rampant smuggling by legal persons and curb widespread corruption, its long-term impact for China's economic governance cannot be overestimated. A major complaint about China's economy has been the lack of a level playing field. When numerous firms made money not by competing on the market but by competing for special privileges, a fair and transparent regulatory framework was not possible. In a sense, the AJPG businesses, particularly the PLA's business empire, had virtually become a "state within the state." The successful divestiture and its expansion thus helped to vastly improve this operating environment and contributed to the making of a fairer regulatory environment and a level economic playing field. Indeed, without the divestiture, China's march to a modern market economy could very well be permanently stunted.

The author is under no illusion that the divestiture has solved all the problems of fairness and transparency in government regulation of the economy. Most prominently, though the relative size of the state sector has declined significantly over time, the state continues to hold vast business assets and remains the dominant player in sectors ranging from airlines to telecommunications. Much remains to be done to equalize treatment between state and private businesses. Nevertheless, it appears a consensus has emerged among the elite to treat businesses of all types of ownership reasonably equitably and, building on the foundations laid by the divestiture and with the international commitments arising from China's entry into the WTO, the promised equal treatment, as enshrined in a constitutional amendment in 2004, should move closer to reality over time. Simply put, the divestiture is one of the most pivotal and market-friendly initiatives China's leaders have ever launched in the reform era.

chapter five

ADMINISTRATIVE RATIONALIZATION AND THE
REORIENTATION OF GOVERNMENT BEHAVIOR

While the downsizing and streamlining of the government have garnered the most attention in the Chinese media, any analysis that focuses
solely on them will miss the essence of these reforms. Likewise the impact
of the divestiture and rationalization goes far beyond the struggle against
smuggling. As was noted in Chapter 2, Chinese reformers have since the
1980s argued that government reforms must seek to transform the functions of government. In the 1988 reforms, there was already recognition
that the government could not and should not take care of everything. The
late 1980s also saw some localities, notably Hainan, pursue initiatives to
promote "small state, big society."[1]

By the time of the 1998 government reforms, the ideological landscape in China had become considerably more variegated than a decade
earlier. Indeed, without much debate and fanfare, the Chinese elite appeared to have accepted matter-of-factly that the power of government
must be delimited, most commonly couched in terms of administration in
accordance with law (*yifa xingzheng*).[2] By the end of Zhu Rongji's tenure as
premier it was no longer controversial for the Chinese media to mention
the need to move from totalistic administration (*quanneng xingzheng*) to
limited administration (*youxian xingzheng*) or even to use the term "limited
government (*youxian zhengfu*)."[3]

In reality, as the 1998 government reforms progressed, reformers
quickly realized the limits of downsizing and streamlining and began to include a program to curb government discretion, boost administrative
transparency, and promote government as service. Central to this program

was a drive to reduce the number of government approvals and licensing requirements and make life easier for businesses and citizens. China's commitments to the terms of the WTO membership both manifest and reinforce the objectives of this program as they lock in requirements for transparency and dramatic reductions in foreign trade quotas.

It should be noted that elements of the central reform initiatives had been adopted in certain localities before. For much of the reform era, local authorities competed for overseas investments by offering special tax incentives and later tax rebates, sometimes even free land.[4] By around 2000, however, this strategy, namely price discounting, had lost much of its edge as the central government imposed uniform tax rules and mandated the use of auctions for commercial land use (Chapter 6). Local authorities now offer similar tax policies to investors. To differentiate themselves from others and gain a competitive advantage in the competition for business investments, local authorities have increasingly turned to the improvement of the so-called soft environment (*ran huanjing*), particularly the enhancement of government service.[5] The competition and emulation among local authorities to improve their investment environment, combined with a public commitment by central authorities to transform government functions in certain ways, have provided important incentives for sustaining the trend to be described in this chapter.

The rest of this chapter proceeds as follows. I first examine the transition from an emphasis on government downsizing to the national drive to reform the administrative approval system. Then I discuss the efforts to improve the transparency of government policy making as well as the initiatives to enhance government service via the establishment of one-stop administrative centers and other mechanisms. By delimiting the scope of bureaucratic discretion and placing bureaucratic behavior under public purview in public hearings and one-stop service centers, these reforms have gone some way toward bringing discipline to wayward bureaucrats. This is particularly the case in coastal municipalities, and in recent years a growing number of them have used public evaluations and telephone hotlines for complaints to hold bureaucrats accountable and thus improve municipal governance. Likewise ongoing civil service reforms have also been an important element in promoting professionalism and limiting discretion in personal recruitment. In the final section, I take into account of the developments described in this and the previous chapters to offer an overall assessment of government reforms.

Administrative Approval Reforms and the
Delimitation of the Administrative State

While all economies impose certain licensing and regulatory requirements on businesses and citizens, Chinese government agencies inherited from the era of central planning an elaborate system of licensing and approval requirements (*shenpi zhidu*). To some extent, the advent of the market reforms has steadily reduced the import of certain regulatory mechanisms that were once widely used in central planning. Most notably, the once pervasive price control and rationing system has largely disappeared. No Chinese today needs a ration coupon to make most purchases. As market competition has expanded, the list of prices subject to government control, maintained by the State Development and Reform Commission (the former State Development Planning Commission), has been whittled down drastically over time. It was still at 131 in 1992 but decreased to just 13 in 2001.[6]

Yet China has continued to maintain one of the most elaborate administrative approval systems in the world, and many of the approval and license requirements have been added in the reform era. Businesses making investments in China generally need numerous chops to gain government approval. While an individual may set up a company in the United States virtually in minutes, the Administration of Industry and Commerce in Beijing, for instance, had a list of 443 examination and approval items for registering a company.[7] Even in Shenzhen, which led the country in reforming government functions, it would require approvals from 13 government departments, more than 50 stamps, and the payment of over 20 fees and levies to move a real estate project from feasibility study to final completion and inspection as of 1998.[8] The expansion of government and the proliferation of government regulation have gone hand in hand in the reform era. The more the government expanded, the more approval and licensing requirements its constituent parts put forth. The proliferation of such approval and licensing requirements has in turn increased the burdens on businesses and citizens alike.

The elaborate administrative approval and licensing system empowers government agencies to make decisions that are often best left to firms and the market. Such a system generates numerous rent-seeking opportunities for bureaucrats and serves as a powerful inducement for them to stay in government. In fact, the myriad fees, levies, and fines associated with the administrative approval system have provided a major source of revenue that is often used as extra income for government employees and for hiring additional personnel.[9] Sometimes bureaucratic agencies fought turf wars to claim the revenue from fees and fines. For example, the Nanjing Construction Bureau went against the Bureaus of Labor and of Quality and Technical Supervision in late 1999 to claim the right to inspect elevators and collect about three million yuan in fees.[10] Given the stakes involved, it is not surprising that the approval and licensing system has become fertile ground for corruption. According to a tally by the disciplinary committee based at the State Development Planning Commission (now State Development and Reform Commission), about two-thirds of the disciplinary and criminal cases at the Commission were economic in nature, and of these most occurred in departments with project approval power.[11]

As market-based prices came to predominate in the economy, reformers saw reduction in administrative discretion as a key indicator of the transformation of government functions. It is conventional wisdom in China that the Chinese government must reduce the scope of the administrative approval and license system and concentrate on doing a smaller number of things, notably the enforcement of laws, more effectively than has been the case. The Chinese media have been especially vocal in calling for reducing the barriers to entry for firms, particularly nonstate firms, and alleviating the regulatory and financial burdens on firms and citizens alike.[12] With central government encouragement, a number of cities, particularly special development zones, began to experiment with initiatives to discipline bureaucratic behavior in order to better attract investments and promote economic growth. In Suzhou, the Suzhou Industrial Park, a collaborative venture between China and Singapore, imported and adopted Singapore's public administration experiences, including one-stop service for administrative licenses and approvals.[13] Shenzhen, which led the nation in administrative reforms, eliminated 310 (out of a total 737) administrative approval requirements over 1997–1999. The remaining approval requirements were standardized and publicized to improve efficiency and facilitate public supervision.[14] The experiences of Shenzhen, Suzhou, and a number of other municipalities have served as models for emulation elsewhere in China even as these cities themselves have continued to promote institutional innovation.

The First Phase of the Administrative
Approval Reform

The government reforms launched in 1998 entailed a revamping of the system of administrative approvals and licenses. Within the central government, the downgrading and then disappearance of most industrial ministries implied a significant reduction in bureaucratic rent-seeking via licenses and other forms of administrative approvals. Shorn of their administrative clout, the ministers chose to leave their bureaucratic posts behind; for example, a number of the vice ministers of the defunct Ministry of Metallurgical Industry became heads of major steel makers. Moreover, pressed to promote fair regulation under the rubric of administration in accordance with law (*yifa xingzheng*), the remaining agency officials became more aggressive in fulfilling their role as regulators. For instance, officials at the Ministry of Construction repeatedly warned construction and real estate management departments at all levels of government not to use their power to establish licensing and approval requirements for the sake of collecting fees. Instead, the departments were urged to sort out their administrative requirements and eliminate or ease those that hindered the development of real estate markets.[15] By the latter half of 2000, it had become conventional to emphasize the use of market incentives rather than regulatory examinations and approvals as much as possible in order to curb government discretion.[16] As will be discussed in Chapter 6, such a philosophy has been adopted in a variety of areas, ranging from government procurement to the allocation of land, mineral rights, and stock listing rights.

As the 1998 government reforms reached the provinces, provincial and sub-provincial authorities were directed to make the reform of the administrative approval system an essential component of government reforms.[17] Local authorities across the country announced targets for and results of provincial and municipal administrative approval reforms over 1999–2001. The Beijing municipal government in April 2000 scrapped 369 administrative approval items and delegated another 85 to district and county governments, cutting the number of approval items by 41.7 percent. The Guangdong provincial government shortened its list of approval items from 1,392 to 414 while the provincial capital city of Guangzhou trimmed its own list from 1,377 to 540. In the port city of Qingdao (Shandong province), the municipal government axed 30 percent of the bureaucratic approval items and instituted a collective examination and approval procedure for major approval items to ensure fairness and curb corrupt behavior. Numerous other cities such as Chongqing and Chengdu made similar moves.[18]

By publicizing plans for and achievements in reforming the system of administrative approvals, local officials not only demonstrated their commitment to the reforms but also sought to cultivate an investor-friendly image. In fact, from Shenyang in the north to Shantou in the south, it is quite common for incoming officials to launch institutional reform initiatives so as to move the locality away from the shadows cast by previous corruption scandals. In Zhejiang's Ningbo, Huang Ningguo became the new party secretary in the aftermath of a major corruption scandal. Shortly after Huang assumed his post, he learned that a real estate firm had spent ten months to get 86 stamps of approval from different government agencies but still could not secure the government's approval for a housing project. Huang enlisted the media to draw attention to this case and then asked government agencies including the Public Security Bureau, the Construction Committee, and the Culture Bureau to rationalize their administrative regimes and introduce mechanisms such as auctions to curb corruption. As a result of this initiative, the Ningpo municipal government cut the number of administrative approval items from 647 down to 227 in 2000.[19] By September 2001, the Zhejiang provincial government had cut its list of administrative approval items by 58 percent while municipal and county authorities reduced theirs by about one-third.[20]

Overall, during this first phase of administrative approval reforms, local authorities canceled or delegated between 30 and 60 percent of pre-existing administrative approval and licensing requirements.[21] Even allowing for some exaggeration and bureaucratic subterfuge (such as by keeping the most important approval requirements and getting rid of less important ones), this round of reforms appears to have helped contain bureaucratic malfeasance, particularly in economic affairs.[22]

While reducing and streamlining the list of administrative approval and licensing requirements, various local authorities also launched initiatives to improve administrative efficiency. The Zhongguancun Science and Technology Park in Beijing announced in 2000 that prospective companies could obtain an operating license in two days, before undergoing an examination by the local office of the State Administration of Industry and Commerce.[23] Fuzhou, the capital of Fujian province, established a set of institutional mechanisms and designated personnel called *shenpi yuan* to help investors handle the process of securing government approvals free of charge.[24] In Xinjiang, the government stipulated that administrative agencies must respond to foreign investors' applications for project approval and related licenses within five days of the receipt of the applications. Failure to respond within five days would be construed as approval.[25]

Administrative Approval Reform as a National Project

Even though the central government encouraged the administrative approval reforms as part of the government reforms, there was no central coordination until early 2001. While the State Council asked the State Economic and Trade Commission and relevant government departments and authorities to sort through the jungle of administrative approval and licensing requirements, the central government ministries were relatively quiet on this front.[26] Instead local authorities enjoyed much latitude. In their eagerness to improve the soft environment for investors, local authorities sought to gain a competitive edge by launching reforms of the administrative approval system. The competition and emulation among localities in turn gave much momentum to the reforms nationwide. Yet significant variations in local practices existed. With some exceptions (such as Sichuan's Mianyang), local governments in the coastal provinces generally outperformed their counterparts in the interior.

In 2001, however, the central leadership, having completed the central government downsizing and reorganization as well as the divestiture, took up the cause of reforming administrative approvals. Rather than viewing the reform solely as an issue of bureaucratic efficiency, the central leadership embraced it as part of the quest to curb corruption (see Chapter 7). This shift in the attitude of central leaders, coupled with the need to prepare the Chinese government for compliance with the terms of WTO membership, imbued the reform of the administrative approval system with a sense of urgency and made it into a national drive. In September 2001, the State Council formally set up an interdepartmental State Council Leadership Small Group on the Reform of the System of Administrative Approvals (Guowuyuan xingzheng shenpi zhidu gaige gongzuo lingdao xiaozu), with its office based in the Ministry of Supervision. Vice Premier Li Lanqing, who was also in charge of the leadership small group on rectifying the economic environment and promoting orderly economic competition (Chapter 3), headed this leadership small group. The following month, the State Council issued a directive titled Opinions on Implementing the Reform of the Administrative Approval System and launched the reform drive via a national teleconference. The directive asked each of the 65 State Council ministries and agencies with powers of administrative approval and licensing to comb through its list of licensing and approval items, analyze each item in the light of a set of principles, and then recommend to the Office of the Leadership Small Group which items were to be retained or abolished. It also directed each central government ministry or agency as well as each provincial-level government to put a leading official, with a dedicated staff, in charge of the reform.

Vice Premier Li Lanqing and other officials have justified the reform of the approval system on the following principles. According to Li, the government should concentrate on doing a relatively small number of things and doing them well. It should resolutely retreat from micromanaging a lot of things the government is incapable of doing, let alone doing well. Generally speaking, the government should focus on macroeconomic issues, on setting the rules of the market, and on effectively enforcing these rules as administrator and regulator. It should stay away from using regulatory power for the benefit of parochial interests (as had been the case with the various sectoral ministries). In economic affairs, Li called for abolishing administrative approval requirements that violated the principles of separation between government and enterprise and between government and not-for-profit organizations (*shiye danwei*) as well as those requirements that hindered market entry, fair competition, or those that simply could not be effectively implemented. In the allocation of commercial land use rights, construction project contracts, government procurement, and the sale of state enterprise property rights, market mechanisms (public and competitive bidding, tendering, or auctions) ought to be adopted (see Chapter 6). The remaining approval items must be streamlined, delegated where possible, and subjected to stricter standard operating procedures and a system of administrative accountability.[27] Strict procedures must be followed in abolishing and adding approval requirements. Local government departments, in particular, are not allowed to institute new approval requirements, and leaders of these departments should be held accountable for doing so. In general, the remaining approval items must be based on law and be reasonable; the exercise of administrative authority and power must be disciplined and bureaucratic discretion reduced through the specification of the contents, conditions, technical standards (where applicable), processes, and time required for conducting the administrative examination and approval.[28]

The national drive to reform the system of administrative approvals and licensing was spearheaded by the super-ministerial State Economic and Trade Commission (SETC) and State Development Planning Commission (SDPC). Shortly before the formation of the leadership small group on administrative approval reforms, the SETC announced that eventually it would replace the government approval system with a registration system for investment projects.[29] Such a statement of intentions was clearly well ahead of the times, but nonetheless in November 2001 the SETC announced that it would abolish 30 types of administrative approval requirements as a down payment for the national drive.[30] Not to be left behind, the SDPC announced that it would cancel five major categories of administrative examination and approval requirements.[31] Meanwhile, as China's WTO entry neared, the State Council made a widely publicized move in October 2001 to annul 64 administrative regulations and decisions promulgated prior to 2000.[32] Local authorities also undertook similar housecleaning to bring local legislation and regulations into compliance with the terms of WTO membership.

Prompted by the central government, local authorities quickly followed with a second and even a third round of announcements of approval-reduction initiatives. The Beijing municipal government, for example, in 2001 scrapped another 30 percent of its administrative approval items concerning the economy on top of the 41.7 percent reduction announced a little earlier. Shanghai decided in November 2001 that the number of economic-related approval and licensing requirements would be cut by another half in order to comply with the terms of the WTO. Ningbo sought to reduce the number of approval items by another third in 2002 on top of the 48 percent reduction made in 2000–2001. The provincial government of Heilongjiang vowed in December 2001 to cut administrative approval items by a further 40 percent following the 55 percent reduction made over 2000–2001. The provincial-level authorities also began to introduce institutional mechanisms to regularize the administrative approval process, make it more transparent, and make officials accountable. Shanghai emphasized holding joint approval meetings in order to reduce the opportunity for a single individual to trade influence for bribes. Both Chongqing and Shanghai (later joined by others) started to hold civil servants accountable for errors and misbehavior in granting licenses and administrative approvals.[33]

A particularly interesting case was Shandong province, which welcomed Zhang Gaoli, the former Shenzhen party secretary, as its new governor in October 2001. Shortly after he moved to Shandong, Zhang launched a Government Acceleration Project (Zhengfu Tisu Gongcheng) under which the Shandong provincial government cut the number of administrative approvals by half first and then the remainder by another half, all in a matter of months. Government agencies were also directed to respond to any requests for administrative approval and licensing within specified time periods. As a result of these reforms, the time needed to register a company dropped from 30 to five days.[34] The result in Shanghai's Pudong was similar. Whereas the establishment of a company used to require a laborious examination process, the reforms have made it possible for a company to register after the company's legal person representative (usually the chairman or president) pledges to comply with government conditions and regulations. As a result, new companies in Pudong can usually obtain their operating licenses in two to three days and generally no more than seven.[35] Even for the super-regulated real estate sector, the time to obtain final approval for a real estate project in Shanghai was reduced from 355 working days to 100, with the number of stamps of approval required having been cut to 40, down from the previous 157.[36]

Yet it was obvious that the Shanghai real estate approval process remained laborious as was also the case in a variety of other areas. Speaking at a work conference on administrative approval reforms in June 2002, Vice Premier Li Lanqing noted that some State Council ministries and agencies had dragged their feet and urged them to better recognize the importance and urgency of the reforms.[37] Such attention from Li and others moved the reform process along. In late August 2002, the leadership small group announced that the State Council commissions, ministries, administrations, and other agencies had sorted out a total of 4,159 approval items, about half of which were about economic regulation and the other half social. Of these items, 1,657 were established on the basis of laws and administrative regulations, 773 were set up on the authority of Party Central Committee and State Council directives, and the rest were based on ministerial regulations (874), ministerial directives (771), and directives of sub-ministerial departments (66). The State Council ministries and agencies recommended retaining 3,297 approval items (79.3 percent), scrapping 767 (18.4 percent), and changing the supervisory style for 95 (2.3 percent).[38]

After vetting the ministerial recommendations, the State Council, upon the recommendation of the leadership small group, announced the cancellation of 789 approval items from 56 government ministries and agencies on November 1, 2002. In line with the drive to improve economic performance, most (560) of the approval items that were scrapped were economic in nature, with the rest being about social affairs (167) and administrative matters (62). Most of the canceled approval items were initially established on the basis of ministerial regulations (279) or directives (303) and sub-ministerial directives (38); the rest were based on administrative laws or regulations (81) or State Council directives (88).[39] A few months later, the State Council announced the abolition of a second batch of 406 approval items. While a majority (241) of the second batch still concerned economic affairs, a greater proportion were about social affairs (105) and administrative matters (60).[40] As of fall 2003, a third batch of approval items to be abolished was also in the pipeline.

Following the State Council announcement, each government commission, ministry, or administration followed with details of their respective reforms. For example, according to a list of 32 approval requirements scrapped by the China Securities Regulatory Commission, foreign securities firms would no longer need to get "primary" approval to set up representative offices or to appoint chief representatives; law firms would no longer need approval to do securities law business; securities firms also would not need regulatory permission to underwrite corporate bonds or to establish investment consulting units.[41]

Since most central government requirements have local equivalents, the State Council announcement gave new impetus to provincial and municipal efforts to rationalize their administrative approval/licensing regimes. Take the case of Guangdong province. Prompted by the central reform initiative, the Guangdong leadership began a new round of administrative approval reforms in October 2001 and sorted through 1,638 existing approval and licensing items controlled by 49 provincial government agencies. Building on the earlier round of approval/licensing reforms, this new round abolished another 318 items (19.4 percent), delegated 132 items to lower-level authorities, and eased requirements on 153 other items.[42] Moreover, in response to the second round of State Council announcements on approval/licensing reforms, the Guangdong provincial leadership also began to consider the further streamlining and reduction of the approval/licensing regime in spring 2003.

These efforts to rationalize the administrative approval system are complemented by measures to replace administrative approval regimes for construction projects, land allocation, stock listings, and a variety of other scarce resources and rights with market-oriented processes to constrain the discretionary power of bureaucrats (see Chapters 6–7). More needs to be done; and government officials are already on the lookout for more administrative approval and licensing items to axe. Taken together, one can safely conclude that the administrative approval reforms have helped reshape the nature and spirit of government functions away from that of the gate-keeping rent-seeker.

Sustaining the Spirit of Administrative Approval Reform

The combination of government downsizing and streamlining with the reform of the administrative approval system has made more room for markets to function in the allocation of resources, particularly in areas long known for rent-seeking and graft (Chapter 6), and appears to help delimit the role of government. This does not mean that government regulation will disappear, however. Indeed, as Vogel has noted for other countries, deregulatory reforms in many areas necessitate the introduction of more rules, whether to ensure the efficiency and fairness of land auctions or to protect patients in the case of procurement reforms in hospitals.[43] And the number of administrative approval items being retained by the central government underscores the fact that there is no withering away of the state in China.

While some elements of the administrative approval reforms are not reversible, the remaining size of the regulatory apparatus raises the question of whether the spirit of the current reforms can be sustained. As mentioned earlier, competition among local authorities for investments, China's commitments to WTO membership, as well as a newfound conviction to use the reforms to curb corruption, have been important factors behind the impetus for reforms. Yet the record of past government reforms points to the challenges of sustaining the momentum of reform: while most industrial ministries were abolished, most regulatory agencies or administrations have been upgraded. There is little doubt that, given the chance, various bureaucratic interests would want to resurrect some of the lost administrative approval requirements and even create new ones.[44]

To sustain the spirit of the reforms, reformers have sought to use legislative means to bind the hands of bureaucracies. In 2000, the State Council Office of Legal Affairs took up the preparation of a draft law on administrative licensing (permission) and had the draft ready for comments shortly before the central leadership launched the national drive for administrative approval reforms. While waiting for the legislature to take up the Administrative Licensing Law (ALL) and as a stopgap measure to help bring government behavior into compliance with WTO membership terms, the State Council in late 2001 promulgated two regulations, one setting forth the procedures for formulating administrative laws and regulations and the other stipulating the procedures for formulating departmental regulations. These procedural rules, which became effective on January 1, 2002, included provisions for interdepartmental collaboration, public hearings, and legal review and were designed to improve the unity and coherence of government regulations and mitigate government arbitrariness.[45] The State Council formally transmitted the draft ALL to the ninth NPC for review in June 2002. In August 2003, after four readings rather than the prescribed three, the ALL was finally enacted into law by the tenth NPC Standing Committee (with a final vote of 151 to 0 and one abstention).[46] It took effect on July 1, 2004.

Consisting of 83 articles, the ALL builds on and locks in existing reform measures and provides a legal framework for further reforms.[47] To begin with, the ALL represents a fairly systematic effort to delimit the scope of administrative licensing and specify the standards and norms for the establishment and administration of administrative requirements. It stipulates that only the National People's Congress and provincial-level People's Congress (under certain circumstances) have the authority to establish administrative licensing requirements. While the State Council can impose interim administrative approval requirements, it needs to seek formal legislative enactment through either the NPC or its Standing Committee in a timely manner. More stringently, provincial-level governments cannot implement interim requirements for more than a year without securing formal legislative enactment through the corresponding legislatures (Article 15) and then only within certain limits (such as not imposing restrictions on inter-regional trade or employment). In a major departure from past practice, agencies within the State Council or local governments can no longer impose administrative licensing requirements on their own. This means that about half of the existing administrative requirements will need to be either reauthorized by the legislatures or modified and abolished.

The ALL also sets forth a set of principles for the establishment of administrative approval or licensing requirements. Generally speaking, licensing requirements are to be confined to areas concerning national security, public safety, macroeconomic control, ecological and environmental protection, and personal health and safety. While the ALL allows for exceptions, the regulation of professions, industries, legal persons as well as equipment, and products and commodities must be justified on the basis of public interest.

Under this principle, a rule of minimalism applies: no administrative approval requirement should be established where citizens, legal persons, and organizations can decide for themselves, where the market is sufficient, where the industrial association or intermediaries can self-regulate, or where the administrative agency can supervise after the event (through the fire-alarm style of regulation).

Against the background of excessive government interference in business and personal life, the balance of the ALL is tilted toward the protection of the rights and interests of businesses and citizens. Many articles in the ALL are designed to promote transparency, fairness, and good service:

—To further the goal of a unified national market and combat local protection, local authorities are enjoined from establishing administrative licensing requirements that harm inter-regional trade or services. Individuals and businesses may litigate to remove such requirements.

—Drafters of laws or regulations entailing administrative licensing requirements must solicit comments through hearings and forums and justify the need for the requirements and discuss the requirements' impact on economy and society.

—When an application for administrative permission directly affects another party (parties), the administrative agency should inform the applicants and the affected party of their right to a hearing (with the costs for convening the hearing to be borne by the administrative agency). The reasonable implementation of this provision alone will have revolutionary implications for how business is conducted in China.

—Existing license holders have the right to compensation when the terms of the grants are revoked or altered for the sake of public interest.

—Article 27 includes specific provisions against bribery and extortion in processing applications for administrative approvals. Applicants are to be informed of incomplete applications within five days of receipt of the application. Decisions on applications need to be made right on the spot as much as possible and generally within 20 days of the receipt of the application.

—To curb bureaucratic rent-seeking, lawmakers included fairly strict rules about the collection of fees. Article 58 states that in implementing administrative licensing requirements and conducting inspections, an administrative agency may not collect any charges unless otherwise stipulated by law or regulation. The agency must not charge for the application form. Instead, the funds needed for the administration of licensing requirements should be provided via the government budget. When charges are collected, information on the charges must be publicly available, and the funds collected must be *fully* remitted to the government exchequer (Article 59; see also Chapter 7).

All in all, in spite of some compromises made along the way, enactment of the ALL is without question a milestone in reforming the administrative approval system and in government reforms as a whole. The ALL joins extant laws on administrative procedure, administrative litigation, administrative punishment, and administrative supervision to make up a growing administrative law system to delimit the reach of the administrative state.

The Drive toward Transparency

Despite more than a decade of economic reforms, China's leadership has jealously guarded its power and has vigilantly cracked down on potentially subversive elements such as the Falungong sect. As the SARS crisis of 2003 highlighted, Chinese government officials are not above hiding information that reflects badly on their performance or on China's image.

While these old habits die hard, the Chinese government has nevertheless become more transparent toward the public, particularly in economic governance. In fact, the transparency in economic governance is a key component of the terms of China's WTO membership [I-2(C)].[48] The trend toward greater government transparency should help make better policies, curb government arbitrariness in policy implementation, and improve relations between elite and masses. It is thus a vital component of the efforts to transform government functions.

Information Availability

The drive toward greater transparency of government begins with the availability of basic information. For a government that at the start of reforms hoarded even the phone numbers of government departments, China has come a long way, aided by popularization of telecom services, including short-text messaging, and the rise of the Internet.

Not surprisingly, the improvement in transparency has been especially pronounced in the areas of foreign investment and trade. Driven by the need to compete for investments and at the urging of the Ministry of Foreign Trade and Economic Cooperation (MOFTEC, now part of the Ministry of Commerce), much of the foreign trade bureaucracy has adopted measures to boost regulatory transparency. Starting in 2000, partly in anticipation of WTO membership requirements, MOFTEC began to publish its policies and regulations in its *Public Notices* rather than through internal documents. It has also publicized the procedures and regulations regarding various administrative approval requirements to make life easier for businesses.[49] To anyone who has been dealing with China for the past two decades, a quick visit to the Commerce Ministry's Web site at www.mofcom.gov.cn reveals an aspect of China that would have been unimaginable at the start of the reform era. Most provincial and municipal governments' Web sites also offer a wealth of information. Moreover, various local authorities provide written guides to potential investors. Some have purchased space in the mass media to offer service guides for investors.

China's entry into the WTO has institutionalized the trend toward government transparency in foreign trade. The terms of China's WTO Accession Protocol state that "China shall make available to WTO Members, upon request, all laws, regulations and other measures pertaining to or affecting trade in goods, services, TRIPS or the control of foreign exchange before such measures are implemented or enforced [I-2(C)]." And the Chinese government has largely complied with this requirement. Indeed, in a major departure from past practice, major cities led by Shenzhen, Shanghai, Jinan, Chongqing announced in 2001 that henceforth they would publish documents and regulations on red letterheads (*hongtou wenjian*), previously available only internally, for public release and subscription. Many of these documents are now accessible via the Internet, particularly for local governments in the coastal region. The archives of cities such as Shanghai have begun to allow the public to access red-letteredhead documents from the past.

Transparency and Government Discipline

The sort of transparency in foreign trade governance has increasingly been extended to other aspects of government under the rubric of administrative transparency (*zhengwu gongkai*). The Ministry of Justice has set up the "148" phone numbers nationwide so that the public can dial for legal information and services.[50] Following the ouster of its minister in 2003, the Ministry of Land and Resources has become a leader in making publicly available important information and administrative decisions on land and resource use. With a few exceptions, central government ministries and commissions such as the Ministry of Water Resources and the State Administration of Environmental Protection release vast amounts of historical information and data on their Web sites.[51]

By 2000, the concept of administrative transparency had become a key indicator of the transformation of government functions and a weapon to hold bureaucrats in check. In December 2000, the Party Central Committee and the State Council jointly directed local authorities to promote administrative transparency (*zhengwu gongkai*) at the town/township level so that the local state could better connect with ordinary citizens.[52] While townships and urban neighborhood offices were directed to disclose key financial data, government departments at the county level and above were also encouraged to experiment with various measures to place their operations under public view.[53] According to data from the Central Discipline Inspection Commission, more than 80 percent of China's townships and villages had adopted some measure to boost administrative transparency by fall 2001.[54] In mid-2002, the general offices of the Party Central Committee and the State Council also urged public enterprises (SOEs, collective enterprises, and firms majority-owned by the state) to further promote the transparency of enterprise affairs.[55] Needless to say, these demands for transparency are not always fully met and in some cases only met perfunctorily. Nevertheless, combined with other institutional mechanisms, including improvements in accounting and auditing, the promotion of transparency is an essential element in the drive toward the improvement of government functions.[56]

Public Involvement in Policy Making

The transparency drive has also reached policy making. Following the enactment of the Legislation Law in 2000, the National People's Congress and local legislatures have routinely made available draft laws, such as the amended Marriage Law, for public comment.[57] Government agencies have also sought public input in formulating development programs. In a highly symbolic move, the State Development Planning Commission, once the secretive core of the planned economy, invited the public to offer suggestions on the tenth five-year plan (2001–2005) in 2000. Over a two-month period, the public could log on to the commission's Web site to send in their suggestions, and they did, with some questioning the existence of the commission itself. In addition, the SDPC also convened various consultative symposia on the broader contours of the plan as well as specific subjects.

Other government agencies have taken similar steps. Most prominently, the China Securities Regulatory Commission, whose regulatory initiatives affect the value of investments of millions of families, published drafts of the rules and regulations on a proposed second board in October 2000 for public comment and has since done the same for newly proposed regulations.[58] The Ministry of Land and Resources sought public comments on a proposed regulation on the requisition of farmland. It specifically asked farmers to discuss the issue of compensation, which had become and remains a deeply contentious issue in various localities.[59] Some local authorities have also invited public comments and suggestions in making up local five-year development plans.

As the Chinese government has progressively introduced competition into network-based industries, it has responded to public complaints about services by promoting more public involvement in utilities pricing and planning for various projects. In 2000 the Ministry of Information Industry (MII) and the SDPC held a hearing on telecom tariffs. Cities such as Beijing and Qingdao held hearings on the prices of taxi rides. In Guangzhou and Nanjing, proposals for raising the prices of water and liquefied gas were vetoed by local legislatures or at public hearings. To be sure, the quality and transparency of these hearings are highly uneven. The Qingdao municipal government won accolades for televising its hearing on the price of taxi rides while the Chinese media expressed deep dissatisfaction with the MII's hearing on telecom charges.[60]

The above experiences made regulators realize that it was good public policy to hold hearings on utilities pricing in accordance with the PRC Price Law. In July 2001, the State Development Planning Commission (SDPC) issued order No. 10 on the procedures and methods for holding public hearings on the prices of water, power, coal, telecom services, and railway transportation effective August 1, 2001. The order states that citizens have the right to be informed about the prices for public goods and services provided by natural monopolies through public hearings.[61] Later in 2001 the SDPC specifically directed provincial pricing authorities to hold hearings on ticket price increases during the Spring Festival peak travel season.[62] These central directives gave momentum to the promotion of public hearings. In December 2001, the Guangdong provincial authorities held a public hearing on public transportation pricing. The hearing was attended by regulators, business and consumer representatives, and experts; and the interested public could provide their input via a telephone hotline as well as on the Internet (www.gdpi.gov.cn). China Central Television televised this hearing live so that officials in other parts of the country could learn from the Guangdong experience.[63]

The impact of public hearings on public policy making has been mixed so far. On the one hand, increased transparency and public involvement appear to have helped moderate the magnitude of price hikes in some instances. For example, in the public hearing on highway passenger transport prices in Henan, the provincial transport association requested a seasonal price hike of 23.4 percent. Eighteen of 23 public representatives were against the price hike or its magnitude. Invoking the opposition, the Henan provincial planning commission and the communications (transport) bureau approved a 10 percent price increase, which was only half of the average 20 percent rise that had been granted in the decade prior to the hearings.[64] In other provinces, notably Guangdong, local planning officials also believed that the public hearings served to moderate the demands of transport interests.[65] Likewise, following a hearing and with comments received from the public via telephone and email, the SDPC cited public pressure in permitting the Ministry of Railways to raise ticket prices by a maximum of 15 percent during the Spring Festival holiday season instead of the 30 percent applied for. It also cut the number of days for the higher holiday prices from the proposed 33 days to 20.[66]

On the other hand, as is to be expected, the quality and impact of public hearings have been uneven across the country. In certain cases, such as the MII's hearing on telecom charges mentioned above, the results of the hearings were not released to the public, and it was not clear whether the hearings had any actual impact on policy making. Even in Guangzhou, a fairly large percentage of the public surveyed in 2002 believed that the hearings had become less substantive than promised.[67] Partly to alleviate public complaints about the quality of the hearings, the SDPC amended its regulations and issued the Methods for Hearings on Government Price Decisions (effective December 1, 2002). The amended regulations added provisions to broaden the range of participants as well as to require price regulators to publicly release the final results of the price hearings.[68] On the heels of the SDPC initiative, some provincial authorities tightened their own rules for holding public hearings. The Guangdong provincial government, for example, announced that public hearings must be held for setting and changing the pricing of nine categories of products and services, including residential power, medical services, education, water, gas, cable TV, public transportation, city parking, and environmental services.[69]

Party Control, the SARS Crisis, and the Promise of Transparency

In promoting greater administrative transparency, albeit ironically not always for themselves, China's national leaders apparently hope that the sunshine will empower the interested public to hold bureaucrats to their words and standards, make bureaucrats more disciplined, and enhance the legitimacy of the ruling elite. Slowly but surely, administrative transparency has improved substantially since the end of the 1990s. Yet the progress has been highly uneven spatially and in terms of the policy arena. The improvement has been the greatest in the economic sphere but less so in other areas.

These limits to the trend toward transparency are to be expected given the continuation of Communist Party rule. There are fundamental contradictions in the party leadership's pursuit of greater transparency. It is thus not surprising that, despite repeated calls for legislative action by some NPC delegates, efforts to produce a set of Regulations on Government Information Disclosure, stimulated by China's anticipated entry into the WTO, have dragged on for several years. With the participation of representatives from the national legislature, the State Council Office of Legal Affairs, the Ministry of Public Security, the State Secrets Bureau (Guojia Baomi Ju), and other legal experts, drafting of these regulations began in 1999–2000, and a draft was circulated in 2003 for comment. Reformers hope to use legal rules to force government agencies to open up and thus endow the people with the right to information (*zhiqing quan*). The draft regulations stipulate that officials are negligent if they disclose false information or obstruct the disclosure of information that has not been ruled as secret.[70] For reformers, this emphasis on transparency builds on theories of principal-agent relationship and implies an effort by the state to enlist the people in supervising officialdom. They argue that greater transparency would help produce all sorts of benefits, including clean administration and economic development.[71] In contrast, the status-quo interests are afraid that mandating information disclosure may upset the current regime and want to release information at their pleasure.

While the national regulations on transparency were being discussed, Guangzhou, capital of Guangdong province, began to implement a set of municipal regulations on government information disclosure on January 1, 2003. The Guangzhou regulations stipulate that government information should be available to the public and that the public (individuals and organizations) has the right to government information. Except in exceptional circumstances, transparency (*gongkai*) is a matter of principle that should be fulfilled legally, truthfully, fairly, and in a timely manner. The regulations include a long list of information that should be publicly available, including development plans and their implementation, major decisions, regulations and related policy measures, and how major local emergencies are dealt with.[72]

The Guangzhou regulations go a long way toward specifying what information should be available to the public and have led to substantial improvement in government practice. Yet they fail to offer a solution to the following problem: Who makes the decision when the government representatives and the public disagree on whether a particular piece of information should be released to the public?[73] Ironically, this issue was put to a quick test during the SARS crisis as Guangzhou became the epicenter of the SARS disease. For weeks the Guangzhou municipal government and the Guangdong provincial government, under pressure from the Guangdong party secretary and the propaganda apparatus, withheld vital information from the public. Moreover, the city of Beijing, which had also adopted various measures for administrative transparency, was soon found to have covered up the incidence of SARS in that city. Unlike in the past, the media control and cover-ups were far from ironclad as the public was able to share information via the Internet and mobile phones. Yet it was not until April 20, 2003, that the Chinese leadership finally came clean on SARS with the firing of the health minister and the Beijing mayor and the launching of a national campaign to contain the spread of SARS. Beginning on April 21, the Chinese government began to release data on SARS on a daily basis.

As a key ingredient of the war on SARS, the Chinese leadership demanded that officials provide full and accurate information on the incidence of SARS. On May 9, 2003, Premier Wen Jiabao signed into effect a set of hastily devised Regulations on Emergency Public Health Cases, which cover major infectious diseases, food poisonings, diseases of unknown causes that affect a large number of people, and other major public health events. Besides empowering the State Council and local authorities to set up emergency command headquarters to provide unified leadership in dealing with the emergency cases, the regulations make strong demands on the timely reporting of information. Provincial-level authorities must report to the State Council health authorities within an hour of getting reports of emergency cases, while authorities at the county level or above are to report to superordinate health departments as well as the State Council health authorities within two hours of getting reports. Most importantly for our discussion, the regulations state that organizations and individuals have the right to report cases to the government or related departments as well as the right to expose negligence on the part of government and its departments.[74]

Many commentators, including myself, noted that China's SARS crisis would not have the same effect on openness as the Chernobyl nuclear accident did in the former Soviet Union in the 1980s. Even as the Chinese press emphasized the need for greater transparency, the Chinese courts continued to hand out jail terms to cyber-dissidents for "incitement to subversion."[75] The propaganda department also continued to exercise its muscle and in the first half of 2003 caused purges to occur at several newspapers, including *Southern Weekend, Twenty-first Century Global Report,* and *Youth Reference.* Nonetheless, in the aftermath of the SARS crisis, the trend toward greater transparency has clearly ratcheted up and moved beyond economic governance. Since the SARS crisis the Ministry of Health has reacted with more alacrity to several mass food poisoning cases, and the Chinese media have reported more freely on these cases as well as various accidents, crimes, and disasters.[76] Meanwhile virtually all media forms have published articles or comments promoting the citizen's right to information. All these developments appear to have given another, although still limited, boost to the process leading to the promulgation of State Council Regulations on Information Transparency.[77]

The Promotion of a Service-Oriented Government

So far we have focused on reforms that curb or reduce the role of the bureaucracy. For the Chinese bureaucrat, however, perhaps the most revolutionary aspect of the government reforms is the idea that government is not simply about control or giving orders but about service. In the words of former Personnel Minister Song Defu, "government civil servants should acquire the mentality of serving taxpayers."[78] One institutional innovation that epitomizes this vision as well as the values of transparency and efficiency is the one-stop administrative service (*yizhanshi fuwu*). Pioneered in China by special zones such as Shenzhen, Hainan, and the China-Singapore Industrial Park in Suzhou, a typical administrative service center brings together in one physical location representatives from various government offices so that businesses and citizens may interact with these offices conveniently and more efficiently.[79] Because an administrative application can now move from one office representative or counter to another in assembly line fashion and ideally under public view, the chance for rent-seeking is sharply curtailed, prompting some journalists to refer to the service centers as "anticorruption agencies."[80]

With the progression of the 1998 government reforms, the one-stop government service centers have spread across the country. By 2000 central government ministries had become strong supporters of the one-stop service model. The Ministry of Construction, for example, urged local departments to offer such service, with all fees paid together, in property rights transactions.[81] The Ministry of Land and Resources announced that its offices would adopt "service windows" (*chuangkou bangong*) to replace its laborious regulatory system and promote administrative transparency at the county level.[82] Many cities around the country have emulated the early pioneers to establish government service centers cater to the needs of investors. In Jiangsu's Lianyungang, the Administrative Examination and Approval Service Center houses 36 government departments and organizations in charge of 210 government approval or licensing requirements. Whereas previously an application for a business license took at least a week, the one-stop service center could issue approval within a day.[83] By 2002 the one-stop service model had spread even to Tibet.[84]

Because of unwillingness on the part of some government bureaus to delegate power to their representatives at the service centers, some one-stop service centers have failed to fulfill their promise. One striking failure occurred in Inner Mongolia's Baotou city, where a one-stop administrative service center was launched with much fanfare in mid-2000. By spring 2002, however, reporters found that the Baotou administrative service center was all form and no substance and at best played the role of a reception room. Instead, investors had to continue to ply the corridors of the myriad government bureaus. Government rent-seeking also remained at a high level; even though the Baotou municipal government reduced the number of fees and levies collected from 498 in 1996 to 246 in 2002, the amount collected actually rose.[85] Similar cases could also be found in other places, such as Jiangxi's Yichun city.[86] Yet these appear to be exceptions to the rule; overall the quality of government service in the interior regions has also seen some improvement over time. In the case of Baotou, attention from the national media prompted the municipal authorities to move key bureau personnel from 38 bureaus and agencies to the administrative service center.[87] A number of interior cities, such as Yunnan's Kunming and Jiangxi's Nanchang, have become innovative models in improving government service via one-stop centers. Nanchang, the capital of Jiangxi province, has given particular emphasis to combining service with public finance reforms after Meng Jianzhu moved from Shanghai to Jiangxi to serve as party secretary. All fees and charges for the examination and approval of investment and construction projects were printed on a list compiled by a special municipal committee overseeing the exam-approval process for investment and construction projects. Investors going through the exam-approval process get an invoice for the fees from the service center but pay the fees at designated banks before collecting the final approvals and licenses. This mechanism separates the fee payment from the government approval process so as to prevent embezzlement by civil servants involved in the exam-approval process.[88]

The pioneers along the coast have moved further ahead. After spearheading the reduction in administrative approval requirements, Shenzhen in late 2001 launched a program to systematically codify government organizations and discipline administrative behavior through laws: government functions and staff size; administrative procedures, approval requirements, administrative fees and penalties; government procurement; government investment; and administrative law enforcement and accountability.[89] Or take Suzhou. The government administrative service center in the Suzhou Industrial Park started with about 100 fee/levy collection items. The number of fees/levies collected dropped to 27 in November 1998 and stood at around 10 in spring 2002, helping make Suzhou one of the world's most attractive destinations for foreign investment.[90] All of Beijing's 18 districts and counties had set up reasonably well-functioning one-stop administrative centers by 2001.[91]

While the one-stop administrative centers were initially introduced to attract overseas investments, by 2001–2002 local authorities had moved beyond the narrow focus on business development to improve service to residents. The trend was set in Xiaguan District of Nanjing, capital of Jiangsu province. In October 2000, Xiaguan launched five government service centers, known affectionately as administrative supermarkets (*zhengwu chaoshi*). At these "supermarkets," which received "excellent" ratings from the public in their first year of operations, residents can obtain nearly 50 kinds of government services ranging from marriage licenses to unemployment assistance.[92] The idea of a "supermarket" where "customers" could pick up just about any type of government "product" and service soon captured the imagination of local officials in various places. Whether these officials were genuinely dedicated to improving government performance or simply looking for a scheme to generate publicity and burnish their reformist credentials in the hope of promotions, a healthy competition ensued among some localities to set up service centers.

By late 2001, many cities had also established community administrative centers (*shequ zhengwu zhongxin*) to bring various forms of government and community services to urban neighborhoods. Some counties in interior provinces also started to jump on the bandwagon to offer government "service like supermarkets."[93] Meanwhile, provincial governments, which had lagged behind municipalities, began to open their own centers. When the Anhui provincial government inaugurated its Administrative Service Center (Zhengwu Fuwu Zhongxin) in December 2001, the center was heralded as the "supermarket for government service." It housed representatives from 31 government departments handling 233 licensing and approval items. All of Anhui's 17 prefecture-ranked cities also set up their own service centers, as did a growing number of counties.[94] With allowance for variations in performance in different places, the centers have become more professional over time and are an important institutional measure for improving bureaucratic efficiency and transparency.

Finally, local governments, notably Beijing, Guangdong, and Shanghai, have made strides in harnessing the Internet to release information and provide services, including a Web platform for government procurement.[95] In fall 2001, the Shanghai municipal government started to use its consolidated shanghai.gov.cn portal to promote e-government. Shenzhen had by mid-2002 set up 1,000 electronic convenience stations in neighborhoods to provide about 150 different services, including government information. Some local governments in Guangdong and the Zhejiang provincial government also began to introduce Web-based licensing and approval programs that serve the same purpose as the physical one-stop government service centers.[96] As is to be expected, the quality of the government Web sites is highly uneven. A third-party evaluation of the Web sites offered by 36 provincial capitals and cities with independent planning status (*jihua danlie shi*) reported in 2002 that only a small number of the sites were graded as superior in terms of content and helpfulness.[97] Nonetheless, by 2002–2003 the Chinese central government, via the State Council Informatization Office, had become a heavy promoter of e-government and, based on my own observation, most major cities have made meaningful upgrades to their Web sites.

Bureaucracy, Accountability, and Municipal Governance

How can government agencies be forced to stay focused on providing good service? In tandem with the promotion of transparency and service (above) and civil service reforms (see below), various local authorities have set up mechanisms to respond to public complaints and deal with wayward bureaucratic behavior. This is most obvious in the area of foreign investment, where intensive competition has often prompted local authorities to bend over backwards to offer attractive terms and sound service, particularly for multinational firms. In late 2001 and early 2002, the foreign trade bureaus of Shanghai and Shenzhen each set up a Coordination Center for Complaints by Overseas Investors (Waishang Tousu Xietiao Zhongxin) to accept complaints, suggest solutions, and propose policy measures for improving government work.[98]

Going beyond the area of foreign investment, the terrain becomes treacherous for the researcher. While studies have documented a variety of mechanisms by which ordinary Chinese can make their influence felt despite the lack of competitive elections, the Chinese bureaucracy is not known for being nicely responsive to the demands of individuals.[99] Yet around 2000 a growing number of local authorities began to establish complaint centers, and the practice has spread. The port city of Ningbo, for instance, set up a Clean Administration Complaint Center (Lianzheng Tousu Zhongxin) in summer 2000 to deal with complaints about violations of government licensing approval rules; excessive and arbitrary levies by party and government agencies; problems in government financial management; and violations of regulations on competitive bidding.[100] Likewise, the city of Qingdao has become well known for taking complaints about civil servant behavior by phone and acting on these complaints, which numbered more than 3,600 in 2002. In response to the complaints, 188 people were admonished, 26 were criticized in public within the government, 33 were asked to formally apologize to the complainers, 30 had their bonuses docked, and 12 were removed from their posts.[101] In Fujian province, the provincial government directed all subprovincial governments to establish Government Efficacy Complaints Centers (Jiguan Xiaoneng Tousu Zhongxin) to supervise the administrative agencies. These centers handled 18,700 complaints in 2001.[102] In Shijiazhuang, the capital of Hebei province, a municipal administrative efficiency supervisory center (*xingzheng xiaoneng jiancha zhongxin*) was established in May 2001 to accept complaints from individuals and businesses on arbitrary collection of fees, administrative procrastination, and a host of other related problems. According to a Municipal Discipline Inspection Committee official, this mechanism also was set up for all counties and districts in Shijiazhuang. The municipal center had received 12,500 complaints by May 2002 and was able to resolve about 9,000 of them.[103]

Since the statistics from the above cases do not indicate the degree of responsiveness on the part of the local leadership, it is useful to dissect some cases. Here I would like to focus on two cities: Zhuhai, one of the earliest special economic zones, and Nanjing, the historic capital city of Jiangsu province. In 1999, Zhuhai's leaders were jolted by criticism from overseas investors that Zhuhai had the hard (physical) infrastructure but lacked the soft environment (*ruan huanjing*) for sustaining development. In one case, orchard trees planted by a Taiwan investor with approval from the head of the Department of Land and Resources were later uprooted by that same department because the director's approval was misplaced. Invoking cases such as this, Party Secretary Huang Longyun thundered that Zhuhai would lose not just investment projects but an entire generation if government staff focused on personal or departmental gain by using their power to erect barriers.[104]

To improve bureaucratic behavior, Zhuhai's leaders in late 1999 launched an initiative to allow the public to evaluate the performance of government agencies and staff (literally, *wanren ping zhengfu,* or "10,000 people evaluate the government"). What surprised the bureaucrats, however, was not the public evaluation itself but what the leaders did with the evaluation results. At the end of January 2000, the leaders announced that, based on the evaluation results, the directors of the three lowest-rated departments would lose all bonuses for the year while all the section heads (*kezhang*) would lose their civil service positions. It was also announced that the director of any department that was rated one of the lowest for two consecutive years would lose his or her position. By September 2000, more than 160 section heads and department directors had lost their posts, including all section heads at the bureaus of pharmaceutical supervision, civil affairs, and land and resources.[105] In addition to the annual public evaluation, the Zhuhai municipal authorities in July 2000 set up a powerful Municipal Complaints Center for Administrative Efficiency (Shi Xingzheng Xiaolü Tousu Zhongxin) within the Supervision Bureau.[106] The Center is empowered to investigate the public's complaints and suggest solutions. Government agencies that are the subject of public complaints are required to respond within a specified time period of between three and seven business days.[107]

Amid much complaint about abuse of power in China, the Zhuhai experience has given the public real power to hold bureaucrats accountable. In response to such institutional incentives, bureaucrats in Zhuhai have made efforts to connect with the public through administrative innovations, including well-staffed telephone hotlines and Web sites. Indeed, the Zhuhai government Web site (www.zhuhai.gov.cn*),* with ample links for making complaints on the front page, is one of the most user-friendly to be found in China. If Zhuhai is an outlier because of its special economic zone status, tradition-laden Nanjing, with a population of 5.3 million (2001), certainly belongs to the mainstream, and its efforts to involve the public in improving municipal governance are therefore of broader relevance. At the end of 2001, the Nanjing leadership under recently appointed Party Secretary Li Yuanchao asked the public to evaluate the performance of government bureaus and organizations. As a result of the survey, the directors of the two lowest-ranked bureaus (Housing and Municipal Appearance [*Shirong*]) were removed from their posts and demoted. Directors of three other bureaus were reprimanded.[108]

As in Zhuhai's case, the demotions on the basis of public ratings gave a jolt to the bureaucracy in Nanjing and prompted bureaucrats to make serious efforts to improve service quality.[109] In the words of Nanjing's Jiangning district vice secretary Zhan Shuangding, "we draw a salary supported by taxpayers. If in doing our work [we] make our 'gods' unhappy, we'll really lose our jobs."[110] Such shifts in bureaucratic attitudes were reflected in the results of the public evaluation conducted at the end of 2002. While the response rate improved significantly, the number of respondents indicating their satisfaction with the government administration also rose by 9.7 percentage points, and those choosing "dissatisfied" dropped by 9.8 percentage points (the sum of "satisfied" and "relatively satisfied" was an impressive 98.8 percent).[111]

Nanjing's adoption of *mowei taotai*—the last shall be the first to be eliminated—through public evaluations came on the heels of the arrest of leaders in Shenyang and Xiamen on corruption charges. While the massive corruption scandals in Shenyang and Xiamen and other localities are negative examples, the developments in Nanjing and elsewhere have served as positive models. Space limitations do not allow me to present more cases, but judging by the spread of the one-stop administrative service centers in interior provinces, even authorities in backwater areas have begun to partake of this trend toward better public administration.[112]

The combined effect of reforms in the administrative approval system, civil service, and public finance and the drive to promote transparency and service has resulted in improved governance in a growing number of cities. Urban leaders in Beijing, Shanghai, and other cities, partly prodded by increasingly demanding municipal people's congresses, have made massive efforts to build urban infrastructure and improve public services. And, in spite of their lack of a mandate through public elections, the "can-do" attitudes have helped these urban leaders win some measure of public support. Results from surveys conducted by the independent opinion survey firm Horizon Survey Group lend credence to such an interpretation. When respondents were asked whether they would vote for their current mayors if they were permitted to vote directly, the mayors of eight of the ten cities surveyed in 2002 and the mayors of all 13 cities surveyed in 2003 enjoyed ratings of more than 50 percent.[113] Comparing these numbers with the far poorer showings of county magistrates, it appears reasonable to conclude that China's major cities have become centers for progressive governance reforms.

Civil Service Reforms and Good Governance

Even before the 1998 government downsizing, there had been some efforts to regularize civil service recruitment through competitive exams. The government downsizing has made bureaucratic positions scarcer and thus more valuable, spurring existing staff members to work harder to retain their positions. During the central government streamlining in 1998, staff members voted on divisional and departmental directors, who then chose those to be retained in their respective divisions or departments. Such competitive bilateral selection processes helped make the downsizing a fairer and less contentious operation and helped boost morale among staff retained.[114]

Encouraged by the results of competition in some departments and worried about the incidence of corruption in official promotions (*pao guan*), the Party Organization Department and the Ministry of Personnel encouraged all government departments to introduce competition to personnel selection in a set of "Suggestions for Using Competition for Positions in Party and Government Agencies" issued in mid-1998. These guidelines stipulated eight steps by which the competitive personnel selection process should be managed, including announcement of available positions, open registration, examination of candidate qualifications, written examination, speech and interview, democratic opinion survey, Party evaluation, and final appointment.[115]

The adoption of competition in personnel selection during government downsizing is part of an overall program to improve the civil service system that had been gradually put into place since around 1993. In March 1999, the Personnel Ministry reinforced its earlier Suggestions by requiring governments at all levels to recruit middle-ranking party and government cadres through open and fair competition in order to promote clean and efficient government. In response to the central authorities' order on regularizing the competitive personnel selection process, competition was widely adopted in downsizing and streamlining the provincial level bureaucracies. In Guangdong, for example, the positions of divisional directors and deputy directors in all 46 departments except the Bureau of Supervision were opened to competition between March and July 2000. In all, 2,490 applicants vied for 1,235 positions. The applicants took written tests (this counted for 20 percent of the total score), gave talks and face-to-face interviews (20 percent), were voted on anonymously by staff members

(30 percent), and vetted by the Party Organization Department (30 percent). The combined evaluation results were then announced for public notice for three days before final appointments were made. As a consequence of this process, 1,136 of the original pool of applicants won appointments while 170 divisional directors and deputy directors were demoted or reassigned. The process won overwhelming support. In a survey of 4,655 civil servants, 91 percent were in favor of the competitive selection process, and 94 percent were satisfied with the selection results.[116]

Similar practices have also been adopted in other provincial units.[117] Indeed, competition has become a widely accepted principle for recruitment in Chinese bureaucracies ranging from central government departments to localities, with major cities opening a substantial number of positions to talent from all over the country. By the end of April 2000, about 350,000 positions ranging from major government agencies including the Ministry of Public Security (105 positions), the Ministry of Personnel, the Supreme People's Procuratorate, the State Development Bank, to government offices in 29 provincial units had become available for competitive recruitment, with over 800,000 applicants for these positions.[118] It is now common to find, in Chinese newspapers and on the Internet, announcements of competitive recruitment for government posts at the deputy director (*fuju*) level and below.

The competition for civil service positions has helped improve the professional quality of the civil service staff and ended the era of strict upward mobility in the bureaucracy.[119] According to one report, as a result of the introduction of competition into civil service recruitment, 2,400 county-divisional cadres and 63,000 section (*ke*) level staff members were demoted, reassigned, or forced out of their government posts.[120] Extensive media coverage of the competitive recruitment, such as the process by which 16 directors were chosen at the Supreme People's Procuratorate, has helped to improve the image of the Chinese bureaucracy, if only to a limited degree.

In an important departure from past practice where the Communist Party's personnel choices were final, nominations for various official positions must be posted for public notice (*renqian gongshi zhi*) for a period of usually about ten days and may be withdrawn in cases of significant public criticism (such as corruption). In Jiangsu's Shuyang county (Suqian municipality), which pioneered the public notice system beginning in August 1997, 25 of 651 nominees had their promotions denied or delayed because of unfavorable public comments after the nominations were publicized.[121] In other provinces, 91 of 7,712 nominees in Heilongjiang and 17 of 1,600 nominees in Fujian at the divisional level (*chu*) or below had their appointments delayed or canceled in response to public comments between 1999 and mid-2000.[122] In 2000 the party center urged local authorities across the country to adopt the practice of public notice. In Beijing municipality, all districts and counties adopted the practice following trial runs in Pinggu county and Xicheng district.[123] In fall 2000, the Guangdong provincial Party Committee announced that it would fully adopt the *gongshi zhi* for all cadres subject to the approval of the provincial organization.[124] Since then a growing number of cities have also made similar announcements, and cities such as Zhuhai have made such announcements on government Web sites. In early 2001, the Party Organization Department formalized the *gongshi zhi* for cadre appointments with a directive that included detailed guidelines on the procedures for publicizing proposed appointments and the contents to be publicized.[125]

The increased transparency about nominees for official appointments has induced behavioral changes among potential nominees as well as by officials making the nominations. Whereas previously officials seeking promotions devoted their energies to pleasing superiors, sometimes by bribery, the introduction of the public notice system has to some extent forced officials seeking promotions to pay attention to the wishes of the common folk as well. Meanwhile, the public notice system has prompted party leaders to be more diligent in vetting the credentials of nominees, at least to avoid public embarrassment.[126]

Besides introducing competition and transparency into the appointment process, the Personnel Ministry has also adopted annual performance appraisals, rotations, and dismissal of incompetent officials in order to enhance performance and reduce corruption in the civil service.[127] Take the rotation of posts, which we have briefly mentioned in Chapter 1. Between 1995 and 2000, more than 500 cadres on the center's nomenklatura, 10,000-plus prefecture-bureau level cadres, and 160,000 county-division level cadres were rotated. As a result, 96 percent of the county-level party secretaries and 97 percent of the county (city) magistrates went through exchanges or rotations.[128] As the system of rotations took hold, the Personnel Ministry announced in 2000 that civil servants in positions concerning personnel, finance, resource management, certificates, and licenses must be rotated more extensively, by more than 30 percent per year. In the Ministry of Finance, for example, 55 percent of the bureau directors and 30 percent of the staff members were rotated to different posts in 2000.[129] As rotations trigger end-of-term audits for officials (Chapter 7), they have become a crucial link in the enhancement of the cadre disciplinary regime.

Many of the civil service reforms are driven by the need to combat corrupt practices in personal recruitment and promotions. The incidence of *maiguan maiguan*, which literally means the buying and selling of official posts, is widely known in China, not to mention the use of appointments as patronage opportunities. Between 1995 and 2001, authorities in China dealt with 1,963 personal management cases, disciplined 519 officials ranked at the county-divisional director (*xian chu ji*) level, and nullified 5,991 cadre appointments.[130] To combat what official documents refer to as "unhealthy tendencies in personnel appointment," the Party Central Committee and its Organization Department have set up a telephone hotline to allow informants to report on abuse in personnel selection and promotion. By the end of 2000, 40,200 tips were received via the hotline, including tips on major cases of corruption in Gansu and Shanxi.[131] They have also introduced various regulations to improve personnel management procedures and promote competition and public notice (*gongshi*). In May 2001, the Organization Department and the Central Discipline Inspection Commission issued a joint directive on preventing unhealthy tendencies in cadre selection and appointment. A little later the Organization Department publicized details of three major cases of such corruption from Guangxi, Hebei, and Shanxi.[132]

The initiatives for personnel management reforms culminated in a revamp in 2002 of the Central Committee "Regulations for Selecting and Appointing Leading Party and Government Cadres," previously issued in 1995. While continuing to emphasize party leadership in selecting and appointing cadres, the 2002 regulations, comprising 74 articles in 13 chapters, include more elaborate procedures to enhance the transparency and fairness of appointments for cadres ranked at the county-divisional director-level and above.[133] Specifically, nominations for official appointments must be vetted via interviews and opinion surveys, voted on collectively by committee, and announced to the public for comment. In addition, there are rules governing open selection and competition for posts; exchange and avoidance; dismissal, resignation, and demotion; and discipline and supervision. Most of these rules and procedures were tried out in some localities before they were incorporated into the 2002 regulations.

Implementation of the regulations has proceeded relatively smoothly, particularly in more developed areas of the country. Take the collective decision making on nominations. In Guangdong, candidates for party secretaries and mayors of prefectures and cities must be voted on by the provincial party committee and receive a simple majority of the votes cast before they can be appointed or, in the case of mayors, nominated to the people's congress for ratification. When the provincial committee is not in session, the appointments are to be decided on by the Provincial Committee Standing Committee following the solicitation of written opinions of the members of the provincial party committee.[134] In Zhejiang, which had tried out the system in most cities and counties by 2002, 4,222 appointments had been made through collective decision making. Of these, 88 were put on hold, and only five were rejected for not winning half of the votes cast.[135]

In conclusion, if the Pendleton Act of 1883 initiated the shift from patronage to a merit-based civil service system in the United States in response to problems of corruption and inefficiency, China's civil service reforms, together with changes to the anticorruption apparatus (Chapter 7), have arisen in response to similar concerns. Benefiting from international experience, the Chinese civil service reforms have proceeded rapidly since the mid-1990s and might similarly help with the cleanness and effectiveness of the Chinese bureaucracy over time.[136] Yet genuine improvement will take time and sustained political commitment from the central leadership, particularly in less developed areas, where nongovernment employment is relatively scarce and less lucrative. Moreover, the civil service reforms have been limited to relatively low levels of the bureaucratic ladder of success; the selection of national leaders, as the sixteenth National Congress of the Communist Party held in November 2002 highlighted, remains as secretive as ever.

Assessment and Conclusions

We have, especially in Chapters 2 and 5, examined the reforms of the Chinese administrative state and how this transformation has helped reshape the Chinese state to suit an age of markets. Shorn of the ministries that were at the core of central planning, the Chinese government has nevertheless steadily boosted its regulatory capacity to sustain and police the markets and cope with various forms of market failure. In this chapter, we have gone beyond the structural changes to examine initiatives that seek to impose discipline on bureaucratic behavior through institutional curbs and to promote service-oriented government.

In Chapter 2, we mentioned some of the benefits of government downsizing and streamlining. Yet the ultimate test of government reforms broadly defined is how the reforms relate to the lives of businesses and individuals. Keeping China's regional disparities in mind, it is safe to say that both businesses and ordinary citizens have genuinely benefited from the government reforms broadly defined to include not only the downsizing and streamlining but also the efforts to reduce red tape and promote transparency and service. One Hong Kong source suggested that downsizing and streamlining of the central government helped improve government efficiency by about one-third.[137]

Generally speaking, the government reforms have been well received by the public. A survey of residents in three major Chinese cities found a majority of the respondents had a favorable impression of the government reforms.[138] More specifically, ordinary citizens can point to a range of benefits from the reform of the administrative approval reform. Under experiments introduced by the Ministry of Public Security, it has become far easier for Chinese citizens to obtain passports (in major cities) and transfer household registration. With the introduction of a law on population planning, provincial authorities have introduced regulations to permit newly-weds to conceive their first birth without prior government permission. Procedures to file for marriage and divorce have been simplified. In another significant initiative for China's increasingly mobile population, the Ministry of Public Security has introduced a drastic overhaul of vehicle registration procedures to make it easier for vehicle owners to obtain license plates.[139] These and others were areas plagued with rent-seeking behavior, and the reforms were designed to reduce agency discretion and curb, if not eliminate, rent-seeking. Surveys of the public indicate growing satisfaction with government administration. In a tracking poll conducted by Horizon Survey, residents in ten major cities are asked to rate their confidence in government management (*zhengfu guanli xinxin du*). The survey results indicate a significant spike in the confidence level, rising from 3.07 in 2000 to 3.87 in 2001 (and 3.8 in 2002) on a scale of 1 to 5 (with 5 being the maximum).[140]

Though efficacy of the reforms varies by locality, businesses have generally been the biggest beneficiaries of the government reforms. In Zhejiang, a 2001 survey of the managers of 258 state companies—traditionally people who most complained of government interference—found that 90.7 percent were satisfied with the policy environment for enterprise reforms and 88.7 percent were satisfied with the quality of government services.[141] With China's entry into the WTO, which was itself a milestone in reforming the government, foreign investors have given good marks to China's investment environment. According to a survey of major multinationals in the chemical industry conducted by a consulting firm, the overwhelming majority of companies surveyed responded that China's environment for investment continued to improve in 2001. The most improved areas of improvement were reduction in bureaucratic hurdles, the legal environment for dispute resolution, and equal treatment for foreign and Chinese firms.[142]

Surveys by the Hong Kong–based Political and Economic Risk Consultancy (PERC) on bureaucratic work style also recognized China's improvements in 2001–2002. PERC's early 2002 survey results gave special praise to China for doing the most among Asian countries in removing many functions from the public sector altogether by getting rid of most industrial ministries and drastically reducing the size of government staff. China's overall score (8.0) in bureaucratic regulation remained much worse than that for Singapore (3.10) and Hong Kong (3.64).[143] But such comparisons are not very meaningful; it would have been far more appropriate to compare Singapore and Hong Kong to cities such as Shanghai, Shunde, Suzhou, and Qingdao. The latter type of city-to-city comparisons would show these cities to be significantly more business friendly than China's overall score suggests and help make sense of China's attractiveness as one of the world's leading foreign investment destinations. Indeed, the 2002 and 2003 annual sentiment surveys by the Global Business Policy Council of CEOs, CFOs, and other top executives of Global 1,000 companies revealed that China overtook the United States as the most attractive foreign investment destination.[144] These sentiments were soon backed up by real investments, as China became the largest recipient of foreign direct investment in 2002.

In conclusion, Chinese leaders have learned from doing and moved from the earlier focus on downsizing and streamlining to a comprehensive program to reform the administrative approval system, boost government transparency, and transform the mentality of bureaucrats from that of gatekeepers to service providers. While still a work in progress, the rationalization of the Chinese administrative state can not only benefit businesses but also contribute to the alleviation of tensions in state-society relations.

chapter six

MARKET INCENTIVES AND THE DISCIPLINING
OF GOVERNMENT DISCRETION

*The Rationalization of Public Projects, Government
Procurement, Land Allocation, and Stock Listing*

As the Chinese leadership worked hard on the high-profile government reforms and the divestiture campaign, a quiet revolution also gath-
ered pace in the way the government spends its money on projects and
procurement and allocates valuable rights, particularly the right to use
state-owned land and to list stocks on the securities markets. The introduction of new institutional mechanisms in government procurement
and other areas is part of a general trend of using institutional innovations to transform the administrative state and combat corrupt practices.
Like the divestiture campaign and the administrative innovations discussed in Chapters 4 and 5, the reforms in government procurement and
other areas shed important light on the rationalization of government behavior and of state-business relations. We discuss these reforms here separately before moving on to the general topic of corruption in the next
chapter.

Government spending, including government purchasing of goods
and services and spending on public projects, has constituted a major
arena for official corruption in China. In the absence of competition and
transparency, those who become suppliers and contractors for government
procurement and projects have tended to be the well-connected and those
who know how to bribe.[1] It is well known that the management of many
government-funded projects was undermined by shady dealings. Construction contracts were subcontracted again and again, forcing the final
contractor to cut corners to make ends meet, with quality becoming the
casualty in the process. There have been numerous Chinese media reports

of poor construction quality leading to collapsed bridges and buildings, with the Rainbow Bridge case—discussed in the following chapter—being one of the most spectacular in recent memory. Complaints about shoddy construction rose sharply in the late 1990s and reflected badly on the government's reputation.[2] While by 1998 most internationally funded projects in China were subjected to rigorous management and quality standards, less than 20 percent of public projects in China used public bidding as of 1998.[3] Similarly, the decentralization of government purchasing to diverse bureaus and institutions, coupled with lack of transparency and lax supervision, not only led to much waste of state funds but also provided ample opportunities for officials and employees in charge of procurement to receive kickbacks and bribes. Likewise, the bureaucratic allocation of state land-use rights at negotiated prices and the listing of stocks on securities markets on the basis of listing quotas also spawned much corruption.

Simply put, "black box operations" that gave bureaucrats much discretionary power but little supervision induced widespread corruption. According to one estimate, at the end of the 1990s as much as 40 percent of all corruption cases in some localities were connected to the issuance of contracts for construction projects, ranging from 34 percent for Guangzhou, capital of Guangdong province, to 70 percent for Xiangfan of Hubei province.[4] In Guangdong province, it is estimated that one-third to one-half of all corruption cases involved the allocation of state land for commercial use.[5] There is a saying in China that "as rows of buildings get built, groups of cadres fall [for corruption]."[6] Meanwhile, China's government purchases for 1997 amounted to 923 billion yuan, but at least 5 percent of that amount was estimated to have ended up in private purses in the form of kickbacks and bribes.[7]

Since the late 1990s, fiscal pressures as well as growing commitment to curbing corruption have served as the twin engines driving the widespread adoption of new institutional mechanisms that are designed to improve the transparency and fairness of the allocation processes and discipline bureaucratic discretion. Given the enormous size of each of the areas discussed here, curbing corruption in them would make a real dent in corruption in general. Moreover, serious reforms in these areas would help create the conditions for fair competition in the economy. In the rest of this chapter, I document the reforms to rationalize the management and supervision of construction projects, government procurement, as well as the allocation of land-use rights and securities listing.

Rectifying State Project Construction

In both government procurement and the supervision of government-funded projects, 1998–1999 was a major transition point toward fairness and accountability. Again it was the Asian economic crisis that provided the major impetus for institutional reforms. On the one hand, the downfall of national leaders in several Asian countries amid the Asian financial crisis accentuated the Chinese leadership's commitment to reducing corruption. On the other, in response to the global economic slowdown, the Chinese leadership decided to promote economic growth by stimulating domestic demand. Because much of the fiscal stimulus was spent on government-funded projects, there was serious concern that the central government spending would be wasted owing to corruption and poor management. Such concern was accentuated by the occurrence of a spate of high-profile accidents, including the collapse of Rainbow Bridge in Chongqing, which killed 40 people on January 4, 1999, and the leaky Western Railway Station in Beijing.[8]

In this context, enhanced supervision of government construction projects was not only good economics but also good politics. Efforts to promote accountability would help save money and improve the government's bruised reputation. During 1998, the leading government agencies introduced a variety of measures to address problems in supervising government-funded construction projects. Most prominently, as part of the 100-billion-yuan infrastructure program initiated in the latter half of 1998 and financed with long-term treasury bonds, the State Development and Planning Commission set up an Office of Special Inspectors for Major Projects to monitor and inspect the projects.[9] The inspectors were given training in the World Bank's procedures for project supervision. Similarly, the Ministry of Finance tightened its supervision of central government–funded projects by setting up a center to take over the monitoring functions previously housed in the China Construction Bank.[10] In a circular issued in spring 1999, "Enhancing Infrastructure Construction Fund Management and Supervision," the Ministry of Finance urged local officials to make every effort to ensure strict compliance with the financial and fund-management rules and regulations.[11] Specialized ministries also came up with their own measures. For example, the Ministry of Communications, which oversees highways and waterways, promulgated ten measures in 1998 to strengthen quality management in highway construction.[12]

The central government inspectors quickly went to work in late 1998. By January 1999, the inspectors had inspected new government-funded highway and water projects in 17 provincial units. The enhanced monitoring unmasked serious problems, including violations of bidding and construction procedures, lax supervision over the qualifications of construction companies, poor project financial management, as well as corruption. The SDPC Special Inspectors' Office found that, of 78 newly approved projects funded with proceeds from the special treasury bond issue, only 23 percent used competitive bidding to choose the project designers, and only 44 percent used competitive bidding to select the project supervisors (*jianli*).[13] The Ministry of Finance discovered that the treasury bond funds earmarked for some infrastructure projects had been diverted to make loans, repay borrowings, or even to pay for overseas junkets.[14] As a State Council circular noted in February 1999, "some localities and departments ignored the quality of their infrastructure projects, violated construction codes, and were lax in supervision and law enforcement. Their construction markets are chaotic and infested with corruption, thereby causing frequent and vicious accidents in construction projects, inflicting heavy losses on the state and on people's lives and property."[15]

Gravely concerned, the State Council leadership convened a national work conference in February 1999 on the quality of infrastructure projects and launched a nationwide inspection drive targeted at housing and infrastructure projects costing 500,000 yuan or more. Inspectors were asked to uncover malpractice in design, construction, and personnel and promote compliance with laws and regulations governing bidding, supervision, and quality control.[16] To back up the nationwide inspection, the State Council also issued a directive with a list of 24 measures. Topping the list is the establishment and implementation of an administrative leader responsibility system for project quality.[17] If poor quality results in a major accident, those to be held responsible will include not only the construction firm and those in direct charge of the project but also the relevant administrative leaders overseeing project approval, compliance with construction codes, cadre appointment, and project supervision. Moreover, administrative leaders in charge of project quality, legal representatives for the project, as well as the legal representatives of the surveying, designing, construction, supervision, and management units must assume lifelong responsibility for the quality of the projects they undertake.

Besides making administrative officials accountable, the State Council directive placed special emphasis on using bidding and tendering to cut costs and corruption for different stages and aspects of a construction project, including surveying, design, construction, project supervision, as well as purchases of equipment and materials. This was intended to end the long-standing but incestuous practice of having one firm design, build, and supervise a project. To curb the abusive practice of repeat subcontracting and corner-cutting by the subcontractors, the directive stipulates that the winner of a bid or tender is prohibited from transferring the contract to a third party and can subcontract part of the project to a third party only with approval. The subcontractor is not allowed to further subcontract.[18]

For a bureaucratic system best known for keeping its skeletons in the closet, the central government's drive for accountability in project construction took on unprecedented publicity in 1999. In a special investigation of urban water supply projects in Jiangxi province, the Ministry of Finance discovered that some localities there had set up phony projects to defraud the central government of funds; diverted specially earmarked funds without permission; and made up fake accounts and contracts to cover up. In April 1999, the Ministry of Finance and the State Development Planning Commission announced that they had halted funding to Jiangxi province for projects that were funded from the special government bond issue. Examination and approval of the province's capital construction projects were also suspended.[19] For the first time in the history of the PRC, the central government essentially turned off the financial spigot for one province. The Jiangxi authorities were told that funding would be resumed only if all problems had been addressed by early May. Cast in unwelcome limelight, the Jiangxi leadership immediately went into overdrive, launching investigations to retrieve misused funds and punishing those responsible for the misdeeds. In June the MOF and the SDPC expressed satisfaction with the remedial measures in Jiangxi and resumed the flow of funds.[20]

The central government had demonstrated that it meant business. In fact, Jiangxi was but the most egregious violator. In response to the inspection results, the central government also ordered remedial measures be taken for projects in Shaanxi, Shanxi, Hebei, Chongqing, Jiangsu, Hunan, Qinghai, Heilongjiang, and Jilin.[21] Feeling the heat, provincial authorities set up their own inspection offices to promote compliance with central government guidelines. Some provincial authorities also publicized their own major cases of violations.[22]

While stepping up monitoring and punishment, the central leader-

ship also promoted sound institutional practices. With the encouragement
of the central government, 284 of the 335 prefecture-ranked cities in China
had by August 1999 set up dedicated centers for construction project tendering and bidding so as to strengthen oversight and curb corruption. In
the first half of 1999, 97.8 percent of the projects that were mandated to be
subject to competitive tendering were so, though most of these remained
invited tenders and only 48.2 percent were truly public tendering and bidding.[23] According to Wei Jianxing, secretary of the Central Discipline Inspection Commission, the establishment of these "markets for construction
projects" resulted in a decline in violations of law and discipline in project
contracting.[24] In Shanghai, for example, the number of bribery cases related to construction projects declined sharply and construction quality
improved after all public tendering, and bidding for construction projects
was conducted in the Shanghai Tangible Construction Market (Shanghai
Youxing Jianzhu Shichang).[25]

Meanwhile, the State Council sought the national legislature's support for a law on public tendering, which had been in preparation since
mid-1994. In this case, the National People's Congress did not need much
persuasion. Many NPC delegates had been vocal advocates for using institutional mechanisms to fight corruption, and the dramatic collapse of the
Rainbow Bridge in early 1999 not only underscored the need to strengthen
regulation of the construction industry but also helped galvanize the NPC
into action. On August 30, 1999, the eleventh meeting of the ninth NPC
Standing Committee voted overwhelmingly for the Law on Public Tendering and Bidding by 131 votes in favor, none against, and one abstention.[26]
The Law on Public Tendering and Bidding, which went into effect on January 1, 2000, mandates public bidding for projects funded with state funds
or financing as well as for other projects that are legally required to adopt
competitive bidding (for example, infrastructure projects bearing on the
public interest or public safety).[27] It stipulates an "open, fair, and just"
process for inviting, appraising, and deciding on bids and provides corrective mechanisms for failure to comply.

The enactment of the Law on Public Tendering and Bidding marked
a turning point in the oversight and management of public expenditure in
China. Nonetheless, the law's enactment is no guarantee of its implementation. Indeed, even in developed democracies such as Japan, the construction industry, notwithstanding elaborate rules and laws governing industry practices, is known for being corruption-prone.[28]

As the Chinese central government publicized the Law on Public

Tendering and Bidding, the Chinese media dissected a variety of major cases. Sometimes officials limited bidding to a select few companies while others violated rules by erecting obstacles for certain potential bidders. In Guangxi's Nanning, for example, the local government adopted restraints on bidding so that cash-strapped state-owned construction companies would not bid too low just to get the projects and then ask the government to make up their losses.[29] Bid rigging was also reported. In 1997 Cheng Kejie, then the chairman of the Guangxi Autonomous Region, directed government agencies to alter the outcome of competitive tendering in favor of a company that paid him a bribe of 1.8 million yuan.[30] Examples of favoritism and irregularities in awarding construction contracts abound in the Chinese press.[31]

The cases discussed here as well as others were exposed in the media after the corrupt officials had been punished. Cheng Kejie, who rose to become a vice chairman of the National People's Congress, became the highest-ranked Chinese official ever executed for taking bribes. Yet these cases also point to the daunting challenges facing reformers and corruption fighters in an industry with high stakes and a lot of power players. To deal with these challenges, Chinese policy makers and regulators in central and local governments have undertaken a growing number of initiatives to standardize the tendering and bidding processes, improve transparency, strengthen enforcement, and enhance accountability. These measures, in connection with the Law on Public Tendering and Bidding, do not eradicate corruption and fraud, but they go a long way toward curbing corrupt practices.

Information Disclosure

In July 2000, the SDPC issued a set of interim regulations stipulating that information regarding projects open to bidding must be widely disseminated. Under these regulations, *China Daily*, *China Economic Herald*, *China Construction News*, and www.chinabidding.com.cn (a Web site under the SDPC and now State Development and Reform Commission) were designated as outlets for announcing projects or purchases for public bidding.[32] With the exception of residential building projects, for which bidding is regulated separately, all public-bidding announcements are to be made via these media outlets so as to ensure the timely and accurate dissemination of information.[33] The Web sites also release the results of various bids and tenders.

Standardization of Construction Markets

As noted earlier, the establishment of dedicated markets for construction tendering and bidding has proved to be an effective mechanism for improving the transparency and fairness of the tendering and bidding processes. As part of the national drive to rectify market order launched in spring 2001 (Chapter 3), the Ministry of Construction worked with a number of government agencies to give special attention to regulating these construction markets.[34] In May–June 2001, the Ministry of Construction inspected construction markets in 12 provincial units and found that 109 of the 169 projects subjected to investigation had failed to fully comply with the Law on Tendering and Bidding.[35] These results prompted the Ministry of Construction to dispatch another five teams in August to inspect construction markets in ten provinces, with special attention to the issuance of permits, compliance with tendering and bidding processes, and contracts.[36] Meanwhile, the anticorruption establishment (the Central Discipline Inspection Commission and the Ministry of Supervision) has also pushed for better supervision of the construction markets and directed that the percentage of projects subject to competitive public bidding be increased.[37]

These central initiatives helped boost the number of prefecture-ranked cities with dedicated markets for the bidding and tendering of construction projects to 328 (out of a total of 338) by 2002. Through the use of competitive tendering and bidding, Guangdong alone was estimated to have saved 7 billion yuan over 1998–2002.[38] To ensure the fairness of market regulators, the Ministry of Construction also asked local authorities to accelerate the divestiture of ownership of construction markets and finish the divestiture (which was 60 percent completed in spring 2002) by the end of June 2002.[39] The divestiture was designed to remove the conflict of interest situation whereby the owner of the "construction market" is simultaneously participating in project bidding. At the same time, the Ministry of Construction decided to link up all construction markets via computer networks in 2002.[40] This move was intended not only to facilitate the dissemination of information but more importantly to enable regulators to promote national integration of construction markets and curb the phenomenon of local authorities' limiting project bidding to local firms.

To improve the integrity of the bidding process, various local authorities have gone to great lengths to make the bidding process transparent and to level the playing field. Because of space limitations, I report only some cases. In 2001, Fujian's Nanping started to provide potential bidders with the criteria for evaluating bidders. These criteria are normally kept secret and are often sought by bidders offering bribes.[41] The Shenzhen Municipal People's Congress amended the Shenzhen SEZ Regulations on Tendering and Bidding for Construction Projects at the end of 2001 and abolished the "negotiated tendering" category, thus removing a mechanism that was easily susceptible to manipulation and corruption. Moreover, the amended regulations fundamentally altered the meaning of the "bottom-line figure" (*biaodi*) by making it the maximum and publicly available amount that may be bid for a project.[42] The selection of experts for the bid evaluation panels has also received much attention in various cities.

Building on findings from its own inspections and local experiences, the State Development Planning Commission, in association with the Ministry of Construction and five other government agencies, promulgated two sets of regulations on the bidding and tendering for construction projects and on the selection of experts for the panels that assess bids.[43] Designed to promote the integrity of the bidding and tendering processes through detailed procedural rules and safeguards, these two regulations went into effect on April 1 and May 1, 2003, respectively.

Monitoring and Policing

Even with the best-designed systems, monitoring and policing are needed to ensure all parties follow the rules. Much of the official effort to curb irregularities and illegalities in the construction industry has been to improve monitoring and policing. Indeed, in a move that signaled the central government's determination to ensure quality and inspire public confidence, builders of the $24 billion Three Gorges Dam recruited U.S. and French inspectors in May 1999 to make sure that Chinese inspectors would not be bribed to hide shoddy work. Engineers from the Atkinson Construction Company of the United States oversaw concrete pouring while engineers from a French power consortium inspected the building of power generators in Canada and Brazil. The inspectors could report directly to the State Council Three Gorges Construction Committee headed by Premier Zhu Rongji (Wen Jiabao succeeded Zhu in 2003).[44]

Of particular importance is the involvement of third parties in helping ensure the integrity of the bidding process and to ward off irregularities and illegalities. Increasingly notaries public (*gongzheng ren*) are present to observe the bidding process and certify that it is conducted in accordance with law.[45] The growing importance of such third parties led to the founding of the Beijing Shoujian Zhaobiao Company in August 2000. Not affiliated with any government agency, this company's mandate is to help guarantee the efficient use of government funds and the quality of construction projects by providing project monitoring from bidding to completion.[46] Another mechanism is the use of price audits (*jiage shenji*) to ensure that purchases for construction projects and ongoing operations are reasonably priced. Such audits can help keep costs down as well as uncover cases of bid rigging. In September 2000 the National Audit Office convened a conference on price audits on procurement and project management. Based on experiences in Jiangsu and Shandong provinces, the conference decided to promote the practice of price audits nationwide.[47]

For important projects, the presence of personnel from the anticorruption establishment has become de rigueur. In launching its new subway projects, the Beijing Subway Group worked with the municipal procurator's office to design a Sunshine Project by requiring officers and contractors to pledge responsibility for eradicating corrupt practices.[48] Likewise, the Guangzhou procurator's office worked closely with the Guangzhou Subway Corporation and contractors on the second phase of the Guangzhou subway project (2000–2002). The Subway Corporation was able to avoid the scandal that plagued the project's first phase (completed in 1998) by getting the procurator's office involved in the bidding and contracting process and by introducing rules to deal with conflict-of-interest situations and other potentially corrupt practices.[49] Other cases include Shenzhen's Dongjiang-Shenzhen water project, Sichuan's major railway and water works projects, and Wuhan's Ring Road project. In all these, inspection personnel from the anticorruption agencies are present to monitor the fairness of bidding.[50]

As mentioned earlier, a number of central government agencies including the State Development Planning Commission (renamed State Development and Reform Commission in 2003) and the Ministries of Construction, Communications, and Supervision have stepped up the inspection of government projects. The Office of Special Inspectors for Major Projects has publicized bidding problems in a number of major projects (for example, airports for Sichuan's Chengdu and for Gansu's Dunhuang and Lanzhou; and Zhangzhou Hospital in Fujian) and directed local governments to amend or abolish local laws or regulations that conflicted with the Law on Public Tendering and Bidding.[51] High-profile national and local projects such as the Three Gorges Dam and the Beijing Olympics have been under special scrutiny, with the international and domestic press playing a growing role in asking questions about corrupt practices. In launching the preparations for the 2008 Summer Olympics, Beijing officials stressed the need to strengthen project management and financial supervision in order to prevent corruption that had plagued previous Olympic events. After Beijing won the right to host the Olympics, the Beijing leadership pledged to fully adopt competitive bidding and tendering for all Olympics-related construction projects. It has set up an Inspector's Office for Major Construction Projects within the Municipal Planning Committee, enacted regulations for its inspections, and invited the public to help supervise the projects by reporting improper behavior.[52] Thus the Olympics have provided the impetus for cleaning up the scandal-ridden construction industry and promoting overall administrative transparency in Beijing.[53]

Accountability

Rampant bribery in China's construction industry is not preordained. In a situation where companies fight fiercely for a limited amount of work available, a company that scrupulously follows the law would lose out to those that use bribery unless there is vigorous policing and punishment of those that offer bribes. In reality, however, construction companies were rarely punished for offering bribes. A sort of Gresham's Law thus prevailed.

As regulators have gotten serious about curbing corruption, this situation appears to have begun to change. Moreover, in addition to the mechanisms mentioned earlier, new measures to hold construction companies accountable have been introduced. The Ministry of Communications (Transportation), for example, has introduced a blacklist mechanism under which the names of those caught offering bribes or taking kickbacks are blacklisted and banned from participation in tendering and bidding for transportation projects.[54] Amid the national drive in 2002 to improve "trust" (*xinyong*), the construction bureaus or committees in a growing list of cities (including Beijing, Shenzhen, Wuxi, Xiamen, as well as Zhejiang province) began to blacklist construction firms found to have engaged in bribery or anticompetitive practices such as bidding below cost.[55] In Nanjing's No. 2

Yangtze Bridge project, the bidding document stipulated that bidders found offering bribes would automatically be disqualified and be barred from projects in Nanjing for two years.[56] Some cities have begun to make information on the reputation of companies available on the Internet. At the Web site of the Beijing Municipal Construction Committee (www.bjjs.gov.cn), one can file complaints about the real estate and construction markets as well as check up on the qualifications of specific companies.

Last, but certainly not least, a growing number of officials in charge of construction and transportation projects have been put in jail for taking bribes, including a succession of three directors of the Henan provincial Transportation Bureau.[57] As many of these cases were revealed, some local authorities have introduced measures to hold officials accountable. In Guangdong, which led in the adoption of competitive bidding, provincial authorities in August 2000 banned officials from involvement in project bidding. In the words of Wang Yuanhua, secretary of the provincial Discipline Inspection Committee: "Any official found to be interfering in [construction] projects, regardless of whether bribery is found, will be punished for violation of discipline."[58] Since then, it has periodically publicized cases of abuse and the punishment meted out to officials.[59]

All in all, under the combined efforts of central and local authorities, the regulation of the construction industry has undergone a sea change in China since the late 1990s. Important measures, particularly the systematic use of competitive tendering and bidding, have been adopted. According to the results of inspections of major government projects by the Office of Special Inspectors for Major Projects, between 1998 and late 2001, the percentage of tendering and bidding that were competitive and public rose by 31.6 percentage points to account for 84.3 percent of the total contracted value. For the construction portion (vs. design) of the projects 91.8 percent of the contracted value was decided through competitive tendering and bidding.[60] Competitive tendering and bidding have been adopted for virtually all water works projects built with treasury bond funding.[61]

The SDPC inspections covered a small sample, albeit some of the largest projects (valued at 42 billion yuan). Perhaps more indicative of the progress made in regularizing the construction industry is the number of violations uncovered. Because efforts expended on monitoring and enforcement have increased, more violations should be uncovered over time if there were no improvements in curbing irregularities. In fact, according to data from the Ministry of Supervision, the number of serious violations of discipline and law uncovered in construction projects has dropped steadily, from 4,700 in 1995 to 2,197 in 2000 and 1,423 in 2001.[62] These numbers seem to suggest that in a few years' time the sustained efforts at inspections and enforcement have indeed helped bring about some improvement in the construction industry. To be sure, the official figures also suggest that more needs to be done. In particular, there remain substantial variations in industry practices across the regions. While various coastal cities are moving closer to the best international practices, egregious violations have been found in inland provinces such as Guizhou, Henan, Jiangxi, and Sichuan.[63] Nonetheless, the continuation of vigorous monitoring and enforcement from the State Development and Reform Commission and the Ministries of Construction and Supervision seems assured, and it seems reasonable to expect further improvement in industry behavior.[64]

Reforming Government Procurement

As noted at the start of this chapter, much of government procurement in China was decentralized throughout the bureaucracy and easily susceptible to corrupt practices, especially bribery and kickbacks. It is well known that competition in government procurement can help reduce procurement costs and curb corruption.[65] Properly conducted, public and competitive bidding for government procurement contracts tends to drive prices down and thus reduce procurement costs. Equally important is the nature of the bidding process: whereas administrative discretion in purchases invites bribery, abuse of power, and corruption, fair and competitive bidding can help level the playing field for bidders and enhance government legitimacy.

Yet the introduction of competitive bidding for government procurement was until recently grindingly slow. The World Bank and the Asian Development Bank have required internationally competitive bidding for their projects in China.[66] Certain sectors, notably machinery and electronics, also introduced competitive bidding for equipment imports in the mid-1980s. Overall, however, the value of government purchases made through competitive bidding was small as a proportion of total government procurement.

As the economy slowed down in the latter half of the 1990s, some local officials, under pressure to reduce fiscal outlays, began to introduce competitive bidding in government procurement as a cost-saving measure. Meanwhile, the introduction of the responsibility system in anticorruption (see Chapter 7) also provided impetus for local leaders to consider government procurement reforms as a mechanism for curbing corruption. The city of Chongqing, which became one of four centrally administered municipalities in early 1997, received much publicity nationwide when it invited tenders for its purchase of 65 vehicles in late 1997. This move saved the city 3.5 million yuan.[67] The Beijing municipal government began to introduce procurement reforms following the downfall of party boss Chen Xitong for corruption. In 1997, Beijing signed contracts with car repair shops to take care of government vehicles so as to eliminate the discretion drivers and other gatekeepers had and reduce their rent-seeking opportunities.[68] In fall 1998, the municipal government started buying its equipment through public bids as part of its anticorruption program. By 2002, Beijing had also begun to use competitive bidding to purchase insurance for all 15,000 vehicles operated by municipal agencies and organizations; Ping'an Insurance won the four-year contract.[69] Limited experimentation with procurement reforms could also be found in Shanghai, Shenzhen, and Hebei.[70]

As local authorities began to adopt competitive bidding in government procurement, they started to establish dedicated institutions for government procurement. Rather than the decentralized and corruption-riddled status quo, the new institutions emphasized centralized processing. Anhui province set up a purchasing center in Hefei in September 1998. In Beijing, the municipal government established a purchasing department in 1998 in order to broaden the scope of procurement reforms beyond automobiles.[71] Shanghai formed a Committee on Government Procurement and a government office for procurement management and for the first time released a centralized procurement catalog in early 1999.[72] Until the end of 1998, local governments led in devising supporting rules and organizations for government procurement reforms. The Guangdong provincial government, for example, issued a set of interim regulations on government procurement through public bidding in September 1998. The regulations stipulated that the bids must be competitive and fair and subject to public monitoring.[73] The city of Shanghai followed suit and began to implement a set of regulations on government procurement on January 1, 1999.[74]

While local authorities introduced procurement reforms in 1998, Premier Zhu Rongji was preoccupied with his fireman's role amid the Asian financial crisis. Nevertheless, the central government made clear its commitment to government procurement reforms in its blueprint for central government reforms: the Ministry of Finance was enjoined "to draw up and implement government procurement policies."[75] Once the central government had put into place a fiscal stimulus program, it began to earnestly promote government procurement reforms, which were now considered a key ingredient of the "clean government and honest administration" program. In fall 1998, a membership-based Web site, www.chinabidding.com.cn, was launched under the auspices of the State Development Planning Commission to promote the use of competitive tendering and bidding for government procurement and projects. In January 1999, the State Council stipulated that all central government departments should introduce competitive bidding for purchases of automobiles, office equipment, and other necessities.[76] In March, public bidding was extended to services (such as insurance) and engineering contracts. These central initiatives provided much impetus for government procurement reforms to spread across the country.

Institutionalization

As the procurement reforms spread, demands grew for standardizing and institutionalizing such practices. It was noted that the reforms not only faced opposition from current government contract suppliers but also needed to be complemented by reforms of China's antiquated system of accounting and fiscal management (Chapter 7).[77] Members of the National People's Congress and the CPPCC were also vocal advocates for national legislation on government procurement. For example, legislative proposal no. 1 at the second session of the ninth NPC in March 1999 called for enacting a law on government procurement as an anticorruption measure.[78] By then, the government procurement law had been put on the NPC's five-year legislative agenda.[79]

In the absence of a procurement law, the Ministry of Finance stepped into the breach by offering its own regulations. In his report to the National People's Congress, Finance Minister Xiang Huaicheng pledged to reform government procurement to "plug the loopholes." The following month (April 17, 1999), the Ministry of Finance issued its Interim Methods for the Administration of Government Procurement. Drawing on local experiences and international practices, the Ministry of Finance document applied to all levels of government as well as state units and social organizations financed by government budget. To promote transparency and fairness, the Interim Methods included detailed guidelines on the qualifications of participants and the procedures for procurement. In early fall, the Ministry of Finance issued two more detailed regulations on the procedures to be used in inviting bids and bidding and on the supervision of procurement contracts.[80]

The Ministry of Finance regulations spurred both the State Council administration and local authorities to speed up government procurement reforms.[81] In May, the cities of Beijing and Shanghai set up dedicated government procurement offices or centers. Meanwhile, local authorities, including those in Beijing and Jiangsu, took their cues from the central government and issued their own government procurement regulations.[82] By late 1999, around 30 provincial governments and major cities had promulgated regulations on government procurement.

Back in the central government, the State Council in mid-1999 centralized procurement of equipment and supplies for ministries and agencies by requiring them to file procurement plans for the coming year with the Government Offices Administration (Jiguan Shiwu Guanliju). This administration would then pool the procurement requests together and use public tender or competitive bidding to purchase designated goods or services. In connection with this reform and amid reports of misuse of funds by government agencies, the Government Offices Administration and the State Development Planning Commission, and the Ministries of Finance, Construction, and Supervision set up a joint group to oversee procurement by government ministries and institutions.[83] For some central government agencies, the launching of procurement reforms offered an opportunity to burnish their battered image. The Customs Administration, then reeling from major corruption scandals, announced with much fanfare that it would use competitive tendering to purchase the main engines for new antismuggling boats.[84]

Whereas the Ministry of Finance regulations applied to government agencies and affiliated organizations, the State Economic and Trade Commission (SETC) took procurement reforms to state-owned enterprises (SOEs) as part of its campaign to fight corruption (kickbacks) and improve managerial efficiency.[85] In its "Interim Provisions on Managing Material Purchasing in State-Owned Industrial Enterprises," which came into effect on May 1, 1999, the SETC directed large state-owned industrial enterprises to establish standardized procurement systems for raw materials, fuel, production and office equipment, and other production materials.[86] The provisions also stipulate that the close relatives of a company's factory director and purchasing manager, including spouses, parents, children, and siblings, are not allowed to take decision-making positions in the company's purchasing department.

In tandem with the issuance of these regulations, the SETC, the Ministry of Supervision, and the National Audit Office directed local economic and trade commissions to strengthen supervision over purchases by state enterprises and curb abuse of power and other forms of malfeasance.[87] According to Shao Ning, director of the SETC Department of Enterprise Reforms, if China's large and medium-sized SOEs could reduce their procurement costs by 2–3 percentage points, they would save 50 billion yuan, which was more than all the profits generated by state-owned industrial enterprises in 1998. The SETC hoped that the cost savings from procurement reforms and managerial improvements would be enough to return a significant number of money-losing SOEs to profitability.[88] In Liaoning, burdened by a large number of state enterprises and a reputation being sullied by massive corruption scandals in Shenyang, the provincial government launched Project Sunshine Procurement in 2000. In the first eleven months of 2000, 402 of the 431 large and medium-sized state enterprises in Liaoning adopted procurement reforms, shaving an estimated 2.7 billion yuan off procurement costs.[89]

An Idea Whose Time Has Come

By 2000, the idea of introducing competition to procurement had become conventional wisdom in China and was being extended to a growing range of settings, including schools, hospitals, and even the military establishment. In early 2000, the Ministry of Health, in conjunction with the State Development Planning Commission and a number of other government agencies, made market-based procurement reforms a key component of its guidelines for reforming the urban health care system. As in the other procurement reforms, the twin goals were to reduce costs and curb rampant corruption in the health care profession.[90] In the fall, Health Minister Zhang Wenkang directed medical institutions in prefecture-ranked cities to adopt centralized competitive procurement practices by the end of 2001. The provinces have generally followed up on the central government's call, with Guangdong and a number of other provinces moving up the target date to mid-2000.[91] In Hainan, a Web portal for hospital procurement was launched in late 2000. The Hainan Health Bureau stipulated that hospitals in Hainan must purchase from winning bidders listed on the Web site.[92] With the introduction of hospital procurement reforms, the prices for drugs and medical supplies subject to procurement saw significant declines in various cities for the first time in years.

Even the military establishment, which had a self-contained system for the production, maintenance, storage, and supply of military equipment, began experimenting with public bidding for its supplies. In military procurement negotiations between the PLA's General Armaments Department (GAD) and the Commission of Science, Technology and Industry for National Defense (Costind), an agency in charge of most defense factories, Costind reportedly asked the GAD to pay market prices for its products.[93] Following some trials, the armed forces began comprehensive reforms in procurement and project bidding in 2002.[94] Under the reforms, a system of checks and balances for procurement management was established. A central procurement agency to amalgamate procurement requests from different departments is in charge of procurement bidding; the finance department disburses payments, and auditors offer monitoring and supervision.[95]

The adoption of competitive bidding has coincided with the Internet revolution in China. It is thus no surprise that the central government (www.ccgp.gov.cn; www.chinabidding.com.cn) as well as local authorities in Shanghai, Henan, Jilin, Sichuan, Zhejiang, and various smaller cities have set up Web sites dedicated to government procurement.[96] In Guangdong, government procurement has been a major emphasis of the Digital Guangdong initiative.[97] It was also a pleasant surprise to find that the Beijing Military Region had set up a well-functioning Web site (www.jdzfcg.com) to handle its procurement of office equipment, medical supplies, and other types of purchases. By publicizing information about procurements as well as accepting bids on the Internet, these Web sites help improve both the efficiency and transparency of the procurement process and are an important factor in propelling China into the front ranks of e-government.

All these efforts to promote government procurement reforms have paid off in the growing scale of government procurement. According to the Ministry of Finance, in 1998 governments at all levels in China purchased 3.1 billion yuan worth of goods and services via government procurement processes. This figure rose to 10.1 billion yuan in 1999, 32.8 billion yuan in 2000, 65.3 billion yuan in 2001, and 101 billion yuan in 2002, and 150 billion yean in 2003. For 2002, the actual government procurement expenditure was 12.6 billion yuan less than the budgeted amount of 113.5 billion yuan, representing a savings rate of 11 percent. Just six provincial units along the coast (Guangdong, Jiangsu, Shanghai, Zhejiang, Shandong, and Beijing) accounted for nearly 48 percent of all local government procurement expenditure.[98]

Growing Pains

The proliferation of procurement programs in a relatively short time has been accompanied by significant variations in regional practices and other problems. As in the case of construction bidding, some localities erected institutional obstacles to protect local producers in making procurements. There have also been reports of intermediaries manipulating government procurement operations in the purchase of elevators in Guangdong and Fujian.[99] Most glaringly, while the amount of purchases made through government procurement programs grew by 54.7 percent from 2001 to 2002, the percentage that was done through public and competitive bidding actually fell from about 53 percent in 2001 to 48 percent in 2002.[100]

Another area of emphasis in procurement reforms has been the centralization of purchases. Both central and local governments have centralized government procurements in specially designated centers to improve monitoring and supervision. In 2002, 73 percent of the purchases made via government procurement programs were centralized, up by 7 percentage points from 2001.[101] Nonetheless, a substantial number of local authorities have allowed different departments to run separate operations.[102] In Hebei province, site of a brewing corruption scandal as of 2001, the provincial government procurement center made only a fraction of the provincial government purchases in its two years of existence. Instead, provincial government departments and affiliated organizations worked hard to avoid having their budgetary purchases go through the procurement center.[103]

There have also been industry-specific problems with procurement reforms. While space constraints make it impossible for me to elaborate on these problems, it is widely known that procurement reforms in public hospitals were to some extent subverted by perverse incentives plaguing China's medical care industry.

Consolidation and Regulation

As government procurement reforms spread around the country, efforts to enact a formal procurement law also increased. Several years earlier, various domestic interests successfully delayed legislative initiatives on a proposed procurement law partly by arguing that enactment of such a law would reduce China's bargaining leverage amid China's marathon negotiations on accession to GATT and then the WTO.[104] By 1999, China's WTO membership finally appeared within grasp, and it was hard to justify further delaying work on the procurement law. In April 1999, as Premier Zhu Rongji launched his high-profile WTO negotiations with the United States during his visit to North America, the National People's Congress formally established a leading group, a working team, as well as a team of advisers to work on a Government Procurement Law.[105] In October 2001, following the conclusion of Chinas' WTO negotiations, the draft Government Procurement Law was finally submitted to the National People's Congress Standing Committee for deliberation. Because China would start negotiations on participating in the WTO's government procurement agreement two years after China's WTO entry, there was some sense of urgency to get the domestic legal and institutional framework for government procurement in order.[106] After going through the due process of legislative deliberations, the NPC Standing Committee approved the PRC Law on Government Procurement on June 29, 2002, by 117 votes in favor, 2 votes against, and 2 abstentions.[107]

The belated enactment of the procurement law provides a much-needed legal framework for improving the regulation of the burgeoning government procurement programs. In advance of the Procurement Law going into effect on January 1, 2003, the State Council in November 2002 directed all central government agencies based in Beijing to adopt procurement reforms and comply with the Procurement Law, with the goal of full adoption by 2005. The Ministry of Finance announced that the amount of purchases made through government procurement programs would rise in 2003 to 150 billion yuan (of which the central government would account for 40 billion yuan).[108] Meanwhile, the Ministry of Finance has been busy drafting the implementing regulations for the procurement law and preparing a series of other regulations concerning bidding, information disclosure, expert panels, appraisal of procurement offices, supplier complaints.[109]

In practice, authorities have devised a variety of safeguards, particularly third-party monitoring, to improve the integrity of the government procurement process. The involvement of representatives from the government's Finance and Supervision departments and the Audit Office in government procurement has become standard practice in many places.[110] In Jiangsu province, bids for government procurement are opened in the presence of officials from the Finance, Supervision, and Audit departments and offices, representatives of bidders, and notaries public. In the case of negotiated purchases and purchases from a single source, the negotiations must be conducted with at least two government representatives, and the final prices must be countersigned by supervisors.[111]

The management of procurement funds has also received much attention. As is the case with construction projects, a major reform initiative the Ministry of Finance has promoted is to combine procurement reforms with government budget management reforms.[112] Such a combination is known as an effective way to prevent fund diversion, embezzlement, and other forms of malfeasance by the units doing the procurement.[113] In compiling the government budget, the Finance Ministry now explicitly requires procurements by administrative and organizational units to use competitive bidding that is supervised by third parties. In such procurement, the Finance Ministry (or local bureau) no longer directly transfers funds to the administrative and organizational units that have the budget allocations but pays suppliers directly following the completion of bidding.[114] The Ministry of Supervision disclosed that 30 percent (about 45 billion yuan) of the government procurement were paid for via direct disbursement in 2003.[115]

Bidders/suppliers have also begun to play an important role in monitoring the integrity of the bidding process. In one prominent case, a Zhejiang company launched a lawsuit in Beijing against two major affiliated organizations of the Ministry of Agriculture for violating procurement rules, seeking to recover losses and a public apology.[116] This case is notable because one of the defendants also held the power to inspect the plaintiff and apparently used its administrative authority to rig the inspection process and the bidding results. With the Government Procurement Law coming into effect and as part of its program to protect the rights of bidders/suppliers and promote the integrity of procurement processes, the Ministry of Finance has called for establishing regular procedures to enable suppliers to file complaints.[117] The Ministry of Finance decided on the first complaint, filed by the Beijing Currency Printing Plant against the State Administration of Press and Publications, in September 2003.

In 2003, the Ministry of Finance also began to champion "checks and balances" in the institutionalization of government procurement. It recommended that local authorities adopt a sort of "separation of powers" arrangement in 2003. The MOF's model comes from Shenzhen. Previously government procurement tended to be handled by the government finance bureau alone. In Shenzhen, however, the Municipal Government Procurement Center (with a vice-bureau rank), which reports directly to the municipal government, is separate from the municipal finance bureau. While the Procurement Center handles procurement operations, the finance bureau formulates regulations and policies on procurement and is empowered to supervise procurement activities.[118] In some other places, including Henan, Hainan, Xiamen, and Qingdao, procurement is simply entrusted to intermediary organizations.[119]

Since the amount of purchases made through government procurement programs was still less than 1 percent of GDP as of 2002, the room for further growth and expansion is obvious. Because various institutional safeguards have been adopted, and with the implementation of the Government Procurement Law, it appears that the government procurement reforms are on track. In spite of some growth pains, the introduction of government procurement programs has become one of the most important initiatives in China's struggle to improve governance and curb corruption.

Disciplining Administrative Discretion: Commercial Land Allocation and Stock Listing

Where bureaucrats control scarce resources and have much discretion in allocating such resources, there is likely to be corruption, whether in China or elsewhere. Besides construction projects and government procurement, the allocation of the right to use state-owned land and the right to list stock on securities markets also became afflicted with rampant corruption. Can graft fighters tame corruption in these two areas? In this section, I examine reforms in these two areas.

The Promotion of Auctions for Land Use and Other Rights

A large number of the corruption cases in China have involved the allocation of land use rights. In these cases, officials in charge of or with influence over the allocation of state-owned land gave well-connected individuals or businesses the right to use land plots at below market prices. Administrative control and discretion thus gave rise to bribery; even legitimate businesses had to resort to shady practices in order to stay competitive. At the same time, the backroom deals cost government at all levels dearly in terms of forgone revenue.

Since the late 1990s, the central government has stepped up the prosecution of land-related corruption cases, including those of Cheng Kejie (an NPC vice chairman) and Mu Suixin (Shenyang mayor)—both were sentenced to death—and numerous others. Between 1998 and 2001, authorities dealt with more than 710,000 cases of violations of land use laws and regulations, including 120,000 in 2001 alone.[120] The Ministry of Land and Resources (MLR) has had a running campaign to rectify the market for land use rights.[121] In 2003 the MLR joined hands with the State Development and Reform Commission, the Ministries of Supervision and Construction, and the National Audit Office and dispatched high-powered teams of superintendents (Tudi Shichang Lianhe Ducha Dui) to inspect land markets in the provinces.

While stepping up the crackdown on irregularities and corruption, regulators have increasingly turned to institutional reforms to prevent abuse of power in land allocations. In conjunction with the implementation of the Law on Land Management, which came into effect on January 1, 1999, the Ministry of Land and Resources began to promote the use of auctions for land use rights. In early 1999 it announced that use rights for land earmarked for commercial use (commerce, tourism, entertainment, and real estate) should use public tendering or auctions as much as possible.[122]

Development in Guangdong province illustrates the importance of anticorruption for the introduction of land auctions, though over time fiscal considerations have assumed greater prominence. In the late 1990s, Guangdong started to systemically promote sunshine measures in land use under a new party secretary—Li Changchun—dispatched to Guangdong by the central leadership to tame the freewheeling province that had become known as the land of financial scandals. In fall 1998, the Guangdong provincial government issued regulations for managing auctions for state land use rights. While punishing officials for illegal land use, the province began to promote the establishment of designated markets (*youxing shichang*) or centers for land-use transactions. These government-sponsored centers, with a published schedule of fees, were designed to ensure the transparency and fairness of transactions and prevent the collection of unauthorized levies or surcharges.[123] By the end of 1999, all 21 prefecture-ranked cities as well as more than 70 counties in Guangdong had set up designated markets or centers for land auctions.

Yet most land transactions in Guangdong still occurred outside the land markets. This situation finally changed with the prosecution of a number of high-profile corruption cases.

In Shenzhen, former vice mayor Wang Ju and a number of other officials in charge of land and urban planning were found to have allocated land to real estate developers at reduced prices in exchange for bribes. The investigation and prosecution of Wang Ju and his associates gave impetus to reforms in early 2000.[124] The Guangdong Construction Committee announced that it would henceforth require all land earmarked for commercial use to go through auctions in designated markets (*youxing shichang*) or centers. In the first eleven months of 2000, Guangdong auctioned off 85 hectares of land for commercial use for 1.6 billion yuan. The auctions not only effectively curbed corruption in land deals but also raised more revenue for the government than the allocation of land by administrative fiat. Meanwhile, land prices for noncommercial use also came under strict supervision.[125] These institutional developments led the local media to conclude that it would be almost impossible for other Wang Jus to succeed in the future.[126]

A number of other cities that had major land-related corruption cases, including Shenyang and Shanghai (the Zhou Zhengyi case), also became eager converts to land auctions in order to demonstrate their commitment to fighting graft. Most prominently, Liaoning's Shenyang, which saw the downfall of Mayor Mu Suixin and numerous others, finally adopted land auctions toward the end of 2001. Whereas under the corrupt Mu Suixin regime the Shenyang municipal government only received 70 million yuan from the commercial development of 33 million square meters of land, the city raised 128 million yuan in November 2001 by auctioning off a single plot of 83,000 square meters. Altogether 14 cities in Liaoning were directed to adopt auctions for allocating commercial land in

2001. Though the amount of land they disposed in 2001 decreased by 25 percent from the previous year, the amount of revenue these cities raised from land sales was 2.6 times greater than the 2000 amount.[127]

As the amount of land revenue from auctions has risen sharply, the fiscal imperative has joined the anticorruption drive as the twin drivers for the adoption of land auctions throughout the country. Led by the city of Hangzhou in Zhejiang province, many cities have not only introduced land auctions but have emulated Hong Kong to establish land banks or reserves.[128] By varying the supply of land made available via auctions, authorities can use the land banks as levers for adjusting housing prices indirectly and for maximizing revenue from land sales.

The State Council leadership was impressed by the local initiatives to build land banks and yet concerned about the incidence of corruption. In 2001 the State Council directed local authorities to earnestly combat irregularities in land allocations, adopt bidding and auctions to guarantee the transparency and fairness of land use rights transactions, and use land reserves to strictly control the supply of land for commercial development.[129] At the same time, punishment for land-related corruption and irregularities has been increased. The Ministry of Land and Resources and the Ministry of Supervision jointly announced in 2002 that, regardless of whether money is involved, any government official found not using public auctions or seeking to influence the results of land auctions is deemed to have violated disciplinary rules and will be subject to punishment.[130] According to a director of the Ministry of Supervision, an official found to transfer land at below market prices, regardless of whether or not the official received a bribe, will be given a warning or severe admonishment if less than one hectare of land is transferred. The official will be demoted or dismissed from office if between one and two hectares of land are involved and dismissed outright if the size of land is more than two hectares. Finally, at the urging of the Central Discipline Inspection Commission and the State Council, the Ministry of Land and Resources mandated that land intended for commercial use must be allocated via auctions or open tender to the highest bidders beginning on July 1, 2002.[131]

The twin imperatives of anticorruption and revenue generation have prompted local authorities to embrace bidding. In Beijing municipality, which has been under international spotlight since it won the bid to host the 2008 Olympics, all land for commercial use has since May 2002 been sold by tender or auction through the Beijing Land Trading Market. Moreover, municipal authorities promised to issue all necessary permits for construction within 100 days of an auction.[132] In the economic powerhouse of Jiangsu province, government revenue derived from land rose from 12 billion yuan in 2000 to 20 billion yuan in 2001 and 40 billion yuan in 2002. At the same time, the percentage of government land revenue derived from land auctions and similar market-based transactions jumped from very low to 36 percent in 2001 and 50 percent in 2002.[133] The development in Shandong province is similarly instructive. In 2001, Shandong had a fiscal deficit of 18 billion yuan but generated only 4 billion yuan from government land auctions and rents, compared with 12.9 billion yuan for Zhejiang, 20 billion yuan in Jiangsu, and 10 billion yuan for the city of Shenzhen. To help cover the provincial budget deficit, newly appointed governor Zhang Gaoli, who had served as party secretary of Shenzhen, called for raising the revenue from land auctions and rents to 10 billion yuan in 2002. To fulfill this objective, sub-provincial authorities made major efforts to adopt land leasing and auctions and build land reserves. These efforts paid off as net revenue from land auctions and rents rose to 10.6 billion yuan (including 2.7 billion from auctions) in 2002.[134]

The institutionalization of auctions for allocating state land designated for commercial use has helped improve transparency and fairness of land use, curb corruption, and increase government revenue from land sales.[135] By 2002, 1,258 cities and counties had established land banks, and 1,198 cities and counties had set up markets for land transactions (*tudi youxing shichang*). Propelled by both central and local initiatives, the value of land allocated at auction has risen rapidly nationwide. In 1999, the amount of revenue raised from auctioning off land use rights was 11.4 billion yuan. This figure rose to 34.6 billion in 2000 and 49.2 billion yuan in 2001. As the central government mandated commercial land auctions, the amount of revenue raised jumped by 97 percent to 96.9 billion yuan in 2002.[136] For a growing number of local governments, proceeds from land auctions have become a major source of government revenue. It is an understatement to say that more and more municipal governments, led by Shanghai, have become hooked on land revenue.

As land auctions have spread, regulators led by the Ministry of Land and Resources have given much attention to standardizing and enforcing auction procedures.[137] Whereas previously local authorities designed their own bidding procedures, which varied substantially among the regions, the Ministry of Land and Resources put out stipulations to promote fairness of the bidding processes. It requires organizers to release bidding information 20 days before the auction date, give all qualified bidders the same information, make the selection on winning bids collectively, and announce the bidding results to the public. As these regulations are implemented, the release of information about land prices and auctions has improved. It is now commonplace to read public notices about land auctions in major newspapers and on major Internet sites, including the Web site of the Ministry of Land and Resources. Moreover, some local authorities have used their official Web sites to provide greater administrative transparency. In Nanjing, for instance, the Web site of the Bureau of Land and Resources provides information on administrative procedures, land grades, applicable fees, as well as information on various land auctions and auction results.[138]

As the idea of auctions has won wide acceptance, regulators have also extended its use to new areas. At the end of 2001, the Ministry of Land and Resources decided to phase out administrative grants of mineral exploration and extraction rights and adopt market mechanisms such as bidding, auctions, and negotiated transfers to enhance the value of state assets and promote the principles of "fairness, justice, and transparency."[139] To promote such practices, the MLR committed itself to terminating 179 and amending 47 rules and regulations (out of 495). In compliance with central guidelines, provincial authorities also issued rules and regulations governing the sale and transfer of mining rights and the procedures for conducting auctions. In the first half of 2002, provincial authorities realized 217 million yuan from auctioning off rights to mineral exploration and extraction.[140] In a time of fiscal austerity, such additional revenue has been a welcome addition to local offers. A breakthrough of a different sort was also made when a private firm won the bid for the mining rights to a gold mine in Jiangxi province in August 2002. The mine was a small one, but the sector had previously been closed off to private investors.

Introduced independently of the land use system, competitive bidding has also been adopted in the allocation of vehicle licenses (Shanghai) and export quotas (the former Ministry of Foreign Trade and Economic Cooperation and now Ministry of Commerce). In the case of export quotas, MOFTEC conducted bidding for some export categories on the Internet.[141] Moreover, various municipalities have invited bids for public projects and auctioned off the right to operate service companies such as bus routes. Auctions have also become the preferred method for disposing of other state assets. The asset management corporations associated with the big four state-owned commercial banks have used auctions and competitive tendering to sell off ill-performing bank assets.

Stock Listing Reforms

Another area that was rife with corruption was China's stock listing process. For the first decade of post-Mao China's stock markets (about the first 1,000 firms listed), the right to list was rationed. Getting a quota or the permission to list was license to gather money from eager investors. To obtain the right to list, enterprising managers falsified information and bribed gate keepers. This writer personally heard the manager of a state-owned firm say that he gave a car to the influential wife of a deceased state leader in the hope that she would help him secure the right to list (he failed).

As regulators have promoted IPO reforms and improved the regulation of the securities markets, many corruption cases have come to light in recent years. For example, Zhang Yuren, the former director of the Sichuan provincial securities regulation and supervision office, took shares from several companies in 1993 before he granted these companies the quotas needed for the China Securities Regulatory Commission (CSRC) to approve their listings.[142]

The case of the Kangsai Group, formerly the Huangshi Garment Factory in Hubei province, offers striking illustration of the bribery that enterprise managers engaged in to secure the listing quota. For several years (1993–1996) before Kangsai was listed, Kangsai's management offered internal shares to more than 100 officials who could potentially help with getting the firm listed. The internal shares were offered to officials at one yuan each but had a value of 6.37 yuan per share; they debuted at 11 yuan per share on the first day of trading in 1996 and reached more than 30 yuan per share at one time. Those who received the internal shares included Xu Penghang, a former Huangshi mayor then serving as vice minister of the State Economic and Trade Commission, and Wu Wenying, then minister of the National Council of Textile Industry, Li Xiong, a deputy department director of the Reform Commission, as well as many lesser officials in the central government and Hubei province. Xu and Li were instrumental in helping Kangsai gain the designation as an enterprise for conducting trials in shareholding reform in late 1993. When Kangsai was still not getting the Hubei provincial government's recommendation to list in spring 1996, Wu Wenying used her influence to persuade Hubei's leaders to give the green light and signed off on the document recommending Kangsai to the China Securities Regulatory Commission.[143] Armed with cheap pre-IPO shares and other bribes, Kangsai paved its road to the Shanghai Stock Exchange. The Xu family netted 1.1 million yuan, Li made 1.2 million yuan in profits, and Wu's son generated 890,000 yuan in profits from the sale of Kangsai shares.[144] Having come to market with bogus numbers, Kangsai soon began to lose money after its IPO. Even before the corruption scandal broke, the Shanghai Stock Exchange condemned Kangsai and its majority shareholder for related transactions that harmed the interests of Kangsai shareholders. The corruption scandal further pushed the stock to junk status in 2000. Both Xu Penghang (having become vice minister of the Commission on National Defense Science, Technology, and Industry and alternate member of the Central Committee) and Wu Wenying (member of the Standing Committee of the Chinese People's Political Consultative Conference) lost their posts in 2000 and were publicly disgraced.

The IPO quotas and high stakes made China's stock listing a hotbed for corruption and turned Chinese investors into cynics. In fact, for the first decade of China's stock markets, the CSRC, with one possible exception, did not reject a single one of the companies local governments and ministries recommended for stock listing. As with dual prices and the administrative allocation of land, the rationing of stock listing quotas became an important avenue for the powerful to convert their power and influence into wealth. Local governments cobbled together state enterprises so that they could use their listing rights to raise funds from investors for underperforming state concerns. The firms would debut on the stock markets with seemingly excellent performance, only to disappoint investors a year or two after in what is known as "face change" or *bianlian*.

To curb corruption and win back the confidence of investors, the CSRC changed the administrative approval system (*shenpi zhi*) for stock listing to a market-oriented U.S.-style registration system (*zhuce zhi*). The new system abolished the right of local officials to recommend stock listings. Instead, underwriters can recommend firms for initial public offerings as long as the firms satisfy listing requirements. The applications are then examined for approval in expert committees. Those underwriters as well as law firms and auditors found to have provided fake information can be severely penalized. Other measures to reform corporate governance and protect minority shareholders have also been pursued. In the first year after the Securities Law came into effect (July 1, 1999–June 30, 2000), the

CSRC rejected 40 percent of the IPO applications. Equally impressively, with threat of sanctions for falsifying information, 60 percent of the legal and auditing reports on the applicant firms contained negative opinions.[145] No longer could a firm devote its energies to getting a listing quota and being assured of final listing.

Conclusions

This chapter has examined a number of areas, including government construction projects, procurement, and the allocation of rights to use state-owned land and to list on stock markets. Each of these areas was noted for rampant corruption: officials and bureaucrats had much discretion but little accountability in deciding who got what scarce resource. As the gate keepers enriched themselves, the state lost both revenue and legitimacy.

Since the late 1990s, major institutional reforms have been undertaken in each of these areas under the twin imperatives of fighting corruption and increasing government revenue. As in other countries, the introduction of competitive bidding, tendering, and auctions into the management of construction projects, government procurement, and the allocation of land use and other rights brings private incentives into public administration, enhances the government's fiscal situation, and helps improve public ethics. Thus, as with Margaret Thatcher's reforms in Britain, "[t]he private sector penetrated the public sector at every level through compulsory competitive tendering."[146]

To be sure, the reforms are so recent that much effort is needed to promote full compliance. Moreover, continuing refinements need to be made, and newly emerging issues need to be addressed. Most prominently, while auctions have been introduced for the allocation of land designated for commercial development, land earmarked for industrial use is still mostly allocated through negotiations. Local authorities eager to attract investors often offer the land at cutthroat prices, which may be an open invitation to bribery. Some cities, such as Shenzhen, have started to mandate public displays and other forms of transparency concerning the allocation of land for industrial use. Less developed areas dying for outsider investors are likely to continue to use backroom negotiations unless the central government steps in to impose transparency requirements. Overall, the economic and political appeal of the reforms coupled with strong commitment on the part of the Chinese leadership suggests that more progress will be made in implementing these reforms.

Fundamentally, the reforms have centered on reducing the excessive discretion of bureaucrats and replacing administrative discretion with competitive mechanisms or processes that level the playing field for competing businesses and place the exercise of governmental power under the constraints of relatively impersonal processes and institutional mechanisms. Seen in this light, these reforms complement the divestiture described in Chapter 4 as well as the administrative reforms in that all these developments contribute to making a more efficient and rational administrative state.

Because these areas figured prominently in China's landscape of corruption, the major institutional reforms described in this chapter go some way toward curbing corruption in these areas. According to Supervision Minister He Yong, the number of cases of violations of laws and discipline in the construction industry has begun to decrease.[147] One can make similar statements about the other spheres discussed in this chapter. Indeed, it is particularly encouraging that the Chinese anticorruption establishment has become the most avid promoter of these reforms. Even a cursory survey of the Chinese media suggests that the reforms, including competitive bidding and auctions, have become the new orthodoxy of the day and have sunk roots as progressive measures to be embraced. Since conventional wisdom continues to point to massive corruption in China, it is worthwhile to examine whether the reforms examined in this chapter are exceptions to the general trend or harbingers of what's to come.

chapter seven

INSTITUTIONAL REFORMS AND THE STRUGGLE AGAINST CORRUPTION

Most of the myriad reforms discussed in previous chapters bear on the issue of corruption, roughly defined as the exchange of official power for private gain in violation of laws and regulations. The initiatives to fight smuggling and financial fraud, to improve government efficiency through transparency and the reform of the administrative approval system, as well as to divest businesses operated by the armed forces and other state institutions not only helped to ferret out numerous criminal corruption cases but also resulted in the introduction of institutional mechanisms more resistant to corruption. Likewise, the changes to the way in which land and mineral rights are allocated, government procurement is made, and construction projects are contracted out and supervised have helped mitigate corruption in these specific areas.

For all these efforts, however, the conventional wisdom in both the press and the scholarly literature remains that China is a land riddled with corruption.[1] The Western press has been virtually unanimous in calling attention to China's "cancer of corruption" and in dismissing official attempts at corruption fighting.[2] Among the scholarly, the general sentiment is that China's anticorruption initiatives are too little, too late, and "half-hearted."[3] Lü, in particular, has pointed to the persistence of bureaucratic indiscipline, or what he calls "organizational corruption" in China.[4] For many, only through a regime change in the direction of democratization and freedom of the press can China truly tame the scourge of corruption. As Zengke He argues, despite the Chinese leadership's efforts, "the current anticorruption campaign is quite inadequate in combating corruption, in large part due to the character of the present political system. Further political reform and movement towards democracy are essential if China is to control corruption in an effective fashion."[5]

While the primary focus of this study is not on corruption per se, the issue of corruption can greatly illuminate our understanding of the contemporary Chinese state. Having already examined institutional reforms in several key areas, this chapter looks more directly at China's struggle against official corruption.[6] After a brief discussion of the incidence of corruption and the effects and limits of anticorruption campaigns, we shall examine efforts to enhance official accountability and recalibrate the incentives for official behavior. In addition, we shall discuss the introduction of financial reforms such as the use of real names for bank accounts and the imposition of financial audits on officials as well as how the government manages and monitors its finances. In conjunction with the reforms discussed earlier, the current chapter should allow us to better assess the construction of an institutional framework for disciplining the behavior of officials and civil servants in areas of economic governance. In the final section, we offer an interim assessment of the impact of these reforms on corruption fighting.

The Incidence of Corruption and the Evolution of Anticorruption Campaigns

The liberalization of society and economy in post-Mao China has dramatically increased both the temptation and the opportunities for low-paid officials and civil servants to accept bribes and kickbacks. As the Chinese press has widely noted, a lot of the new riches in reformist China have been made not by economic entrepreneurship but by exchanging official power over scarce state resources for rents and other forms of benefits. For much of the 1980s, the simultaneous existence of different prices for the same goods was an open invitation for "arbitrage"; those who gained access to low-priced products within the plan could immediately reap bountiful profits by selling (the right to) the products at higher free-market prices. It often required corrupt practices such as bribes and kickbacks to obtain the quotas for products within the plan. As most product prices converged to market prices by the 1990s, the incidence of corruption moved on to other highly regulated areas including land, securities listing, and licenses as well as access to government projects and procurement. The reform of state-owned firms through sale, leasing, reorganization, and other institutional forms also created many an opportunity for siphoning off state assets. Meanwhile, growing socioeconomic diversification and government permissiveness made it easier for corrupt officials to hide their wealth. In fact, the Chinese government permitted the use of false names in making bank deposits and opening brokerage accounts in order to encourage domestic savings and investments.[7] Such practices, needless to say, also provided safe havens for dirty money.

Like many underground activities, the extent of corruption in China is hard to quantify accurately. It is generally agreed that China in the 1990s was one of the most corrupt countries in the world. Various Chinese sources have made suggestive estimates of the costs of corruption. According to the social critic He Qinglian, corruption resulted in astronomical losses of state assets estimated at around 50 billion yuan per year.[8] The Chinese media report that, in infrastructure construction alone, corruption is estimated to affect nearly 100 billion yuan worth of projects a year. Such corruption has resulted in cost overruns as well as collapsed buildings, bridges, dams, and losses in lives.[9]

By one simple measure, namely the amount of money involved in each corruption case, the scale of corruption has gone up exponentially during the post-Mao era. Whereas in the immediate post-Mao years the amount of money involved in each corruption case rarely surpassed the 100,000 yuan mark, by the late 1990s many corruption and financial fraud cases involved tens of millions and even billions of yuan. For example, Li Jiating, the governor of Yunnan province, was found to have accepted bribes and other benefits totaling more than 50 million yuan.[10] The executive vice mayor of Shenyang reportedly gambled away more than 40 million yuan of state funds over a three-year period.[11] The case of Cheng Kejie, a vice chairman of the National People's Congress, the highest ranked official ever sentenced to death for taking bribes, is particularly instructive. Between 1994–1998, Cheng, the former chairman (governor) of the Guangxi Autonomous Region, directed Guangxi government agencies and banks to channel real estate and construction projects as well as bank loans to his favorite companies. He was found to have accepted kickbacks and bribes worth 41 million yuan (including bribes from subordinates seeking promotions).[12] The list can go on and on.

Besides causing economic losses, corruption also poisons morals and undermines regime legitimacy. Discontent with pervasive corruption was a major factor behind the student demonstrations of 1989 and various social protests of later years.[13] The Tiananmen demonstrations of 1989 provided a wake-up call to the Chinese leadership. Recognizing the need to rebuild popular support, Deng Xiaoping, speaking in June 1989, urged the leadership to persist in reform and opening up on the one hand and strengthen the fight against corruption on the other. For Deng, the party risked defeat if it did not crack down on corruption.[14] While incoming party general secretary Jiang Zemin did pay lip service to Deng's instructions on fighting corruption, anticorruption was at best secondary to the consolidation of power for Jiang for several years. Meanwhile, Deng's push for hypergrowth and rapid liberalization provided fertile soil for corruption as businesses set up by party, state, and government agencies mushroomed in much of the 1990s (Chapter 4). Indeed, the widely touted "China Miracle" of the early 1990s was made possible by a sea of corrupt deeds and financial irregularities.[15] China's banking system remains saddled with bad loans made during that time.

As central leaders began to combat inflation and stabilize the financial system in 1993–1994, they also revved up the drive against corruption. The Chinese approach to anticorruption was, until recently, a mixture of exhortation plus periodic crackdowns. Like good Confucians, the Chinese leadership has placed much emphasis on education in party spirit, work style, discipline, and clean government in order that the leading cadres be honest and self-disciplined amid reforms and dramatic social change.[16] Documents issued by the CCP's Central Discipline Inspection Commission have time and again urged leading cadres to practice honesty and self-discipline. Such exhortation has been complemented by periodic campaigns to crack down on corruption and other misdeeds.[17] The anticorruption crackdowns, however, tended to be sporadic and politicized.[18] They frequently punished lesser offenders while leaving untouched those with powerful backing. Some cases also appear to be driven by political considerations. When Chen Xitong, the former Beijing party boss and member of the Political Bureau, was put behind bars for corruption, Beijing residents generally believed that Chen was the victim of political struggles.[19] To some extent, the severity of punishments varied not on the basis of legal norms but according to the dictates of national leaders, fueling popular cynicism about the party's commitment to anticorruption. Indeed, many local officials believed that some corruption was to be tolerated to oil the machinery of economic growth. For these local leaders, such "small climates" of tolerance and connivance were necessary to ensure economic growth as a "hard target."[20]

While corruption was already a major issue in the mid-1990s, by the end of the 1990s it was unmistakably the most prominent sociopolitical issue in China. According to a survey conducted in late 1998 by the *Far Eastern Economic Review*, top managers, senior cadres, educators, and entrepreneurs in three major centers (Beijing, Shanghai, and Guangzhou) ranked anticorruption as the most important measure for promoting economic development.[21] In a variety of Chinese surveys conducted in 1999 of scholars, officials, as well as the general public, the respondents invariably ranked corruption as the most serious issue confronting Chinese society.[22] The seething public discontent with corruption was also palpable in the national legislature. Substantial numbers of NPC delegates have in the 1990s and 2000s displayed their dissatisfaction with crime and corruption by voting against or abstaining from voting on the work reports of the Supreme People's Court president and of the procurator general of the Supreme People's Procuratorate.

Amid rising unemployment, the righteous discontent with corruption increasingly became a major factor motivating social protests.[23] The political elite clearly felt the heat. According to a 1998 survey of prefecture-level officials attending the Central Party School, 65 percent of the 121 officials believed curbing corruption was the key to winning public confidence.[24] Partly in response to growing public discontent with rampant corruption and in view of the downfall of corrupt regimes in Asia during the Asian financial crisis, anticorruption rose to the top of the political agenda. Tapping into the rhetoric of crisis, Jiang Zemin and other leaders have on many occasions echoed Deng Xiaoping to emphasize the importance and urgency of anticorruption. For Jiang, China's fate rested on the fight against corruption. "If we do not fight economic crimes and corruption," Jiang thundered in 1999, "we will disappoint the people. Serious social disturbance would then arise, and the possibility that people will rise and strike us down cannot be ruled out."[25]

Some economists have suggested that the anticorruption campaigns are ineffective and risk hurting economic growth.[26] China's leaders, however, came to see anticorruption as a stone that can kill two birds in that anticorruption can help improve the economic environment and win public support. As previous chapters have noted, a conjunction of events, including the Asian financial crisis, domestic economic difficulties, and rising social discontent, prompted China's leadership to pay greater attention to various forms of irregularities and illegalities toward the end of the 1990s and to adopt various institutional reforms to curb bureaucratic discretion. To counter pervasive public cynicism about whether the crackdown on corruption only affected the little fish but left untouched corruption by high-level officials, the anticorruption establishment has prosecuted a growing number of high-profile cases since the late 1990s. For President Jiang Zemin, catching "big tigers" was the easiest way to improve "the Party's relations with the masses."[27] He reportedly emphasized that the introduction of the death sentence for corruption of senior cadres was designed to "drive home the point that the central authorities are serious about busting graft."[28] The most prominent cases include Chen Xitong, a member of the Political Bureau and Beijing party boss who was sentenced to 16 years in jail for embezzlement and dereliction of duty in 1998.[29] In 2000, Cheng Kejie, a vice chairman of the National People's Congress, and Hu Changqing, vice governor of Jiangxi province, were sentenced to death for corruption. Numerous lesser officials have been put behind bars or given the ultimate penalty for corruption.

Indeed, much of the anticorruption establishment's attention was by 1999 focused on groups of corrupt officials in scandal-ridden localities. After the central leadership dispatched Li Changchuan and Wang Qishan to freewheeling Guangdong, the Central Discipline Inspection Commission investigated a series of scandals including the bankruptcy of GITIC and the disgrace of former vice governor Yu Fei for abuse of power; a host of lesser local officials in Guangdong's Leizhou, Zhanjiang, and other places were arrested. This crusade strategy has netted a record number of major arrests in Daqing, Ningbo, Shenyang, Zhanjiang, Xiamen, and other cities around the country. In the Xiamen smuggling case already mentioned in Chapter 4, dozens of top-level government and customs officials as well as banking officers, including Shi Zhaobin, the party secretary of Xiamen and deputy secretary of Fujian province, were sentenced to death or lengthy jail terms. Certain sectors have also attracted special attention from the anticorruption apparatus. Chapter 3, for example, mentioned the banking industry reforms, and by 2003 several top industry leaders and many local banking officials had been caught in the anticorruption dragnet. In these localities and sectors, new leaders have been installed, invariably with a pledge to fight corruption. Such intense crackdown has garnered much publicity and helped jump start major reforms in the locality or sector targeted. Even before the anticorruption drive revved up at the end of the 1990s, Yan Sun concluded that, for all the imperfections of China's anticorruption efforts, the Chinese leadership had displayed far more resolve and established far better institutions in the fight against corruption than their Russian counterparts in the Yeltsin era.[30] The major anticorruption initiatives since the late 1990s have demonstrated an even higher level of political commitment.

Recalibrating the Institutional Incentives for Corruption

For a country infested with corruption, however, there is a paradox with anticorruption: at least in the short and intermediate term, the arrest and exposure of corrupt officials tend to reinforce the public's perception of widespread corruption. This appears to have been the case in China, as even casual conversations with ordinary people can easily suggest. Despite the arrest of a large number of officials, many people inside China as well as media analysts abroad remain convinced about the rampancy of corruption and are adamant that central leaders have pulled their punches on politically sensitive cases involving top-level officials.[31] This paradox of anticorruption, coupled with the limits of sporadic anticorruption campaigns, has led China's leaders to gradually concede that moral exhortation and campaigns can only deal with the symptoms but not remove the causes of corruption. Local officials are even less enamored of the utility of party exhortation. According to a survey of prefecture-level officials attending training courses at the Central Party School, 22 percent of the respondents surveyed at the end of 1997 still believed public education and publicity of role models could improve public morals. By the end of 1998, the percentage had dwindled to just 5.8 percent.[32]

The growing recognition of the limits of anticorruption campaigns has led the anticorruption establishment to gradually shift its focus, especially since the Asian financial crisis. While the anticorruption crackdown continues, the emphasis has increasingly turned to revamping institutions and incentives, a strategy that is recommended by most analyses of corruption. The Central Discipline Inspection Commission, in particular, has repeatedly called for comprehensive management (*zonghe zhili*) to check corruption at the root. The rest of this section first reports on efforts to empower the anticorruption organizations. It then describes the adoption of various initiatives to alter the incentives for corruption, including amendments to antigraft laws, the adoption of real names in financial services, the implementation of rules on accountability and conflicts of interest, and the introduction of end-of-term auditing on official performance.

Enhancing Organizational Discipline for Anticorruption Institutions

One problem afflicting China's anticorruption apparatus has been its centrifugal organizational structure. Because the local supervision bureaus (and/or discipline inspection committees) report to the local party leaders, they have tended to encounter difficulties in investigating major local corruption cases that often touch on a web of local officials. To mitigate these tendencies, China's top leaders, beginning with the sixth plenary session of the Central Discipline Inspection Commission (January 1996), have put in place a number of important guidelines and measures to empower the anticorruption establishment. Among the measures, the CDIC would send vice minister–ranked officials to inspect local authorities and central government agencies so that the central party leadership, via the CDIC, can learn about how local and ministerial officials implement the party's policies and promote clean administration. In dealing with cases of discipline violations by members of a party committee, the discipline inspection commission ranked at the same level is empowered to conduct preliminary investigations and report to the discipline inspection commission at a higher level. In appointing leaders of a discipline inspection commission, the party organization department must seek the approval of the superordinate discipline inspection commission (ranked one level above).[33] Generally speaking, these measures were designed to enhance the hierarchical organizational integrity of the discipline inspection system and make it more independent of local and departmental interests.

In spite of these measures, some reports have noted that CDIC officials encountered stiff resistance from the "patrons" and accomplices of corrupt officials when they investigated high-profile cases in Hebei, Xiamen, Shantou, Shenzhen, and Nanning. According to Supreme People's Procuratorate officials, the public often complains about local prosecution offices shielding local officials.[34] The local embededness of the anticorruption establishment has forced the Central Discipline Inspection Commission (CDIC) and the Ministry of Supervision to involve themselves heavily in various local cases in order to overcome resistance from local political interests. In April 2000, for example, CDIC chief Wei Jianxing, also a member of the Political Bureau, went to Shenzhen to arrange for the investigation of Wang Ju (then a vice mayor), bypassing the Shenzhen Party Committee. In early June, Wang was appointed vice-chairman of the Shenzhen people's congress by the unsuspecting local leadership. By late June, however, Wang was cooped up for intense investigation. Other senior officials of the CDIC, such as the legendary CDIC deputy secretary Liu Liying, also traveled to localities in the name of inspection or research and sometimes bypassed local bosses to directly launch antigraft investigations.[35] In fact, the CDIC became so busy in 2000 that it enlisted a significant number of officials who had lost their positions during the government downsizing to join special corruption case examination teams (*zhuan'an zu*) being dispatched to practically every provincial unit.[36] To reduce entanglements with local interests, investigation of some major cases, such as that of Shenyang's Mu Suixin and associates, was taken away from the provinces where the cases had occurred.

That the CDIC has to be engaged in work that should usually be handled by local anticorruption agencies underscores the organizational challenges facing China's discipline and inspection system. A variety of reform proposals have been put forward to make the anticorruption establishment more independent and powerful. Since 2002, a series of noteworthy reforms have been introduced to enhance central direction and coordination. To begin with, the Supreme People's Procuratorate (SPP) announced in fall 2002 the formation of a Command Center for Corruption Investigation to strengthen the SPP's leadership over local prosecution offices. In cooperation with the SPP's Bureau for Anticorruption and Bribery, the center would set up special task forces to supervise investigations of major corruption cases that cross provincial boundaries and thus combat local protectionism.[37] Secondly, the heads of provincial-level discipline inspection commissions have been made deputy party secretaries so that these officials will have more political clout in anticorruption work. During the transition of provincial leadership leading up to the sixteenth National Party Congress, each provincial-level discipline inspection commission director was simultaneously appointed deputy party secretary.[38]

Thirdly, in a move that signals a potential institutional breakthrough, the CDIC has begun to make its discipline inspection agents seconded to various ministries and organizations more independent. Previously these agents were under the dual leadership of the CDIC/Supervision Ministry and the host government agencies, but in reality the host agencies had greater influence over the behavior of the agents by virtue of their control over appointments and other resources. For example, the State Administration of Industry and Commerce (SAIC) houses a nine-person discipline inspection team/supervision bureau. Previously these individuals belonged to both the SAIC and the Discipline Inspection Team/Supervision Bureau seconded from the CDIC/Ministry of Supervision. In fall 2002, under an experimental scheme, the CDIC/Supervision Ministry began to exercise unified management over the discipline inspection team/supervision bureau being seconded to other ministries and administrations. The experiment started with the discipline inspection teams seconded to the Ministry of Health, the State (Food and) Drug Administration, and the State Administration of Industry and Commerce and was in 2003 also extended to five other ministries/commissions, including the State Development and Reform Commission and the Commerce Ministry. The move, evidently designed to reduce the influence of the host ministries/agencies, is intended to strengthen the monitoring of the key leaders of the government ministries. The discipline inspection agents are empowered to directly deal with corruption cases without seeking the approval of leaders in the host ministry.[39] As of 2003, the CDIC/Supervision Ministry only directed the work and promotion of the seconded personnel but did not pay their salaries and related benefits.[40] Such incongruities will take time to sort out, but full implementation of the scheme, announced in April 2004, will undoubtedly make the anticorruption establishment more independent and potent in its work.

Finally, the CDIC and the Central Organization Department (COD) formed five roving inspection teams led by ministerial-ranked CDID or COD officials in 2003. Based in the CDIC Party Style and Clean Administration Office (Zhongyang Jiwei Dangfeng Lianzheng Jianshe Shi), the five teams, consisting of a total of 45 inspectors, are empowered to inspect provincial leaders and assess their performance on compliance with party policies, corruption, work style, and cadre promotions. Beginning with five provinces (Guizhou, Hunan, Jilin, Jiangsu, and Gansu), the roving inspection teams will cover all provincial units over a four-year period.[41] In a sign of the coming of age of the institutional approach to anticorruption, the above initiatives to augment the anticorruption establishment and strengthen monitoring of leading officials were formalized in the Interim CCP Regulations on Internal Supervision, which the CDIC approved in early 2004. These regulations give special emphasis to the monitoring and supervision of top officials at various levels of the political hierarchies, including members of the Political Bureau, and ask the CDIC and the CCP Organization Department to strengthen the roving inspection system. The CDIC/Supervision Ministry is authorized to exercise "unified management" of the units seconded to other government agencies and state institutions. All in all, these reforms go some way toward making the Chinese anticorruption establishment more powerful and independent vis-à-vis local and departmental interests.

Strengthening Antigraft Laws and Corruption-related Enforcement

In the late 1990s, several simple but important changes were introduced into the incentive structure for corruption. To begin with, changes in the criminal law shifted the burden of proof to corrupt officials. Officials investigated for corruption must be able to prove that their assets and income are legitimately acquired; those caught with large sums of money but who could not offer such proof could be charged for possessing illegitimate income (*shoulu laiyuan buming zui*).[42] Punishment for those offering bribes was also increased. Until recently, those offering bribes were rarely punished, putting the burden of uprightness solely on the shoulders of officials. Until the revision of the criminal law in 1997, the maximum penalty for those offering bribes was three years in prison while officials taking the bribes could be given the death penalty. Many people believed that this asymmetry of punishments was a major reason behind the rise in corruption cases. The amended criminal law (1997) increased the maximum penalty for bribe givers to life imprisonment (plus confiscation of personal property). The judicial institutions have gradually paid more attention to bribe givers. In March 1999, the Supreme People's Court and the Supreme People's Procuratorate issued a joint circular directing prosecutors and judges to give more attention to the punishment of bribe takers as well as bribe givers and to impose heavier penalties for bribe giving.[43] So far the number of bribe-taking cases still dwarfs the number of bribe-giving cases prosecuted. Nonetheless, the prosecution of various high-profile corruption cases has increasingly included the punishment of bribe givers. For instance, in the case of Hu Changqing, a vice governor of Jiangxi, more than ten of the bribers were put in prison; Zhou Xuehua received a life sentence for having given Hu Changqing more than three million yuan in bribes.[44] In the Cheng Kejie case, the trial court (Nanning Intermediate Court) imposed a fine of $8 million on Guangxi Yinxing Industrial Development Company for offering bribes of 28 million yuan to Cheng and others. The former manager of Yinxing was sentenced to five years in jail.[45] The list can go on and on.

Adoption of Real-name Financial Services and Anti–Money Laundering

As noted earlier, the widespread use of fake names for bank accounts was a convenient way for corrupt officials and other criminals to launder money and a major headache for investigators of corruption cases. Some Western-trained economists argued that anonymous banking helped limit government predation and thus promoted economic growth.[46] Yet anonymous banking also made virtually meaningless an important sunshine measure introduced in 1995 that required officials at the county and department levels or above to report their incomes.[47] For example, Zhang Kuntong, formerly director of the Henan provincial construction bureau, deposited his dirty money in dozens of bank branches using fake names and was able to evade detection for years.[48] Overall anonymous banking helped provide fertile soil for a variety of undesirable behaviors, including money laundering, embezzlement, and tax evasion. It is thus not clear what the net effect was of the growth-enhancing and growth-distorting effects of anonymous banking.[49]

In 1999, two years after the People's Bank of China imposed restrictions on banking transactions involving large sums, the central bank, against the advice of the economists, decided in favor of real-name accounts for bank deposits.[50] Though actual adoption of the real-name system was held up to ease the fear of financial instability associated with the collection of taxes on interest income, the State Council finally ordered the adoption of real names beginning on April 1, 2000.[51] Unlike in the past, bank customers would need to present proof of identity when opening bank accounts and making withdrawals for transactions above a certain amount.[52] For fear of unleashing a flood of money rushing out of banks, the State Council chose to grandfather existing accounts, requiring the use of real names only for new accounts.⁵³ In May 2000, the real-names system was also extended to the purchase of treasury bonds.⁵⁴ Finally beginning on June 1, 2002, investors opening new stock accounts were required to use their real names. Around the same time, securities regulators barred stock accounts that failed to bear the real names and personal identity numbers of account holders from participating in initial public offerings (IPOs), thus closing a major loophole by which institutions (particularly brokerages) had used profitably to bid for IPOs. Overall the effort to end anonymity in banking, stock transactions, bond purchases, and insurance constitutes a crucial link in the fight against corruption. Yet there have been reports of poor compliance in some bank branches, particularly those in remote areas, which are under more pressure to attract deposits, and until 2003 the efforts to promote the use of real names in stock transactions was far from systematic.⁵⁵

After the terrorist attacks in September 2001, however, U.S. pressure to stop terrorist financing provided fresh impetus for China to fight money laundering amid rising domestic concerns about corruption and financial fraud. Shortly after 9/11, as part of the Chinese government's cooperation with the United States in the war against terrorism, the People's Bank of China established a small leadership group to combat money laundering. In 2002 the Ministry of Public Security set up a division for investigating money laundering in the department for investigating economic crimes while the People's Bank of China established an anti-money laundering division and a department for monitoring payments (Payment Transaction Monitoring Department). On September 11, 2002, a national conference on fighting money laundering was held, signifying a new level of central commitment to combating money laundering.⁵⁶ As a result of these initiatives, there has been increased cooperation between financial institutions and the police to combat money laundering.⁵⁷ The enforcement efforts are backed by the Regulations on Countering Money Laundering by Financial Institutions, which the People's Bank of China issued in January 2003 (effective March 1, 2003).⁵⁸ The regulations require customers of banks and other financial institutions (notably brokerages) to use their real identities and present proof of such identities. They also stipulate that financial institutions must seek to track suspicious transactions, keep records of transactions for at least five years, and cooperate with judicial institutions, the Customs Administration, and the Tax Administration to track and interdict dirty money flows. Financial personnel found to have violated the regulations will be penalized to the extent of decertification. The *Financial Times* of London concluded that these rules "may help China finally get a reliable system to monitor underground cash flows."[59]

The Accountability System

The year 1998 witnessed the full promotion of the leader-accountability system for officials, which had been evolving for several years. Initially, leading officials were asked to play an exemplary role and be clean and self-disciplined in performing their duties. Then officials were told to not only exercise self-discipline but also take responsibility for the behavior of their spouses, children, and staff working under them.[60] At the end of 1998, this system of accountability was extended further.[60] As stipulated in a directive of the Party Central Committee and the State Council, titled "Provisions on Implementing the Responsibility System for Improving Party Style and Building a Clean Government (November 21, 1998)," top officials in party and government departments (including judicial institutions), government-funded social organizations, and state enterprises were to be held responsible not only for their own behavior and that of their family members and close subordinates but also for major corruption cases in the regions or departments under their jurisdiction.[61] It stipulated that leading officials must offer to resign or would otherwise be removed from their official posts if serious corruption cases in their jurisdiction resulted in major losses of state or personal property, loss of life, or serious damage to the image of either the party or government.[62]

By making leading officials responsible for fighting corruption, the accountability system requires leaders of party and government departments to adopt effective management and supervision mechanisms. In the judiciary, Procurator General Han Zhubin vowed that the head of a local procuratorate shall be forced to resign if any serious crime, either of corruption or in the enforcement of the law, is committed by anyone under his charge.[63] The Supreme People's Court warned top judges in local courts that they would face punishment if judges in their courts are found to be obstructing justice by accepting bribes.[64] Similar incentives have also been introduced into other areas such as the police, the Customs Administration, and for local officials. The Ministry of Public Security pledged to hold local police chiefs responsible for malpractice under their jurisdiction. Local police chiefs are required to resign their posts if vicious cases such as smuggling, harboring smuggling, or death caused by extorting confessions occurred within their jurisdiction.[65] Many local governments have adopted the principle of resignation for major lapses in safety, performance, and other indicators.[66]

It did not take long for the accountability system to be put to use and get national attention. On January 4, 1999, the 100-meter-long Rainbow Bridge in Chongqing's Qijiang county suddenly collapsed, killing 40 and injuring 14. The bridge was built with county government funds but in violation of proper approval procedures and construction codes. Following the bridge collapse, a number of local officials were detained for dereliction of duty and bribery. In trials televised nationwide, thirteen suspects were found guilty. Lin Shiyuan, former deputy party secretary of Qijiang county, was sentenced to death for taking bribes and dereliction of duty during the construction of the bridge. Zhao Xiangzhong, vice magistrate of the county, was sentenced to a five-year jail term for causing a serious safety accident in key projects. Also punished for dereliction of duty were Lin's assistant, the director of the local quality supervision center, the former director of the county's key project construction office, as well as the steel and construction materials suppliers, the general contractor, the former director of the local construction designing institute, and a construction engineer. In a later trial, Zhang Kaike, the party secretary of Qijiang, was sentenced to life in prison for taking bribes and exempting a company from paying taxes. Zhang was also sentenced to five years in jail for allowing the Rainbow Bridge to open to traffic before proper inspections had been completed.[67]

The Rainbow Bridge collapse pushed the long-awaited law on tendering and bidding onto the NPC's legislative agenda (Chapter 6). It also prompted the Supreme People's Procuratorate to issue a circular, right after the televised trials, directing local branches to crack down hard on dereliction of duty in construction projects.[68] In any case, the verdicts underscored to local officials the risk of tolerating misconduct, particularly because corruption and disregard for regulations were widespread in the construction industry.[69] A deputy county chief in charge of construction noted that his county's situation was similar to Qijiang's. The Rainbow Bridge trials made him sweat with fear.[70] He had good reason to be afraid. The Rainbow Bridge trial has been followed by others. In Hubei's Badong county, the collapse of a bridge during construction landed four people including the deputy director of the transportation bureau in jail for major safety violations and dereliction of duty.[71] Overall, in the first year (November

1998–October 1999) of the nationwide adoption of the responsibility system, 6,300 officials were disciplined after their subordinates committed crimes.[72] More recently, the SARS crisis of 2003 led to the sacking of the health minister, the mayor of Beijing, and numerous local administrators.

While far from perfect, the enforcement of the accountability system appears to have started to reshape the behavior of local government officials that the long-standing emphasis on party discipline has failed to elicit. In some areas, local officials overreacted by resurrecting tedious rules and regulations.[73] Whereas previously local officials tended to cover up for their subordinates in exchange for support, the introduction of the accountability system amid the crackdown on corruption has given local leaders incentives to seek to prevent corrupt acts from occurring in the first place. As a result, the adoption of good practices such as competitive bidding for projects and government procurements has accelerated.

Conflict-of-Interest Rules

Shortly after introducing the responsibility system, the Central Discipline Inspection Commission and the Ministry of Supervision began to promote the systemic enforcement of conflict-of-interest rules for government officials ranked at the provincial (ministerial)-prefecture (bureau) levels. According to these rules, the spouses and children of officials ranked at these levels are not permitted to engage in businesses directly regulated by the officials. For provincial-level party and government officials, their spouses and children are specifically banned from engaging in the following businesses in their jurisdictions: real estate, advertising, law, service establishments (clubs, dancing halls, and massage parlors).[74] Various ministries have also adopted conflict-of-interest rules tailored to their specialties. The Ministry of Public Security, for example, banned the spouses and children of police officials from operating service establishments such as dancing halls and engaging in the manufacturing and sale of police and fire fighter uniforms, insignia, and equipment. The State Development Planning Commission, the Ministries of Finance, Health, Land, and Resources, as well as the State Administration of Taxation, also adopted similar regulations. The Central Discipline Inspection Commission conducted a round of inspections on compliance with these rules in late 2000.[75]

End-of-Term Audits (liren shenji *)*

Of special significance and complementing the emphasis on accountability has been the growing use of audits. At the end of 1986, the National Audit Office began to audit state enterprise managers leaving their posts. This practice of performance audits was extended to party and government officials in some localities in the mid-1990s, led by Shandong's Heze prefecture.[76] To add teeth to the demand for accountability, the Party Central Committee and the State Council in May 1999 issued interim regulations for expanding economic responsibility auditing to cover the managers of state enterprises and state-controlled holding companies as well as government and party officials at the county level or below. Under this system of "end-of-term audit" (*liren shenji*), all officials must undergo financial audits before they leave their positions for other appointments or retirement. The Central Discipline Inspection Commission, the Central Organization Department, the Ministries of Personnel and Supervision, as well as the National Audit Office set up a joint conference system to promote such audits.[77]

Data on the results of the audits suggest that a nontrivial percentage of those audited were penalized. Between 1998 and the first half of 2000, 40,418 party and government officials and enterprise managers were audited. Based on the audited economic performance, 2,581 received promotions while 2,814 were demoted or dismissed. The audits also uncovered various financial irregularities and crimes; 343 people received disciplinary warnings from the party or government while cases for 724 people were turned over to the procurators' offices for criminal investigation.[78]

The teeth of the auditors cut deeper in some provinces than in others. In Hubei province, which acquired notoriety for corruption scandals in securities listing (Chapter 6) and infrastructure, end-of-term financial audits were performed on 2,487 leading cadres in government, state firms, and government-sponsored nonprofit organizations between 1998 and the end of 2000. As a result of the audits, 525 of the audited cadres or 21 percent of the total received punishments, including dismissal and demotion (381), party and administrative discipline (69), and criminal prosecution (75). The strict auditing procedures adopted in Hubei attracted national attention and were recommended nationally.[79] Guandong performed end-of-term audits on 2,683 party and administrative officials in 2002 and uncovered 4 billion yuan of funds used in violation of laws and regulations. As a result of the audits, 243 were removed from their posts, 11 were demoted or fired, 14 were given disciplinary punishments within the party while the anticorruption establishment and prosecutors took up the cases of 45 others.[80]

The audit system is not without its problems. Some auditors, not surprisingly, have faced an uphill struggle as they perform the audits on those in power. While it is relatively easy to assess the work of government officials based on data about economic and financial performance, it is nevertheless harder to assess the performance of party officials. Nevertheless, impressed with the results of the audits of lower-level officials, the central leadership saw the audits as a major weapon in the fight against corruption and decided to extend the audits to senior government officials. In the first half of 2000, the National Audit Office conducted audits on the retiring chairman of the China Securities Regulatory Commission as well as the departing presidents of the four largest state commercial banks plus the China Agricultural Development Bank who were then being rotated. Beginning in 2001, all government and party officials at the ministry level (including governors) or below were required to be audited when they left their posts. Major government financial institutions such as the Bank of China have received special attention. Some agencies, such as the Customs Administration, began in March 2001 to require audits of customs chiefs whenever they leave their present posts (including promotion, transfer, rotation, retirement, resignation, and dismissal).[81] Meanwhile, to correct for the limits of end-of-term audits, some corruption-ridden localities, such as Shenyang and Xiamen, have started to carry out audits on the performance of officials while the officials are still in office. As it divested its commercial businesses, the military also strengthened audits on officers in charge of financial matters.[82]

In Chapter 8 we shall discuss the rise of the National Audit Office as an institution. For the moment, it appears reasonable to agree with Auditor General Li Jinhua that the routinization of end-of-term audits has helped to uncover corruption, determine whether an official has violated financial regulations and rules, and assess whether the official has fulfilled his or her duties. The rate of penalty, at several times the rate of IRS audits, should also serve as a warning for officials still in their posts and has in fact brought down the rate of audited officials receiving punishment. Whereas in 1999 the percentage of audited officials who were punished was at 10 percent, the figure came down to 2.4 percent for local officials in the first three quarters of 2001.[83] One could argue that officials became more skilled in evading detection over time. While there is an element of truth in this alternative argument, I think the reasonable conclusion, in consideration of the overall picture, is that officials have become more careful in adhering to laws and regulations on financial matters. Equally important, as will be discussed below, the audits have helped uncover problems in existing institutions and contributed to institutional improvements that make financial malfeasance less likely to occur than before.

Reform of Government Budgeting and Management

As will be discussed in Chapter 9, the Ministry of Finance began a major reform of government budgeting practices in 1999 at the prodding of the National People's Congress, which set up a Budgetary Work Committee in 1998. The immediate impetus for this reform, which the Ministry of Finance had put on the agenda earlier on, was the NPC's review of the finance minister's budget report and of the auditor general's report. With the discovery of massive accounting irregularities and fraud, the NPC's vociferous demands for reform of government financial management in general and of the budget in particular had to be heeded. As there was growing recognition of the need to use institutional mechanisms in the fight against corruption, the Zhu Rongji administration was happy to oblige.[84] The result has been a dramatic empowerment of the Ministry of Finance as well as local finance bureaus in overseeing the flow of government funds, including revenue from fees, levies, and fines that were previously off the budget.

Reform of Government Budgeting

While Article 4 of the PRC Budget Law (1994) states that the central government budget consists of the budgets of central government departments, the government budget was until recently aggregated and compiled from top down. Moreover, the budget submitted to the NPC (and local legislatures) was presented in broad functional categories of numbers such as national defense, basic construction, education, and so on rather than specific details, making it difficult for legislators to offer detailed comments, let alone amendments. Since each of the ministries had spending on different functions, each reported to several Finance Ministry departments in charge of spending in the functional areas (such as education). In the meantime, government agencies often had hidden treasuries within the budget as well as vast amounts of extra-budget or off-budget funds that were beyond legislative oversight. In short, until the late 1990s China's government budget was one that maximized executive discretion at the expense of legislative oversight.

Under the watchful eyes of the NPC Budgetary Work Committee, the State Council began to fundamentally reform government budget making. To begin with, the reform seeks to include all incomes and expenditures in the budget rather than leave a huge chunk of government incomes, particularly the extra-budget slush funds that were a source of much corruption, off the budget.[85] In 2001, the State Council General Office and the Ministry of Finance issued a directive (Guobanfa [2001] no. 93) on strengthening budgetary management and stipulated that from 2002 on all incomes from fees, fines, and levies for state agencies (including public security, courts, customs, industry and commerce, environmental protection, and family planning) must be included in the government budget and turned over to the government exchequer. The agencies are prohibited from drawing on these incomes directly to meet their budget needs and are instead provided for by the government finance departments.[86] In the same spirit, the State Council also centralized the management of China's thriving lottery business. While previously lotteries were issued by the Ministry of Civil Affairs (the welfare lottery) and the State Administration of Sports (the sports lottery), the reform of 2001 decided that these two agencies could only keep 20 percent of the profits above a certain base amount and must remit 80 percent to the Ministry of Finance for inclusion into the Social Security Fund. The move was undertaken in response to irregularities in the issuance of lotteries, but it allows the central government to allocate lottery proceeds according to its own agenda.[87] Rental income from government buildings, currently under the disposal of the ministry or organization that controls the space, will also likely be included in the budget as part of an initiative to centralize management of government real estate and other assets.[88]

Second, the budget reform moves the basis of budget making from functional categories to that of the government department (*bumen yusuan*). Previously the budget of a government ministry or administration was dispersed in various functional categories. In contrast, with the introduction of the *bumen yusuan*, each government ministry or administration compiles a comprehensive or consolidated budget of all revenues and expenditures. To accomplish this shift, the Ministry of Finance undertook a major internal shakeup in mid-2000. It abolished six functional bureaus (Economy and Trade; Public Expenditure; Foreign-related Finance; Capital Construction; State Asset Management; and Asset Appraisal) and established six new bureaus (Exchequer or state treasury; National Defense; Administration, Political, and Judicial Affairs; Education, Science, Culture; Economic Construction; and Enterprise). The names of six other bureaus were also modified.[89] With the administrative shakeup of the Finance Ministry, each ministry or administration needs only to work with a single Finance Ministry bureau in making its budget.

Third, the budget reform replaces incrementalism with zero-based budgeting, forcing claimants to justify each budget item. In contrast to the top-down budgets of the past, the new budget-making process starts item by item with the grass-roots units and moves up level by level to final compilation by a government ministry or administration. The ministry then submits its draft budget to the corresponding bureau of the Ministry of Finance for examination and approval. Next the Finance Ministry compiles the government budget by department (*bumen*) and submits it to the NPC for deliberation and amendments before the ratified budget goes into implementation.

Actual adoption of the *bumen yusuan* was accelerated in 2000. In spring 2000, the Ministry of Finance submitted a budget (and supplementary items) to the NPC that was more detailed than ever.[90] As a first step of the budgeting reforms, budgets for four ministries (Education, Agriculture, Science and Technology, and Labor and Social Security) were prepared for 2000.[91] A year later, the NPC received detailed *bumen yusuan* from 26 ministries and commissions, significantly ahead of expectations. Moreover, the contents of the budgets included not only the central government–allocated funds but also extra-budget funds, government-approved special-purpose funds (*jijin*), as well as other incomes. Some ministries also included proposed spending on projects and payroll. Beginning with the 2003 budgets, all central government ministries and organizations are required to implement the budget reforms as well as to include the extra-budget funds (administrative fees and levies) in the exchequer accounts.[92] Moreover, the armed forces had also shifted from incremental to zero-based budgeting and undertaken financial management reforms by 2001.[93]

The budgetary reform has also been promoted at sub-national levels of government administration. Some provincial administrations, including those of Guangdong, Hebei, and Beijing, were ahead of the central government in reforming budget making.[94] By the spring of 2001, about 20 provincial units had put in place regulations governing the supervision and management of extra-budget funds.[95] With the passage of time, each provincial unit has expanded the reforms of budget making to encompass more government departments and government-funded organizations. In Guangdong, for example, the number of government departments and organizations included in the revamped budget-making process rose from seven in 2001 to 27 in 2002 and 102—the entire lineup (including funding to government-funded colleges, the women's federation and so on)—in 2003. Not surprisingly, the printed budget expanded from several dozen pages in 2000 to 605 in 2003. Nonetheless, these departmental budgets accounted for only 22 billion yuan (including 11.5 billion yuan of spending previously categorized as extra-budget funds) of a 50 billion yuan–plus budget in 2003, with the rest still being presented in broad categories.[96] Nonetheless, in terms of coverage and specificity, the 2003 Guangdong provincial government budget was a milestone in government transparency.

The budgetary reform, by including funds previously off budget and moving to *bumen yusuan* and zero-based budgeting, is a major institutional improvement over previous practices. First, the reform tightens government financial management and promises to reduce discretion in budget implementation. It thus significantly enhances the power of the Ministry of Finance (and of local government finance bureaus) vis-à-vis that of other government agencies and should help curb diversion of funds and other forms of malfeasance that had been prevalent throughout the government administration.

Second, even while the budgeting reforms enhanced the clout of the Ministry of Finance, Finance Ministry officials, keenly aware of the need to prevent corruption and mismanagement within the ministry itself, also adopted a number of measures to strengthen internal control. Whereas previously each bureau in the Finance Ministry had a substantial discretionary account to cover shortfalls in the budget, these discretionary accounts were abolished over 2000–2001. Meanwhile, the ministry sorted out and reduced the scale of earmarked funds (*zhuankuan*) by 6–7 billion yuan and instead increased the amount of transfer payments to local authorities. Finally, in light of the fact that 42 percent of the corruption cases uncovered in the Finance Ministry were connected to the use of the Finance revolving fund, the ministry abolished that fund in 1998.[97]

Third, presently the Chinese legislature, compared with its counterparts in most democracies, has a relatively feeble influence over budget making and expenditures. The availability of greater budget details not only dramatically improves the transparency of the government budgets but, together with increased interaction with the NPC Budgetary Work Committee, should also enhance the NPC's input into budget making and enhance the NPC's monitoring of the budgetary process. This point will be discussed further in Chapter 8.

The Separation of Revenue and Spending for Extra-budget Funds

The government budget reforms were heralded by a simple but extremely important innovation in government financial management known as *shouzhi liangtiao xian*, namely the separation of the powers of revenue collection and spending in the case of fines, levies, and other forms of government income. Previously government agencies, including the police, the industry and commerce administration, and other regulatory agencies with the power to impose and collect fines, fees, and levies, took in the funds directly, deposited the funds in their own bank accounts, and expended the funds with minimal external supervision. While some of the fees and surcharges (such as for energy use and education) are legitimate, many types of fees and levies can be best described under the rubric of state corruption. According to statistics from the Ministry of Finance, the transport, construction, and public security departments collected 530 types of fees and funds (*jijin*) totaling 162.6 billion yuan in 1997. Of these fees and levies, the Ministry of Finance believed that 245 were collected without proper authorization.[98] Even when these agencies surrendered the funds to finance departments, they often were given a share of the revenue from fines and levies to cover inadequate budgetary funding for bonuses and operations. In Shenzhen, for example, the share was 30–40 percent, providing a high-powered incentive for these agencies to collect such extra-budget funds aggressively.[99] The decentralized management of these funds created many opportunities for malfeasance and was a major source of corruption and widespread public discontent. Some police units set quotas to force policemen to generate revenue, leading to capricious behavior in the enforcement of traffic rules and urban management regulations and the collection of fines.

In order to reduce such malfeasance as well as corruption, the Ministry of Finance issued the Financial Regulations on Administrative Units and other rules to encourage the separation of revenues and expenditures for various forms of government income including surcharges, levies, and fines beginning in 1998.[100] Local governments and departments were also prohibited from issuing quotas for collecting administrative fees and fines. In a major departure from the Deng-era decentralization, the Finance Ministry regulations stipulated that henceforth budgetary and extra-budget funds (administrative charges, fines, levies, and add-on [*fujia*] incomes) are defined as government revenue and subject to government financial management. While previously government offices and administrative units collected and disposed of the extra-budget funds, the redefinition by the Finance Ministry requires that the extra-budget funds be first surrendered to designated accounts under the supervision of government finance departments before they can be spent with approval of the finance departments. Hence there is one line or fund flow going from the government department to the finance department and another from the finance department back. Extra-budget incomes and expenditures must thus be mediated by the finance department or bureau under what's known as the *shouzhi liangtiao xian*. In practice, with the emphasis on the separation of revenue and expenditure, government agencies or institutions that collect fees and levies no longer take in the funds themselves. Instead they issue a special payment form printed by the government finance department to the payer. The payer then takes the form and makes the requisite payment to bank accounts set up and centrally supervised by the finance departments.[101] Such a mechanism can generally ensure that those who collect funds do not simply spend the funds on themselves. In fact, as this reform was fine-tuned and as the funds from levies and fines became incorporated into government budgets, the agencies or offices collecting the funds generally lost the right to dispose of the funds collected.[102]

The *shouzhi liangtiao xian* was promoted in earnest beginning in the latter half of 1998 alongside the divestiture of businesses operated by the military and other state agencies and an education and rectification campaign among public security and judicial personnel.[103] As the divestiture promised the police and judicial institutions that their operating expenses would be funded from the government budget rather than from their own business operations and collection of fees, the adoption of the *liangtiao xian* in these institutions was accelerated. By the end of 1998, as the divestiture campaign was near completion, police departments, procuratorial offices, courts, and the industry and commerce bureaus in major cities as well as cities at sub-provincial levels had largely separated accounting for revenues and expenditures.[104] In 1999 the Central Discipline Inspection Commission, the Ministry of Supervision, and other government agencies made the separation of income and expenditure for revenue from administrative charges and fines a top priority for implementation in different government departments and down to the county level. In order to establish effective supervision and management mechanisms and prevent malfeasance, these central agencies also issued standards governing the approval of fee-collection items, the opening of bank accounts, the submission of funds to higher authorities, the use of standardized receipts, and the administration of expenses.[105] In February 2000, the State Council issued interim regulations which stipulated the administrative penalties for violations of the *liangtiao xian* method of financial management.[106]

As the *liangtiao xian* reduces the financial discretion of officials, it was natural that some officials were unhappy about making the change. Nonetheless, the strong commitment by the central leadership made the day and elicited another round of conversions around the country.[107] By spring 2000, the State Administration of Industry and Commerce had adopted the *shouzhi liangtiao xian* practice in all local administrations. The county administrations must submit all administrative fees and fines to the finance bureau as part of the administrative reforms that put SAIC administrations within provinces under vertical administration. With the adoption of the *shouzhi liangtiao xian*, the amount of funds handed over to the finance bureaus rose rapidly. It doubled in 1998 over 1997 and was 1.5 times the year-earlier amount for the first ten months of 1999.[108]

Local authorities have also adopted similar reforms at the urging of the State Council. Indeed, when a foreign writer for the *National Geographic* was fined by the local police for illegally intruding into a remote town at the western end of the Great Wall, he was not allowed to pay the police directly but was escorted to the local post office to transfer the money to the designated account.[109] Moreover, the practice was also promoted for certain not-for-profit institutions. Recoiling from the bad publicity surrounding its former Health Quarantine Bureau (see below), the Ministry of Health urged state hospitals to adopt the *liangtiao xian* as part of its effort to curb the widespread practice of doctors' prescribing certain medicine for kickbacks from manufacturers.[110]

By 2000–2001, most government departments at the county level and above that collect administrative fees and have the authority to issue fines had adopted the *liangtiao xian*. Following the popularization of the *liangtiao xian* in the localities, the central leadership decided to adopt the *liangtiao xian* for all central government units (*zhongyang yusuan danwei*) in 2003. In fall 2002, the Ministries of Finance, Supervision, the PBOC, and the National Audit Office undertook examinations and inspections of bank accounts that the central ministries and organizations had for extra-budget incomes. Following the inspection, the remaining accounts were turned into designated accounts for extra-budget incomes subject to Finance Ministry supervision. For these central units, all incomes from levies and fines are henceforth to be under the direct supervision of the government exchequer (*guoku*), and their spending must fall under budgetary purview.

In connection with the conversion to the *liangtiao xian,* 39,306 unauthorized bank accounts and 67,994 bank accounts for incomes from fees and fines were canceled to improve financial supervision. Monitoring and punishment of wayward behavior were also stepped up. Together with the audit offices, provincial authorities uncovered and corrected financial irregularities that amounted to 480 million yuan in Guangdong and 629 million yuan in Hebei. For the first eleven months of 2000, authorities dealt with 1,723 cases of violations of State Council regulations on the *liangtiao xian* in 31 provincial units. Seven hundred eighty-six officials, of whom 460 were at the county and township levels, were disciplined for setting up unauthorized slush funds (*xiao jinku*) and dividing up such funds among employees.[111] The most prominent case occurred at the Ministry of Health's former Health Quarantine Bureau, which was found to have accumulated an illegal slush fund of more than 190 million yuan between 1993 and 1997. The funds were collected, without proper authorization, in the name of frontier health quarantine development and social security. In addition, various departments, offices, and units within the health quarantine system also collected 286 million yuan. Rather than surrendering these funds to the government exchequer, officials used the funds for "such degenerate behaviors as reckless expenditure, lavish squandering, corruption, and embezzlement." As a result of the investigation, Qu Xulu, director of the former HQB, Liu Weiliu, head of State Assets Management Department of the former HQB, and Hao Gang, head of the Laws and Regulations Department of the former HQB, were dismissed from their official posts.[112] This continuing crackdown on financial fiefdoms has resulted in a significant rise in the percentage of extra-budget funds handed over to the government exchequer or finance accounts.

The adoption of the *shouzhi liangtiao xian,* together with the divestiture drive discussed in Chapter 4 and the consequent improvement in funding for government agencies, and more vigorous crackdown on financial malfeasance, appears to have helped reshape the ethics of basic-level law enforcement officers. This is especially true in more developed localities where adequate funding for payroll and operations is available from the government budget and the incentives for self-aggrandizing rent-seeking are reduced. Whereas previously cash-strapped traffic police departments depended heavily on fines for routine operations and traffic policemen worried about meeting their quota of fines were bound to be more aggressive in treating drivers, the introduction of the *liangtiao xian* and associated reforms divorced the collection of fines from the amount of funding for agency operations and staff bonuses and, as a result, has curbed the potential for malfeasance, especially in major urban centers. Take the case of Guangzhou, the capital of Guangdong province. In 1998, Guangzhou's urban management enforcement officers collected more than 100 million yuan in fines. With the introduction of the *liangtiao xian* and more adequate budgetary funding for operations arising from the divestiture, the amount of fines dropped to 80 million yuan in 1999 and only 27 million yuan in 2000.[113] In Beijing, reporters noted that, as a result of the implementation of the financial reforms, personnel from the traffic, industry and commerce, environmental protection, and urban management departments no longer rush to impose fines in order to meet their fine collection targets at year end.[114] The less aggressive collection of fines has served to ease some of the strains between law enforcement officers and the populace. Unfortunately in localities with cash-strapped governments, the situation has been less rosy than in major cities.

Centralization of Expenditure Management

Besides tightening up government budgeting, major reforms of government expenditure management have also been launched. To ameliorate the pitfalls of an extremely decentralized and convoluted government accounting system, the Ministry of Finance, the People's Bank of China, and the State Administration of Taxation began in 2000 to overhaul the government accounting system. For the central government, the overhaul introduces a consolidated account for all the central government's revenues and expenses and thus promises to help curb embezzlement and other forms of financial mismanagement and improve the efficiency and transparency of fund usage.[115] Local authorities have also undertaken similar changes.

Because of the technical difficulties of wholesale change, the Finance Ministry began to reform the disbursement of funds for major projects and in certain areas first. In 2000 the Ministry of Finance began to disburse funds for major projects directly to the government projects, bypassing sub-national governments and agencies that might withhold and misuse the funds. The Three Gorges Dam project (excluding the scandal-riddled resettlement, which is contracted out to Chongqing and Hubei) also set up a centralized financial management system with stringent auditing requirements. In the case of the construction of state granaries, the direct disbursement of funds to contractors meant the bypassing of the State Grain Bureau and lower levels of the bureaucracy.[116] On January 1, 2001, in connection with the collection of a new vehicle purchase tax, the Finance Ministry chose to allocate funds from the special transportation fund directly to contractors in Heilongjiang, Jiangsu, Hainan, Yunnan, Shanxi, and Xinjiang rather than let the funds flow through provincial-level bureaucracies known to be prone to rent-seeking.[117]

In early 2001, the Ministry of Finance and the PBOC laid out a comprehensive plan for introducing the state exchequer (*guoku*) direct disbursement system. With the approval of the State Council, the plan was first implemented for the Ministries of Water Resources, Science and Technology, and Finance, as well as the State Council Office of Legal Affairs, the Chinese Academy of Sciences, and the State Natural Science Foundation. In spring 2002, the reform was further extended to about 40 central government ministries and organizations. As in the case of reforms for government project disbursement, the reforms have centralized the fund flow through the state treasury or exchequer system rather than let the government ministries and organizations handle the flow of funds. Take the Ministry of Water Resources, for example. With the disbursement reforms, the Ministry of Finance (via the banking system) directly paid for the salaries of employees at the Ministry headquarters as well as various affiliated organizations. It also directly paid for the materials procurement by the ministry as well as for the ministry's seven major projects. By 2002, the Ministry of Water Resources had fully adopted the disbursement reforms for lower-level units.[118] With the reforms, the flow of funds is under the constant monitoring of the finance departments, and fund diversion and embezzlement, a major problem for which the Ministry of Water Resources had gained notoriety (see Chapter 8), have largely become a thing of the past.

The disbursement reform has been made possible by the adoption of new technologies such as the wire transfer through the banking system. Another simple but important change occurred in the management of salary payments. Faced with fiscal pressure, the Shaanxi provincial government sorted out its salary and pension payments and introduced direct bank deposits for such payments by bypassing government units that tended to inflate the number of employers. To the pleasant surprise of the reformers, the direct-deposit scheme cut the number of payees by a whopping 5,100 (out of a total of about 80,000 in 1997). The successful elimination of ghost payrolls saved the provincial government 36 million yuan per year. It also prompted the Shaanxi provincial government to popularize the direct-payment scheme down to local levels.[119] Likewise, Hebei's reforms in 1999 uncovered 5,096 "ghosts," saving the government 37 million yuan per year.[120] Other provinces such as Guangdong quickly emulated the direct-deposit method in order to make it difficult for government departments and government-funded institutions to add staff without proper authorization. In 2000, the Ministry of Finance promoted the direct bank deposits nationwide for all employees whose salaries are covered by the government budget (including personnel from government departments, organs of the Communist Party, institutes of the People's Congress and Chinese People's Political Consultative Conference, People's Procuratorate, People's Court, and relevant nongovernmental organizations at all levels, as well as schoolteachers). The provinces have followed up with their own plans to comply with the Finance Ministry order even though the direct-deposit scheme may not solve the problem of delayed salary payments in some of the poorest communities. Some provinces such as Hainan have expanded the disbursement reform to include salary payments for employees and retirees in government-sponsored nonprofit organizations.[121]

In many ways, the direct salary deposits served as the precursor of the budgetary disbursement reforms in the localities. As the Ministry of Finance launched disbursement reforms for central government agencies and institutions in 2001, a number of provincial units (Anhui, Chongqing, Fujian, Heilongjiang, Jiangsu, Liaoning, Shandong, Sichuan, and Zhejiang) were also authorized to experiment with similar reforms by consolidating bank accounts and centralizing the disbursement of budgetary and designated funds through the provincial (municipal) finance departments.[122] The initiation of the broader reform in turn helped to give impetus to the adoption of the direct salary deposits. Building on these local experiences, the Ministry of Finance has made it a priority to promote the disbursement reform in the provinces beginning in 2003. Provincial-level governments have devised programs for implementing the central directive. For example, the Hunan provincial government put forth a plan to adopt the centralized disbursement reform for all provincial government departments and institutions (*shengzhi danwei*) by the end of 2005.[123] As part of this initiative, dedicated government exchequers (*guoku ju*) or centers have been established in provincial and municipal financial bureaus.

Centralization of Government Accounting Services

As a complement to the disbursement reform, many local governments have changed government accounting services. In Hubei's Jingmen municipality, the centralization of accounting services between 1998 and mid-2000 led to the elimination of 3,960 decentralized bank accounts and the reduction of 1,700 accounting personnel, with savings of more than 100 million yuan per year.[124] In Zhejiang's Jinhua municipality, each municipal department and organization was asked to keep only one bank account (this led to the cancellation of 1,150-plus accounts). Accounting services for all 56 government departments or organizations were centralized in a single government accounting center. This reorganization, by "using one faucet to control 56," forced government staff to abide by regulations and not to misuse funds through various accounting gimmicks. For small expenditures, government staff received reimbursements directly from the accounting center; for large procurements, the center directly paid suppliers. As a result, the average departmental expenditure in 1999 decreased by 11.2 percent from 1998. Meanwhile, the municipal government office was in 2000 able to cut the number of accountants to only 13, down from 112 prior to the reorganization.[125] These reforms also spread to the interior provinces, notably Shaanxi. Altogether, the centralization of government accounting services in these localities has helped to improve the monitoring of both budget and extra-budget funds, curtail administrative expenses, and rein in corruption.[126]

The centralization of government accounting services was one form of accounting organizational reform. Another interesting mechanism has taken the form of the accountant secondment or assignment system (*kuaiji weipai zhidu*).[127] A district in Zaozhuang municipality of Shandong province was one of the first to adopt the accountant secondment system in Shandong. In 1998, the district put the supervision of all accountants under a newly founded Accounting Management Bureau (*kuaiji guanli ju*) and then dispatched 115 certified accountants to 75 government departments and units. By making the accountants report to the Management Bureau rather than individual departments and units, the system was intended to empower the accountants against officials or managers who tended to pressure accountants to cook the books and make unwarranted reimbursements. Moreover, to prevent the co-optation of accountants by the units to which they are dispatched, the Accounting Management Bureau held training sessions for the accountants every month and instituted a rule of rotation for accountants every three years. The introduction of this accounting management system dramatically improved the quality of accounting and reduced waste and malfeasance. For example, the change helped reduce food and entertainment expenses, for which Chinese officials are notorious, by 58 percent in 1998. Moreover, the accountants on secondment uncovered 1.7 million yuan in hidden funds.[128]

By the end of June 2000, 125 cities (prefectures) and 494 counties in 29 provincial units had introduced the accountant secondment system (*kuaiji weipai zhidu*), involving about 60,000 accountants.[129] Convinced that accountant secondment improved financial discipline and governance, the Ministries of Finance and Supervision issued a joint directive in fall 2000 to promote the accountant secondment system nationwide. The directive stated that party and government agencies, government-funded organizations, as well as institutions empowered by the government to collect fees and fines should introduce the accountant secondment system. An official of the Finance Ministry emphasized that such a system was conducive to ensuring the independence and integrity of the accountants and thus the authenticity of accounting information.[130] The central government promotion of the accountant secondment system helped increase the number of accountants on secondment to about 110,000 by the end of 2000.

These accountants were dispatched to 44,000 administrative and nonprofit organizations and 79,000 firms in 31 provincial units.[131] In late 2000 the State Economic and Trade Commission launched a three-year program to enhance financial management in state enterprises and improve the management of state assets. Under this program, the SETC would help state enterprises establish centralized financial management and budgeting systems and tighten control over cash flow in subsidiaries. Supervision is to be improved by having accountants on secondment and by strengthening audits.[132] Finally, the emergence of major pools of new funds for housing and social welfare also calls for vigilance and has prompted regulators to introduce institutional mechanisms to ensure that the funds are managed and used properly.[133]

To conclude, all these reforms in government financial management have helped reduce administrative costs and curb misuse of funds amid an ongoing fight against false information and for financial discipline. They have also improved government performance in the eyes of the public. Indeed, as the centralization of accounting makes it more difficult for government officials to divert funds to their own use, the appetite of officials for the collection of unreasonable fees, levies, and fines has been somewhat moderated.[134] Thus the better supervision of government fund use has the effect of improving the environment for both investors and citizens.

Institutional Reforms and Anticorruption: An Interim Assessment

As noted earlier, the paradox of the anticorruption drive has been this: in recent years so many officials have been charged with corruption, and the amount of money involved in each corruption case has risen so much, that even optimists about the antigraft drive must question their own judgment about whether corruption can be tamed in China. In 1998, 12 provincial-ministerial-level officials were tried and publicly humiliated. The numbers were 17 for 1999 and 22 for 2000.[135] In 2001, besides the prosecution of the massive corruption scandals in Xiamen and Shenyang, a vice minister of the Ministry of Public Security, the governor of Yunnan, two deputy governors in Anhui and Hebei, as well as numerous lesser officials were put in jail or were under criminal investigation. Shortly after Hu Jintao succeeded Jiang Zemin as party general secretary and state president, another series of high-profile corruption cases was announced, including the disgrace of Cheng Weigao, the former Hebei party boss, Tian Feng-shan, minister of land and resources and former governor of Heilongjiang province, and the sentencing of Wang Huaizhong, a vice governor of An-hui province, to death. Yet, despite and indeed partly because of such rev-elations, most of my interviewees remain viscerally skeptical about the Chinese leadership's commitment to anticorruption and invariably note that the anticorruption drive has failed to get anyone in the very center of political power except for former Beijing party boss Chen Xitong.

Two Conventional Perspectives on Corruption

Before we analyze the evolving public perceptions about corruption and assess the impact of the anticorruption initiatives, it is useful to first discuss a widely accepted view of anticorruption in China as well as abroad. On this view, much of the anticorruption work is politically driven, raising questions about its effectiveness. As Joseph Fewsmith writes: "Charging one's opponents (or their close followers) with corrup-tion—a charge that seems increasingly true of most officials—had become the weapon of choice for political maneuver."[136] In interviews about cor-ruption in China, the flow of conversation frequently becomes a discussion of political struggle. In the downfall of Beijing party boss Chen Xitong, for example, the conventional wisdom is that he was put behind bars not for corruption, since numerous lesser officials could have been charged with far more ill-gotten gains, but for opposing Jiang Zemin.[137] As China moved closer to the sixteenth National Party Congress in 2002, the Hong Kong media, notably magazines such as *Zhengming* and *Qianshao*, were rife with speculations about who was trying to get at whom through the prosecution of corruption cases. For example, the removal of banker Wang Xuebing and other financial leaders was said to be aimed at Zhu Rongji. Revelations of corruption at the State Power Corporation and protests against the gov-ernment's handling of the Xinguoda futures fraud case were interpreted to be targeted at Li Peng, who had started his career in the power industry, and whose son Li Xiaoyong was allegedly connected with Xinguoda.[138] In-deed, in fighting extradition to China in Canadian courts, a major argu-ment advanced by smuggling kingpin Lai Changxing and his lawyer was that the Chinese government's charges against Lai were politically motivated and aimed at getting at Jia Qinglin, who moved on from being Fujian governor and then party secretary to become Beijing party secretary and then member of the Political Bureau Standing Committee.[139]

There is little doubt that the reputation of national leaders can be dented if their followers are found to be involved in major corruption cases, particularly if the corruption occurred while the followers worked immediately for the national leaders. After all, as discussed earlier in this chapter, official rules already point to a degree of responsibility if an official's subordinates are found to be corrupt. Nonetheless, it is obvious that, generally speaking, corruption remains corruption even if there are political motivations behind the prosecution. In fact, if the revelation of corruption cases rises with the intensity of power struggles in the political system, then the political motivations for digging up dirt, factional or not, can over time play a role in combating corruption similar to that played by inter-party competition in political systems with open political contestation. If a political aspirant knows that his or her opponent may use charges of corruption to discredit his or her career, then he or she will do well to be prudent in financial dealings. Therefore, the existence of political motivations behind the prosecution of certain corruption cases does not necessarily reduce but may in fact enhance the effectiveness of the anticorruption drive.

A second issue we should briefly discuss is the relationship between democracy and corruption. Again, as was intimated at the start of this chapter, it is conventional wisdom that political reforms, particularly the introduction of democracy, are needed before China can succeed in curbing corruption. On this view, whatever China's leaders have been doing in fighting corruption can and should be dismissed. Thus the *Wall Street Journal* editorialized in summer 2000 that a major exhibition on corruption in Beijing was yet another act of "China's Charade." The editorial writer went on to argue that political reform—"free speech, rule of law and an expansion of democracy"—was the only way for the Chinese leadership to demonstrate "real commitment to clean government."[140] In the words of Bao Tong, the former policy secretary to Zhao Ziyang (the party general secretary at the time of the 1989 demonstrations): "Any anticorruption measures that are implemented without fundamental political reforms are superficial and ineffective."[141]

What the *Wall Street Journal* editorial writer and others did not mention, however, was that through the early twentieth century, the United States, with free speech, the rule of law, and democracy (though certainly not universal franchise), was also quite corrupt and indeed was renowned for its spoils system. Some local, especially municipal, governments boasted political machines that lasted well into the twentieth century and were known to possess the capacity to deliver the votes to desired candidates. In today's Asia, a number of democracies, including India and the Philippines, have also been known for systemic corruption and indeed now rank behind China on the Transparency International's Corruption Perceptions Index.[142] Even while China's elections occur in severely constrained political circumstances, vote buying has already been reported in various provinces including Guangdong, Shanxi, Jilin, Guangxi, and Hebei.[143] Competition arising from political reforms may thus bring discipline to some areas but open up new arenas for corruption.

In the meantime, some of the cleanest governments in the world today, including those of Hong Kong and Singapore, are not renowned for their practice of democracy in the form of competitive elections. While more democracy is desirable, it does not appear to be necessary for curbing corruption. In fact, an important recent study of corruption has found that the extent of democracy does not show a statistically significant impact on the incidence of corruption in post-communist countries.[144]

The Impact of Institutional Reforms and the Anticorruption Drive on the Incidence of Corruption

While the *Wall Street Journal* editorial writer and many others appear to have mistaken democracy as the panacea for corruption and other ills, he was correct in noting that China's struggle against corruption should not rely on exhortation and the availability of upright officials but must place its emphasis on the construction of an institutional framework that reduces the incentives for corrupt behavior. What the writer and other writings missed, however, is that China has since the mid-1990s not only strengthened anticorruption laws and enforcement but also introduced and adopted a long list of institutional mechanisms that help discipline the exercise of bureaucratic power, curb corrupt practices, and improve governance. These institutional mechanisms include the implementation of accountability and conflict-of-interest rules and end-of-term audits; systemic revamping of government budgeting, expenditure management, as well as accounting and auditing practices; the adoption of real name financial accounts and other measures to combat money laundering; government and state enterprise procurement reforms; the introduction of competitive bidding and tendering to public projects; land auctions; and stock listing reforms. Various other initiatives, such as the growing resort to civil service examinations, the reform of the administrative approval system, the WTO-related drive to boost government transparency, the efforts to rationalize the collection of fees and levies, as well as reforms of the Customs Administration and of the banking system, also bear on the incidence of corruption in these areas.

Many of these reform areas, such as the construction industry, were corruption-prone and produced a very high percentage of the corruption cases that were uncovered. With the institutional reforms already or being implemented, it should require no stretch of the imagination to expect the reforms to help rein in corruption in the areas concerned. For example, Guangdong province, under a new leadership, launched a major program to set up transaction centers for construction projects and land in all 21 prefecture-ranked cities in 1999 and brought all land, construction projects, and real estate transactions into these markets. The total amount of transactions amounted to 32.1 billion yuan for 1999. With the adoption of bidding and tendering and thus a corresponding decrease in the number of discretionary back-door deals, the number of cases of violations of laws and regulations by officials dropped by 83.3 percent in 1999 compared with 1998.[145] We have no comparable data for other parts of the country. Nevertheless, the spread of similar institutions can also be expected to bring about improvement in official behavior elsewhere.

More stringent and highly publicized audits coupled with the reforms in public management have also helped reduce the amount of government funds used in violation of laws and regulations. In 1998, the National Audit Office's audit of 53 State Council ministries and institutions uncovered 16.4 billion yuan of funds misused in violation of laws or government regulations. In 1999, a similar audit of 55 State Council ministries and institutions ferreted out 9.5 billion yuan of misused funds. The 2000 audit of 63 State Council ministries and institutions yielded 5.6 billion yuan of misused funds. Likewise, the amount of funds auditors found to have been diverted from originally budgeted purposes declined from 3.1 billion yuan in 1998 to 2.1 billion in 1999 and 0.5 billion in 2000.[146] Since the rigor of government audits has increased in recent years (see also Chapter 8), the 66 percent decline in the amount of misused funds uncovered over the 1998–2000 period indicates that the reforms in the management of government finances coupled with more rigorous auditing have started to pay off. To be sure, the amount of misused funds remains large, but the trend suggests some sort of a turnaround in a relatively short time period and gave Auditor General Li Jinhua the confidence to predict further improvement ahead.[147]

Sweeping corruption crackdowns have also turned some sectors and cities around. The Customs Administration, as documented in Chapter 4, has undergone a pretty thorough cleansing, with the arrest of customs chiefs in some two dozen cities. In Xiamen, where nearly 300 people were tried for smuggling or taking bribes from smugglers, the impact was quite immediate. Before the scandal broke, even Taiwan investors hesitated about investing in Xiamen because of the rough-and-tumble environment there. According to a Taiwanese investor, graft had by 2001 become "almost invisible since the scandal broke," making the city "much better here than elsewhere."[148]

It would be an indication of growing public confidence in anticorruption if and when more informers were willing to sign their real names to their letters exposing corruption. Informants who provide their real names tend to supply better information, making it easier for anticorruption agencies to nail their cases. In the city of Nanjing, capital of Jiangsu province, the percentage of informers willing to sign their real names rose by 80 percent between 1999 and 2000. In Fujian, 39 percent of the leads on corruption cases for the first eleven months of 2000 came from informers who signed their real names, up from less than 15 percent in the same period of 1999. Local procurators' offices have adopted a variety of measures to protect the identity of informers while paying out awards to them. Some local offices such as Fujian's Zhangping city even purchased special life insurance for informers/whistleblowers to encourage whistleblowing.[149] Other cities, including Shenzhen, also had more people informing on official waste and corruption. This development suggests informers in these cities have become less fearful of reprisals and more confident that the government will follow up on their information.[150]

The Changing Incidence of Corruption:
A Survey of Surveys

Given the nature of corruption, it is impossible to obtain a totally accurate measurement of corruption in China and how it has changed over
time. Nonetheless information from the anticorruption establishment suggests that the rising tide of corruption peaked and began to subside in certain sectors by the turn of the 2000s. According to Wei Jianxing, until late
2002 the head of the Central Discipline Inspection Commission, the
largest number of major corruption cases were committed over 1993–1997,
and fewer such cases were found to have been committed after 1998, when
the antigraft campaign intensified.[151] As noted above, the number of major
corruption cases in construction and finance appears to have peaked and
has come down somewhat. Meanwhile, according to a research institute
under the Central Discipline Inspection Commission, the likelihood that
a new corruption case is uncovered in the year it occurs has risen from 10-
plus percent in 1997 to 28 percent in 2001.[152] Thus it makes sense that a
growing number of corrupt officials have committed suicide or fled China
for fear of being caught, though the Chinese government has also made
major efforts to capture them.[153] At the same time, the number of informant letters and public petitions received by the anticorruption agencies (the
discipline inspection commission, the procuratorate, and the Supervision
Ministry and its local bureaus) has declined each year since 1999.[154] Since
this decline coincided with the intensification of the anticorruption drive
and the introduction of various institutional reforms as well as growing informant willingness to sign their names on such letters, the decline appears
to be suggestive of a real decrease in the incidence of corruption. Seen from
this perspective, 1999 appears to be a sort of inflection point in China's
struggle against corruption.

To be sure, corruption remains a highly salient issue in China. Given
the paradox of anticorruption (revelations of cases tend to reinforce the
public's view that corruption is rampant) and insights from cognitive psychology about the persistence of beliefs, it is expected that shifts in public
opinion would lag behind the efforts in anticorruption and institutional reforms.[155] Nonetheless, by the early 2000s, there were tentative indications
that China's corruption situation, which deteriorated badly in the 1990s,
had stabilized and begun to improve. This is indicated by data from a tracking poll of urban residents conducted by the independent survey firm Hori-

zon Survey. In this poll, based on random sampling of residents aged 18–65 in ten major cities (Beijing, Shanghai, Guangzhou, Shenyang, Wuhan, Nanjing, Xi'an, Zhengzhou, Jinan, and Chengdu), respondents (N = 4,728 in 2001) were asked to choose the three most important issues they were most concerned with. "Clean government/anticorruption" ranked number three in the mid-1990s (1995–1997), but then rose to number two in 1998 and number one in 1999. As the Chinese leadership intensified the crackdown on corruption and began to focus on institutional reforms to curb corruption, the ranking of "clean government/anticorruption" moved down to number five in 2000 and number seven in 2001. Remarkably, in the survey conducted in 2001, "clean government/anticorruption" ranked below "unemployment," "social welfare," "health care reform," "environmental protection," "housing reform," and "children's education."[156] Horizon's 2002 poll of 2,622 residents in smaller cities and towns in seven provinces, conducted in April-May 2002, also showed results that are similar to the 2001 urban survey, with "Clean government/anticorruption" coming in seventh, behind unemployment, environment, economic development, social welfare, crime, and housing reform.[157] Thus corruption rose to become the foremost public issue in the late 1990s but had by 2001 receded in importance relative to issues such as unemployment after the Chinese leadership combined crackdown with institutional reforms in its quest to curb corruption.

As corruption has receded somewhat as a public concern, public confidence in the anticorruption fight has slowly improved. Data from a tracking poll sponsored by the Central Discipline Inspection Commission offer us an alluring glimpse of the evolving situation. When this survey was initiated in 1996, only 32.8 percent of the respondents indicated that they were satisfied with the anticorruption work (*fanfu changlian gongzuo*). This figure stayed below 40 percent until 2000 (42 percent) and has since steadily risen to 48 percent in 2002 and 52 percent in 2003. Interestingly, the worst-performing indicator also showed the greatest improvement: whereas in 1996 only 23 percent of the respondents agreed that the Chinese leadership was tackling corruption cases with vigor or some vigor, the figure rose to a more encouraging 54.6 percent in 2002 and 59 percent in 2003.[158] These figures, still realistically low, suggest grudging but growing public recognition of the Chinese leadership's increasing commitment to anticorruption and the interim results that have been achieved.[159]

Western surveys, skewed toward the views of expatriates in multinationals, also point to similar trends. Of these surveys, Transparency International produces the most widely followed Corruption Perceptions Index (CPI), which draws on other polls and surveys of business people, country analysts, as well as both local and expatriate residents. According to the CPI, which ranges between 10 (highly clean) and 0 (highly corrupt), China's score started out at 4.73 for 1988–1992 but fell to 2.16 in 1995. Since then China's score has gradually improved, albeit still at a pretty bad level, and stabilized at the 3.4–3.5 level for 2001–2003.[160] For 2002, China, at 3.5, ranked number 59 out of 102 countries/economies included in the Transparency International index.[161] This put China on an even keel with Mexico but more than 10 places better than India, Russia (2.7), and other former Soviet republics.[162] As a result, and surprisingly, China's score in corruption index is actually substantially better than what its nominal per capita GDP would predict.

The survey of expatriates by the Hong Kong–based Political and Economic Risk Consultancy appears to reflect well the shifting perceptions of corruption in China over time. As was expected in our discussion of the paradox of anticorruption, China's corruption score jumped to 9 in 1999–2000 as the Chinese leadership intensified the antigraft drive in the late 1990s. As the effects of the anticorruption drive and institutional reforms became known, however, China's corruption score fell from 9.11 in 2000 to 7.88 in 2001 and 7 in 2002, bringing the Chinese score to the South Korean level.[163]

While these survey figures point to improvement in China's corruption situation, they must be taken with a big grain of salt. First of all, they are mostly based on perceptions. In this sense, the CDIC data, based on surveys of the Chinese population, may be better indicators of corruption in China. Second, the scores are for China as a whole, and as such they mask vast regional differences across China and raise questions about the utility of comparing Hong Kong or Singapore with China. Indeed, it may be more appropriate to compare Hong Kong or Singapore with Shanghai, Shenzhen, Suzhou, and other cities. Such comparisons will likely show some Chinese cities in much better light than the aggregate figure for China suggests. Last, but certainly not least, the improvement in the corruption scores has been modest, and the absolute level of corruption perceptions remains high and underscores the need to fully implement existing reforms and launch new ones.

China's top leaders have been realistic about what lies ahead. Speaking at a press conference following the conclusion of the NPC's annual session in March 2000, Premier Zhu Rongji noted that China had punished more corrupt officials than any other country in the world.[164] But he noted that around 700 of the over 2,700 NPC deputies did not vote in favor of the work reports of the Supreme People's Court and the Supreme People's Procuratorate during the NPC session. Zhu concluded: "This shows that people are not satisfied with our anticorruption work".[165] In his directive to the National Conference on Auditing Work held in January 2002, Zhu Rongji stated that the results revealed by auditors led him to believe that "corrupt and degenerate elements" remained "undaunted and reckless."[166] Likewise, Jiang Zemin stressed the arduous nature of the anticorruption struggle at every annual meeting of the CDIC.[167] In his political report to the sixteenth Communist Party National Congress, held in November 2002, Jiang warned that "If we do not crack down on corruption, the flesh-and-blood ties between the party and the people will suffer a lot and the party will be in danger of losing its ruling position, or possibly heading for self-destruction."[168] Toeing the same line, the new generation of leaders succeeding the Jiang Zemin generation has vowed to step up the anticorruption fight and further contain the trend toward rampant corruption by "truly strengthening the supervision of cadre power and basically establishing the mechanisms for the prevention of corruption."[169]

Conclusions

The reforms discussed in this and other chapters suggest that China has moved well beyond its earlier emphasis on campaigns to combat corruption. A host of institutional mechanisms has been introduced to make corrupt practices less likely. As in other countries and areas, the combination of tougher law enforcement and institutional reforms should prove more effective in curbing corruption than the singular focus on campaigns. Yet because most of the reforms were launched only recently, we should not expect a drastic reversal of the corruption perceptions in China. It is nonetheless encouraging that the deterioration of the 1990s was halted and the corruption scores and indices began to show improvement by the turn of the century.

Most of the institutional reforms we have discussed relate to economic governance. In this realm, one can write with reasonable confidence that most of the reforms we have discussed, once adopted, are not likely to be reversed in the absence of major shocks to the system as a whole. Competitive bidding in government procurement and land auctions, for example, has become the new conventional wisdom; over time participants will be socialized into these practices from the very beginning. Likewise the revamping of government budgeting and financial management practices will be locked in once they are fully implemented. It is also hard to imagine any leader would publicly want to revert back to anonymous financial services after real names have been introduced or to roll back competitive bidding. In fact, most of these reforms are known to serve the twin purposes of saving money and curbing corruption and have become the new political orthodoxy that no politically attuned leader would openly seek to end. Equally important, it is important to note that the anticorruption establishment has not only embraced most of these institutional reforms but has also made it part of its mission to suggest further improvement of institutions, mechanisms, system, as well management in order to eliminate the conditions that are conducive to corrupt practices.[170]

Yet this author has no illusions; it is too early to pronounce China's anticorruption program a success. Not only does sustaining the progress made in recent years require continual political commitment, which can be undermined by political uncertainty, but even with the implementation of the reforms discussed so far China's corruption situation remains serious. First, the adoption of the reforms has been uneven spatially and across issue areas. While some cities have comprehensively adopted the best practices available, many localities remain mired in the rough-and-tumble world, and in various places it is common practice to give packets of money to officials at year's end.[171] The reforms in land allocation and government financial reforms, among others, have yet to be fully implemented. It will thus take time and continuous modification and improvement for the web of institutions to become truly effective against various forms of corruption in the country as a whole. Moreover, while some old forms of corruption have been contained, new ones have emerged and call for the refinement of governance practices and heightened vigilance from law enforcement agencies. The introduction of land auctions, for example, has helped eliminate much corruption in the land allocation process, but it has also coincided with the rise of the land reserves or land banks that are concentrations of enormous resources and wealth and thus potential spawning grounds for new corruption. Finally, while newly available technologies have been harnessed to fight corruption, they may also become facilitators of new forms of corruption. Our guarded optimism about China's anticorruption struggle must therefore be tempered by these and other considerations.

chapter eight

INSTITUTIONS OF HORIZONTAL
ACCOUNTABILITY AND GOOD GOVERNANCE

Legislative Oversight and Government Audit

So far we have examined numerous reform initiatives that contribute to the rationalization of government, the strengthening of regulatory authority and power, and the improvement of governance. Yet such developments also raise concerns about whether the enhancements in governance can be sustained and whether the government itself is accountable and to whom. The latter concern is a universal one and especially important. Through an examination of aspects of intrastate relations, I seek in this chapter to assess this latter aspect of Chinese political development, namely whether the government is constrained from without. The central question I ask will be whether China has witnessed the growth of institutions for horizontal accountability in the post-Mao era.

By horizontal accountability, I mean the legal empowerment of some state agencies to oversee and even take legal action against other state agencies.[1] There has been growing awareness of the importance of horizontal accountability by scholars interested in democratization and governance. A liberal democracy requires not only periodic elections but also other institutions such as checks and balances between the executive and legislative branches, election commissions, anticorruption agencies, and judicial systems that constrain the state and its leaders.[2] Electoral democracies that are deficient in institutions of horizontal accountability tend to succumb to various forms of corruption and abuse of power.[3]

While China is not an electoral democracy, I suggest that China's turn toward constitutionalism in the post-Mao era has, for all its weaknesses and contradictions, not only enabled the introduction of basic-level elections but also provided substantial room for the development of the institutions of horizontal accountability.[4] In this chapter, I use the development of two major institutions in the post-Mao era as a window on the webs of relationships that are beginning to impose some constraints on the government. I shall first review the evolving relationship between the people's congress and the government at different levels of the Chinese political hierarchy. I provide evidence for the growing institutional prominence of the National People's Congress (NPC) and local legislatures and discuss the implications of an ascendant NPC and of the people's congress system in general for legislative-executive relations, government leadership behavior, as well as patterns of China's political change. Then I shall discuss the establishment and growth of the National Audit Office, which has become a powerful institution in fighting financial malfeasance and corruption, to illustrate the growing interest in building institutions to discipline the government.

The National People's Congress and Legislative Oversight

By virtue of the constitution promulgated in 1982, the relationship between people's congresses and governments is the most consequential principal-agent relationship in China.[5] While the constitution stipulates that all power belongs to the people, that power is exercised through the people's congresses. Section I of the Chinese constitution states that the NPC is the highest organ of state power. In other words, unlike systems with checks and balances, the Chinese NPC, as the highest organ of state power, *is* the principal. All power emanates from the people's congress system; the NPC can not only legislate but also can emend the constitution (Article 62).

Most pertinently for our purpose, the NPC is empowered to supervise the enforcement of the constitution; to elect the president and the vice president; and to vote, on the president's nomination, on the appointment of the premier, vice premiers, state councilors, and cabinet ministers. In addition, the NPC elects the chairman of the PRC Central Military Commission (CMC) and, on nomination by the chairman, votes on other members of the CMC. It also ratifies the appointment of the president of the Supreme People's Court and the procurator general of the Supreme

People's Procuratorate. By the same appointive power, the NPC can also recall or remove officials whose appointment requires its ratification.

Skeptics who have read thus far will be quick to note that all of the above have so far occurred at the pleasure of the Communist Party and that most NPC members are party members. The preamble to the constitution makes reference to the leadership of the Communist Party of China as well as to Marxism-Leninism, Mao Zedong Thought, and—following a recent amendment—Deng Xiaoping Theory. This, plainly, is a blunt reminder of the heavy axe the party can wield.[6] Major initiatives at the NPC, such as the establishment of a special committee on agriculture in 1998, have required the party leadership's approval, which is not granted automatically.[7] Seen from this perspective, it was logical that Shirk's important book on leadership selection in Chinese politics should focus on the choice of party leaders.[8]

A quick survey of the Chinese literature on people's congresses indicates that Chinese scholars and policy makers are united in believing that the NPC has been weak in exercising oversight over the organs of government (*yi fu liang yuan*).[9] The leading Chinese text on the topic laments that, in spite of its high democratic aspirations, China's people's congress system is "more in name than in reality."[10] The widespread dissatisfaction among scholars and NPC leaders with the state of legislative oversight is a reflection of the increasing acceptance of the idea of oversight over government. In fact, in spite of the political constraints, successive NPC leaders in the reform era—Peng Zhen, Wan Li, Qiao Shi, and Li Peng—have steadily played up the NPC's institutional role.[11] Emerging from the core of the party establishment, the various NPC chairmen have generally been advocates for the rule of law and for NPC oversight over government. Shortly after Li Peng, the former premier, took on the NPC chairmanship in 1998, he noted that the NPC, the State Council, the Supreme People's Court, and the Supreme People's Procuratorate are all state organs under the leadership of the Communist Party.[12] But he was quick to point out that the party must follow established legal procedures when it converts its wishes into the will of the state. Thus Li concluded, "while the party leads the people in formulating the law, the party and the people should obey the law together. All are equal before the law."[13] Indeed, the party should become "the model for obeying the constitution and laws."[14] Using this rhetoric and a series of concrete measures, Li Peng—a decade after his name became indelibly associated with the Tiananmen crackdown of

1989—thus followed in the steps of his predecessors. Indeed, such rhetoric has become de rigueur for the party leadership. The first major speech by incoming party General Secretary Hu Jintao in late 2002 was on the commemoration of the twentieth anniversary of the 1982 constitution. In the speech, Hu gave strong emphasis to obeying the constitution and upholding its authority.[15]

Scholars and legislators are agreed that China's legislatures have been tame in exercising their powers of oversight. For their part, NPC leaders as well as their local counterparts have not hesitated to refer to the weak legislative oversight over the government and the judicial institutions to justify greater efforts at supervision. Following his assumption of NPC chairmanship, Li Peng stated again and again that, while the NPC strengthened its lawmaking capacity, it still had much room for improving congressional oversight over law enforcement and the work of government.[16] During the 2001 NPC annual session, Li Peng noted in his NPC Work Report that "power without checks and supervision inevitably leads to corruption." He stated that legislative supervision over the government, the courts, and the procuratorates was essential to the prevention and containment of corrupt behavior so that these institutions would govern in accordance with law and promote judicial fairness.[17]

Lawmaking

There is growing evidence that the NPC is shedding its rubber-stamp image and slowly taking on its institutional role as defined by the constitution. Take the case of lawmaking, which has received careful examination in a number of studies, especially Tanner's book, and thus only needs to be briefly touched on here.[18] Over the past two decades the NPC has significantly strengthened its ability to control the legislative agenda and shape the substance of laws. Not surprisingly, the growth of the NPC's legislative capacity has sometimes pitted the NPC's staff against the Legislative Affairs Bureau of the State Council.[19] Although the government side still plays a significant role in generating and drafting legislation, it is the NPC's clout that has been gaining over time. The NPC has from time to time asserted its institutional prerogative and held up approval of proposed legislation. The Securities Law, for example, was submitted to the NPC several times from 1993 to 1998 before the NPC Standing Committee finally enacted it at the end of 1998. Another high-profile case was the amended Highway Law, which Premier Zhu Rongji sought as part of an initiative to eliminate numerous levies and fees on vehicle owners. Unfortunately for Premier Zhu Rongji, the NPC Standing Committee first delayed a vote on the amendments in late 1998 and then narrowly voted them down in April 1999 before finally approving it.[20] Although some commentators viewed the legislative rebuff as evidence of the long-standing animosity between NPC Chairman Li Peng and Premier Zhu Rongji, it is nevertheless worth commenting that the outcome was accepted as legitimate. This event has served as a warning to Zhu and future premiers to do a better job at legislative lobbying.[21]

A major institutional mechanism to enhance the NPC's control over the legislative agenda is to regularize the legislative process for new laws to make it less subject to politicians' whims. This was one of the first issues tackled by the ninth NPC Standing Committee in spring 1998. Following the rules laid down by the NPC Standing Committee, a draft law must go through three readings instead of just two as in the past.[22] First, the Standing Committee hears the explanations from the sponsors of the law and conducts preliminary deliberation (*shenyi*). Second, Standing Committee members conduct further hearings and deliberations after a period of two months or more and following full investigations into the draft law. Third, after the draft law is revised on the basis of these discussions, the Special Committee in charge would make its report before the Standing Committee convenes another review. When there are no major criticisms, the draft law will be reported to the full committee for a vote.[23] This growth of the NPC's clout over lawmaking reached a logical conclusion when the Legislation Law, or law on lawmaking, was approved in March 2000. Supporters for the Legislation Law have argued against excessive reliance on government departments in drafting laws and called for strengthening the NPC's own legislative capacity and curbing the incidence of "legislative corruption" that caters to the parochial interests of government departments.[24] The enactment of the Administrative Licensing Law, despite some of its inherent compromises, points to the influence of the above legislative spirit.

Appointment Ratification and Annual Policy Reviews

Our attention now turns to the NPC's role in appointing officials and monitoring government performance. So far the NPC has not removed a government official from office on its own initiative.[25] Indeed, except when it has had more candidates than positions, it has yet to reject a single candidate put before it for ratification. While this absence of rejection suggests the NPC is quite tame as an institution, it should not be taken as lack of influence on the NPC's part. In fact, aided by the installation of an anonymous electronic balloting system, many NPC members have displayed substantial independence in ratifying personnel appointments. Data collected by Tanner and Chen show a growing percentage of dissenting votes over personnel appointments for the 1988–1997 period. In 1995, for instance, more than 1,000 NPC delegates did not vote for Jiang Chunyun's nomination as a vice premier. In contrast, a resounding majority voted for Zhu Rongji as premier in spring 1998.[26]

A number of mechanisms have been adopted to ensure that party-favored candidates are voted in. For the presidency and vice presidency, for example, there is only one nominee per position, with no competition allowed. The party group within the NPC also instructs party members, about 70 percent of the total NPC membership, to vote for the official nominees. Nonetheless, the party must cope with a structural framework of anonymous voting. In consequence, party leaders have strong incentives to nominate high-caliber candidates. For the candidates, even if they know that their appointments will be ratified, they still do not want the embarrassment of having many negative votes.

The national legislature also hears periodic reports from the premier and other officials. Such policy reviews, including the highly publicized work reports during the annual NPC sessions, quarterly hearings on the economic situation, the annual auditor general's report, as well as special hearings on selected issues, have become crucial elements of legislative oversight. The premier, cabinet members, as well as heads of the Supreme People's Court and the Supreme People's Procuratorate have become increasingly conscious of this oversight relationship. In one interview, then Premier Zhu Rongji commented that he should not talk too much to reporters: "Talking too much makes NPC delegates unhappy. Who will help me if my votes go down?"[27] Such awareness appears to have prompted appointed officials to modify their behavior. In recent annual NPC sessions, government ministers have made a sustained effort to stay in Beijing and attend NPC group discussions in order to explain their work, hear comments, and receive suggestions. The tone of work reports by the premier, the Supreme People's Court president, the procurator general, and the minister of finance, all of which are voted on by the full legislature, has also shifted over time to become more self-critical.

Nowhere has the oversight relationship been more evident than in the realm of law and order. Large numbers of NPC delegates have repeatedly displayed discontent with corruption and rising crime rates by voting against or abstaining from voting on the work reports of the Supreme People's Court president and the procurator general. The recent cycle of criticism and reaction began in spring 1998, when former railways minister Han Zhubin won NPC approval as procurator general of the Supreme People's Procuratorate by one of the smallest margins in history. More than 1,000 NPC delegates either voted against him or abstained. The negative votes prompted Han to launch a public relations offensive to win NPC support. He instructed government prosecutors to "strengthen relations with National People's Congress members, and actively and consciously accept supervision by the members."[28] Procurators were directed to promptly meet requests from NPC delegates for meetings, humbly listen to the views of NPC delegates, attach great importance to proposals from NPC delegates, and report on the results of any investigations into complaints and petitions. Each local procuracy was urged to designate a department or office to respond to NPC members.[29] The Supreme People's Court, with Xiao Yang as president, also vowed to pay more attention to the NPC's wishes. It set up a special liaison office, together with a hotline, for the NPC and pledged to promptly and carefully investigate all allegations of judicial misconduct and mishandled cases. In early 1999, both the Supreme People's Court and Supreme People's Procuratorate announced that, in response to NPC criticism, they would improve the quality of law enforcement personnel by adopting stricter internal and external supervision of procurators and judges.[30] These initiatives quickly led to some improvement of judicial behavior. In the procuratorate, cases of public complaint about possible corruption by procurators declined by 17.5 percent in 1999, and the number of formal charges filed declined by nearly 60 percent.[31] With the media stoking the public imagination by asking whether the government and judicial reports can pass muster at the NPC by good margins, the NPC delegates' votes have become a powerful leverage reshaping the legislature's relationship with the State Council and the judicial institutions.

The initiatives by the procuratorates and the courts to respond to legislative criticisms and reform themselves produced some quick payoffs.

At the NPC plenary session in March 1999, the procurator general's report won approval from 78 percent of the NPC delegates, up substantially from only 55 percent the previous year.[32]

Legislative Oversight and the Power of the Purse

The NPC has also sought to gain real supervisory authority and power over the government budget. Until recently, the NPC relied on its 30-strong Finance and Economic Committee to oversee China's massive economic legislation program as well as budget control and other matters. Overextended, the Finance and Economic Committee could not effectively monitor the increasingly important area of budget and outlays. It tended to approve the aggregate budget figures sent over by the Finance Ministry with little input of its own.

Things finally began to change in 1998, when the NPC Standing Committee established a special Budgetary Work Committee (Yusuan Gongzuo Weiyuanhui) to audit and supervise the national budget.[33] With a dedicated staff, including trained accountants, the Budgetary Work Committee has enabled the NPC to examine government spending with more intensity and detail. It has also enhanced the NPC's capacity for drafting laws relating to finance, budgets, and taxation.

The State Council leadership has been willing to oblige the NPC. In August 1998, the NPC Standing Committee approved a State Council request for an emergency bond issue of 100 billion yuan to fund a fiscal stimulus program amid the Asian financial crisis. It is an encouraging sign that the State Council requested the NPC's approval for this fiscal measure that more than doubled the central government's projected budget deficit for 1998. Since then, the NPC Standing Committee has approved other State Council requests for treasury bond issuance, with provisos requiring the State Council to strengthen supervision of fund use and to report back to the NPC on the use of proceeds.[34]

Control over budget making is arguably the most crucial aspect of the legislative-executive relationship. As is well known, the NPC had until recently played a perfunctory role in budget making. The government budget submitted to the NPC tended to be late. Presented in broad categories, it was aggregated by purpose (such as education) rather than being broken down by departmental details. And the NPC was largely relegated to a rubber-stamp role in budget making. Following the establishment of the Budgetary Work Committee in 1998, the NPC began to push for a law on budget supervision. The Ministry of Finance was understandably uneasy about such a law but the legislature produced a legally binding resolution, Resolution on Strengthening the Examination and Supervision of the Central Government Budget, at the end of 1999.[35] The resolution promises to improve transparency and close various loopholes in budget making. It stipulates that the State Council must provide certain details and meet a schedule so that the NPC can have enough time to examine the proposed budget.[36]

As the resolution on budget supervision went through parliamentary deliberations, government officials saw the writing on the wall and quickly began to reform the budget-making process to head off legislative criticism. In fall 1999, the State Council instructed the Ministry of Finance to provide a more detailed budget, broken down by government department rather than by purpose. As of result of this change, the Ministry of Finance has to start the budget-making process three months earlier than before. As noted in Chapter 7, the State Council ministries had converted to detailed departmental budgets by 2001. The availability of budget details broken down by government department has made it possible for NPC delegates to scrutinize government spending like never before. During the 2001 annual session of the NPC, the NPC budget review was especially critical of the diversion of funds, a common practice in budget implementation. The review emphasized the binding authority of the approved budget and demanded that funds be spent for their earmarked purposes. Indeed, the NPC's efforts to claim the power to oversee the purse of state have helped promote the major reforms in budget making and budget management discussed in Chapter 7.

Local People's Congresses and Legislative Oversight

The Chinese constitution also specifies a set of principal-agent relationships between local people's congresses and governments that are similar to those between the NPC and the State Council, the Supreme People's Court, and the Supreme People's Procuratorate. Article 95 of the constitution provides for the establishment of people's congresses and people's governments in provinces, municipalities directly under the central government, counties, cities, municipal districts, townships, nationality townships, and towns. Article 99 gives local people's congresses at and above the county level the authority to examine and approve the plans for economic and social development and the budgets of their respective administrative areas, and to examine and approve reports on the implementation of these plans and budgets. Article 101 gives local people's congresses the power to elect and recall government officials. Article 110 states that local governments are responsible, and report on their work, to people's congresses at the corresponding levels.[37]

In reality, the development of the various capacities of the local people's congresses has been highly uneven, but the trend has been toward greater institutionalization.[38] By the turn of the 1990s, there was clear evidence of growing legislative activities at the provincial level, giving provincial people's congresses increasing say in lawmaking.[39] Nevertheless, in most localities and with relatively few exceptions such as Chongqing and Shenzhen, lawmaking is still dominated by the government side, which commands more resources as well as expertise. Government departments rather than the legislative committees of the local people's congresses have produced the majority of local legislation and dominated the legislative agenda.[40]

Compared to lawmaking, the oversight relationship between local legislatures and governments is more dynamic. Whereas the NPC is more ponderous and more attentively constrained by the central party leadership, it appears that a true breakthrough in the relationship between local legislatures and governments has already occurred in some localities. Rather than the government dominating the people's congress, a growing number—albeit certainly not all, and not even a majority—of local people's congresses seem to be taking the power that is rightfully theirs by virtue of the constitution. By 1998, more than 20 provinces and municipalities had already passed laws and regulations spelling out congressional oversight over government in these localities.[41] This trend has continued to spread in recent years. In early 2000, for instance, the Hubei provincial legislature approved regulations to empower all levels of people's congresses in the province to strengthen oversight over the government, the procuratorates, and the courts. The Hubei regulations stipulate that local legislatures monitor local compliance with the constitution, laws, and administrative regulations, supervise and evaluate the work of government, courts, and procuratorates, and monitor the performance of officials appointed by legislatures. They also empower local legislatures to provide supervision in cases of gross violations of the law and when there is public consternation over abuse of power, arbitrary punishment, and violations of the legitimate rights of citizens, legal persons, and other organizations.[42] In other words, the local legislatures have put in force provisions that the NPC has sought through a proposed Supervision Law.

The ascendancy of local legislatures can be seen in appointment ratification. In 1997–1998, in a bout of activism last seen nearly a decade earlier, several provincial legislatures voted down candidates that the party leadership had proposed for the post of governor. Deputies in some provinces also dismissed incompetent government officials without authorization from the party leadership.[43] The Chinese press has also begun to publicize such rejections and dismissals at lower levels. For example, there was much attention when Luo Bisheng, the mayor of Yueyang in Hunan, failed to win the MPC's support for another term in January 2003 even though he was the sole candidate put forward.[44] To avoid the embarrassment of defeat, the views of the local people's congresses are to some extent factored in before nominations for government appointments are made public and presented to the congresses.[45]

One major strategy local people's congresses have used in wielding their power of appointment ratification has been to require appointees to meet certain qualifications. In April 1998, the Wuhan People's Congress Standing Committee passed a resolution requiring all nominees to take and pass a law exam before they can be ratified for their appointments.[46] Other major cities, including Chengdu, Guangzhou, and Shenyang, have followed suit and made passage of legal knowledge tests mandatory prior to the ratification vote.[47] Though such tests are perfunctory in some localities, with nominees given various forms of assistance in passing the tests, the very existence of the tests does require nominees to give some attention to issues of law in governance.[48] There have been various reports of nominees failing the tests. In Chongqing, three appointees to the courts and the procuracy were not appointed because of failing their tests in August 1998.[49] In Henan's Xihua county, 10 of 121 nominees for judicial positions failed their legal knowledge tests in spring 1999 and couldn't secure their appointments. Moreover, passage of law tests was no guarantee of ratification of appointment. Another seven of the nominees in Xihua were voted down because of low ratings in public evaluations (*qunzhong pingyi*).[50]

Local people's congresses have also invoked the rule of law to promote oversight over local government performance. This assertion of supervisory power over government started in one of the poorest inland provinces. In 1993, Shaanxi initiated "democratic evaluations" of key government leaders, chief judges, and prosecutors. By early 1999, people's congresses at provincial, city, and county levels in Shaanxi had summoned over 1,000 officials, including one vice governor, to report to legislators and face questioning. Following the hearings, the legislators wrote formal evaluation reports on the merits and shortcomings of the officials, who in turn would work out proposed solutions and report back to the people's congresses.[51] By the late 1990s, major cities including Beijing and Shanghai had introduced such hearings on a regular basis. For example, at the end of 1998, the standing committee of the Shanghai Municipal People's Congress asked the director of the city's Industry and Commerce Bureau to report on his work and to hear the committee's evaluation. The chairman of the Shanghai People's Congress indicated that Shanghai would institutionalize such a practice in the future and evaluate a number of key municipal officials each year.[52]

Yet local legislatures do not automatically gain their influence vis-à-vis the governments. To overcome existing structures of power and influence, the crucial opening for the rise of the legislature's influence has tended to appear with certain turning points. Beijing and Guangdong have been exemplars of such development.

Corruption Scandal and Legislative Empowerment in Beijing

In Beijing municipality, the party secretary has enjoyed membership on the Political Bureau of the Party Central Committee and generally dominated the political scene as well as municipal finances. It was not until the downfall of party boss Chen Xitong in a major corruption case that the local party leader's dominance was severely weakened. Following the suicide of Wang Baosen, Chen's deputy and the vice mayor in charge of finance, and the fall of Chen himself, it was found that Chen and associates had hidden more than 10 billion yuan in fiscal revenue from the Municipal People's Congress (MPC) in the mid-1990s.[53] In response, the Beijing MPC began to assert itself. Starting in September 1996, land management, which had been subject to much discretion and corruption, came under the legislature's scrutiny. In 1998, the Beijing MPC rejected the official nominee for the MPC chairmanship.[54]

Meanwhile, the MPC and people's congresses at the district (county) and township levels have pushed for more supervision over budgeting and spending and have stepped up oversight over other aspects of government work. Most significantly, in response to overwhelming demand by MPC delegates for strengthening supervision over government spending, the MPC enacted a set of detailed rules, effective on January 1, 1997, to strengthen its role in budget making. Prior to the enactment of these rules, the MPC received the government's budget proposals only a few days before its MPC Standing Committee met. In consequence, members of the Standing Committee approved the budget without having had the time to examine it in detail. To add insult to injury, municipal leaders also made extensive use of extra-budget items to avoid scrutiny of much spending altogether.[55] The adoption of the budget supervision rules in 1997, however, went a long way toward redressing the unbalanced legislative-executive relationship in Beijing city. It symbolized an extraordinary shift in these relations and heralded the similar shift between the NPC and the State Council discussed earlier. First, the new rules stipulate that the MPC Standing Committee conducts a preliminary examination of the budget plan one month before the full congress meets. Once the Standing Committee has reviewed the budget plan and issued its suggestions for revision, the municipal finance department is required to respond to the suggestions within 15 days. Second, the budget supervision rules include provisions on extra-budget funds (*yusuan wai zijin*). Besides stipulating the areas in which these funds are to be utilized, the new rules require government departments to report, for the record (*bei'an*), to the MPC Standing Committee on how these funds are to be used. The attention to extra-budget funds was later enhanced by efforts to tighten government financial management, including the separation of revenue and expenditure streams discussed in Chapter 7.[56]

How have the budget supervision rules been implemented in Beijing? The government side began by testing the nerve of the MPC leadership in 1997. After the MPC's Finance Committee had conducted its preliminary review of the budget plan and offered suggestions for revision, the municipal finance bureau took time to respond to the suggestions. By the morning of the fourteenth day following the review, the MPC Finance Committee still had not received the Finance Bureau's responses. Giving up hope on getting the Finance Bureau to respond in time, the MPC Finance Committee submitted its preliminary budget review to the MPC vice chairman in charge of finance for approval. In a display of political will, the MPC vice chairman refused to accept the committee review and insisted on getting the municipal Finance Bureau's responses first. Upon learning of the MPC's strong stand on following the rules and wary of a public confrontation with the municipal legislature, the Finance Bureau caved in and provided its responses to the Finance Committee that afternoon. Since the game of chicken in 1997, the Finance Bureau has learned to respond to the MPC Finance Committee promptly; it took only seven to eight days for the Finance Bureau to respond to the MPC Finance Committee's suggestions in 1998 and 1999. As far as the budget is concerned, a new norm in legislative-executive relations has come into being.

In addition to a longer and more interactive budget review process, the Beijing MPC has strengthened its monitoring over government finances in several other aspects. In 1998, it set up an expert group to advise the MPC Standing Committee on the government budget and conduct research on topics of interest to the MPC Standing Committee. Whereas previously the MPC heard the government fiscal report only once a year, the MPC Standing Committee now asks the government to report on fiscal matters twice a year, and the MPC Finance Committee now hears quarterly reports on budget implementation. As the MPC delegates have gained more information and influence over the budget-making process, they have become more forceful in demanding changes to the government budget proposals. In 1999, the government Finance Department made more than 70 revisions to the budget plan in response to MPC suggestions. These suggestions led to increased spending for social welfare, enterprise renovation, as well as public health.

The principle of legislative oversight has thus become the new routine in practice. At the end of 2001, the MPC amended the budget supervision regulations and gave special attention to the monitoring of budget implementation through hearings and audits. To combat the diversion of funds from one budget item to another, the regulations put restrictions on such practice and require the municipal government to seek the approval of the MPC Standing Committee in cases of spending cuts for items related to agriculture, education, science and technology, and social security.[57] Moreover, starting in 2000, the MPC Standing Committee began to request government officials to appear before it to report on their work and be evaluated by the committee. In early 2001, the MPC Standing Committee voted into effect a set of rules governing such reports and evaluations, stipulating, inter alia, that mayors and bureau directors must report back within three months on the corrective measures being taken after receiving the congressional evaluations of their work. Under these rules, the hearings on the work of government officials have become institutionalized.

In short, political crisis became a turning point for reconfiguring legislative-executive relations in Beijing. According to one report, delegate activities (inspections, motions, and so forth) through the Beijing MPC have reached "unprecedented" levels in recent years.[58] As a result of the institutional changes, the discretionary spending power of local officials has been curbed.

Financial Crisis and Legislative Empowerment in Guangdong

In the case of Guangdong province, members of the provincial legislature had questioned the provincial land and transportation bureaus in 1994–1995.[59] In an augury of the future, 11 delegates to the Guangdong Provincial People's Congress (PPC) in 1995 proposed that the PPC should enact legislation asserting its authority over major policy issues. The proposal did not go far, however, as party and government officials dominated the political landscape in Guangdong at that time.

In the aftermath of the Asian financial crisis in 1997–1998 and coinciding with a centrally engineered change of local leadership (the central leadership dispatched Li Changchun to Guangdong to serve as party secretary, taking over the position from a Guangdong native), the surge of legislative activism in Guangdong has become known as the Guangdong Phenomenon (Guangdong *xianxiang*). As the GITIC bankruptcy and distress at other financial institutions put severe fiscal pressure on the provincial government, PPC leaders called for more oversight over the financial sector. They also declared that PPC supervision over economic and financial matters would focus on the implementation of the development plan and the budget. Moreover, PPC deputies unanimously adopted an amendment to the Rules of Procedure to increase democracy and transparency at the PPC. The amendment promises deputies a greater role in nominating officials and hearing work reports from government officials. It also provides for more public input into lawmaking.[60] Governor Lu Ruihua apparently took the congressional demands to heart by vowing to revamp local financial institutions and Guangdong window companies listed overseas.[61]

While the provincial leadership focused on economic and financial issues, the Guangdong PPC began to systematically assert its authority vis-

à-vis the government. This was evident in two areas, personnel appointments and environmental policy. On personnel appointments, the Guangdong PPC Standing Committee voted down two of the 15 nominees for
government bureau directors in February 2000.[62] On environmental policy, delegates to the PPC severely criticized the provincial Environmental
Protection Bureau (EPB) for misuse of funds and for negligence in overseeing environmental work. In a case that captured national attention, delegates to the third session of the ninth PPC in January 2000 castigated the
Guangdong EPB for allowing a heavy-polluting electroplating park to go
into operation in the city of Sihui without proper environmental impact
study. Electroplating firms at the industrial park caused serious pollution
to Guangdong's water system. After rejecting the EPB's responses as insin-
cere and evasive three times, 21 delegates requested the provincial legislature to impeach Wang Zikui, the deputy EPB director, for incompetence.
Under heavy fire, the EPB shut down the electroplating park. Tang
Bingquan, the vice governor overseeing environmental work in the provincial government, accepted the delegates' criticisms and agreed to conduct
an investigation and follow up on the demands of the legislators.[63]

Besides the Guangdong PPC, the Guangzhou Municipal People's
Congress has also shown its mettle. During the annual session of the
Guangzhou MPC in April 2000, delegates confronted government officials
on a whole host of issues, including the location of a heavy-polluting ce-
ment plant, land use, and unauthorized road toll collection.[64] The delegates' sharp questions and criticisms directed at government officials led
the local media to conclude that, for the first time in Guangzhou, MPC
delegates had exercised their rights to decide on major issues. Media comments noted that the questioning by delegates meant that government officials no longer talked down to the people and that the delegates had finally begun to represent the interests of the common people.[65]

As the provincial and municipal legislatures asserted themselves, the
Guangdong PPC in November 1999 began consideration of the bill, first
proposed in 1995, that would enshrine the legislature's authority vis-à-vis
the government. The following summer, the Regulations on Discussing
and Deciding on Major Issues by the Standing Committees of People's
Congresses at Various Levels in Guangdong were enacted. According to
the regulations, approvals must be sought from the People's Congress
Standing Committee in the following areas: major policy measures concerning population, environment, and resources; development plans for

education, science, culture, health, and sports; government-proposed amendments to the government budget; major judicial issues as requested by the chief procurator where the chief procurator disagrees with the majority of the procuratorate committee. In many other areas, such as price changes for water, power and gas, health care, and public transport, policies concerning unemployment insurance, and housing funds, the local government is required to report to the People's Congress Standing Committee, which in turn has the right to make suggestions.[66]

In essence, the enactment of the regulations marked the institutionalization of actual practices and offers a legal framework for people's congresses at all levels in Guangdong to exercise their constitutional authority over the government. A variety of developments following the enactment of the regulations suggests the ratcheting up of legislative assertiveness in Guangdong. Most notably, the Guangdong PPC, following on the heels of the national legislature, put in place the Regulations for the Discussion, Approval, and Supervision of Budgets in Guangdong in March 2001. These regulations, applicable to provincial, municipal, and county levels, direct governments at these levels to provide detailed department budgets 45 days before the people's congresses meet. Moreover, whereas previously funds earmarked for one purpose were often diverted to other uses, the regulations stipulate that such changes require the approval of the legislatures.[67]

As mentioned in Chapter 7, following the enactment of the budget supervision regulations, the Guangdong provincial government budget, now compiled on a departmental basis, has since 2003 come to encompass all 102 fiscal units, including government departments as well as organizations funded by the provincial government. Moreover, the departmental budgets are broken down by allocations for salary, administrative expenses, retirement benefits, and so on, as well as figures on specific projects, complete with brief explanations and justifications for the projects. Assisted by a newly created office of budget supervision under the Finance and Economy Committee, members of the Guangdong PPC have not been shy about asking questions and demanding explanations for some spending items.[68] While so far the legislature's input into the final government budget remains limited, not the least because most members of the PPC still have only a very limited window of time to examine the thick book of budget numbers, the reforms in Guangdong, and increasingly in other localities, clearly mark a major ratcheting up of legislative supervision over budget making.

Legislative Activism in Other Localities

Local people's congresses in other localities have also begun to assert their power over social-economic issues, albeit unevenly. The NPC's resolution on budget supervision, in particular, has provided a model for local legislatures to emulate and given local legislators the authority to claim a power that has historically been taken over by the governor's office. For example, the Guangxi legislature adopted its own rules for supervising economic work by invoking the NPC resolution as well as the relevant laws and regulations.[69] In Shanghai, the Baoshan district legislature vetoed a major budget adjustment proposed by the district finance office.[70] Most interestingly, Shenzhen in mid-2000 enacted the Shenzhen Municipal Regulations on Government-invested Projects. Under these regulations, Shenzhen became the first major Chinese city to require legislative approval for major government-funded projects. In late 2002 the Shenzhen MPC joined forces with the municipal discipline inspection commission and the bureau of supervision to inspect the implementation of the regulations and concluded that they were successful in preventing wasteful projects designed for short-term political benefits.[71]

A variety of social and environmental issues have attracted the attention of local legislatures. In Jiangsu province, the provincial people's congress filed a high-profile complaint in summer 2000 about the government's lackluster efforts to clean up Lake Tai.[72] In Shenyang, which had been plagued by problems of crime and corruption that culminated in the resignation and arrest of the mayor and deputy mayor, the municipal legislature rejected the work report of the Shenyang Intermediate People's Court—a first in the history of PRC legislatures—and barely approved the procuratorate's work report in February 2001. Only after the court, under new leadership, had undertaken months of emergency reforms did the Shenyang MPC approve its work report at a specially convened session.[73]

An excellent illustration of the sort of legislative-executive confrontation occurred in Hubei's Wuhan. On April 24, 1998, the Wuhan Municipal People's Congress, having conducted careful investigations of its own, vetoed the municipal government's report on the city's reemployment project. The MPC concluded that the government report had failed to provide a sound description of the situation, specify concrete goals, and provide for effective measures. It specifically criticized the municipal government for citing 1,400 press reports on Wuhan's employment situation as evidence of success and noted that the number of furloughed workers had steadily increased between 1994 and 1997. The municipal government abided by the veto and immediately started to respond to the criticisms.[74] By early 1999, Wuhan municipal officials had adopted a series of measures, including making available additional funds and telephone hotlines, to boost reemployment and publicly committed to helping 60,000 unemployed workers to find jobs.[75] In this particular case, the local people's congress chose a potentially explosive issue to put the government on the defensive. The government side could choose to cooperate with the MPC or defy it and popular opinion at a time when central leaders were holding local leaders responsible for keeping unemployment down. By choosing the former option, the government acknowledged the authority of the people's congress.

The developments in Guangdong, Beijing, Wuhan, Chengdu, and Shenyang are not isolated cases but appear to fit a broad trend. By accepting the legislative veto and taking tests mandated by people's congresses and by appearing at the people's congress to report on their work, government officials effectively acknowledge and reinforce the constitutional authority of the local people's congresses. Local officials may complain in private about having to go through hearings and other parliamentary procedures, but their participation has nonetheless helped legitimize these procedures.[76]

Political Alliances for Horizontal Accountability

It should be pointed out that the legislative-executive relationship at the local level is not destined to be confrontational. For top government leaders presiding over complex bureaucracies must contend with their own monitoring problems while they themselves may be held accountable by the national government if their subordinates commit major crimes such as corruption. In consequence, top local leaders have some incentive to welcome criticism and oversight from people's congresses as well as the media.

This alliance between top local leaders and people's congresses (as well as the media and to some extent the public) against lower-level bureaucrats is especially likely to endure if the congresses are seen to act in a constructive manner. Some provincial officials, such as Guangdong party secretary Li Changchun (until 2002), an outsider dispatched to tame the localist impulses in Guangdong, saw people's congress delegates as a powerful supervisory force to be harnessed. For Li Changchun, Guangdong's 150,000 people's congress delegates should have direct access to party and government officials at various levels so that the delegates can safeguard the people's interests according to law.[77] In March 1998, the Guangdong provincial party and government leadership opened "express trains" for people's congress delegates as well as members of local political consultative conferences so that government officials can quickly receive and respond to comments, criticisms, and suggestions. Eight months later, the measure had generated 320 letters and proposals. The letters and proposals prompted provincial leaders to deal with both pressing and emerging problems.[78] It was only with the approval of the Standing Committee of the Guangdong Provincial CCP Party Committee that the Guangdong People's Congress Standing Committee was able to enact the controversial law empowering people's congresses at all levels mentioned earlier.[79]

Constitutional Empowerment and the National Audit Office

The legislative institutions, including the National People's Congress and local people's congresses, are the most salient institutions for horizontal accountability that have invoked the constitution to enhance their authority and expand their influence. In addition, the procuratorates, themselves subject to legislative oversight, also play a role in holding other institutions and individuals accountable. Other institutions of horizontal accountability that have seen their profile rise include the Ministry of Supervision, the Central Discipline Inspection Commission, and the National Audit Office. In this section, I examine the short history of the China National Audit Office to show how a minor constitutional provision provided the basis for the growth of this important institution.

Constitutional Foundation

During the Mao era, there was no national audit agency, and the government relied on financial supervision, periodic accounting inspections, and revolutionary spirit to elicit compliance. Systematic auditing was resurrected only in the reform era. As the initial wave of reforms decentralized power, it became ever more urgent to strengthen the financial monitoring of government departments, state enterprises, and other government institutions. Article 85 of the 1982 constitution makes the auditor general a constituent member of the State Council. Article 91 specifies the tasks and authority of the auditing institution to be established as follows:

The State Council establishes an auditing body to supervise through auditing the revenue and expenditure of all departments under the State Council and of the local governments at different levels, and those of the state financial and monetary organizations and of enterprises and undertakings. Under the direction of the premier of the State Council, the auditing body independently exercises its power to supervise through auditing in accordance with the law, subject to no interference by any other administrative organ or any public organization or individual.

Conceived in the new constitution, the National Audit Office was inaugurated in September 1983. The establishment of provincial, municipal, and county audit institutions followed. The Audit Law of 1994 stipulates that "Local audit institutions at various levels shall be accountable and report on their work to the people's governments at the corresponding levels and to audit institutions at the next higher levels." In practice, organization of the audit office has gravitated toward vertical administration since the 1990s. While the auditor general reports to the premier, local audit institutions, according to the National Audit Office, "should be directed mainly by audit institutions at the next higher levels and report to their corresponding-level governments as well as the next-higher-level audit institutions."

Humble Beginnings

In spite of the authority granted by the 1982 constitution, the National Audit Office started with little institutional clout. Indeed, until it moved to its present headquarters in May 1994, the National Audit Office had to rent space for its offices. Hampered by bureaucratic resistance (most other government departments had the same bureaucratic ranking as the National Audit Office), shortage of qualified personnel (there were few qualified accountants), a weak legal framework, and ever-shifting policies and politics, the auditors, whose mission was to step on other people's toes, had to make their moves with great care.

To begin with, the National Audit Office went about its work as the audit institutions at different levels of government were still being built up. At the end of 1985, the total staff of the audit institutions nationwide reached 28,600, many of whom had only gone through short-term training classes. The audit offices were able to audit 81,000 units that year, only a tiny fraction of the number that should be audited. By 1989, the total staff of the National Audit Office had reached 63,000, and the number of units audited had risen to 243,000.[80]

Second, while the constitution empowered the National Audit Office against interference by other government departments, the details for that power needed to be worked out. As is typical in Chinese lawmaking, the State Council sent the auditors to work with interim regulations. In 1985, the State Council issued a set of Interim Regulations on Strengthening Audit Work. Two years later, the State Council put forth the People's Republic of China Regulations on Audit.[81] Needless to say, these were administrative regulations rather than laws enacted by the National People's Congress. The absence of formal legislation sometimes put the auditors on the defensive.

In light of these challenges, the government auditors at first emphasized conducting audits on government construction projects, state enterprises, and nonprofit institutions (*shiye danwei*), as well as financial and commercial institutions and sectors such as agriculture. They moved more slowly in audits of government departments, starting with county-level government financial departments and some provincial departments. Simply put, the National Audit Office first took on units and government departments that it clearly outranked bureaucratically. When the auditors had to take on provincial government agencies, they faced bureaucrats who were more powerful and less cooperative. As a report by the General Office of the National Audit Office noted in 1989, the audit institutions "had not worked out smooth relationships with some financial and economic management departments, and there still existed various obstacles in the work conditions for audit institutions."[82] It was not until 1990, in the aftermath of the Tiananmen crackdown and amid the central leadership's drive to rein in local authorities, that the National Audit Office took on the "arduous task" of auditing the revenues and expenditures of 31 provincial-level governments and cities with separate budget status (*jihua danlie shi*).[83] Audits of central government finances still had to wait.

These limitations notwithstanding, the importance of government auditors was becoming apparent in the late 1980s. In 1989, government auditors audited 243,000 units and uncovered 24 billion yuan of funds that were used in violation of financial rules. Of this amount, 5.2 billion yuan belonged to the government treasury and 3.7 billion yuan was recovered. As a result of the audits, 367 corruption cases were cracked and criminal proceedings were launched against more than 2,200 people.[84]

Economic Transformation, the Demand for Monitoring Institutions, and the Institutionalization of Auditing

As with the development of other macroeconomic and monitoring institutions, the major turning point for the National Audit Office came with the central leadership's formal commitment to the market economy and the need to rectify China's economic chaos in the early 1990s (Chapter 3).[85] As the Chinese leadership struggled to stabilize the economy and deal with various forms of irregularities, the central government worked in concert with the national legislature to improve the legal environment for enforcing economic order. At the end of 1993, the NPC Standing Committee amended the Accounting Law. In 1994, the NPC enacted the Budget Law and the Audit Law. These and other laws such as the Banking Law have provided concrete foundations for the National Audit Office to exercise its constitutionally provided authority.

The major reason for the central leadership's eagerness to strengthen the auditing institutions is the desire to strengthen central monitoring and control over the government's vast and complex financial empire. We have already discussed the effort by the central leadership to use vertical administration as a weapon against local protectionism. But central leaders recognized that they could not count on the institutions they want to monitor to discipline themselves. In September 1994, for example, Vice Premier Zhu Rongji compared the audits on the branches of the People's Bank of China by the PBOC itself and the National Audit Office. Zhu noted that the National Audit Office's report uncovered more problems at the PBOC than the PBOC's internal audit. While the PBOC's internal audit found 430 million yuan in unauthorized short-term loans, the National Audit Office uncovered more than one billion yuan.[86] The difference in the audit results prompted Zhu to ask the PBOC to send five work teams to PBOC branches to straighten things out. Another striking example was the management of the government's strategic grain reserves. In an audit report submitted in July 1995, the National Audit Office concluded that local authorities had cheated the center with fake numbers. The audit report prompted Premier Li Peng to consider separating central and local government reserves, which eventually occurred under the watch of Premier Zhu Rongji.[87] In short, for central leaders worried about declining central government capacity and corruption, the auditors were potentially a powerful force that could be marshaled to monitor and discipline the sprawling bureaucratic establishment.

The empowerment of the National Audit Office has also given the National People's Congress an additional weapon to augment its authority. The Audit Law invokes the constitution and states that China practices the system of audit supervision (Article 2). In an important victory for the legislature, Article 4 of the Audit Law stipulates that audit offices from the State Council down to county governments should report to the legislature of the corresponding level each year on their work.

The enactment of the Audit Law in 1994 provided the National Audit Office with the legal wherewithal to institutionalize the role of the audit offices in auditing government finances, particularly of the central government departments. Two months after the enactment of the Audit Law, the National Audit Office put forward a draft of the Implementing Rules for Auditing and Supervising Government Fiscal Revenue and Expenditure.[88] While the rules for auditing the central government itself were still being worked out, the National Audit Office, with the support of the Political Bureau leadership, invoked the Audit Law to launch audits of the implementation of the 1994 budget in selected central government departments. Guo Zhenqian, then the auditor general, plainly stated that these audits would help the auditors prepare for full-scale audits of central government budget implementation in the future. Between February 18 and March 8, 1995, the National Audit Office conducted audits on budget implementation by 46 central government ministries and departments. The audits uncovered 13.8 billion yuan in misused funds. When the audit results were presented to the State Council, Premier Li Peng commented: "There are quite a number of problems; some [of the problems] are quite serious. Effective and feasible reform measures should be adopted."[89] Suddenly accountability was in the air.

The year 1996 became the first for systematic auditing of central government budget implementation (for the 1995 fiscal year). Throughout this process, the fledgling National Audit Office carefully negotiated its relationship with the leaderships of the State Council and of the National People's Congress. Put baldly, the National Audit Office needed to demon-

strate the effectiveness of its work to the National People's Congress by uncovering some problems. Yet it risked the wrath of the State Council leadership if it was seen as overly aggressive in digging up financial problems in
central government departments. Mindful of their delicate position, the
auditors general of the National Audit Office stayed in close touch with
leaders of both the State Council and the National People's Congress as
they planned and audited central government finances. On March 25,
1996, Deputy Auditor General Li Jinhua reported on the plans and
arrangements for auditing the implementation of the central government
budget to the Finance and Economic Committee of the National People's
Congress. When the audit results became available, Guo Zhenqian and Li
Jinhua briefed Cao Zhi, secretary general of the NPC Standing Committee and Yang Jingyu, deputy secretary general of the State Council, on May
9, 1996. At the end of May, the National Audit Office submitted its report
to Premier Li Peng on the audit results of the implementation of the 1995
central government budget. Li instructed the National Audit Office to put
together an Audit Work Report to be presented to the NPC Standing
Committee. In June, Auditor General Guo Zhenqian rehearsed the pres-
entation of the audit work report to the State Council leadership first. On
July 3, 1996, Guo Zhenqian, representing the State Council, made the audit work report to the eighth NPC Standing Committee.

Until 1996, the Minister of Finance reported each year to the NPC
on the implementation of the previous year's government budget and presented a budget outline for the current year. The auditor general merely sat
there to listen as a guest. Beginning in 1996 the auditor general stepped
into the spotlight, epitomizing the national legislature's authority to supervise government operations. Though for the moment the auditor general's
work report pulled its punches, a chain of accountability had come into
being.

Most importantly, the central government audits have had real impact on central government financial management. In a sort of annual performance ritual that has fundamental political implications, the auditor
general each year presents to the legislature and the public on the problems
in central government finances. The government leaders in turn promise
to undertake remedial measures and introduce reforms.[90] In 1996, for example, Premier Li Peng instructed that the auditor's report should emphasize adopting measures to strengthen budgetary constraints and reduce irregularities in government expenditure.[91] Similarly Premier Zhu Rongji,

who succeeded Li Peng in 1998, directed the State Council departments to deal with the problems uncovered by the auditors.

The audits have been an important driving force behind the rationalization of government budget management discussed in Chapter 7. Moreover, oftentimes the Audit Office is mobilized to undertake targeted audits and is thus able to make very specific recommendations on institutional reforms. For instance, the National Audit Office in 1997 conducted an audit on the bank accounts of central government budgetary units. The audit found that these government agencies and organizations tended to have multiple bank accounts that undermined financial supervision and sometimes became loopholes for malfeasance. The audit prompted the State Council to limit the number of accounts each government agency was allowed to open. In another case, the Supervision Ministry, the National Audit Office, and the People's Bank of China in early 1999 conducted an investigation into the extra-budget funds collected by central government departments. The investigation uncovered a whole host of problems: 700 million yuan of levies and special purpose funds that were collected in violation of regulations; 6.3 billion yuan in budget funds and 12.5 billion in special funds (*zhuanhu zijin*) that should have been turned over to the government exchequer; half a million yuan of public funds deposited in private accounts; 4.2 million yuan in hidden funds; and 36 million yuan that were collected without issuing proper receipts.[92] In short, government agencies at all levels had hidden a lot of funds from the purview of the Ministry of Finance. Partly to overcome the problems uncovered by such audits, the Ministry of Finance promoted reforms of government financial management that strengthened oversight over government revenue and expenditure (Chapter 7).

By 1998, the constitutional status, mission, and functions of the National Audit Office had been settled, and the institutionalization of government audits was well on its way. In that year, government auditors helped recover more than 17 billion yuan of revenue for the treasury, cut the amount of financial appropriations and subsidies by 3.1 billion yuan, and helped uncover 19.8 billion yuan of misused funds.[93] Indeed, in field interviews, I found that government officials and managers already held the auditors in awe, and the mention of doing an audit (*shenji*) would invariably elicit serious attention. Even in villages, farmers who suspect corruption by village leaders have from time to time sought the assistance of auditors.

The Zhu Rongji administration (spring 1998–spring 2003) not only vigorously pursued government reforms but gave greater prominence to the National Audit Office in its drive to impose organizational discipline and combat corruption. To empower the auditors and improve their independence, the auditing institutions, armed with more adequate budget allocations for operations, have covered the expenses of the audits on their own rather than accept payments from the government agencies and firms being audited.[94] Meanwhile, the National Audit Office has since March 2000 adopted a set of behavioral norms to ensure the independence of the auditors. The norms stipulate that auditors should not accept lodging arrangements, meals, transportation, and other benefits from the institutions being audited.[95]

Besides conducting audits of government budgets and of state enterprises and financial institutions, the central government has also enlisted auditors to enhance the audit of key funds and government-funded projects. In the meantime, in conjunction with the ongoing government reforms, the National Audit Office, now headed by Li Jinhua, assumed a higher public profile in the name of boosting transparency and promoting administration according to law.[96] Not only has the annual auditor's report to the National People's Congress become more hard-hitting, but the National Audit Office has also released various audit results at other times, such as the embezzlement of 473 million yuan of resettlement funds earmarked for the Three Gorges Dam project. Such visibility highlighted the authority of the National Audit Office and gave momentum to government reforms and the fight against corruption. In a variety of ways, government auditors have portrayed themselves as guardians of state interests, uncovering malfeasance, promoting good governance, and protecting the dignity of law.

Take the case of Auditor General Li Jinhua's 1999 report to the NPC Standing Committee. In the report Li offered details of the NAO's audits on 53 State Council agencies and 173 major state-owned firms. He revealed that the 53 agencies had misused 16.4 billion yuan and singled out the Ministry of Finance and the Ministry of Water Resources for criticism. The Ministry of Water Resources was found to have misused 116 million yuan earmarked for water conservancy projects to build luxurious offices, buy apartments for its staff, and invest in stocks over 1994–1998 at a time when the country faced major problems of flood control. The State Council confiscated the buildings to recover misused funds. Some of the apartments were later auctioned off, with proceeds going to the government treasury.[97]

The auditor general's report won much praise from legislators. In response to the report, the NPC Standing Committee directed the State Council to rectify the problems uncovered and punish those responsible. The State Council was also asked to report back to the legislature within six months on the measures taken to reform financial management in central government departments. NPC Chairman Li Peng asked the Ministry of Finance to set an example for other agencies. Moreover, the discovery of serious problems prompted the NPC to demand more audits. Upon the recommendation of the Finance and Economic Committee, the NPC Standing Committee ordered a special audit on the use of the special treasury bonds for infrastructure development.[98]

In December 1999, Auditor General Li Jinhua reported back to the NPC Standing Committee that the problems discussed earlier had basically been corrected. Misappropriated funds and uncollected taxes had been recovered, and real estate of illegal provenance had been confiscated for public auction. Those found responsible had been disciplined. Li noted that, following the National Audit Office's recommendations, the departments concerned were adopting measures for strengthening internal management and improving budgetary management.[99] In the case of the Ministry of Water Resources, former Minister of Water Resources Niu Maosheng was given "a big demerit point" (*daguo*) by the Ministry of Supervision for his part in misappropriating state funds allocated for water conservation projects. While Niu had been transferred to become governor of Hebei province, the administrative penalty effectively ended his upward mobility. A vice minister of Water Resources also received a "demerit point." Further investigations on personal corruption were launched, with various personnel directly connected with the misuse of funds facing criminal prosecution.

In the early 2000s the National Audit Office launched several high-profile initiatives, including audits of the major state banks and the massive State Power Corporation. In the audit of the Bank of China headquarters, seven provincial-level branches, and 150-plus sub-provincial branches, the auditors uncovered evidence for 22 major fraud cases involving 2.7 billion yuan and sent 35 people to the procurators for criminal proceedings.[100] In 2002 the Audit Office directed its attention to the China

Construction Bank, where the disgraced Wang Xuebing served as president between 2000 and his ouster in early 2002.[101]

Partly in response to demands from the National People's Congress, the auditors have also devoted more and more attention to highly visible national projects. In the case of the Three Gorges Dam project, auditors found that the Ministry of Finance had taken pains to ensure that the project's management had a strict fund-management system in place from the very start. Extensive use of competitive bidding and strict contract management helped to keep spending below projected costs. Audits of the dam project itself by the Ministry of Finance and the State Audit Office between 1993 and 2000 did not uncover major problems. In contrast, the auditors uncovered significant misuse of resettlement funds, which were prone to abuse because they were allocated to local officials.[102] In 2000, the National Audit Office also reported that between 1997 and the first half of 1999 more than 4.3 billion yuan in poverty relief funds, about one-fifth of the total allocated, was misappropriated or diverted to other purposes.[103] These findings led to reforms in the disbursement of government funds.

Some local legislatures have also become prominent champions of government audits. In Guangzhou, the capital of Guangdong province, MPC delegates in August 2000 vociferously complained that the municipal audit office's four-page report on government finances was inadequate. They asked for more details and demanded that specific cases be discussed.[104] Likewise, members of the Guangdong provincial legislature have called for the Audit Office to establish special institutions charged with auditing top officials.[105] Gone are the days of Mao and Zhou Enlai, when government financial affairs were conducted in great secrecy.

The Western press has justifiably given much prominence to government reports of massive fraud. In the attention-grabbing style typical of newspaper editors, the *South China Morning Post* headlined its report "Reaching to New Heights of Fraud."[106] The *New York Times* similarly reported that "Graft in China Flows Freely, Draining the Treasury."[107] What the press has failed to note, however, is that these corruption cases were uncovered through institutionalized audits of government finances. Moreover, such audits have spurred State Council to undertake systematic reforms of government financial management. With these reforms as well as the extensive use of end-of-term audits discussed in Chapter 7, government departments have more closely followed laws and regulations on financial management and improved internal management. In consequence, as Auditor General Li Jinhua proudly noted in his 2003 Audit Work Report to the NPC, the value of problem funds uncovered in the State Council's constituent ministries and agencies declined from 16.4 billion yuan in 1998 to 2 billion yuan in 2001.[108] Of course Li did not stop there. He went on to discuss a long list of other problems in government financial management and the remedial measures that had been taken, and recommended further reforms. For Li, who has himself become a subject of much Chinese media attention, the government auditors are on a permanent mission to improve China's governance.

Conclusions

A hallmark of state socialist countries was the ease with which top leaders rewrote the constitution. Constitutions proclaimed grandiose goals and bore little resemblance to reality. They were drawn up and rewritten as if party leaders were working on a speech about the future rather than the most fundamental political document about the governance of a society and polity. In real political life, the annihilation of opponents became the cardinal rule of political life.

It may be too early to tell whether the post-Mao constitution will be as durable and important as those that have been held as conducive to well-ordered societies. Nevertheless, our empirical examination of the relationship between the people's congress and the government and of the rise of the National Audit Office points to growing respect for the terms of the constitution: the NPC as well as the local legislatures have increased their influence over lawmaking, appointment ratification, budget and policy reviews, and the monitoring and supervision of the behavior of agencies and officials. The activism of the National People's Congress has risen despite its rubber-stamp image.

To be sure, the NPC's clout in various areas remains limited in comparison to its Western counterparts. Yet there does appear in practice to be growing acceptance in China of legislative oversight over government and judicial institutions. Indeed, the very thought that the National People's Congress ought to put into practice its constitutional power to supervise the government is a remarkably recent development in China, suggesting the emergence of some sort of a "constitutional faith" in China.[109]

As the profile of the legislatures has grown, the legislatures are no longer simply dumping grounds for retirees or government leaders who have lost influence. At the first session of the tenth NPC, in March 2003, 19 individuals in the prime of their career paths were elected to the NPC Standing Committee. A growing number of provincial party secretaries have taken on the chairmanship of provincial people's congresses. In mid-1998, 13 of the 31 provincial-level party secretaries did so; by 2003, the number had risen to 23 out of 31.[110]

The growing number of top party officials serving concurrently as legislative leaders suggests that local party apparatuses, which have traditionally focused on personnel selection, have increasingly turned their attention to using the local people's congresses as levers over appointments and policy and even to confront the governments.[111] This means that party leaders are behaving as if they recognize that the local people's congresses are the principals vis-à-vis local governments. While some members of legislatures appear to regard this trend as evidence of party control and interference, it seems that, as the local legislatures become more authoritative, this trend may be taken to constitute evidence of growing respect for the constitution, albeit a constitution implemented under the Communist Party's shadow.

The legislatures are but the most prominent institutions that have begun to provide some element of checks and balances vis-à-vis other state institutions, particularly the government and the judicial institutions. A variety of other institutions have also come into being within the Chinese political system that promise to enhance the demands for accountability. Among these, the Ministry of Supervision and the National Audit Office have especially acquired visibility and clout. The rise of these institutions of horizontal accountability has strengthened monitoring of government behavior and helped lock in the improvements in governance. Looking to the future, these institutions are set to promote further governance reforms.

chapter nine

CONCLUSIONS

At the start of the post-Mao reforms, the Chinese state was known for its totalistic orientation. Today we still see some of this old streak in certain major aspects of Chinese governance, such as the confrontation between the state and certain quasi-religious sects (particularly the Falungong), the lack of toleration for open political dissent, and the initial mishandling of the SARS crisis in early 2003. Yet more than two decades of economic liberalization and socioeconomic diversification have already transformed the Chinese economy and society beyond the recognition of any Rip van Winkle who went to sleep in the late 1970s. In fact, China has not only made major progress toward the goal, officially adopted in fall 1992 at the CCP's fourteenth National Congress, of building a socialist *market* economy but has also witnessed significant reforms in the way the state works. Indeed, as the quote from Polanyi in Chapter 1 would imply, without the remaking of the state, China's relatively successfully market transition would be hard to conceive, and sustained economic development would be difficult.

We have so far examined myriad reforms and adaptations in the mechanisms of governance in China, especially in the post-Deng years. These governance reforms, ranging from the streamlining of government and the simplification and rationalization of administrative approvals, to the divestiture of military businesses, the reforms of government financial management, and the utilization of competitive mechanisms for government procurements and land allocation, and others, have already helped enhance the efficiency, transparency, and fairness of the administrative state, strengthen the regulatory apparatuses, remove various institutional incentives and loopholes for corrupt practices, and improve the environment for business. Elements of these reforms, particularly the SEZ (special economic zone) model, have engendered emulation in other economies, including India, Japan, and even North Korea.[1]

Nonetheless, as this book goes to press, the governance reforms remain a work in progress (China is certainly not unique in this regard). The major contours of the new institutional framework, particularly for governing the economy, are in place, but many important details need to be filled in, tested in practice, and refined. Moreover, much as the SARS crisis of 2003 has spurred the spread of transparency and accountability to the area of public health and the regulation of risk in general, it also highlighted the limits of the governance reforms beyond the economic realm. For their part, China's technocratic leaders continue to see the improvement of the governance mechanisms as a major mission.[2]

The governance reforms, singly and in combination, have significant implications for state-society relations. Some of the reforms, notably the divestiture of businesses operated by the armed forces and other state institutions and the abolition of most sectoral ministries, force state institutions not to do certain things and thus offer more space for nonstate actors to develop. Many others, such as the land auctions and the reforms in government financial management, introduce mechanisms of checks and balances to established procedures so as to discipline the behavior of state agents. Moreover, there have been regulatory reforms to reshape the role of industry regulators such that the regulators do not simultaneously serve as both owner and regulator.[3] Finally, the rise of various institutions of horizontal accountability promises to offer impetus for further refinements of existing reforms and the introduction of new ones. In general, these developments delimit the government's role. Multiple constraints have begun to be exerted on the government to make its behavior more predictable and less capricious. Just as life as an emergent phenomenon is far larger than the elements that make it possible, the improvements in the governance mechanisms described in this volume seem suggestive of a transformation of government behavior in the making.

In the rest of this chapter we shall first review the politics that have attended the reforms of governance and state-business relations and look at the Chinese experience in light of the experiences in contemporary Russia and the Progressive Era United States. We then offer a quick summary of the trends toward the constraining of governmental power in terms of actual practices and elite attitudes. The chapter ends with a discussion of the significance and implications of the governance reforms for China's political development.

Market Transition and the Political Economy of Governance

Before we consider the emergent properties of China's governance reforms, let us first review some central themes that have been covered. The most important of these themes concerns the politics of institutional changes needed to sustain China's transition to a well-functioning market economy.

As is well known to most observers of transitional economies, the Chinese economy moved away from prices set by planners toward market-based pricing between the late 1970s and early 1990s. Much of this transition was facilitated by the dual-track pricing mechanism that provided the incentives for producers and consumers to enlarge the sphere of the market. The evolution of the economy from plan toward the market, particularly the arrival of buyer's markets for most products, transformed attitudes, altered incentives, and furnished a hospitable soil for reforms of the government and of government-business relations.

Yet the transition to market-based prices, while a signal achievement, does not make a modern market economy. In fact, accompanying the arrival of market prices has been a proliferation of fake and shoddy products, local protectionism, and rampant corruption. These elements of market disorder prompted many observers to worry about the direction China's economy and politics would take and ask whether China might end up in the worst of both worlds. As Karl Polanyi's classic *The Great Transformation* made abundantly clear, the making of a market economy on a national scale is neither natural nor painless. Moreover, market making is far from simply the liberation of the economic sphere from governmental control. Instead, "the market has been the outcome of a conscious and often violent intervention on the part of government."[4] This has especially been the case with the transformation of the planned economies of the twentieth century. In most of these economies, notably Russia, politicians buoyed by the joys of the fall of communism quickly inflicted painful "shock therapies" on their economies and societies in order to produce market economies, albeit not always with therapeutic results.

With the benefit of insight from the pains of the former Soviet Union, Chinese leaders have been doggedly determined not to fall into the same traps, particularly because China's own aborted price reforms in 1988 contributed to the political crisis of 1989. In an ironic historic twist, the Chinese Communist Party, shortly after surviving the crisis of 1989 and the fall of communism in the Soviet Union and Eastern Europe, committed to the construction of a market economy under its own leadership, the better to survive politically. According to General Secretary Jiang Zemin, a new economic system to be known as the socialist market economy would be built to harness the vitality of market forces for the cause of socialism.[5] In late 1993, the Party Central Committee formally approved and promulgated its Decision on Various Issues Concerning the Building of a Socialist Market Economic System.[6] As part of this reform platform, the Chinese leadership reiterated the need to transform the functions of government, separate government and enterprises, and establish the institutions needed to nurture and sustain the market. There was thus a clear recognition on the part of China's leaders to build the institutional infrastructure for a market economy. Gone were the days when the motto of reform was crossing the river by feeling the stones.

Yet subsequent developments did not occur according to plan or a script. Faced with myriad challenges, national leaders undertook specific reforms largely in response to pressing problems, especially real and perceived crises that got their immediate attention. In view of declining government revenue as a share of GDP and rising inflation and fearing the political consequences of such trends in light of the fall of communist regimes in the Soviet Union and Eastern Europe, the Chinese leadership in 1993–1994 undertook to rebuild the foundations of government revenue by reapportioning taxes between central and local governments and by establishing an independent revenue collection apparatus for the central government. Equally importantly, the central leadership reclaimed the prerogative to set the tax and fiscal structure and has since used that right again and again, exiling the notion that China has a federalist system.

After pushing through the 1993–1994 tax and fiscal reforms, the central leadership coasted a little; with the health of Deng Xiaoping failing, Jiang Zemin was much more concerned about shoring up his political base than with launching painful new reforms. It took another crisis from abroad, the Asian financial/political crisis, to drive home the message that China urgently needed new reforms at a time of escalating public discontent with corruption. Occurring after the Chinese leadership had weathered the death of Deng Xiaoping, the Asian financial crisis thus became the precipitating event for a host of new initiatives. By then the relative success of the tax and fiscal reforms had furnished the central leadership with the financial wherewithal to undertake important but costly policy initiatives. In the event, the appointment of the hard-charging Zhu Rongji as premier also infused the reform drive with fresh energy and focus.

To begin with, the Asian financial crisis underscored the importance of financial security and prompted the Chinese government to revamp the central banking system and the regulatory apparatuses for the securities and insurance industries. Along with regulatory restructuring, serious reforms of the banks, investment and trust companies, and other financial institutions have been launched. With the banking system having become the Achilles' heel of the economy, such reforms were sorely needed and have made significant headway.

Equally important, rampant smuggling during the Asian crisis severely hurt the national government's revenue base and prompted the Chinese leadership to finally come down hard on smuggling and to launch a dramatic divestiture program. By getting the People's Liberation Army, the armed police, judicial institutions, as well as a host of other party and state institutions out of the business of doing business, the divestiture program removed the special privileges these businesses enjoyed and often abused (in smuggling and other activities). It made them subject to the regulation of government agencies, including the Customs Administration (which was also cleansed). In consequence, the divestiture, surely one of the most momentous but least noticed events in the late 1990s, not only helped bring rampant smuggling and related corruption under control but was also critical to the development of a level economic playing field.

Moreover, while every incoming State Council administration has proposed reforms of the governmental structure, the drastic government reforms Premier Zhu Rongji unleashed in 1998 were made both to catch up with changes in the economy and to preempt the possibility of governance failure. Last but certainly not least, the fall of crony governments in South Korea, Indonesia, and other countries steeled the leadership's resolve to crack down on corruption and to promote a series of institutional innovations designed to close loopholes and prevent corruption from occurring in the first place.

Leaders in most countries rarely need or are able to reshape their governance structure in a wholesale manner. In contrast, China's leaders have had the rare albeit arduous task of remaking China's institutions of governance in many areas, all within a relatively compressed time period. Moreover, unlike in many developing countries of China's level of economic development, the Chinese leadership has largely been able to implement the reforms discussed in this volume and look set to push through others in the next few years. Taken together, the institutions for a functioning market economy have taken shape, and the nature of the state itself has undergone a subtle but profound transformation.

Why has China been able to accomplish this transformation of its institutions? As indicated earlier, the steady expansion of the market not only created demands for institutional change but also powerfully altered the incentives for individuals and organizations. Ultimately, however, the construction of market-sustaining institutions and the transformation of governance have required political leaders to recognize the need for such reforms and to carry the reforms out. The 1993 Decision indicates that such recognition already existed then. Moreover, as domestic and international circumstances changed, these changes as well as new knowledge were taken into account. The most obvious example of such global learning was the restructuring of the People's Bank of China into something like the Federal Reserve System of the United States (albeit without the independence of the Fed).

The recognition of the need for reforms does not mean that the reforms will be carried out. Whether in the formerly communist countries or Latin America, too often leaders with the vision and the courage for reforms are met with strong resistance and obstruction from powerful vested interests.[7] For China, however, the Communist Party has remained in the driver's seat of the political machinery. This institutional underpinning, most notably through the power to appoint and remove officials that leaders in most other countries such as Russia could only dream of, has provided China's national leaders the luxury and leverage to promote and implement both short-term stopgap measures and long-term fundamental reforms.

Even with this strong political machinery, central leaders have nevertheless been solicitous about social and local interests, generally taking steps to protect the interests of potential losers as new reform policies are introduced. In remaking the fiscal and taxation systems, central leaders adopted a divide-and-rule strategy vis-à-vis provincial officials and ensured that the provinces would not see a reduction in their current spending power. Likewise, in forcing the armed forces and other state institutions to divest of their business interests, the central leadership offered to increase budgetary allocations to these interests to make up for incomes lost. And with the downsizing of the state sector and rising unemployment the Chinese government has made a serious effort to provide a minimum cushion for the least advantaged.[8]

In short, without the CCP's political machine, most of the contentious institutional reforms described here, from the revamping of the fiscal system to the divestiture of the late 1990s and the continuing improvements in governance, would most likely have been far more difficult to accomplish, if not downright impossible. Using this political machine as leverage, the Chinese leadership has been able to promote administrative redesigns that enhance the sinews of governance and provide the foundations for a regulatory state.

It should be emphasized that the efforts to alleviate the decompository fissures through a reconfiguration of the system of political and especially economic governance have not meant a return to the status quo ante of the Maoist era and the stifling of local initiatives. While the fiscal reforms have strengthened the central government vis-à-vis the localities, the system of tax assignment still offers local authorities economic incentives to promote growth and generate revenue. While the central government upgraded the various regulatory agencies, it also abolished most of the industrial ministries that were at the heart of the command economy. Thus it appears that a middle road for organizing China has been found that would provide the means for implementing the will of the central government while leaving room for local initiatives. The resultant organizational form is a crossbreed between strict hierarchy and excessive decentralization. Though China has not adopted federalism, local governments continue to have room to maneuver. As the state has retreated from micromanaging enterprises, the realm for private and individual businesses has continued to expand. Altogether the myriad institutional reforms that have been undertaken since the 1990s, by offering stability and greater protection for property rights, have helped provide an improving institutional environment for investment and growth.

China in the Russian Mirror

We can gain more perspective on China's governance reforms by looking at developments in Russia and the United States. Much has been said about the divergent paths of reforms taken by China and the former Soviet Union.[9] It is useful to recall that there have been persistent doubts about the viability of the Chinese system, especially in the 1990s. Drawing on parallels with Russia, Yugoslavia, or China's own history, various commentators both in China and abroad have pointed to the disintegrative forces in China.[10] Charles Fairbanks, Jr., for example, postulated in 1999 that "[t]he decomposition of the Chinese Communist regime is approaching inevitably and probably quickly."[11]

Despite and to some extent because of these gloomy prognostications, China's leaders have leveraged their political machinery to gradually refit the ship of state. Not only has China been able to sustain an enviable economic record, but the leadership in China has also been able to push through important institutional reforms concerning tax, customs, police, central banking, and standards, as well as laws to undergird the institutional sinews of governance. It has also achieved much in leveling the playing field for all economic actors. These reforms helped bring China into the WTO at the end of 2001 and ahead of Russia, even though China still lags behind Russia in terms of nominal per capita GDP.[12]

In contrast, Russia's shock therapy did not produce a sound market economy but instead a sort of anarchic capitalism riddled with corruption. Amid the dramatic political and economic transformations in progress, the Russian central state has been notably deficient in the delivery of various forms of public goods and services, including the enforcement of laws.[13] Instead, private mafia-type law enforcement has thrived.[14] The Russian state became a vehicle for rent-seeking and freeloading and had trouble collecting taxes to pay its bills until it was bailed out by the rise in oil prices at the end of the 1990s. Meanwhile political power and authority largely passed into the hands of Russia's 89 governors as well as local government leaders.[15] Some governors ran their localities like fiefdoms, and various provinces had charters that contravened the federal constitution. The economic and political morass in turn has made it difficult to consolidate Russia's fledgling democracy.[16]

Why was there such divergence between Russia and China? The most critical difference between these two giants lay in the different manners decentralization occurred. In China, the decentralization of power and authority to the provinces was introduced at the discretion of the central leadership to stimulate local initiatives in the 1980s.[17] For all the talk about federalism in China, it is clear that Chinese central leaders have retained the prerogative to manipulate the political machinery and have used that prerogative as a lever for revamping the fiscal and taxation systems and other institutions.

The contrast with Russia cannot be starker. Even before Russia pursued shock therapy under Yeltsin, the Soviet state was already in paralysis. The disintegration of the Soviet Union saw Yeltsin lead Russia toward electoral democracy as well as the further enervation of Moscow. Indeed, Russia itself was in danger of territorial disintegration. According to Treisman: "One by one, different ethnic republics within the Russian Federation declared themselves sovereign states, adopted constitutions, flags, and even national anthems, announced that their laws took precedence over federal law, asserted rights over resources in their territory, and refused to remit the taxes Moscow demanded."[18] At the height of the tax revolt about one-third of the regions in Russia, led by Chechnya and Tatarstan, withheld some or all of their assessed taxes and used various strategies and threats to wring concessions from Yeltsin.

While Moscow tried hard to crack down on Chechnya, it adopted a policy of selective fiscal appeasement for other regions, using transfer payments and tax breaks to buy electoral support for central incumbents and proreform forces. The fiscal appeasement policy helped prevent bandwagons of opportunistic protest and tax withholding from escalating, but it was also very costly and burdensome for the cash-strapped federation government.[19] Whereas China's fiscal decentralization of the 1980s was designed by central leaders to stimulate local initiatives, Russia's was adopted in desperation to stave off territorial disintegration.

Indeed, rather than the center controlling local politicians, the locals gained power independently of the center. Moreover, the upper house of parliament (the Federation Council) under Yeltsin was made up of regional governors and the heads of regional assemblies. As members of the Federation Council, they enjoyed political influence as well as legal immunity, thus giving them significant influence in Moscow by virtue of their regional positions. According to Russian president Vladimir Putin, a fifth of the provincial laws were at odds with federal law.[20] The Russian state simply did not possess the power to reasonably regulate and enforce. In the words of Stephen Kotkin, "Russia's dysfunctional state apparatus is the world's biggest parasite. It has a self-serving culture that is inimical not just to the tasks of regulating a market society, but also to the commands of any would-be authoritarian ruler."[21] Some studies even suggested that Russia might become like China after the 1911 Revolution, with the central government present in name only and real powers vested in the regions.[22]

To a significant extent, the malaise afflicting most postcommunist countries has been a crisis of governance.[23] Without the capacity to extract, regulate, protect, and police, a fledgling democracy would be hard pressed to survive, let alone thrive. It was thus no surprise that, following Yeltsin's resignation, Vladimir Putin, who was inaugurated as president in spring 2000, would seek to rein in the regional politicians and strengthen the central state. In one major move, Putin chose to remodel the Federation Council, the upper house of parliament, along the lines of the U. S. Senate prior to the Seventeenth Amendment of the U.S. Constitution (1913).[24] Under Putin's plan, the 178 regional governors and heads of regional assemblies who served in the council are replaced with full-time representatives appointed by the regional governors and legislatures.[25] The plan also gives the president the power to dismiss elected provincial governors and dissolve local legislatures if their policies break federal law. Remarkably, it is a sign of the demand for change that not only the Duma but also the Federation Council went along with Putin to enhance the power of the federal government.[26] And, predictably, Putin introduced major initiatives to boost the central government's fiscal strengths by, among other things, sharply reducing the share of income taxes kept by the regions.

The program to rein in regional interests is only part of Putin's efforts to build a "managed democracy" with a strong central government, though hardly one accountable to ordinary Russian citizens.[27] While Russia got far ahead of China in terms of electoral contestation, it has followed in the steps of China in strengthening the sinews of governance, thereby underscoring the importance of the governance reforms that China has pursued since the early 1990s.

China in the American Mirror

Whereas the contemporary histories of China and Russia are a study in contrasts, there are significant historical parallels between China and the United States of the Progressive Era.[28] Before I point to these parallels, however, it is important to keep in mind that the two countries differ greatly in terms of political system, that the historical circumstances have changed substantially, and that the levels of technology are vastly different in today's China from a century earlier. Yet, for all the technological and other differences separating today's China and the United States a century earlier, there are amazing parallels that point to certain themes in the process of economic and political development in countries of a continental size.

Let me begin with a quick and undoubtedly oversimplified review of the Progressive movement in the United States that followed on the heels of the closing of the frontier. Progressivism refers to a diverse set of reforms that came in response to issues engendered by rapid industrialization and urbanization, including corruption and machine politics in cities; protection of labor, consumers, and the underprivileged in general; and financial legislation as well as railroad and trust regulation. Those who demanded reforms sought to enhance democratic governance, protect economic freedom, and promote social justice. The urban reforms sought to get rid of corrupt city bosses. As corrupt local governments were overthrown, urban services were improved and new city management forms came into being (albeit unevenly). In state capitals, reformers brought about greater regulation of railroads and public utilities, introduced various social policies, and brought about the popular election of senators to replace their selection by state legislatures.

At the national level, the Progressive movement was especially identified with the policies of two presidents, Theodore Roosevelt's Fair Deal and Woodrow Wilson's New Freedom. Theodore Roosevelt used the Sherman Anti-Trust Act of 1890, which had not been enforced under previous administrations, to break up various forms of trusts or monopolies such as the Standard Oil Company. He was also able to revitalize the Interstate Commerce Commission to strengthen control over the railroads. The regulatory state was further enhanced with the passage in 1906 of the Meat Inspection Act and the Pure Food and Drug Act, which aimed to protect the interests of consumers.

After the interregnum of William Howard Taft, Woodrow Wilson's election in 1912 revived the Progressive agenda. Wilson's New Freedom platform emphasized antimonopoly, tariff reductions, and banking reform. These goals were quickly fulfilled with the Federal Reserve Act of 1913, which created the Federal Reserve system that has been the linchpin of the American financial system, the Underwood Tariff Act of 1913, which reduced average tariff rates from 40 percent to 25 percent, and the Federal Trade Commission Act of 1914, which empowered the newly created Federal Trade Commission to fight monopolistic business practices. Next Wilson moved on to social and economic legislation that promoted the interests of farmers, labor, and children.

In the aftermath of the World War I and the victory of Warren Harding in 1920, various Progressive Era reforms, particularly those concerning unions, minimum wage, and child labor, came under attack. Nonetheless, it was in this era of retrenchment that the early budget reforms in New York City and other places became crystallized at the federal level with the Budget and Accounting Act of 1921, which placed the federal administrative apparatus under presidential control through the newly created Bureau of the Budget and paved the way for the interventionist policies of the New Deal.[29] Indeed, the New Deal of Franklin D. Roosevelt went far beyond Progressivism to include large-scale social programs and greater government participation in the economy.[30]

Now let's turn to the Chinese reforms, which followed on the heels of the Cultural Revolution, China's own version of a political civil war. Unlike the Progressive reforms of the United States, the wellspring of the Chinese reforms is not the Protestant passion—the desire to redeem the world.[31] Yet both reform movements are shaped by dynamic interactions between state and society. In the United States, it was demands from society (minus blacks, immigrants, labor unions, and to some extent women) in an open political system that drove the agenda for reform. In China, the Chinese reforms are far more reliant on the state and more driven by fear of social protests, although over time different interests such as consumers, businesses, property owners, and so on have become more vocal and even influential. Nevertheless, China also witnessed some expansion of popular political participation, notably district-level elections to local people's congresses and village elections. The Communist Party is unwilling to relinquish its hold on power, but the urge to retain power has prompted it to introduce reforms designed to streamline government, make the state more transparent, and curb abusive power. Where the American Progressives sought to realize a cleaner and more efficient government by breaking the power of the bosses through the introduction of the secret ballot and the direct primary, the Chinese leaders have tried to accomplish similar objectives by introducing new institutional mechanisms and incentives including reforms of the civil service and of the administrative approval system.

In this perspective, the Chinese reforms are managerial, businesslike, and technocratic, and the Chinese state has in turn moved closer to becoming a managerial state. Professional men and college graduates as well as businessmen in large enterprises led the Progressive movement in the United States; China's reforms have seen the flourishing of technocrats.[32]

Muckraking brought the diffuse malaise of the public into focus and provided the fuel for action in American Progressivism. For America's Upton Sinclair, China has Wang Hai and Consumer Rights Day (March 15). The Chinese press, though severely limited in the political sphere, has been an extraordinary force in exposing problems with product and food quality, construction fraud, and environmental damages. CCTV, the Chinese Central Television, now provides regular and frequent updates on air quality in cities; major newspapers such as *The Economic Daily* regularly print information or results of quality surveys on products, as do programs on CCTV. Such exposures have helped shape the agenda for the consumers association, the reform of the construction industry, and major efforts to deal with the environment. By the end of the 1990s, the State Administration of Quality and Technical Supervision and the State Environmental Protection Agency, two agencies that hardly existed at the start of the reform era, had become household names with augmented power and authority. Regulation of food and drugs has also been enhanced through the installation of the State Food and Drug Administration. Indeed, it seems the SARS crisis of 2003 has ratcheted up the trend toward administrative transparency and propelled reforms into previously neglected noneconomic areas, including public health and social rights.

The championship of consumer rights by the press has helped propel China's embrace of competition. Extensive discussions of unfair fee structures and practices have been a major factor behind the Chinese leadership's commitment to bringing competition into the telecom, airline, and power industries.[33] The government-engineered competition in telecommunications has helped bring down charges and improve service. Meanwhile, comprehensive government budget reforms have been introduced under the direction of technocrats to make the administrative apparatus more amenable to central control and less prone to corruption.

In banking, finance, and tariffs, China has followed the American road. China's Banking Law adopted the principles embodied in the Glass-Stegall Act. The Chinese leadership chose to remodel the Chinese central bank upon the Federal Reserve in terms of its regional structure. And, partly at the prodding of the United States, China's reformers have steadily reduced its tariff rates to meet the requirements for joining first GATT and then the World Trade Organization. It is conventional wisdom that the Chinese economy is now much more open to foreign direct investment than the economies of Japan and other Asian tigers at a comparable stage of development.

Just as the age of reform in the United States lasted several decades, the age of reform in China has yet to run its course. Some of the reforms, such as the building of an unemployment system, have only just unfolded in China. In other cases, such as securities regulation, China and the present-day United States face remarkably similar challenges. In still other areas, such as health care and higher education, China's reforms have barely begun, and the SARS crisis has revealed profound problems in the public health system. Overall, in spite of the dissimilarities in the two political systems, the similarities between the Progressive movement in the United States and the recent reforms in China are striking. In each case, the remaking of the state occurred in response to massive economic and social transformations and dislocations.

Institutional Reforms and the Constraining of Governmental Power

The comparisons with Progressive Era United States and contemporary Russia raise serious questions about the implications of China's governance reforms, which have occurred on the watch of the Communist Party leadership. The reforms have furnished the central state with greater fiscal prowess and added nimbler fingers to the arms of the reconfigured state to make it more capable and effective in governing a dynamic economy and society. Since such governing capacity is often in short supply in countries with China's level of economic development, the Chinese reforms are vitally necessary to make available basic public services, maintain order, and provide the institutional conditions for sustained economic growth. Indeed, it may be hard to believe, but China has in the post-Mao era witnessed the longest period of stable economic development since the late nineteenth century.

Equally importantly, China's leaders have gradually adopted the view that the government's role should be delimited, particularly in the realm of economic governance. As Zhu Rongji emphatically stated in 2003 in his last government work report as premier, "What the government should take care of must be done well; but it must not intervene in what it should not take on."[34] In tandem with the changing philosophy of governance, various types of institutional reforms appear to have started to serve as webs of mechanisms imposing discipline and constraints on governmental power, offering glimpses of the possibility of a limited government. Indeed, as will be discussed later in this section, the very concept of limited government has won some important adherents in contemporary China.

The presence of limited government is now largely taken for granted in most democracies. In *Federalist* 51, James Madison succinctly made the case for it: "In framing a government to be administered by men over men, the great difficulty lies in this: you must first enable the government to control the governed; and in the next place oblige it to control itself." In the American constitutional system, checks and balances coupled with federalism have provided the institutional foundations for a sphere of rights.

Yet countries that fought hard in the twentieth century against colonialism and imperialism to gain independence rarely chose constitutional rights as their top priority. For countries such as China, freedom from foreign domination was the first order of business. It was not until after having experienced the terrors of late Maoism that China, like the post-fascist countries in Europe, really began to embrace, however tentatively, a constitutionalist framework.[35] It is against this background that a variety of constraints on government power have emerged in China. These constraints can be roughly grouped as follows.

Economic Constraints. Since the mid-1990s, the Chinese government has relied on the issuance of treasury bonds rather than printing money to meet budget deficits. As a consequence of such public borrowing, government behavior is subject to discipline by bondholders, as occurred in England earlier.[36] A government relying on the bond markets for public financing may still be tempted to alter the terms of the bonds or renege on the promise to repay bondholders. But such options are costly, because they will raise the price of future borrowings and, in the case of default, cause new sources of funds to dry up. Generally speaking, governments with a reasonable long-term time horizon have strong incentives to abide by the terms of the markets. Though various local government-funded investment and trust companies have floundered at great cost to lenders, the Chinese central government has thus far cultivated its reputation as a responsible player in both the domestic and international bond markets.

In the meantime, faced with hard budget constraints and ever-increasing capital mobility, local officials have been under pressure to lure investments and have as a result become more responsive to the needs of business. The inter-jurisdictional competition among local governments to attract investments has served as an important disciplining mechanism on local governments.[37] Development zones such as Sichuan's Mianyang have learned the hard way about the importance of improving the quality of governance. In turn these zones have become the catalysts of governance reforms in the interior, much as Shenzhen, Hainan, Pudong, Suzhou, and other special zones have been along the coast. In fact, as the central government reduced local governments' discretion to offer tax benefits to investors, local officials have increasingly turned to the improvement of the overall business environment—such as the provision of infrastructure, the reduction in red tape, and the improvement in government service—in their drive to attract investments. Indeed, the competition is global, and China's central government reforms as well as willingness to accept global rules are partly attributable to the Chinese leadership's desire to make China a competitive economic player in the global marketplace (also see below).[38]

Intra-governmental Discipline. Broadly speaking, government agencies are required to carry out "administration in accordance with law" (*yifa xingzheng*). But where exhortation may fail, institutional mechanisms have often been proposed and instituted to improve transparency, reduce conflicts of interests, and curb undesirable behavior. The divestiture of businesses operated by numerous state agencies sharply reduced the conflicts of interest arising from regulators serving simultaneously as both player and referee. The streamlining and reorganization of government departments and functions, the reduction in the scope of government approvals and licensing requirements, and the promotion of civil service reforms have begun to improve organizational coherence, raise the quality of civil service, and enhance the uniformity of regulatory enforcement. Systemic reforms in government financial management and oversight, including overhauls of government budget making and budget management, have also taken place. Comprehensive programs to discipline government discretionary power in government procurement, projects, stock listings, and land allocations through the use of market incentives have been introduced.

Also important has been the establishment and increasing prominence of various institutions of horizontal accountability, including the National Audit Office and Ministry of Supervision (Central Discipline Inspection Commission). Such internal mechanisms to discipline the state, including internal checks and balances, have also been promoted, to varying degrees, in the judiciary, the police, the Customs Administration, and other agencies. Earlier in the book we discussed the reforms of the Customs Administration. In the police, officials have admitted the widespread use of torture and have introduced some measures, including both internal discipline and societal supervision, to do something about this problem.[39]

Constitutional Constraints. Whereas the choice of national leaders remains the preserve of the party leadership, there has nevertheless been growing respect for the constitution among the ruling elite. In particular, the legislatures are playing a growing role in the ratification of appointments and in examining budgets. The relationship between the National People's Congress and the State Council increasingly resembles the division of political power commonly found in systems of modern constitutionalism. Provisions in the 1982 constitution for a National Audit Office or for village self-governance have already proven to be enabling mechanisms for institutional development.

In the meantime, though judicial independence is lacking, the broadening and deepening of legal reforms have provided individuals and legal persons an increasingly important means—albeit still far from perfect—with which to hold government agencies accountable.[40] In particular, the enactment and implementation of the laws on administrative litigation, administrative punishment, administrative reconsideration, state compensation, and administrative licensing have served to impose disciplinary constraints on administrative behavior and delimit the reach of the administrative state. Take the case of the Administrative Litigation Law promulgated on April 4, 1989. Whereas there were 9,934 cases filed against government agencies in 1989, the number of cases had risen to 98,000 by 1998. Of the 460,000 cases filed against the government over that period, plaintiffs won about 35 percent of the time.[41] While enforcement of verdicts remains to be improved, the verdicts have provided impetus for administrative agencies to improve their compliance with laws and regulations.[42] Partly in response to the drive to promote administration in accordance with law and partly in response to societal demands through legal channels, local governments have started to pay more attention to the legal aspects of their administration. In 1999, the provincial government of Jilin became the first to hire a team of 15 lawyers and experts to provide counsel to officials to help them make the transition to rule of law.[43] At the national level, the Wen Jiabao administration used the formal implementation of the Administrative Licensing Law in 2004 to promote government administration in accordance with law. It also announced a comprehensive ten-year program on governance in accordance with law in 2004.

International Engagements and Obligations. Related to the above are constraints arising from China's growing entanglements in global rules and norms. One of the first laws China enacted in the reform era was designed to attract and protect investment from overseas. As China has become more deeply integrated into and dependent on the global economy, its behavior has also become more "normalized," marked by its accession to membership of the World Trade Organization. Gone is the fiery revolutionary rhetoric that China sported when it returned to world stage in the early 1970s. Having become one of the world's largest traders, China's interests and stakes in an open global economy have increased steadily. In a surprise to some observers, China has tended to be on the side of free traders at the WTO.[44]

Given the relative underdevelopment of China's legal system, WTO membership has required significant adjustment on the part of China. In late 2001 and early 2002, Chinese government ministries and commissions made announcements concerning the status of existing legislation and regulations. While some laws and regulations not compatible with the WTO membership terms were scrapped, others were amended to comply. The Supreme People's Court alone announced the annulment of 177 judicial explanations and stepped up its internal reforms to make the Chinese legal system more WTO-compatible.[45] Provincial-level authorities also actively amended local legislation to comply with WTO requirements. Legislators have also become more cosmopolitan in proposing new legislation. Take the case of the Government Procurement Law. Anticipating future negotiations on China's participation in the WTO government purchase agreement down the road, legislators considering China's own government procurement law in 2001 noted that China should pay close attention to the WTO rules and stipulations of international organizations in enacting its government procurement law.[46] At the same time, domestic judicial practices, particularly problems in judicial enforcement, have come under international spotlight. Indeed, domestic reformers, concerned about the pace of domestic reforms, have deliberately sought international pressures to promote domestic change. Some Chinese policy makers noted that a major reason for China's joining the WTO was to force China to make further legal reforms and to "familiarize officials with the rule of law in a modern market economy."[47] Likewise, many people hope that China's signing of the U.N. Convention Against Corruption in 2003 would help apprehend corrupt officials who have fled the country and would thus aid the domestic anticorruption drive.[48] China's involvement in international rules and norms is not limited to economic interactions but also reaches other spheres. It is widely believed that pressures from the World Health Organization and foreign governments were a major factor behind the Chinese leadership's dramatic policy reversal in handling the SARS epidemic in April 2003. Fearing an economic abyss as well as a major loss of global prestige, the Chinese leadership sacked the health minister and the Beijing mayor, who were blamed for covering up the epidemic in Beijing, and opted for policies of greater transparency and accountability. Even in the human rights arena, the Chinese government has become enmeshed in the global human rights regime by signing various international human rights agreements, including the International Covenant on Social, Economic, and Cultural Rights and the International Covenant on Civil and Political Rights, and by entering into human rights dialogs with, among others, the United States.[49] While there remains much room for Chinese government behavior to improve, particularly in the human rights area, the corollary of China's growing international entanglements entails that it is increasingly subjecting itself to global rules and norms.

While this quick review does not exhaust all developments that impose constraints on governmental behavior, there remains much room for improvement, not to mention the fact that these developments have occurred with the Communist Party still in power. Moreover, some of the institutional changes, particularly the emphasis on vertical administration and the trend toward the establishment of regulatory agencies—whose chiefs are not voted on by the legislatures—to some extent detract from the growing webs of constraints on government. Nonetheless, in consideration of the multiple developments listed above, I think it is reasonable to detect a trend toward imposing certain constraints on governmental behavior.

It is worth noting that this trend has come into being for varied reasons. Some institutional developments, such as the growing assertiveness of the national and some local legislatures or the increasing clout of the

National Audit Office, represent the realization of provisions in the constitution that the framers may or may not have tended to have real significance. Others, most notably the issuance of treasury bonds to replace the printing of money to cover government budget deficits was driven by the fear of hyper-inflation, which was a major cause of the fall of the Guomindang in the 1940s, and the need to cover the government's fiscal needs. Meanwhile, the various international agreements China has entered into are at least as much manifestations of China's adaptation to the international system as they are part of a conscious strategy to join the international system and be a respectable member of the international community. There was no unified master plan for imposing constraints on the government.

Yet, as more and more institutional reforms have been adopted, the concept of limited government has found growing acceptance in China. By this I mean not simply the usual reference by legislative leaders and advisers to the need for more monitoring and supervision of the government and judicial institutions, or the widely held view that the government should delimit its role in the economy, but the actual adoption of the phrase *youxian zhengfu* (limited government) or its close equivalent in discussing the goals of government reforms.[50] Even a quick Chinese Internet search would reveal the use of phrase *youxian zhengfu* in a range of party and government sponsored newspapers including the *People's Daily*, and it is almost uniformly used in a positive sense to indicate something desirable.

Policy makers and scholars accept that the government in a modern market economy has to be a limited one and argue that the reform of China's government will promote the transformation of the administrative state from a totalistic, unlimited government to a limited government, with its operations moving from compulsory supervision to the provision of public services.[51] Some policy advisers such as Chen Shouyi, vice chairman of the Ningbo People's Political Consultative Conference, argues that corruption cannot be rooted out without transforming the government into a limited government.[52]

Where Chinese scholars and analysts disagree is in their assessment of the extent to which China has moved toward limited government. Some authors simply state that the government in China is making a gradual transition from unlimited to limited government.[53] Others lament that both the elite and the people still lack a proper understanding of the concept of limited government.[54] Occasionally some authors have noted that, after 20 years of reforms, the Chinese government has already been transformed from a totalistic government into a limited one.[55] This divergence in opinions is to some extent a reflection of regional differences in government behavior. The most optimistic assessment cited here, for example, is from Guangdong, the province that borders on Hong Kong. In contrast, there are more reports of government interference with business and other matters in the interior.

Most interestingly, for public officials engaged in the discourse on limited government, the concept itself has become convenient shorthand that can be invoked to provide intellectual coherence for further reforms. For example, in explaining China's WTO membership to the domestic audience, Long Yongtu, then China's chief negotiator for WTO accession, pointed out that 21 of 23 of the agreements for China's WTO membership were about the government, and most of the rules were intended to constrain government behavior. According to Long, a basic requirement of the WTO membership is that the government be a limited government based on the rule of law.[56]

A number of provincial officials have made the promotion of limited government their mission. The province of Fujian has stood out. Fujian party secretary Song Defu, formerly the minister of personnel, called for combining limited government with effective service in pursuing government reforms.[57] Former Fujian governor Xi Jinping, who became Zhejiang provincial party secretary in fall 2002, has given a variety of published interviews invoking the notion of limited government.[58] For these officials, the government should focus on the provision of public goods. The power of government can be disciplined by reducing bureaucratic hurdles (such as licenses and approvals) and inviting public criticisms and supervision. Under the leadership of Xi and Song, all sub-provincial governments in Fujian set up Government Efficacy Complaints Centers (Jiguan Xiaoneng Tousu Zhongxin) so that the public can file complaints on administrative behavior and provide supervision of administrative agencies.

Even Shanghai, known for its ponderous bureaucracy, got a mayor and party secretary in 2002 who called for limiting the government's role. At his inaugural press conference in early 2002, Mayor Chen Liangyu held that the government should retreat from the allocation of social resources and become a referee and supervisor. Chen called for transferring more government functions to social intermediaries to help transform "government with unlimited power" into "government with limited power."[59] The growing acceptance of the idea or notion of limited government, though understood somewhat differently than in liberal democracies, raises the hope of further reforms in this direction. All in all, notwithstanding various problems and even grave deformities in current practices under a one-party regime, China has taken some steps in the direction of limiting governmental arbitrariness. Such limits on the arbitrary power of the government are vitally important for protecting and expanding the liberties that China has gained in the reform era.

The Political Significance of Good Governance

While the post-Tiananmen leaders in China have occasionally, as in 1997, flirted with a more liberal political vision, their governance has largely been defined by the massive economic, social, and ecological dislocations of a country with 1.3 billion people in the throes of market transition, rapid urbanization, and global integration. Caught between the disillusionment with outmoded ideological fantasies and the fear of political eruptions, the Chinese leadership has jealously guarded the party's political dominance while promoting economic liberalization and development. Ideologically they have chosen a distinctively pragmatic middle course, preferring to stay away from either end of the ideological spectrum. From time to time market liberalism had to be compromised for the sake of garnering political support, as had been the case in grain and cotton marketing reforms. Yet these have turned out to be but small digressions in a robust journey to the market.

Put simply, the Chinese leadership's emphasis has so far been on order rather than democratic ideals, technocratic control rather than popular participation (except at the grassroots level), governability rather than regime type. For now, the economic reforms and rapid growth have generated substantial popular support, which helped to limit the appeal of radical student demonstrators in 1989 and continues to provide the social basis for the Chinese combination of economic liberalization and political authoritarianism.[60] Yet the preoccupation with stability and economic growth has come at great costs, including environmental degradation and under-investment in public health. Moreover, the conservative character of Chinese reform politics has left liberals unimpressed and dissidents in disdain. Liberal critics complain that the liberalizing economic reforms alone do not address the fundamental problem of regime legitimacy. They contend that the lack of path-breaking political reforms will cause tensions to accumulate, including those from tens of millions of struggling farmers and urban unemployed. Such strains, if not properly channeled and released, may one day erupt in explosions of great magnitude and overwhelm the regime that has so far placed its bets on short-term tinkering with the status quo rather than thorough rebuilding of the political foundations of their rule. The resulting crisis may open up new political vistas but may also plunge China into some sort of political chaos or paralysis.[61]

This rhetoric of crisis is nothing new.[62] Indeed, the death of CCP rule and the disintegration of China have been predicted many times over since 1989. A quick search on the Internet search engine Google gives a good indication of the bourgeoning literature on this topic. As of fall 2002, there were more than one million items containing both "China" and "crisis," or about one in eight of all Google search items containing the word "crisis."[63] The search for the "China" and "collapse" combination produced more than 700,000 items. Had all the predictions since 1989 about China's collapse materialized, China would have died many times over.[64]

In practice, against the background of Tiananmen and the fall of the Soviet Union, the crisis rhetoric and genuine challenges in navigating the shoals of multiple transitions have served to concentrate the minds of China's leaders on stability and political survival. This preoccupation with order and survival has in turn driven the Chinese leaders' efforts to undertake reforms of economy and administration, rebuild the sinews of governance, and introduce institutional mechanisms for combating corruption while restraining the expansion of popular political participation and cracking down on dissent.[65] If the improvement in the institutions of governance documented in this volume bears any resemblance to reality, then the Chinese state is not only not falling apart but is becoming a sort of managerial state—more efficient, more service-oriented, and more disciplined. Indeed, the new governance mechanisms appear to have helped to compensate for the organizational deficit that has resulted from the declining significance of the *danwei* system and the party-controlled network of corporatist social organizations (labor, youth, and women). Thus the emphasis on order has not meant a paralysis of institutional development. Instead, the Chinese leadership has given much attention to building and remaking institutions to enhance bureaucratic capacity and alleviate tensions in state-society relations with limited popular political participation.

Order has been a major concern of political theorists since at least

Confucius. Modern political theorists from Hobbes to Samuel Huntington have given special attention to it. Nonetheless, the Chinese leadership's preoccupation with order has been, especially since the early 1990s, out of sync with the global trend toward democratization, particularly in former communist countries. Much of the academic literature as well as the media have tended to highlight the slow pace of democratization in China, so much so that one of the foreign leaders that President Jiang Zemin invited to Beijing suggested that the Chinese leadership was on the wrong side of history.

Yet, as the political philosopher John Gray notes, no country can sustain modernization without effective institutions of governance.[66] From a historical and comparative perspective, the ability of the Chinese leadership to govern that vast and poor country effectively, not least to maintain economic growth and weather the Asian financial crisis relatively unscathed, was in itself no trivial achievement. For many countries with per capita income levels similar to China's, the existence of an effective state that can maintain order and provide basic public goods remains a forlorn dream. While some of the new democracies have done well, a significant number of countries, particularly the low-income ones, have been hobbled by state as well as economic breakdowns. Marked by the deterioration of basic education and health services, some of these countries have become breeding grounds for terrorists.[67] Both in terms of world historical comparisons and against the background of Maoist rule, China has accomplished much in economic transformation and institutional development since the late 1970s.

There is much in the English-language press about how the Chinese leadership might misuse China's growing might and political machinery for sinister purposes. Some scholars and commentators as well as dissidents such as Harry Wu liken today's China to Hitler's Germany and Mussolini's Italy.[68] Such comparisons should not be simply dismissed out of hand, but there is little doubt they are more apt for Mao's China than for the China of the reform era. Whereas the rise of Hitler was associated with the diminution of individual freedom and growing state dominance, not to mention ethnic extermination, in post-Mao China we have seen a declining role of the state in the economy and society, expanding freedom for people to change jobs, move around, choose their lifestyles and even gender (there has been a growing number of sex-change operations in China), healthy if still preliminary moves toward legal rule, and increasing (albeit still severely limited) room for popular political participation.[69] In this broader context, the institutional changes described and analyzed in this volume are part of an encouraging trend to improve government transparency and efficiency and curb bureaucratic arbitrariness.

Ideally the further improvement of governance calls for the promotion of democratic accountability throughout the Chinese political system. This is not the place to adequately discuss the prospects for China's democratization, yet it is nonetheless clear that the Communist Party leadership has promoted the governance reforms in order to keep its monopoly on political power.[70] And in the short to intermediate term it may very well succeed in doing so.[71] However, if and when China does become more democratic—whatever the combination of contingent and structural factors involved—there is little doubt that such a democratic polity will need not just competitive elections but also effective institutions for implementing the policies made by democratic institutions, monitoring the effectiveness of such policies, and timely correction and redress of errors and abuses in policy implementation. In this sense, the governance reforms being undertaken to improve the efficiency, transparency, and accountability of the administrative state will prove indispensable for the fledging democratic polity if and when elite politics does make the democratic turn. As Samuel Huntington famously noted several decades ago, "Organization is the road to political power, but it is also the foundation of political stability and thus the precondition of political liberty."[72] The reconstitution of the Chinese state thus has fundamental implications for the expansion of liberty and democracy.

APPENDIX:
THE COMPOSITION OF THE STATE COUNCIL

1992	*2003*
1. Commissions and Ministries [1]	
Foreign Affairs	Foreign Affairs
National Defense	National Defense
State Planning Commission	State Development and Reform Commission
State Economic System Reform Commission	
State Education Commission	Education
State Science and Technology Commission	Science and Technology
Commission of Science, Technology, and Industry for National Defense	Commission of Science, Technology, and Industry for National Defense
State Ethnic Affairs Commission	State Ethnic Affairs Commission
Public Security	Public Security
State Security	State Security
Supervision	Supervision
Civil Affairs	Civil Affairs
Justice	Justice
Finance	Finance
Personnel	Personnel
Labor	Labor and Social Security
Geological and Mineral Resources	Land and Resources
Construction	Construction
Energy	

1992	2003

1. Commissions and Ministries (cont.)

1992	2003
Machinery and Electronics Industry	
Aviation and Aerospace Industry	
Metallurgical Industry	
Chemical Industry	
Light Industry	
Textile Industry	
Railways	Railways
Communications (Transportation)	Communications (Transportation)
Post and Telecommunications	Information Industry
Water Resources	Water Resources
Agriculture	Agriculture
Forestry	(see under 2)
Commerce (Domestic)	
Foreign Trade	Commerce
Materials Supply	
Culture	Culture
Radio, Film and Television	(see under 2)
Health	Health
State Sports Commission	(see under 2)
State Family Planning Commission	State Population and Family Planning Commission
People's Bank of China	People's Bank of China
National Audit Office (Administration)	National Audit Office (Administration)

2. Administrative Agencies Directly under the State Council (Zhishu Jigou)

1992	2003
State Statistics Bureau	State Statistics Bureau (also trans. as National Bureau of Statistics)
State Price Bureau	
State Administration of Technical Supervision	State General Administration of Quality Supervision, Inspection and Quarantine
State Administration of Industry and Commerce	State General Administration of Industry and Commerce
State Administration of Environmental Protection	State General Administration of Environmental Protection
State Land Administration	

1992	*2003*

2. Administrative Agencies Directly under the State Council (Zhishu Jigou) (cont.)

1992	2003
State Administration of Press and Publications	State General Administration of Press and Publications[2]
General Administration of Customs	General Administration of Customs
State Tourism Administration	State Tourism Administration
Civil Aviation Administration of China	General Administration of Civil Aviation of China
State Bureau of Construction Materials Industry	
State Drug Administration	State Food and Drug Administration
State Oceanography Bureau	
State Meteorological Bureau	(see under 4)
State Seismological Bureau	(see under 4)
State Council Religious Affairs Administration	State Administration of Religious Affairs
State Archives Bureau[3]	
State Council Counselors' Office	State Council Counselors' Office
State Council Administration of Government Offices	State Council Administration of Government Offices
	State General Administration of Taxation[4]
	State General Administration of Radio, Film and Television
	State General Administration of Sports
	State Forestry Administration
	State Intellectual Property Office
	State Administration of Workplace Safety Supervision
	State Council State-Owned Assets Supervision and Administration Commission
	State Electricity Regulatory Commission

3. Administrative Offices Directly under the State Council (Banshi jigou)

1992	2003
Legal Affairs Bureau	Legal (Legislative) Affairs Office
Foreign Affairs Office	
Overseas Chinese Affairs Office	Overseas Chinese Affairs Office
Hong Kong and Macau Affairs Office	Hong Kong and Macau Affairs Office
	Taiwan Affairs Office

1992	*2003*

*3. Administrative Offices Directly under the State Council (*Banshi jigou*) (cont.)*

Special Zones Office	
Research Office	Research Office
Press (Information) Office	Press Office
Production Office[5]	

4. State Council Shiye *Institutions*

Xinhua News Agency	Xinhua News Agency
Chinese Academy of Sciences	Chinese Academy of Sciences
Chinese Academy of Social Sciences	Chinese Academy of Social Sciences
	Chinese Academy of Engineering
State Council Development Research Center	State Council Development Research Center
	State Administration College
	China Seismological Bureau
	China Meteorological Bureau
	China Securities Regulatory Commission
	China Insurance Regulatory Commission
	China Banking Regulatory Commission

SOURCES: Xinhua News Agency 1992, *Zhongguo zhengfu jigou minglu* (Directory of Chinese government organs [Beijing: Xinhua chubanshe, 1992]); XWZK 2003 special supplement.

1. Unless otherwise noted, the units under this heading are ministries. The appointments of the ministers, the governor of the People's Bank of China, and the auditor general are subject to ratification by the National People's Congress.

2. Also doubles as the State Copyright Administration.

3. The State Archives Bureau also doubles as the Central Archives Bureau and as of 2003 appears as part of the organizational setup of the CCP Central Committee.

4. Previously subordinated to the Ministry of Finance.

5. The State Council Production Office was succeeded in 1993 by the powerful State Economic and Trade Commission. The SETC disappeared in 2003, and a major part of it became the State-Owned Assets Supervision and Administration Commission (see under 2).

ABBREVIATIONS USED IN NOTES AND BIBLIOGRAPHY

AFP	Agence France Presse
AP	Associated Press
AWSJ	*Asian Wall Street Journal*
AWSJW	*Asian Wall Street Journal Weekly*
BJCB	*Beijing chenbao* (Beijing morning post)
BJYLXB	*Beijing yule xinbao* (Beijing star daily)
BKWZ	*Baokan wenzhai* (Press digest)
BQB	*Beijing qingnian bao* (Beijing youth daily)
BWB	*Beijing wanbao* (Beijing evening news)
CCTV	China Central Television
CD	*China Daily*
CDBW	*China Daily Business Weekly*
CDSB	*Chengdu shangbao* (Chengdu commercial news)
CET	*Zhongguo jingji shibao* (China economic times)
CJRB	*Changjiang ribao* (Yangtze River daily)
CJSB	*Caijing shibao* (China business post)
CJZK	*Zhengquan shibao: caijing zhoukan* (Securities times: finance and economics weekly)
CNR	China National Radio
CNS	*China News Service* (Hong Kong)
CYD	*Zhongguo qingnian bao* (China youth daily)
DJN	Dow Jones Newswire
FBIS	Foreign Broadcast Information Service. Daily Report: China.
FEER	*Far Eastern Economic Review*
FJRB	*Fujian ribao* (Fujian daily)
FT	*Financial Times* (London)
FZRB	*Fazhi ribao* (Legal daily)

GJJRB   Guoji jinrong bao (International financial news)
GMRB   *Guangming ribao* (Illumination daily)
GRRB   *Gongren ribao* (Workers' daily)
GZRB   *Guangzhou ribao* (Guangzhou daily)
HKS   *Hong Kong Standard*
HQBD   *21 shiji huanqiu baodao* (21st-century global report)
HSB   *Huasheng bao*
HXDSB   *Huaxi dushibao* (Western China metropolitan daily)
IHT   *International Herald Tribune*
JCRB   *Jiancha ribao* (Procuratorial daily)
JFJB   *Jiefangjun bao* (PLA daily)
JFRB   *Jiefang ribao* (Liberation daily)
JHCB   *Jianghuai chenbao* (Anhui morning post)
JHSB   *Jinghua shibao* (Beijing times)
JJBD   *21 shiji jingji baodao* (21st-century business herald)
JJCKB   *Jingji cankao bao* (Economic reference)
JJGCB   *Jingji guancha bao* (Economic Observer)
JJRB   *Jingji ribao* (Economic daily)
JJYJ   *Jingji yanjiu* (Economic research)
JNSB   *Jiangnan shibao* (Southern China times)
KJRB   *Keji ribao* (Science and technology daily)
LSWB   *Liaoshen wanbao* (Liaoning Shenyang evening post)
LW   *Liaowang* (Outlook)
MRXB   *Meiri xinbao* (Daily news herald)
NFC   *Nanfeng chuang* (Southern window)
NFDSB   *Nanfang dushi bao* (Southern metropolitan daily)
NFRB   *Nanfang ribao* (Southern daily)
NFZM   *Nanfang zhoumo* (Southern weekend)
NYT   *New York Times*
QB   *Qiao bao* (China press), New York
QDRB   *Qingdao ribao* (Qingdao daily)
RMFYB   *Renmin fayuan bao* (People's court daily)
RMRB   *Renmin ribao* (People's daily)
RMRBE   *Renmin ribao: huadong xinwen* (People's daily: East China news)
RMRBO   *Renmin ribao* (People's daily), overseas edition
RMRBS   *Renmin ribao: huanan xinwen* (People's daily: South China news)

SCB	*Shichang bao* (Market news)
SCMP	*South China Morning Post*
SCRB	*Sichuan ribao* (Sichuan daily)
SDC	*Shidaichao* (Tide of the times)
SHSB	*Shenghuo shibao* (Life times)
SHZQB	*Shanghai zhengquan bao* (Shanghai securities daily)
SLSH	*Sanlian shenghuo zhoukan* (Sanlian life weekly)
SQB	*Shanghai qingnian bao* (Shanghai youth news)
SZRB	*Suzhou ribao* (Suzhou daily)
SZSB	*Shenzhen shangbao* (Shenzhen business)
TJRB	*Tianjin ribao* (Tianjin daily)
TKP	*Ta Kung Pao*, Hong Kong
UPI	United Press International
WHB	*Wenhui bao* (Gazette)
WSJ	*Wall Street Journal*, print and electronic
XDRB	*Xingdao ribao* (Sing Tao Jih Pao)
XDT	*Xinhua meiri dianxun* (Xinhua daily telegraph)
XHRB	*Xinhua ribao* (Xinhua daily)
XKB	*Xinkuaibao* (New and fast [news] herald)
XMWB	*Xinmin wanbao* (Xinmin evening news)
XWCB	*Xinwen chenbao* (News morning herald)
XWZK	*Xinwen zhoukan* (News weekly)
YCWB	*Yangcheng wanbao* (Guangzhou evening post)
YGXXRB	*Yuegang xinxi ribao* (Guangdong and Hong Kong information daily)
YZWB	*Yangzi wanbao* (Yangtze evening post)
ZGB	*Zhongguo gaige bao* (China reform news)
ZGFZB	*Zhongguo fangzhi bao* (China textile news)
ZGGSSB	*Zhongguo gongshang shibao* (China business times)
ZGJJNJ	*Zhongguo jingji nianjian* (China economic yearbook)
ZGJYB	*Zhongguo jingying bao* (China business)
ZGQCB	*Zhongguo qiche bao* (China automotive news)
ZGQGNJ	*Zhongguo qiche gongye nianjian* (China automotive industry yearbook)
ZGSB	*Zhongguo shangbao* (China business daily)
ZGSJNJ	*Zhongguo shenji nianjian* (China auditing yearbook)
ZGTJNJ	*Zhongguo tongji nianjian* (China statistical yearbook)
ZGTJZY	*Zhongguo tongji zhaiyao* (China statistical abstract)

ZHGSSB   *Zhonghua gongshang shibao* (Chinese business times)
ZQB   *Zhengquan bao* (Securities)
ZQSB   *Zhengquan shibao* (Securities times)
ZSB   *Zhongguo shuiwu bao* (China taxation news)
ZTS   *Zhongguo tongxun she* (China reporting agency)
ZXS   *Zhongguo xinwen she* (China news service)
ZZB   *Zhongguo zhengquan bao* (China securities daily)

A Note About Dates

For convenience, dates in the endnotes are written year first, month second, and day last, such as 2000–01–01. In doing so, I follow ISO 8601, which was adopted by the International Organization for Standardization in 1988.

NOTES

CHAPTER I

1. See, e.g., North 1990.

2. Holmes 1997; Linz and Stepan 1996: 11; and Suleiman 1999. In Latin America, however, competence in state bureaucracies has tended not to survive the transition to democracy well (Geddes 1994: 194).

3. Schumpeter 1975: 206.

4. For the concept of governance, see Pierre 2000. The OECD offers the following principles of good governance: "respect for the rule of law; openness, transparency and accountability to democratic institutions; fairness and equity in dealings with citizens, including mechanisms for consultation and participation; efficient, effective services; clear, transparent, and applicable laws and regulations; consistency and coherence in policy formation; and high standards of ethical behavior." (http://www.oecd.org/EN/about/0,,EN-about-11–nodirectorate-no-no-no-11,00.html).

5. My study of policy making has benefited much from Kingdon 1984.

6. Colina MacDougall, "After the Crackdown the Outlook Is Far From Bright," FT 1989–06–14.

7. Fox Butterfield, "Deng Reappears With a Chilling Lesson about Power in China," NYT 1989–06–11.

8. See, for example, Jenner 1992 and Fu 1994.

9. Ling Zhijun 1998: 35–36; 42–43.

10. Ling Zhijun 1998: 43; 55–56. It is likely that Ling touched up his diary and moderated his views for publication. For English account of this period, see Fewsmith 2001, chapter 1.

11. Zhonggong Zhongyang Wenxian Yanjiushi 1998: 420.

12. On September 4, 1989, Deng reminded Jiang and others of the rotation of military commanders in the 1970s (Deng Xiaoping 1993: 319).

13. In 1999 the central leadership formalized the cadre exchange system with "Provisional Regulations on Exchanging Leading Party and Government Cadres."

14. For a further elaboration of these issues, see Bo 2004.

15. WHB 1999–06–14.

16. Quade 2000: 12. In this volume, I use the term "province" or "provincial unit" generically to denote units of territorial administration ranked at the provincial level, commonly known as "provinces, autonomous regions, and centrally administrated cities."

17. Cheng Li 2004.

18. For analysis of the tendency toward localism in elite formation, see Li and Bachman 1989. For a contrary view, see Huang 1996a.

19. The other members are the Minister of Public Security, the Supreme People's Court president, and the chief prosecutor as well as representatives of the Labor Union, the Education Ministry, the People's Bank of China, and the Ministry of Health.

20. Willy Wo-lap Lam, "Jiang Unveils 'Two-fisted' Graft Policy," SCMP 1999–01–07.

21. Wu Guoguang 1997. Wu was a member of Zhao's brain trust.

22. On the internal deliberations that led to the public commitment, see Zhang Liang 2001.

23. In Xinshiqi 1998: 747–761. For an evocative account of this period, see Ling Zhijun 2003.

24. On the interaction between Deng and other leaders, see Baum 1994: 350–352; on the ideological clashes, see Ma Licheng and Ling Zhijun 1998.

25. For a review of the theoretical-ideological debates in China, see Sun 1995.

26. Jiang Zemin 1992. On June 12, Jiang secured Deng's support for his platform. His party school speech was then circulated among central and provincial leaders. Soon the 30 provincial party committees indicated their support for the spirit of the speech. For an insider's account of the debate leading to the fourteenth Party Congress, see Gong Yuzhi 2002.

27. In contrast, the "market socialism" advocated in Eastern Europe was centered on a simulated market still controlled by planners (Kornai 1992).

28. The best English account of the reforms in the 1980s is Naughton 1995.

29. Jiang Zemin 1992. Various Chinese economists had promoted proposals for comprehensive market reforms. See, for example, Wu Jinglian and Liu Jirui 1991.

30. Fligstein 2001: 36.

31. Wiebe 1967. For somewhat different emphasis, see Sklar 1988.

32. Skowronek 1982: 4; see also Bensel 1990 and 2001.

33. See, e.g., Carpenter 2001.

34. Huntington 1968. In recent years there has been much attention to failed states by both policy makers and scholars.

35. For a recent review of the Maoist development strategy, See Lin, Cai, and Li 2001. Many scholars, including Barrington Moore (1967) and Alexander Gershenkron (1962), have noted that development in late-industrializing countries tended to be dominated by a strong state. For a refinement of this argument that notes the different forms of state intervention across time, including in England, see Amsden 2001.

36. On the domination of the Chinese state over society, see Oi 1989; Shue 1988.
37. World Bank 1997.
38. Naughton 1992: 271–275.
39. On bureaucratic decision making in China, see Liberthal and Oksenberg 1988.
40. Chen Ruisheng et al. 1992: 28.
41. CET 1997–10–28.
42. Blecher and Shue 1996; Duckett 1998; Gore 1999; Nan Lin 1995; Nee and Su 1996; Oi 1992; for a review of East Asia, see Wade 1990.
43. Oi 1992, 1999; Pearson 1994; Unger and Chan 1995; Walder 1995; Wank 1995.
44. Che and Qian 1998. The problem was that the local state can be just as predatory, though the degree of local state predation seems to vary spatially.
45. D. Li 1996; see also Weitzman and Xu 1997.
46. It should be noted that some of the scholars cited above have also noted the various undesirable aspects of China's reforms.
47. World Bank 1990a.
48. Shirk 1993: 196.
49. Montinola, Qian, and Weingast 1995: 53.
50. Lyons 1987; Shen Liren and Dai Yuanchen 1990.
51. Wong 1992: 198.
52. Gore 1999: 279.
53. He Qianlian's representative work is *The Pitfalls of Modernization* (1998). He left China for the United States in 2001. Yang Fan, based in the Chinese Academy of Social Sciences, is a prolific writer for Chinese newspapers.
54. This argument is obviously similar to Hellman's next section, though the Chinese writers apparently came to it independently.
55. Zhong Guoxing 1998.
56. Lü 2000b: 289; see also Pei 1999.
57. See, e.g., Y. Sun 1999; quote is from p. 5. It should be noted that Sun did not justify corruption per se. See also Z. He 2000: 256–258.
58. Weber 1978.
59. Root 1996.
60. X. Lü 1999: 365. Elsewhere X. Lü (2000b) uses "booty socialism" to describe China.
61. Lü 2000a: 254; Shue 1988.
62. An enormous literature exists on the earlier reforms in the USSR and Eastern Europe; for a succinct review of the Soviet experience, see Schroeder 1990. It should be noted, however, that a number of these economies had gotten into better shape by the early 2000s.
63. Holmes 1997.
64. Aslund 2001.
65. Hellman 1998.
66. Goldstone 1995; Liu Binyan 1990. The introduction to Naughton and Yang 2004 offers a survey of literature on the disintegration/fragmentation thesis.

67. Wang Shaoguang and Hu Angang 1993.
68. Lau, Qian, and Roland 2000.
69. Polanyi 1957: 139.
70. For a review of the first decade of political reforms, see Goldman 1994.
71. For an overview of Jiang's rise, see Fewsmith 2001, chapter 6.
72. Over 1993–2003, I conducted field interviews in Beijing, Chongqing, Guangdong, Hainan, Jiangsu, Jiangxi, Shaanxi, Shandong, Shanghai, Tianjin, and Zhejiang. I have generally used the field interviews to verify and supplement information from published sources.
73. See, especially, Baum 1994.
74. See, Almond, Flangan, and Mundt, eds., 1973; Grew, ed., 1978.
75. Higgs 1987.
76. Collier and Collier 1991, Gourevitch 1989; Yang 1996a.
77. Simon 2000: 755.
78. It should be noted that limited government does not require full democracy. A major example is England in the seventeenth and eighteenth centuries. See North and Weingast 1989 and Weingast 1997b. For overview of the global public management reforms, see Kettl 2000.

CHAPTER 2

1. RMRBO 2002–06–20. Portions of this chapter are based on Yang 2001b (Routledge Publishers).
2. Oi 1992: 100.
3. Naughton 1992: 263–270.
4. Reform 1984.
5. Wenxian Yanjiushi 1996: 125.
6. Interview with ministerial personnel 1994.
7. Lieberthal and Oksenberg 1988; Shirk 1993.
8. Cited in Wu Guoguang 1997: 72. For more examples, see He Guanghui 1996: 16–25.
9. CET 1997–10–28.
10. Yang 2001b.
11. See Yang 2001b for discussion of the local experiments in government reforms.
12. JJRB 1998–03–08.
13. BKWZ 2001–07–05.
14. LW 2000–07–24 provides details of government growth in Shishi. See also NFRB 2000–09–28.
15. For data on the declining share of prices set by the government for different types of goods, see Cao, Fan, and Woo 1997: 21, table 2.2.
16. ZGTJNJ 1996: 429.
17. Liu Shijin 1998.
18. Xinhua 2002–08–01.
19. CCTV 2001–02–03; JJRB 2000–12–15.

20. RMRB 2002–01–31.

21. The Chinese makes reference to *shiluo gan* or sense of loss. See, e.g., RMRB 1998–09–25.

22. Yang 2001b.

23. CET 1997–11–12; 1997–11–19.

24. RMRBO 1997–12–23.

25. RMRBO 1997–03–07: 3.

26. CD 1997–09–18.

27. CET 1998–2–18.

28. Silberman 1993.

29. Jiang Zemin 1997. In addition, Jiang announced that China would reduce the size of its armed forces by half a million, on top of a reduction of about a million in the 1980s. This was completed by early 2001 (XDT 2001–03–21). A further reduction of 200,000 was announced in 2003.

30. Song Defu 1999: 1708.

31. Unless otherwise noted, all substantive information in this section is based on "Further on Restructuring Plan," Xinhua 1998–03–06.

32. BQB 2001–04–17.

33. The exceptions were the State Administration of Coal Industry, which was converted into a newly established State Administration for Workplace Safety Supervision (Guojia Anquan Shengchan Ju) and the State Tobacco Monopoly (Guojia Yancao Zhuanmai Ju). Parts of the abolished industry administrations became industry associations. With the absorption of the industry administrations, the SETC's authorized staff size rose from 450 to 750.

34. Xinhua 2000–10–07.

35. See, e.g., Lieberthal and Lampton 1992.

36. Xinhua 1999–08–27.

37. The national headquarters officially merged in October 1998; local CIQ offices were merged in August 1999. CIQ has 500–600 labs nationwide. See also JJRB 1998–07–10.

38. ZXS 2000–01–12.

39. For complaints about overlapping charges and fees prior to the streamlining, see RMRB 1999–06–28: 9.

40. XDT 1998–08–02; QB 1999–08–11; CD 1999–08–17; BJCB 1999–08–17. CCTV-4 China Report, 1999–09–27.

41. ZGB 2001–07–16; Xinhua 2001–05–30; RMRBO 2002–06–15. Following the merger, CIQ's core functions at the border have not been affected.

42. QB 2000–10–23.

43. JJRB 2001–11–27.

44. The Ministry of Labor and Social Security has taken over functions previously dispersed in the Ministries of Personnel, Civil Affairs, Health, Labor, and the Reform Commission to oversee social security administration (pensions), unemployment insurance, medical insurance, and disability insurance (CET 1998–04–02).

45. Most of these universities have been transferred to the supervision of the Ministry of Education and to local governments.

46. "Further on Restructuring Plan," Xinhua 1998–03–06.

47. CET 1998–03–11.

48. Bian Hongwei, "Reform Doubters Out of Line," CD 1998–03–13.

49. NFRB 2000–07–07; Xinhua 2000–10–07. The NFRB report discusses the difficulties the graduate trainees faced in seeking new jobs following the completion of their retraining programs. See also the full-page coverage in QB 2000–07–16, p. B3.

50. SCMP 1998–08–05.

51. GZRB 1999–05–24.

52. There have been reports that some government staffers let go during the reorganization had been rehired, sometimes because they possessed key skills. But this phenomenon is of minor significance in relation to the overall trend.

53. Interview with Shaanxi vice governor Gong Deshun in CET 1998–03–11.

54. QB 1998–03–09.

55. SCMP 1998–08–05.

56. Xinhua 2000–10–07.

57. QB 2000–01–30.

58. ZGB 1998–03–12.

59. LW no. 29 (1999); GZRB 1999–07–20.

60. CET 1999–05–18.

61. ZGB 2000–01–05.

62. Tian Sui, "Local Officials Resist Streamlining," *Zhengming* (Contention), no. 261 (July 1, 1999): 16–17.

63. As an exception, the provinces of Henan, Shanxi, and Liaoning were each allowed to temporarily retain one industrial bureau.

64. RMRBO 2000–10–04. The authorized staff size for party organizations was trimmed by an average of 20 percent (BKWZ 2001–02–15).

65. NFRB 2000–01–18; YCWB 2000–01–17.

66. TKP 1999–03–07; FBIS-CHI-1999–03–10.

67. CET 2000–01–06. However, a Xinhua report (2000–03–24) suggests that the staff reduction in Hainan was only 16 percent because the Hainan government, based on the "small government, big society" model, was smaller than others.

68. ZXS 2000–04–20.

69. In 2003, the Sichuan provincial leadership decided to prohibit civil servants from engaging in business (HXDSB 2003–07–17).

70. CET 1998–06–17; NFRB 2000–07–27.

71. ZGTJNJ various years.

72. ZGB 2000–09–28.

73. RMRBE 1998–10–30.

74. Xinhua 2001–09–09. For discussion of the political context, see Yang 2002b.

75. Xinhua 2001–02–16.
76. RMRBO 2002–06–20.
77. In Hubei, each town/township would have about 45,000 people, ranging between 35,000 (hilly areas) and more than 50,000 (plains). Each county/city would have 9–13 towns/townships (Xinhua 2001–02–15).
78. I discuss the interrelatedness of these reforms in Yang 2003. For more comprehensive analysis of the burdens on farmers, see Bernstein and Lü 2003.
79. Li Lanqing 2003.
80. RMRB 2001–04–01; 2002–03–29. Similar developments have also been reported in Jiangxi (Xinhua 2002–02–19).
81. Xia Changyong 2002. It should be noted that the fee for tax reforms has not always been stable. See, e.g., "Su Wan shuifei gaige hou nongmin fudan fantan" (Farmers' burdens rise again following the tax and fee reforms in Jiangsu and Anhui), Xinhua 2003–02–12.
82. ZGTJZY 2003: 112.
83. Needless to say, retiring government employees receive government pension payments. For a scholarly study of the *shiye danwei*, see Huang Hengxue 1998.
84. ZGB 1999–04–15.
85. It is valid to use "for life" here because government employees also receive pension payments.
86. RMRB 2000–09–03. The author, Chen Chijun, was a member of the Committee on Government Establishment (bianzhi wei) at Jiangxi's Xinyu.
87. MRXB 2002–08–07. Subtotals may not add up due to rounding.
88. The target year was 2000, but this has been postponed.
89. Xinhua 2003–08–22.
90. By November 2003, 673 newspapers and journals had been closed under this initiative (Xinhua 2003–11–23).
91. GMRB 2001–08–31; Xinhua 2001–01–12.
92. CD 1999–08–29; CET 2000–04–25; CYD 2000–05–27.
93. CD 2000–07–11.
94. RMRB 2000–09–22.
95. CD 1999–08–16.
96. KJRB 1999–11–29.
97. CET 2000–08–11.
98. Xinhua 2001–03–28.
99. CET 2000–02–19.
100. ZGB 1999–11–16; RMRB 2000–02–02.
101. "Guowuyuan Zhongyang Junwei: tuijin jundui houqin baozhang shehuihua" (State Council and Central Military Commission: promote the socialization of military rear services provision), Xinhua 2002–09–29.
102. Researchers at the State Council Development Research Center argued in 2001 that the reforms undermined agricultural technology services and certain basic research facilities in which the government should be involved.

103. Xinhua 2000–08–18.

104. CDSB 2002–07–10; Xia Changyong 2002.

105. See, e.g., the report on Jiangsu in RMRB 2001–05–14.

106. The salary increases were real because of the absence of inflation.

107. Sun Yafei 2002.

108. Sun Yafei 2002; personal interviews.

109. CET 2000–10–21; RMRB 2000–07–09; XDT 2000–01–11; Xinhua 2001–12–09.

110. RMRBO 2001–08–30.

111. RMRB 2002–04–18.

112. For the guidelines, see RMRB 2001–08–06.

113. Lieberthal and Oksenberg 1988; Shirk 1993.

114. Interviews.

115. CYD 2000–08–28.

116. CD 1998–03–09.

117. Quoted in CET 2000–01–11.

118. For an excellent example of such solicitation becoming a burden on private firms in Sichuan, see XDT 2000–04–24.

119. Wang Lingling 1998.

120. Hua Zhongwei, "Guanban hangye xiehui jiasu zhuanxing" (Government-affiliated industry associations accelerate their transformation), CET 2003–05–12.

121. DJN 1998–09–09.

122. J. Fu 1999.

123. Even though the actual level of government subsidies to agriculture is low and for several decades planners had siphoned money from the rural sectors to support industrialization, Chinese leaders wanted it to be known that they were fighting for the interests of farmers. Such a stand also meant that, as the Chinese side gave in somewhat on agriculture, it didn't have to give as many concessions in the service sectors.

124. ZGSB 2000–12–01.

125. As of the end of 2001, the central government had set up supervisory boards in 174 major SOEs the central government owned or controlled (RMRB 2002–02–02).

126. Since the political leadership retains the right to appoint management, the degree of managerial autonomy is debatable.

127. JJRB 2000–08–01.

128. The vice president of a major state bank emphatically told me in fall 2001 that, in the view of management, political control had become stronger in recent years.

129. JJRB 2000–08–01. The difference between the two is not entirely clear; both are holding operations.

130. GZRB 1999–07–08.

131. For example, the State Asset Management Committee of Fujian province planned to put under fiduciary management 80 percent of the assets in major

provincially controlled state firms by 2003. By the end of 2001, 16 firms, accounting for 30 percent of the state assets, had been put under fiduciary management (RMRBO 2001–11–26).

132. For official explanation of the rationale behind the 2003 plan, see Wang Zhongyu 2003.

133. ZGGSSB 2003–03–07.

134. The Reform Office's six bureaus became two of the 26 SRDC bureaus in spring 2003 (Bureau of Comprehensive Reforms and the Bureau of Employment and Social Distriubtion).

135. "Government to Cut Trade Sector Red Tape to Benefit All Markets," CD 2003–03–07.

136. ZQB 2003–03–07.

137. CET 1997–11–19.

138. Yang 2001b.

CHAPTER 3

1. Huang 1996b; Yang 1994, 1999.

2. See, e.g., Cheng Li 2001.

3. See, e.g., Gao Xin 1999; SCMP 1998–12–30; *Zhengming* (Contention) 1999–04–01. Following the restoration of financial order, Wang Qishan was recalled to the center to head the Reform Office at the end of 2000. He became acting mayor of Beijing in 2003 after a short stint in Hainan.

4. Chang 1999.

5. Portions of this and the next section draw on Yang 1994 and Yang 1999.

6. Yuan Shang and Han Zhu 1992.

7. ZGTJZY 1999: 42.

8. DJN 1993–07–20.

9. LW 1993–07–12: 4–5.

10. Chinese studies of the soft landing include Fu Wei 1998 and China Reform Foundation 1998. The former is the basis for a popular CCTV series.

11. CD 1993–07–01; RMRB 1993–07–01.

12. CD 1993–07–19; CDBW 1993–06–21; NYT 1993–07–23. The bond purchase turned out to be highly profitable as the inflation rate dropped subsequently.

13. CD 1993–06–23.

14. Huang 1996b; Wong 1991.

15. Deng turned 89 in August 1993.

16. Interestingly, most former Soviet states also suffered a revenue decline of 10 percent of GDP, albeit over a much shorter time period (1991–1993). Because output also declined in these countries, the amount of revenue also declined. In contrast, the tax ratio in China declined more gradually, and the amount of revenue continued to increase.

17. Yang 1990.

18. Quote from Goode 1990: 121. See Bahl 1999, esp. chapters 2–3, for a summary discussion of the issues.

19. Yang 1994: 76–78; Yang 1999.

20. Delfs 1991: 21–22.

21. Lu Dongtao and Xu Yan 1993: 250–287; Yang 1994: 79.

22. Chen Yuan 1991: 18.

23. A widely reported study at this time was Wang Shaoguang and Hu Angang 1993.

24. CCTV interview with Liu. Transcript appears as Fu Wei 1998.

25. Yang 1994: 85–87.

26. According to the plenum decision (Art. 18) and the Ministry of Finance, the major taxes and responsibilities are allocated as follows. The central government is responsible for funding national defense, diplomacy, armed police, key state projects, the national deficit, and governmental administrative departments, while other expenditures are the responsibility of local governments. Central government revenue comes from tariffs, a consumption tax collected by customs, value-added taxes, and (nationally based) business taxes. Taxes collected by local governments include business tax, income tax of local enterprises, and a personal income tax. Taxes shared by both central and local governments include the value-added tax, securities trading tax, and natural resources tax (TBA).

27. Xiang Huaicheng 1997; Chung 1995; Yang 1994.

28. For a discussion of implementation problems, see Sun Wenxue and Wang Yuwu 1994.

29. These figures are derived from data from the State Statistics Bureau. The revenue figures exclude debts.

30. A major exception was Shanghai, which still had a combined central and local tax administration as of 2002.

31. "Separation of State, Local Tax Systems Nearly Complete," Xinhua 1994–08–15; FBIS-CHI-94–160.

32. XDT 1999–07–22.

33. RMRB 1999–10–25.

34. Shandong interview, 2000–06–26.

35. CJSB 2003–01–06.

36. Jin Man, "Tax Bureaux Roles Defined," CDBW 1994–09–18.

37. GJJRB 2003–06–05.

38. WHB 2000–11–20. For a case of how police officials have abused their control over the tax police, see Dong Yanli, "Shanxi yishi gong'an ju juzhang cehua 'meiren ji' xianhai fu juzhang" (The police chief of a Shanxi city set up a "beauty trap" to frame his deputy), SDC no. 6 (2002).

39. For the impact in Guangdong, see XKB 2003–01–09.

40. Much of the information in this and the next paragraph is based on Hu Haiyan 2002.

41. YGXXRB 2003–01–15.

42. Ter-Minassian and Craig 1997.
43. Xiang Huaicheng 1997.
44. CD 1999–07–19.
45. ZQSB 2000–01–21. Nonetheless, it should be noted that some local authorities, under intense pressure to attract overseas investment, have failed to fully comply with the policy on tax rebates. See, for example, the Xinhua short commentary "Unauthorized Tax Break Policies Are Prohibited," Xinhua 2002–01–31, FBIS-CHI-2002–01–31.
46. Hainan was the last to phase out this policy, in 2003. Shenzhen began to collect the value-added tax in 2002. Products from new firms are subject to 100 percent of the value-added tax while products for older firms are liable to pay only 50 percent of the value-added tax (CJSB 2003–01–06).
47. GJJRB 2002–12–16.
48. Yingyi Qian and Barry Weingast have argued in a number of articles that China has a sort of market-preserving federalism. See, e.g., Montinola, Qian, and Weingast 1995.
49. "Personal Income Tax Grows Fast in China," Xinhua 2002–08–22.
50. However, the central government has retained the right to the corporate income taxes from the railways, the postal service, the big four state-owned commercial banks, the three policy banks, and the China National Offshore Oil Corp. (CNOOC).
51. "PRC Officials on Income Tax Revenue Sharing Scheme Aimed at Common Prosperity," Xinhua 2002–03–12.
52. Lardy 1998: 90–91.
53. World Bank 1990b: xiv.
54. AWSJW 1993–05–31; DJN 1993–06–30; interviews.
55. Lardy 1998.
56. Alesina and Summers 1993.
57. Holz 1992: 31; World Bank 1990c: 3.
58. World Bank 1990c: 5.
59. CD 1998–12–22.
60. Karby Leggett, "China Central Bank Details Reorganization to Bolster Oversight," DJN 1998–11–16.
61. For information about the evolution of the People's Bank of China up to 1992, see Holz 1992.
62. This was further reiterated in the State Council's decision on the reform of the financial system issued in December 1993. The idea of super-regional branches was also mooted in the bank earlier (World Bank 1990c: 5).
63. For background on the drafting of the banking laws, see RMRBO 1993–12–08.
64. A number of Chinese scholars in Beijing think tanks suggested such a possibility in interviews I conducted over 1996–1998.
65. Interview with Dai Xianglong in ZGB 1998–11–18.

66. James Areddy, "China Central Bank Lifts Rates Ahead of Bond Sale," DJN 2003–02–11.

67. For the most vocal prediction of China's collapse, see Chang 2001.

68. Jiang Yong 2002. This was the fifth wave of consolidation of the trust and investment companies. The number of itcs surpassed 1,000 in 1988.

69. My focus here is on the big four state commercial banks, which in 2001 accounted for 84 percent of all bank deposits and the bulk of the bad loans. Phelim Kyne, "Small Chinese Banks May Thrive When China Allows Foreign Rivals," DJN 2002–03–04.

70. SLSH 2002–02–01.

71. Wang Zhi 2002.

72. "Agricultural Bank of China Streamlines Banking System," *Asia Pulse* 2003–01–24.

73. For strong arguments to this effect, see, among others, Clifford 2002.

74. CET 2001–11–02; Pottinger and Wonacott 2002. The second-tier banks have enjoyed healthier balance sheets.

75. Wang Yanjuan 2003.

76. In 2001, the central government decided to lower the business tax rate (*yingye shui*) levied on financial and insurance firms by one percentage point per year from 2002 through 2004 to 5 percent. This reduction is worth an estimated 6 billion yuan per year in additional profits to the banks and insurance firms (ZXS 2003–01–30).

77. PBOC figures as reported by DJN 2002–02–08.

78. People's Bank of China 2003; JJCKB 2003–01–22. According to the more rigorous five-category loan classification scheme, the amount of nonperforming loans was cut by 78.2 billion yuan, and the NPL ratio dropped by 4.92 percentage points but still stood at 26.1 percent at the end of 2002 (People's Bank of China 2003).

79. Data from www.cbrc.gov.cn. Accessed on February 10, 2004.

80. PBOC research reports accessed at www.pbc.gov.cn.

81. For evidence of such optimism, see "China Has Basically Set Up a Banking Supervisory System Conforming to the Basle Core Principles," Xinhua 1999–06–03, FBIS-CHI-1999–06–11; Karby Leggett and Peter Wonacott, "Government's Role in Bank System Is a Vote of Confidence for China," WSJ 2000–09–26. For an earlier and more pessimistic view, see Lardy 1998.

82. Li Junling 2002.

83. DJN 2001–12–24.

84. Xinhua 2002–01–08.

85. CJSB 2003–01–06.

86. "Chinese Central Bank Raps 114 Loan Managers for Malpractice," Reuters 2002–05–16.

87. CJSB 2002–12–13.

88. Replacing Dai is Zhou Xiaochuan, the hard-charging securities regulator and former PBOC vice governor.

89. See, e.g., JJGCB 2003–03–03: A2.

90. BQB 2003–05–09.

91. It helps that both the PBOC and the CBRC started with new chiefs who had previously served as PBOC deputy governors.

92. JJRB 2003–08–14.

93. CD 2004–02–12.

94. I only discuss regulation of the securities industry here. On the regulation of the insurance industry, see Thomas 2002. The China Insurance Regulatory Commission was also given ministerial rank in 2003.

95. I provide a fuller treatment of the topic in Dali Yang, "Governance and Regulation of China's Securities Markets," paper presented at the Conference on Financial Sector Reform in China, Kennedy School of Government, Harvard University, September 2001.

96. Wang Lianzhou and Li Cheng 2000: 91–92.

97. ZZB 1997–08–15.

98. Xinhua 2000–09–29; CJSB 2003–01–06.

99. Sun Jie, "An Important Milestone in the Construction of a Legal System for the Stock Market," Xinhua 1999–06–29; FBIS-CHI-1999–07–15.

100. In June 1999, regulators at the Shanghai Stock Exchange for the first time rebuked a listed company, Lingguang Industry Co., for failure to disclose important information to shareholders. Such public commendations have become fairly common since then.

101. For the views of Arthur Levitt, former chairman of the Securities and Exchange Commission, on the need for unified markets and regulation, see WSJ 1999–09–21; 1999–09–24.

102. Matt Pottinger, "China Is Ahead of Hong Kong in Drive to Clean Up Markets," AWSJ 2003–01–22; John Plender, "Capitalism, Higgs, and the China Syndrome," FT 2003–01–27.

103. Polanyi 1957.

104. The mission of the Customs Administration also includes antismuggling.

105. The State Administration of Industry and Commerce added a new bureau of consumer rights protection in 1998.

106. CD 1999–11–27.

107. QB 2000–07–03; Xinhua 2003–07–25.

108. RMRBO 1999–11–06.

109. JJRB 1999–08–11.

110. Wu Bangguo 1999.

111. Interview 1999–06–22.

112. ZXS 2000–01–18.

113. CD 1998–12–02.

114. Xinhua 2000–04–13; 2000–05–10.

115. Xinhua 1999–12–28.

116. "Central Organs Directly Supervise PRC Waters," ZTS 2000–01–05; FBIS-CHI-2000–01–05.

117. SAWS reported to the State Economic and Trade Commission at first but was upgraded to ministerial rank in 2003 and now reports directly to the State Council.

118. Xinhua 2000–01–10; 2000–03–08.

119. HSB 2000–01–14.

120. CD 1999–03–29.

121. Wu Bangguo 1999.

122. RMRB Commentator 1999.

123. Interview with SAEP official 1999–06–18.

124. YCWB 2000–02–24.

125. Ironically, as a consequence of the adoption of vertical administration, local administrators in the administrations are more attentive to directives from their bureaucratic superiors in the provincial administration but have become less receptive to supervision by local people's congresses (RMRB 2000–08–02).

126. BQB 2000–07–10; see NFZM 2000–07–20 for criticisms of the amended law by Wang Hai, China's controversial consumer advocate.

127. RMRB 2002–12–08; RMRBO 2003–01–24.

128. ZGJYB 2003–08–18.

129. CD 1999–07–03.

130. The guiding document for this national drive was the State Council's Decision on Rectifying and Standardizing Market Economic Order (April 27, 2001; published in RMRB 2001–05–09).

131. "China to Continue to Improve Market, Economic Order," Xinhua 2002–01–24.

132. RMRBO 2002–08–10. Following this announcement, various provincial authorities quickly introduced regulations on product recalls.

133. "Over 10,000 Small Coal Mines Closed in 2001," China Economic Information Network (www.cei.gov.cn) 2002–03–08.

134. Full text of the regulations is in RMRB 2001–04–20.

135. ZXS 2001–10–26.

136. "China Shutters 3,300 Cybercafes," InternetNews.com 2002–12–27.

137. RMRBO 2002–06–28.

138. CD 2003–01–30.

139. For Microsoft's travails in China, see Robyn Meredith, "Long March: Bill Gates' China Conundrum, Big Market, Big Piracy Problems," *Forbes* 2003–02–17. However, Microsoft appeared to have finally turned the corner in China's notorious software market in 2002. All the major Chinese computer makers entered into licensing agreements to preinstall and prepay Microsoft's operating system. The Chinese government also began to earmark funds for purchasing software for office computers (see, e.g., BJWB 2003–01–12). According to a Microsoft executive, "China is really improving the environment across the board for software makers" (Quoted in Kahn 2003).

140. According to a survey released in July 2003 by the Quality Brands Protec-

tion Committee under the China Association of Enterprises with Foreign Investment (CAEFI), more than half of the 213 firms surveyed said the counterfeiting problem had improved since 2001 ("China Steps Up Fight Against Counterfeiting," Xinhua 2003–11–12). For the difficulties Procter & Gamble encountered in fighting counterfeits, see RMRB 2001–05–14, p. 12.

141. "Li Lanqing Addresses Meeting on Rectifying Market Economic Order," Xinhua 2002–06–24.

142. Oi 1992, 1999; Qian and Xu 1993.

143. Gray 1998: 28.

144. Shirk 1993.

145. Quoted in Hennessy 1989: 628.

146. Ye Xiaoping 2000.

CHAPTER 4

1. Chuan Chieh 1998.

2. Zhu Rongji 1998. Zhu's figure was likely for 1997, and it was also probably underestimated. Based on Hong Kong's trade deficit data and their relationship to errors and omissions in China's balance of payments data, an economist with Morgan Stanley Asia estimated that the value of goods smuggled into China was more than 1.5 percent of China's GDP in 1997, or about 112 billion yuan (Andy Xie, "How Good China's Data?" *Asiaweek* 1999–05–28).

3. SCMP 1999–05–24.

4. QB 2000–01–30.

5. Ming Pao 1999–03–08; the figure for Zhanjiang is from QB 1999–03–20.

6. The decentralization of authority gives unit leaders more resources to distribute among employers. This increased the material dependency of employees on the performance of the units, making employees less likely to blow the whistle (Gong Ting 1994: 125).

7. Zhao Zhiwen and Wang Hua 1998.

8. SCMP 1999–09–28.

9. Interviews; CCTV-4 1998–09–21.

10. Xinhua 2001–02–28; 2001–10–22.

11. AFP 1998–12–09.

12. QB 1999–03–20; SCMP 1999–05–25.

13. For an indication of corruption in and around the Customs Administration, see RMRB 1998–10–12. State Councilor Wu Yi refers to a host of problems with the Customs Administration in RMRB 1998–07–18.

14. CD 2000–11–25; XDRB 2002–01–06.

15. FJRB 1998–08–10.

16. Yeh Tan 1998a. In July 1998, the Chinese People's Armed Police Corps Court sentenced Chen to a suspended death sentence and Luo to ten years in jail.

17. *Dongfang ribao* (Oriental daily), as quoted in Chinesenewsnet.com 2000–01–23.

18. Zhao Zhiwen and Wang Hua 1998.
19. SCMP 1998–09–24.
20. Zhao Zhiwen and Wang Hua 1998.
21. Wen Siyong and Ren Zhichu 2002: 330.
22. Zhu Rongji 1998.
23. For an overview of vehicle smuggling, see Shou Peipei, Wang Hua, and Chi Liwei 1999.
24. AFP 1999–02–25.
25. For the case of Nanchang in Jiangxi, see NFZM 1999–02–26; for Qinzhou in Guangxi, see NFZM 1999–05–21; on Guangdong, see QB 1999–01–21. See also report on Jilin and Guangxi in SCMP 1999–02–06.
26. Yang 1999.
27. CDBW 1998–09–21; Zhao Zhiwen and Wang Hua 1998; SCMP 1998–06–29.
28. ZGTJZY 1998: 55.
29. JJRB 1996–05–17.
30. "Taxes Collection Slowing Down," CDBW 1998–06–21; DJN 1998–06–15.
31. For the rampancy of smuggling in Britain and the efforts by Prime Minister William Pitt to bring smuggling under control in the 1780s, see Johnson 1995: 248.
32. Zhao Zhiwen and Wang Hua 1998. Jiang's remarks were reported in "National Conference on Crackdown on Smuggling Opened in Beijing," Xinhua 1998–07–13.
33. See, for example, "Appeal for Intensified Action on Smugglers," SCMP 1998–12–01.
34. CD 1999–01–06. Similar remarks are also found in the speeches by Jiang Zemin and Zhu Rongji.
35. Quoted in Zhu Rongji 1998.
36. Gao Xin 1999: 193–94.
37. For discussion of the broader leadership commitment to the crackdown on smuggling, see Jen Hui-wen 1998; for a useful chronology, see Wang Hua and Zhuang Huining 1998.
38. Zhu Rongji 1998.
39. "National Conference on Crackdown on Smuggling Opened in Beijing," Xinhua 1998–07–13.
40. Cao Zhi, "Major PLA Units Vow to Cease Businesses," Xinhua 1998–08–03.
41. Kuan Chieh 1998.
42. "PLA Logistics Director Calls for Commercial Disengagement," Xinhua 1998–07–24.
43. Zhu Rongji 1998.
44. SCMP 1998–10–24.
45. RMRB 1999–03–14.
46. See, for example, "Smugglers Sentenced to Death, Executed," CD 1998–10–08.

47. CD 1999–06–08; FZRB 1999–09–08; *Dongfang ribao* (Oriental daily), as quoted in Chinesenewsnet.com 2000–01–23.

48. For a partial list, see QB 2001–02–23.

49. Xinhua 2002–12–03.

50. There is a vast amount of Chinese reporting on the Yuanhua case. For English reports, see Leggett 2001 and Beech 2002.

51. Xinhua 2000–11–08.

52. Xinhua 2001–02–28.

53. Xinhua 2001–10–22. Nonetheless, Jia Qinglin, who was from 1991–1996 governor and then party secretary of Fujian, did not suffer for the Yuanhua case despite widespread press speculation that his family was implicated. After Fujian, Jia was plucked by Jiang Zemin to take charge of Beijing and apparently enjoyed Jiang's protection. In November 2002 Jia was promoted to become a member of the Political Bureau Standing Committee.

54. XDRB 2002–01–06. Ji Shengde was sentenced to death with reprieve at the first trial, but the sentence was reduced to life imprisonment on appeal.

55. For a succinct summary of the measures taken, see Cong Yaping 1998.

56. SCMP 1998–12–10; Reuters 1998–11–27.

57. "Smuggling Problems Addressed at Beijing Meeting," Xinhua 1999–02–11.

58. CD 2000–02–01.

59. DJN 1999–08–26.

60. Xinhua 1998–09–20; CD 1999–01–27; "War on Smuggling Bails Out Oil Firms," CDBW 1998–09–21. For accounts of how each industrial sector benefited from the antismuggling campaign, see JJRB 1999–07–27.

61. According to the Customs Administration, China's tariff income for the first half of 1998 was 36.418 billion yuan. After the crackdown on smuggling was launched in July, the amount reached 33.327 billion yuan for the months of July rhrough October.

62. "Smuggling Problems Addressed at Beijing Meeting," Xinhua 1999–02–11; DJN 1999–12–15. The 87.9 billion yuan includes 2.6 billion in extra revenue.

63. BJWB 2000–01–10; QB 2001–02–27; Xinhua 2001–12–23.

64. See, for instance, the discussion in Wang Hua and Zhuang Huining 1998. One legal loophole is that there is little punishment for small amounts of smuggling.

65. QB 2000–01–12; see also Ostrov 2000 for an overview.

66. HSB 2000–03–16.

67. CD 1999–01–22. In mid-2002, the antismuggling police became a part of the regular police, under the dual command of the Public Security Bureau and the Customs Administration (Xinhua 2002–07–17).

68. CD 1999–01–06; 1999–04–26. The border patrol police were also given similar authority in 2000.

69. Ostrov 2000: 47.

70. Xinhua 2002–12–30.

71. Cong Yaping 1998.

72. SHSB 2002–03–22.

73. CYD 2001–05–10.

74. QB 2001–02–23; ZXS 2001–08–09.

75. Xinhua 2000–08–15.

76. ZXS 2000–04–20.

77. Xinhua 2002–12–24.

78. RMRB 2000–04–28; TKP 2000–08–22.

79. Xinhua 2000–08–03.

80. www.southcn.com 2000–12–03.

81. JJBD 2002–12–03.

82. See also Yang 2001a.

83. RMRB 2000–04–28; HKS 2000–05–25.

84. Zhu Rongji 1998.

85. Deng Xiaoping 1984: 270.

86. Official defense spending declined in real terms in the 1980s.

87. Deng Xiaoping 1993: 99. For studies of the conversion of China's military industry for civilian production, see Gurtov 1993; Gurtov and Hwang 1998.

88. Zhang sent a letter, dated March 14, 1985, to the Commission on National Defense Science and Industry. The letter warned that allowing the military to engage in business would inevitably lead to corruption and asked for the cancellation or divestiture of the business operations (QB 2000–08–31).

89. Cheung 1997.

90. Wang Mengkui 2000: 146; see also the data in Cheung 2001: 38.

91. SCMP 1998–12–16. For an overview of the holdings, see "PLA Businesses in all Segments of Economic Pie," HKS 1998–11–23; for more comprehensive treatment, see Cheung 2001 and Mulvenon 2001.

92. Cheung 2001: 171.

93. For a succinct overview of these misgivings, see Cheung 2001: 192–194.

94. Gurtov and Hwang 1998: 190–192.

95. Wang Mengkui 2000: 147.

96. Reuters 1998–10–08.

97. Quoted in SCMP 1993–02–03.

98. "PLA Compensated 1.3 Billion Yuan for Coal Mines," SCMP 1994–08–18.

99. For more extended treatment of the politics of this policy shift, see Cheung 2001: 50–58.

100. Wang Yang and Ma Chunlin, "Whole Army Auditing Supervision Scores Marked Results," JFJB 1995–12–16, FBIS-CHI-96–019.

101. JJRB 1996–08–28.

102. For a list of such enterprise groups, see Cheung 2001: 67.

103. Xue Cheng, "Separation of Army from Business Done," CD 1999–03–21. The quoted figure is most likely for 1998 and is thus likely inflated by the military to gain more compensation from the government.

104. RMRB 1998–09–11.

105. Gao Ying, "Project of Purification," *Renmin luntan* no. 2 (1999–04–15): 23–26; FBIS-CHI-1999–04–21.

106. Xinhua 1998–08–05.

107. Cao Zhi, "Major PLA Units Vow to Cease Businesses," Xinhua 1998–08–03.

108. Bickford 1995; Gurtov and Hwang 1998: 189–191; Joffe 1993.

109. Wang Ke 1998.

110. Wu Hengquan and Luo Yuwen, "Chairman Jiang Zemin Stresses at PLA Delegation Meeting," Xinhua 1998–03–10; FBIS-CHI-98–070.

111. For example, Poly Group, the PLA's main arms dealer with affiliation to the PLA's General Staff Department, was once under the management of He Ping, the son-in-law of paramount leader Deng Xiaoping, and Wang Jun, the son of late Chinese vice president Wang Zhen (AFP 1996–05–23; Lam 1995: 228).

112. JJRB 1998–08–05; ZGB 1998–02–25.

113. "Hu Jintao Speaks on Banning PLA Businesses," Xinhua 1998–07–28.

114. Jen Hui-wen, "New Policy Decision by Chinese Armed Forces to Oppose Corruption," *Hsin Pao* 1997–06–06; FBIS-CHI-97–118.

115. Jen Hui-wen, ibid.

116. Wu Hengquan and Luo Yuwen: "Chairman Jiang Zemin Stresses at PLA Delegation Meeting," Xinhua 1998–03–10.

117. "Military Firms Urged to Cut Ties with PLA," XDRB 1998–03–02; FBIS-CHI-98–06–1. The exceptions were production farms and other operations whose output was consumed within the military.

118. "Jilin Issues Circular on Army-Run Enterprises," *Jilin ribao* 1998–04–02, FBIS-CHI-98–112.

119. "Army Divestiture to Make Military More Professional," AFP 1998–12–16.

120. The downsizing was announced in fall 1997 at the fifteenth National Congress of the Chinese Communist Party.

121. "Jiang Zemin Criticizes Slow Progress in Army Reform," *Ming Pao* 1998–05–19; FBIS-CHI-98–140.

122. Quoted in Yang Yang, Fu Aiping, and Zhao Guilin 1999.

123. Zhu Rongji 1998.

124. John Pomfret, "Chinese Army out of Business?" *Washington Post*, 1998–11–23, A20. Besides foreign models, Jiang was also impressed with the Hong Kong garrison. During the Hong Kong handover, Jiang reportedly noted that the Hong Kong garrison did not engage in commercial activities and was very clean and competent. Jiang was thus interested in extending the SAR Garrison Law forbidding soldiers to do business to the entire military establishment (Lam 1998).

125. "Hu Jintao Speaks on Banning PLA Businesses," Xinhua 1998–07–28.

126. RMRB 1998–10–08.

127. "PLA Logistics Director Calls for Commercial Disengagement," Xinhua 1998–07–24.

128. "Hu Jintao Stresses Five Do's, Six No's," *Ming Pao* 1998–11–20; FBIS-CHI-98–324.

129. Kuang Tung-chou, "Premier Promises to Increase Military Funding to Make Up for 'Losses,'" XDRB 1998–07–24; FBIS-CHI-98–205.

130. Zhang Jing, "Jiang and Zhu Jointly Punish PLA and Police Businesses," in Xiao Chong 1999: 157. There was also compensation for the divestiture by the armed police and fire safety units.

131. QB 2001–02–11.

132. "Hu Jintao Speaks on Banning PLA Businesses," Xinhua 1998–07–28. Also see "Xinjiang Bans Judicial Organs, Police from Enterprises," *Xinjiang ribao* 1998–09–20; FBIS-CHI-98–275, 1998–10–02.

133. Quoted in Wang Hua and Zhuang Huining 1998.

134. "PLA Logistics Director Calls for Commercial Disengagement," Xinhua 1998–07–24.

135. "Law Enforcement Departments Close Commercial Operations," Xinhua 1998–12–08.

136. RMRB 1998–08–04.

137. This statement is based on a comprehensive survey of Chinese media reports.

138. Details on the working conference can be found in "Hu Jintao on PLA Involvement in Commerce," Xinhua 1998–10–07; Wang Xiaobing 2001.

139. "Hu Jintao Stresses Five Do's, Six No's," *Ming Pao* 1998–11–20, FBIS-CHI-98–324. Hu especially warned against 1. concealing, transferring, and selling enterprise assets; 2. the division of enterprise property; 3. fraud to change, transfer, or destroy accounts; 4. transfer and promotion of enterprise personnel during the liquidation period and overseas travel for personnel suspected of violating laws and discipline; and 5. interference with the implementation of the central decision.

140. "Military, Police Disengaged from Commercial Operations," Xinhua 1999–12–14.

141. "Political, Judicial Units Cut Business Ties," Xinhua 1998–12–31; Zheng Hongfan 1999.

142. Lung Hua, "Central Ban on PLA Businesses Enters Implementation Stage," *Hsin Pao* 1998–08–19; FBIS-CHI-98–231.

143. Wei Jianxing 1999.

144. "Hu Jintao on Transfer of Army Businesses," Xinhua 1999–04–26.

145. For a number of examples, see Matt Forney, "China's People's Liberation Army Leaves Rubble Behind in Business," WSJ 1999–05–21; Wang Xiaobing 2001.

146. In the case of service businesses operated by the relatives, especially spouses, of military personnel, those in urban areas were ordered divested while those in isolated locales with few other employment opportunities were retained (RMRB 1998–11–30).

147. "Military-run Enterprises to Be Taken Over," *Ming Pao* 1998–11–03, FBIS-CHI-98–308, 1998–11–04.

148. In summer 2000, the author stayed briefly at a hotel affiliated with a provincial supervision bureau.

149. Most of these firms were closed or merged, and only 900 remained as enterprises with independent accounting status.

150. Cited in Yang Yang, Fu Aiping, and Zhao Guilin 1999; Wang Xiaobing 2001.

151. Lawrence 2000.

152. SCMP 1999–03–26. It is not known whether compensation is involved.

153. Lawrence 2000 reported that 3,530 businesses had been turned over by early 2000. The difference between 3,530 and 2,937 equals 593.

154. "Zhu Rongji on Military-Run CDMA Cellular Telephones," Xinhua 2000–03–15.

155. Matt Forney, "China Orders Army to Transfer Mobile-Phone Network to Unicom," WSJ 2000–07–14; Matt Pottinger, "China Military to Give Up Mobile Business to Unicom," Reuters 2000–07–13.

156. Xinhua 2001–01–01.

157. RMRBO 2000–05–26.

158. Wang Xiaobing 2001; CNR 2001–10–11.

159. According to the finance minister's annual report to the NPC, the budgeted amount was 104.6 billion yuan for 1998, 166 billion for 2002, and 185.3 billion for 2003. In contrast, Lawrence 2000 cites an anonymous official source saying that the government in March 1999 paid the PLA a lump sum compensation of 10 billion yuan, only half of what the PLA had asked for.

160. "China Defends Military Spending," AP 2000–03–07.

161. Lawrence and Gilley 1999. Cf. Lawrence 2000, which presents a different picture.

162. Xinhua 1998–11–19. In March 2001, the Supreme People's Court (no. 8) issued a set of legal guidelines concerning the resolution of disputes related to divested AJPG businesses.

163. Quoted in Pomfret 1998.

164. JFJB 1999–04–21.

165. Cheung 2001: 150.

166. ZXS 1997–12–05. For an in-depth study of the Sanjiu Group, see Nolan and Wang 1998.

167. O'Neill 1999.

168. I came across several such cases during my fieldwork in China.

169. Lung Hua, "Decision to Ban Armed Forces from Doing Business Increases Pressure on Central Government," *Hsin Pao* 1998–07–29, FBIS-CHI-98–216, 1998–08–04.

170. Many AJPG businesses located in Guangdong to take advantage of the freewheeling business environment there. AJPG businesses registered in Hebei, which envelops Beijing, for geographical proximity and convenience.

171. Of these 420 enterprises, 368 were from the armed police, 22 from the military, and 30 from public security, procuratorial, and judicial organs. Payroll totaled 7,009. An earlier wire item (ZXS 1998–11–30) reported on the handover of 390 enterprises on November 30. These enterprises had total net assets of 2 billion yuan and 6,700 employees. They included 368 enterprises owned by the Guangzhou Military Region, the South China Sea Fleet, the Guangzhou Military Region Air Force, the Guangdong Provincial Military District, and the Guangdong Provincial Armed Police Corps, as well as 22 Guangdong-based enterprises owned by the Beijing, Jinan, Lanzhou, and Chengdu Military Regions, and the

Guangzhou Naval Academy. The 420 figure may also include enterprises owned by non-Guangdong-based military units.

172. ZTS 1999–01–13.

173. "Hebei Takes Over Military Enterprises," Xinhua 1998–12–12.

174. Xinhua 1998–12–15.

175. "Party, Government Units Sever Ties with Enterprises," Xinhua 1998–12–31.

176. "PRC Military, Government Bodies to Cease Business Activities," Xinhua 1998–12–14.

177. www.southcn.com.cn 2000–10–15.

178. JJRB 2002–04–14.

179. www.southcn.com.cn 2000–10–15.

180. CCTV 2001–02–04; Reuters 1998–11–30.

181. Matt Pottinger, "China Construction Bank Explains Official's Ouster," WSJ 2002–01–15.

182. For the setup in Jiangsu, see YZWB 2000–05–26.

183. CET 1999–06–17.

184. In 1995, the China Certified Accountants Association and the China Certified Auditors Association were merged to become the China Certified Accountants Association and put under the leadership and supervision of the Ministry of Finance and the National Audit Office.

185. JJRB 2000–06–21.

186. For the development in Shanghai, see JFRB 2001–12–03.

187. CJSB 2003–02–22.

188. QB 2000–06–04.

189. CYD 2002–03–09.

190. ZZB 2000–07–17.

191. Of course, the certification process may potentially become another rent-seeking opportunity for those with the power/expertise to certify.

192. Xinhua 2003–01–08.

193. SHZQB 2002–02–27, 2002–03–02; "China Revokes Licenses for Five Accounting Firms," Reuters, 2002–03–02.

194. Song Yongjian 2003.

195. "Hu Jintao Speaks on Banning PLA Businesses," Xinhua 1998–07–28.

CHAPTER 5

1. Yang 2001b.

2. See, e.g., the discussion by Wang Zhongyu, secretary general of the State Council, in RMRBO 2001–05–17.

3. See, e.g., Zhu Renxian 2002 and Liu Xirui 2000. Zhu's essay was published in the *People's Daily*. I shall elaborate on this development in Chapter 9.

4. Yang 1996b.

5. This is analogous to the case of American airline competition under govern-

ment price controls. Being unable to compete on price, the airlines instead competed on service. See Chen Zhiqiang 2001 for the case of Taizhou, a city in central Jiangsu that competes with cities in southern Jiangsu. One can easily cite many more such cases.

6. RMRB 2001–07–12.

7. XDT 2000–04–24. Fortunately the list of approval items required varies with the type of business.

8. ZGB 1998–07–27.

9. BKWZ 2000–07–31.

10. FZRB 2000–01–23.

11. ZGB 2001–04–25.

12. See, e.g., ZGB 1999–08–17.

13. Suzhou Industrial Park Administrative Committee 2001.

14. RMRBO 2000–06–15; ZGB 1998–07–27.

15. JJRB 2000–02–12.

16. ZZB 2000–12–28.

17. In addition, local authorities formed special teams to vet government documents (directives) and announced the termination of government directives that had become "outdated" or conflicted with national laws.

18. FZRB 2000–08–03; NFRB 2000–11–21; Xinhua 2000–03–24; 2000–04–17; 2000–06–08. For an overview, see ZGB 2001–04–24.

19. RMRB 2000–02–06.

20. ZGB 2001–10–13.

21. For a Chinese review, see Yan Zhenhua 2001.

22. For examples of such subterfuge in Sichuan and Anhui, see XDT 2001–12–08.

23. JJRB 2000–5–14.

24. RMRBE 2000–07–31; ZGB 2000–08–04.

25. XDT 2000–09–05.

26. CET 2000–07–27.

27. Li Lanqing 2002.

28. RMRB 2001–10–25; ZXS 2002–02–23.

29. YGXXRB 2001–06–18.

30. For a list of these approval items, see RMRB 2001–11–16.

31. The five categories were urban basic infrastructure construction; projects in agriculture, forestry, and water works not requiring central government investment; social and cultural investments funded by local governments and enterprises; real estate development projects; and commercial facilities projects. Further details can be found in XDT 2001–11–08.

32. The complete list was published in RMRB 2001–10–19 and 2001–10–20.

33. CNR 2001–12–23; RMRB 2002–03–11; RMRBO 2002–02–25; SQB 2001–11–05; Xinhua 2002–08–25; ZXS 2001–12–13.

34. Wang Xu and Yin Hongdong 2002.

35. FZRB 2002–03–18.
36. FZRB 2002–03–18.
37. Li Lanqing 2002.
38. Xinhua 2002–08–25.
39. Xinhua 2002–11–03.
40. In addition, the administration of 82 other approval items was transferred to industry associations and other intermediary organizations. FZRB 2003–03–02.
41. DJN 2002–12–25; for the list of 25 administrative approval items scrapped by the People's Bank of China, see BJYLXB 2003–01–03.
42. NFRB 2003–05–27.
43. Vogel 1996.
44. For a report of bureaucratic attitudes toward the administrative approval reforms in Gansu, see ZGB 2001–07–19.
45. The two regulations are the Regulations on Procedures for the Formulation of Administrative Laws and Regulations (*Xingzheng fagui zhiding chengxu tiaoli*) and the Regulations on the Procedures for the Formulation of Departmental Regulations (*Guizhang zhiding chengxu tiaoli*). Full texts can be found in FZRB 2001–12–03.
46. Xinhua 2003–08–27.
47. This discussion is based on the PRC Law on Administrative Licensing (Zhonghua Renmin Gongheguo Xingzhen Xuke Fa), enacted August 27, 2003, to go into effect on July 1, 2004. See also the legislative explanation by Yang Jingyu (2002), the director of the State Council's Legislative Affairs Office.
48. Interestingly, the drive toward government transparency has coincided with growing awareness of and emphasis on individual privacy.
49. XDT 2000–02–21.
50. FZRB 1999–06–21.
51. For information about the Ministry of Water Resources and historical information, see www.mwr.gov.cn and www.dydroinfo.gov.cn; for overview of the significance of such information, see RMRBO 2001–10–29. The exceptions are the Ministries of State Security and Supervision.
52. This drive came on the heels of an effort to promote transparency in village affairs initiated in 1997. On transparency and village governance, see Su and Yang 2001.
53. The full document is at JJRB 2000–12–26.
54. RMRB 2001–09–17.
55. Xinhua 2002–06–23.
56. For a useful compendium of essays on the promotion of transparency in different fields, including government administration, judicial institutions, the police, and villages, see Li Buyun, Zhang Zhiming, and Wang Shiqiang 2002.
57. Lin Shiyu 2002.
58. The documents were published in ZZB 2000–10–23.
59. RMRBO 2001–06–21.
60. See the front-page comment on the telecom hearing in CET 2000–09–27. Lin Shiyu (2002) discusses the adoption of public hearings across the country.

61. BQB 2001–07–17.

62. CD 2001–12–13.

63. Xinhua 2001–12–09.

64. Xinhua 2002–01–27.

65. Lin Shiyu 2002.

66. "PRC Planning Commission Limits Rail Price Hikes in Accordance with Public Opinion," Xinhua 2002–01–27.

67. CYD 2002–11–09.

68. ZXS 2002–11–25.

69. ZXS 2003–01–30.

70. FZRB 2003–05–12.

71. See Zhou Hanhua 2002. This is an abbreviated version of Zhou's report.

72. Guangzhou People's Government order no. 8 (2002), "Guangzhou shi zhengfu xinxi gongkai guiding." Accessed at www.guangzhou.gov.cn in May 2003.

73. For discussion of actual improvement in Guangzhou, see Huang Liaoyuan 2003. This report also examines certain knotty issues in the drive toward government transparency.

74. For full text of the regulations, see http://www.people.com.cn/Gshizheng/19/20030512/990224.html (accessed May 15, 2003).

75. See, e.g., "Rights Group Condemn Conviction of Webmaster," AFP 2003–05–20; "Four Dissidents Jailed in Internet Dissent Case," SCMP 2003–05–29.

76. Nailene Chou Wiest, "New Page Opens on the Road to Media Reforms," SCMP 2003–05–20.

77. ZXS 2003–09–02.

78. Quoted in CET 1998–05–21.

79. Suzhou borrowed the model from Singapore.

80. See, for example, the report by Hou Zhiming on Mianyang's administrative service center (XDT 2001–03–26).

81. JJRB 2000–02–12.

82. HSB 2000–12–25.

83. ZXS 2000–10–23.

84. Xinhua 2002–04–12.

85. XDT 2002–04–05.

86. ZGB 2002–05–10; for a general criticism of the poor performance of one-stop government service centers in the western region, see Zhao Xia, "Fuwu zhongzai shixiao" (The essence of service lies in actual performance), JJRB 2001–11–06.

87. XDT 2002–04–05.

88. Xinhua 2002–04–12; for the development of one-stop service centers in the counties and districts of Kunming, see the interview with Kunming mayor Zhang Zhenguo in ZGB 2001–11–12.

89. JJRB 2001–11–22.

90. RMRB 2002–04–14.

91. A survey by a Xinhua journalist found that all but the tax counter performed well at these centers (XDT 2001–10–29).

92. ZGB 2001–10–09. For description of how government staff modified their behavior to become more service oriented, see Gu Yinong, "Fuwuxing zhengfu de xin xingxiang" (The new image of a service-oriented government), RMRB 2002–03–25.

93. JJRB (2002–04–14) reports on the opening of an administrative hall in Lushan county of Henan.

94. CNR 2001–12–07; JHCB 2002–01–05; RMRB 2001–12–30.

95. For an earlier overview, see Yang 2001a.

96. ZXS 2002–01–27; RMRBO 2002–07–24.

97. Sun Ding 2002.

98. NFDSB 2002–03–01; XMWB 2001–12–12.

99. On the varieties of political action, see esp. Shi 1997. For the strikingly different attitudes between receptionists at the Ministry of Civil Affairs (cold) and the Ministry of Finance (nicely professional), see JJRB 2001–09–30.

100. ZGB 2000–09–07. For the case of Wenzhou, also based in Zhejiang, see RMRBE 2000–08–23.

101. QDRB 2003–01–16.

102. RMRBE 2002–03–10. An earlier report says that until between 2000 and April 2001 the centers handled 18,775 cases and resolved 94 percent of them. Disciplinary action was taken in 185 cases (RMRB 2001–05–02).

103. CNR national news roundup, 2002–05–08.

104. Huang was Zhuhai party secretary until 2002. His successor was Mayor Fang Xuan.

105. BKWZ 2000–07–03; QB 2000–08–14; RMRB 2002–09–01.

106. The detailed description of the center's authority and responsibility is contained in a document issued by the Zhuhai Party Committee and the municipal government on July 10, 2000. This and much else can be accessed at www.zhuhai.gov.cn.

107. This account is based on CCTV-4, Jingji Banxiaoshi, 2000–09–07.

108. ZXS 2002–02–21.

109. RMRBE 2002–05–15.

110. ZXS 2002–04–06.

111. In this evaluation conducted in December 2002, 11,902 questionnaires were distributed, and 11,693 were returned. The response rate for 2002 (97.7 percent) was up 21.45 percent over 2001, indicating greater confidence among the respondents that their responses counted. The survey respondents included members of the people's congress and of the people's consultative conference. The two biggest blocks were 3,000 firms and 4,000 ordinary people (Xinhua 2003–02–11).

112. It is important to note that some interior localities undertook important reforms under energetic leadership. Shanxi's Changzhi, led by the redoubtable Lü Rizhou, gained national recognition for enlisting the press to monitor government

performance. The move led to the removal of the director of the environmental and health bureau. What is interesting, however, is that the orientation toward better government service had by 2001–2002 spread to localities not particularly known for such progressive leadership.

113. Horizon Survey Group 2002; Horizon Survey Group 2003. Interestingly, four of the seven county magistrates failed to reach the 50 percent mark in the 2003 survey. See also report in NFZM 2002–08–22.

114. Personal interviews, July 1998.

115. XDT 1999–08–02.

116. NFRB 2000–08–03.

117. In Sichuan, the municipalities of Deyang and Yibin introduced open competition even for the post of county magistrate (SCRB 2002–08–23).

118. Xinhua 2000–08–08.

119. RMRBO 1999–07–19.

120. Xinhua 2000–08–08. The number of civil servants dismissed (*citui*) for cause was 2,680 in 1996, 2,898 in 1997, 2,937 in 1998, and 2,881 in 1999. In addition, 11,624 resigned during these four years (RMRB 2000–07–31).

121. QB 2000–07–27.

122. ZXS 2000–06–27; 2000–08–24.

123. BQB 2000–04–09.

124. YCWB 2000–10–24.

125. ZGB 2001–02–01.

126. For an extensive profile of the origins of the public notice system in Suqian, see RMRBE 2000–05–29. Chinese critics have noted, however, that the public notice system is still limited in its effect and have called for extending its duration, broadening its scope, and involving the public in the selection of nominees in the first place. See, for example, Zhou Faming 2000.

127. CD 1999–07–20. For an example of dismissal in Guangdong's Fogang county, see NFRB 2000–02–19. In August 2000, the General Office of the Communist Party's Central Committee issued a directive, "Summary on Deepening Reforms of the Cadre and Personnel System," which formalized the policies and guidelines for reforming the Chinese cadre system. For an indication of the central leadership's concerns about irregularities in personnel management, see the commentator's article in RMRB 2000–08–09.

128. HSB 2000–08–17; RMRB 2000–07–19; RMRB 2001–06–25.

129. ZGB 2001–07–10.

130. ZXS 2002–09–22.

131. RMRB 2001–06–14.

132. RMRB 2001–08–07.

133. These include the party, people's congress, government, the people's consultative conference, the discipline inspection commission, the people's court, and procuratorate, as well as institutions and mass organizations (union, communist youth league, women's federation).

134. RMRBO 2002–04–06.

135. RMRBO 2002–08–07.

136. There is a huge literature on civil service reforms in the U.S.; see, e.g., Johnson and Libecap 1994. Geddes (1994) provides evidence that merit-based recruitment and promotion strategies helped improve the effectiveness of state agencies in Latin America.

137. "State Council Efficiency Boosted After Staff Cuts," WHB 1999–05–23; FBIS-CHI-1999–0610.

138. This survey was done by the China Economic Sentiment Monitoring Center. The cities were Beijing, Shanghai, and Guangzhou, and the sample size was about 700 (ZGSB 2001–03–27).

139. CET 2001–09–22.

140. For the 2002 survey, interviews were conducted with 3,276 randomly selected households in ten cities (Beijing, Shanghai, Guangzhou, Wuhan, Chengdu, Shenyang, Xi'an, Jinan, Dalian, and Xiamen). The summary results of the survey appear at http://www.horizonkey.com/first/first_jb/539.htm.

141. RMRBE 2001–05–14.

142. The consulting firm is Valushar (Floyd 2002). Because chemical firms require elaborate regulatory approvals for their environmental impact, their views are particularly noteworthy.

143. Chinesenewsnet.com 2001–02–26; "Few Escape Bureaucracy Grip in Asia," AFP 2002–02–24.

144. Global Business Policy Council 2002; WSJ 2003–09–17. There have also been publications critical of FDI in China; see, e.g., Studwell 2002.

CHAPTER 6

1. This statement is based on many conversations I have had with construction industry insiders. It should be pointed out that many other countries, including Japan and South Korea, have also had much corruption in their construction industries.

2. Citing Chinese media, a Reuters wire item (1999–02–24) reported that the number of complaints rose by more than 50 percent since 1997. It is not clear whether the increase was in annual terms.

3. CDBW 1999–05–02.

4. Xinhua 1999–09–09; Li Yinyan 2000.

5. YCWB 2000–10–12.

6. "Yi paipai loufang qilai le, yi pipi ganbu daoxia le."

7. Zhang Dingmin and Li Wenfang 1998.

8. The 5-billion yuan Western Railway Station was built between 1993 and 1996 while Beijing was under the spell of party boss Chen Xitong. Cases of corruption and fraud at the station came to light in 1998 and 1999.

9. The full name of the office is Zhongda Xiangmu Jicha Tepaiyuan Bangongshi. In May 1999, the SDPC issued an elaborate set of rules that invited organiza-

tions and private individuals to report to the special inspector's office on illegalities in key construction projects funded by the government as well as foreign loans (Xinhua 1999–05–17). These rules are available on the Web site of the SDPC (SDRC).

10. ZGJYB 1999–05–18.

11. "Finance Ministry Infrastructure Circular," Xinhua 1999–04–07; FBIS-CHI-1999–0415.

12. QB 1999–03–01.

13. RMRB 1999–09–02.

14. CD 1999–03–25.

15. "State Council General Office Circular on Strengthening Quality Control over Infrastructural Projects," Xinhua 1999–02–23; FBIS-CHI-1999–0225. I have made some modifications in the translation.

16. "PRC Begins Nationwide Check on Construction Sector," Xinhua 1999–03–02; FBIS-CHI-1999–0301.

17. The full text of the directive is translated as "State Council General Office Circular on Strengthening Quality Control over Infrastructural Projects," Xinhua 1999–02–23; FBIS-CHI-1999–0225.

18. The limits on subcontracting would also be included in amendments to the Contract Law.

19. Funding for water conservancy was exempted from the ban.

20. "Ministry Stops Jiangxi Funds over Treasury Funds Misuse," Xinhua 1999–04–24; "PRC Resumes Transfer of State Bonds Funds to Jiangxi," Xinhua 1999–06–16.

21. RMRB 1999–02–12; 1999–04–05; 1999–08–29.

22. See, e.g., "Jiangsu Issues Notice on Bidding Irregularities," Xinhua 1999–04–02; FBIS-CHI-1999–0408.

23. JJRB 1999–08–21.

24. "Wei Jianxing on Construction of Markets," Xinhua 1999–08–20; FBIS-CHI-1999–0828.

25. RMRB 1999–07–28.

26. In Chinese, the law is titled Zhonghua Renmin Gongheguo Zhaobiao Toubiao Fa.

27. For further elaboration, see the SDPC regulations issued on May 1, 2000. These regulations can be found in XDT 2000–05–11.

28. See, e.g., Woodall 1996.

29. Li Yinyan 2000.

30. Xinhua 2000–07–31.

31. These include the Guangzhou Metro (NFRB 2000–01–27) and the Shenzhen Donghu Water Plant (FZRB 1999–07–27).

32. The www.chinabidding.com.cn site is in turn linked to a long list of other sites backed by provincial and municipal authorities as well as sector-specific sites dedicated to bidding and tendering.

33. RMRB 2000–07–07.
34. The Construction Ministry's directives on regulating construction markets as well as other documents can be accessed at www.cin.gov.cn.
35. RMRB 2001–07–17.
36. XDT 2001–08–08.
37. FZRB 2001–08–10.
38. GZRB 2003–04–11.
39. XDT 2002–04–03.
40. JJRB 2002–04–03.
41. CYD 2001–06–19.
42. Xinhua 2001–12–22.
43. These two regulations were available at *www.sdpc.gov.cn* as of May 2003.
44. QB 1999–08–30. For praise of such foreign supervision over quality, see JJRB 1999–08–09 comment on the quality of the Beijing-Tianjin-Tanggu Highway.
45. For detailed reports on this development, see JJRB 1999–07–07.
46. BJWB 2000–08–15.
47. Xinhua 2000–09–24.
48. BJYLXB 2002–10–19.
49. ZXS 2003–01–4.
50. CJRB 2001–05–22; NFRB 2001–12–27; ZGB 2001–09–04.
51. These cases were reported in most official Chinese media in early April 2001.
52. Xinhua 2002–09–17. For initiatives on inspection and public supervision, see BQB 2002–02–25. Ongoing information, including updates on project bidding and how to report on malfeasance, can be found at www.beijing-2000.org.
53. For an overview of Beijing's Sunshine Planning initiative, see BJCB 2003–02–13.
54. JCRB 2001–03–30.
55. JHCB 2002–09–30; *Shenzhen shangbao* (Shenzhen business post) 2002–03–01; Xinhua 2002–05–05; YZWB 2002–09–06; *Zhejiang ribao* (Zhejiang daily), 2002–04–17; ZXS 2002–09–05.
56. RMRBE 2001–04–03.
57. ZXS 2003–02–23. For a dissection of corruption in transportation construction, see *Caijing* (Finance and economy) no. 16 (2003).
58. YCWB 2000–08–19.
59. See, e.g., GZRB 2003–04–11.
60. RMRB 2002–02–25. The rest of the contracts may be decided by invited tenders and so on.
61. RMRB 2001–12–17.
62. XDT 2002–04–03.
63. For an indication of such regional variations, see Wang Zheng 2001.
64. For an overview of the regulatory efforts, see Sun Yubo 2002.
65. McMillan 1998.
66. Dodds 1995.

67. Lou Jiwei 1998: 142; ZXS 1997–11–20, FBIS–CHI– 97–324.
68. CD 1998–08–10.
69. BQB 2002–11–30.
70. Lou Jiwei 1998: 136, 144.
71. CD 1998–08–10.
72. QB 1999–03–22.
73. GZRB 1998–09–10.
74. QB 1999–03–22. The regulations are titled "Shanghai Shizhengfu Caigou guanli Banfa."
75. Ji Bin 1998: 78.
76. Xinhua 1999–01–26.
77. Lou Jiwei 1998: 134–135.
78. "NPC Deputies Urge Rules for Government Procurement," Xinhua 1999–03–04.
79. CDBW 1998–11–15.
80. CD 1999–06–05; RMRBO 1999–05–12; RMRB 1999–09–20. State enterprises are excluded.
81. William Kazer, "China's Anhui Bids to Save Cash, Meet WTO," Reuters 1999–06–03.
82. On Beijing, see SCMP 1999–05–28; on Jiangsu, see CET 1999–08–17.
83. BQB 1999–07–01; "PRC Centralizes Government Spending," Xinhua 1999–06–30; FBIS-CHI-1999–0630.
84. QB 1999–06–19.
85. Under growing competitive pressure, some state firms had already adopted improved procurement systems on their own.
86. These provisions may be found in JJRB 1999–05–25.
87. "SETC Urges Implementation of Procurement Provisions," Xinhua 1999–04–09; FBIS-CHI-1999–0417.
88. "SETC To Standardize State Sector's Purchasing System," Xinhua 1999–05–14; FBIS-CHI-1999–0514; ZXS 1999–12–25.
89. ZXS 2000–12–06.
90. These guidelines can be found in ZGB 2000–04–16.
91. JHSB 2001–09–02; FZRB 2001–12–31.
92. ZXS 2000–10–05.
93. Gilley 1998.
94. Qu Qiyun and Xu Jinzhang, "The PLA Has Taken New Strides in Its Procurement Reform," Xinhua 2002–06–29; FBIS-CHI-2002–0629.
95. RMRBO 2002–01–10.
96. Besides dedicated websites, many local governments announce their procurements at other government and commercial websites.
97. NFRB 2001–11–05.
98. Ministry of Finance 2002; "Zhengfu caigou yinian chao qianyi" (Govern-

ment procurement surpasses 100 billion per year), www.ccgp.gov.cn 2003–05–15, accessed on May 30, 2003.

99. ZHGSSB 2005–05–22.

100. These data are from Ministry of Finance 2002; Hu Hongjun 2003.

101. Hu Hongjun 2003.

102. ZGB 2000–09–06.

103. ZGSB 2001–03–19.

104. For indications of such sentiments, see Zhang Hong 1998.

105. ZGB 1999–06–11. While there is overlap between the Law on Public Tendering and Bidding and the proposed government procurement law, the former is not limited to government behavior while the latter was expected to include detailed rules on government financial management. For extended discussion of these differences, see Zhu Shaoping 1999.

106. ZXS 2001–10–23.

107. The Government Procurement Law can be read at www.ccgp.gov.cn.

108. Xiao Jie 2002.

109. Ministry of Finance 2003.

110. Xiao Jie 2002.

111. JJRB 2001–02–23.

112. The original document by the Ministry of Finance and the People's Bank of China on using direct disbursement for government procurement can be accessed at www.ccgp.gov.cn/web/tz.htm.

113. "China Finance and Economy Report," CCTV 2001–06–05.

114. Li Changhong and Qi Xiaoping 2000.

115. Xinhua 2004–04–01.

116. GRRB 2001–11–13.

117. Ministry of Finance 2003.

118. CJSB 2002–12–20.

119. Hu Hongjun 2003.

120. CCTV Channel Oriental Horizon conducted an interview with representatives of the Ministries of Land and Resources and of Supervision on October 8, 2002, on this issue. For updates on the regulation of local land markets, see the Web site of the Ministry of Land and Resources at www.mlr.gov.cn.

121. See, e.g., Ministry of Land and Resources circular on further regulating and rectifying the land market order issued on May 15, 2003. Last accessed at www.mlr.gov.cn on May 25, 2003.

122. QB 1999–02–04.

123. YCWB 2000–02–19.

124. Wang and his associates were sent to prosecutors' offices to face formal charges in 2001 (ZXS 2001–12–12).

125. NFRB 2000–11–28; XDT 2000–08–25; YCWB, 2000–02–19; 2000–10–12; NFDSB 2001–12–13.

126. NFDSB 2001–12–13.

127. YZWB 2001–11–30; RMRBO 2002–07–08.

128. Hangzhou started its land bank in 1997. CCTV-IV, 2000–06–26; BQB 2001–04–17; Xinhua 2001–12–15.

129. State Council "Directive on Strengthening the Management of State Land Assets," XDT 2001–05–31.

130. This rule is contained in a joint directive on strictly adopting auctions for the transfer of commercial land use rights (XWCB 2002–09–03).

131. ZXS 2002–07–20. The MLR regulations governing the auctioning of land rights were issued on May 9, 2002.

132. Murphy 2002.

133. The land revenue data are for the 13 cities that report directly to the provincial government. Aggregate land revenue was four billion for 1998 and eight billion in 1999 (YZWB 2003–01–29).

134. JJBD 2002–04–24; RMRBO 2003–01–23.

135. Nevertheless, as governments limit the supply of land, some have worried about the emergence of a Hong Kong style nexus between the government and big developers to keep land prices artificially high at the expense of public interest (Murphy 2002; Leng Xiao commentary in NFC 2002–06–21).

136. These data are from Ministry of Land and Resources 2000–2003.

137. See various regulations on the Ministry of Land and Resources Web site (www.mlr.gov.cn), especially MLR Order no. 11 (2002).

138. The Web site is http://s-gt-j.nj.gov.cn/ (YZWB 2001–10–25).

139. Xinhua 2001–11–28.

140. RMRBO 2002–07–11; "China's Shandong Sells Mining Royalty," *Asia Pulse* 2002–07–12.

141. On the auction of export quotas, see QB 2000–02–26; XDT 2000–02–21.

142. *Tianfu zaobao* (Sichuan morning post) 2000–11–30.

143. Two Hubei vice governors have lost their jobs on corruption charges.

144. Fang Zhengjun, Fu Gang, and Wang Shiqiang 2000; NFZM 2000–11–23; ZXS 2001–10–31.

145. ZQSB 2000–07–01.

146. Jenkins 1995: 9.

147. "Zhongguo cong yuantou shang zhili fubai qude mingxian chengxiao" (China achieves noticeable results in curbing corruption at the source), Xinhua 2002–10–25.

CHAPTER 7

1. For discussion of the changing conception of corruption in China, see Hao 1999: 406–407; for discussions of the causes of corruption, see, among others, Gong 1994; Hao and Johnston 1995; Lü 2000a; Kwong 1997; Tang Shenming 1997; White 1996. For a general discussion of corruption, see Rose-Ackerman 1999. Within China, He Qinglian and Hu Angang have been especially notable

for their writings on corruption. Note, however, that He's influential book *The Pitfalls of Modernization* (He Qinglian 1998), was written and published in China, and the author pulled his punches. I have deliberately left out reference to Hu Angang's high-profile writings on corruption. Hu defines corruption broadly to include all sorts of monopolies and is thus of little use in the present context.

2. James Kynge, "Cancer of Corruption Spreads Throughout Country," FT 2002–11–01; Editorial, "China's Charade," WSJ 2000–08–24.

3. Pei 2002.

4. Lü 2000a.

5. Z. He 2000: 269; see also Huang Weiting 1998.

6. The main focus in this chapter is on corruption in economic governance. Much corruption also occurs in other areas, such as personnel promotions. As noted in Chapter 5, extensive civil service reforms should help to reduce the scope for such corruption, but the civil service reforms have mostly been limited to the lower echelons of power. Serious reforms have also been launched in judicial institutions and law enforcement, but it will take time for these reforms to become truly effective against various forms of corruption. For Chinese discussion of judicial reforms, see Liu Renwen and Xiao Junyong 2003; Tan Shigui 2003.

7. Such accounts were also popular in South Korea, which converted to real names in fall 1993. The conversion quickly led to the resignation of various high officials and is known as a bloodless revolution in anticorruption.

8. He Qinglian 1998; see also Huang Weiting 1998; Wang Yaping 1999.

9. SCB 1999–02–11.

10. RMRBO 2001–09–27.

11. QB 1999–07–19.

12. Xinhua 2000–07–31. Cheng and his mistress deposited most of the money in Hong Kong. Various Chinese Web sites, including the *People's Daily's*, offer enormous amounts of information on corruption.

13. On the linkage between corruption and student demonstrations, see Ostergaard and Peterson 1991; Y. Sun 1991; Dingxin Zhao 2001. On corruption and social protests in the post-Tiananmen era, see F. Chen 2000.

14. Deng Xiaoping 1993: 313.

15. He Qinglian 1998.

16. A convenient compendium of documents is Zhongyang Jiwei Jijian Jiancha Yanjiusuo, ed., 2002.

17. For discussion of the role of campaigns in China, see Teiwes 1993, White 1989; on strike-hard campaigns in the 1980s, see Tanner 1999.

18. Manion 1998.

19. Cf. Gilley (1998b), who argues that the case of Chen Xitong and associates was a genuine corruption case.

20. Zheng Hongfan 1999.

21. FEER 1998–11–26. The specific data are as follows: enforcement of anticorruption laws (74 percent), encouragement of foreign investment (60 percent), lowering of government expenditure (55 percent), reduction of tax rates (45 percent).

22. CET 2000–01–11.

23. For the case of labor protests, see F. Chen 2000. On the link between anti-corruption and labor protest in Liaoyang, see Eckholm 2002.

24. Xinhua 1999–01–14; FBIS-CHI-99–014.

25. Quoted in commentator's article, RMRB 1999–10–11.

26. See, e.g., D. Li and Li 2000. Some local officials and businesses complained that the crackdown dampened business activities because those with the money shunned conspicuous consumption for fear of being suspected of corruption (SCMP 1999–01–07).

27. SCMP 1999–01–07.

28. SCMP 2000–03–03.

29. RMRB 1998–08–21.

30. Y. Sun 1999.

31. For examples of such media comments, see James Kynge cited earlier and Willy Lam, "Jiang Surviving on Shaky Ground," SCMP, 2000–09–20; Karby Leggett, "China Treads Carefully on Corruption," WSJ, 2000–09–21.

32. Xinhua 1999–01–14; FBIS-CHI-99–014.

33. Zong Hairen 2002: 287–288.

34. SCMP 2000–09–15.

35. Liu retired in November 2002.

36. "Zhong jiwei gaoceng sichu fanfu" (Senior officials of the Central Discipline Inspection Commission fight graft in various areas) *Ming Pao* 2000–08–08.

37. SCMP 2000–09–15.

38. ZXS 2002–02–15.

39. This discussion is largely drawn from JJBD 2003–03–31.

40. ZXS 2003–09–04.

41. Yu Bin 2003. The roving inspection team is not new. In 1996, seven teams were sent to inspect 18 provincial units, and in 2001 three teams were dispatched to eight provincial units. The difference in 2003 is that the roving inspection team is seen as a formal institution to inspect all provincial units.

42. In an ironic twist, however, a growing number of corruption cases have included huge "unaccounted incomes." Suspects are at most sentenced to five years in jail for possessing such unaccounted incomes; they can be sentenced to death if they give a clear account of the sources of their funds (JCRB 2000–11–22). As can be expected, such perverse incentives have prompted growing demands for amending this provision of the Criminal Law that has apparently fallen behind times.

43. CD 1999–03–10; SCMP 1999–03–20; RMRBO 2001–02–02.

44. Xinhua 2001–07–03.

45. Xinhua 2001–11–16.

46. Bai et al. 1999.

47. The income report is of limited utility in itself because it does not include assets. Moreover it appears that implementation of this regulation on income declaration has been spotty at best (NFRB 1999–6–11).

48. XDT 2001–04–06.

49. See, e.g., Tao 2002.

50. RMRBO 1999–08–28; ZGB 1999–08–19. For details on the regulation of large-sum banking transactions, see QB 1997–04–15; 1997–05–02.

51. The use of real names and the provision of additional information have also helped banks conduct appraisals of creditworthiness.

52. Previously bank customers only needed to present proof of identity in the case of early withdrawal of time deposits.

53. CYD 2000–01–21; RMRB 2000–03–31.

54. CYD 2000–05–01.

55. For a good overview of the pros and cons of using real names, see Cheng Bin, "Chuxu shimingzhi yuezou yuejin" (The real name system in savings is coming ever closer), RMRB 1999–05–17.

56. JJDB 2002–09–25.

57. See, e.g., RMRBO 2002–11–21.

58. "Jinrong jigou fan xiqian guiding," Xinhua 2003–01–13. These regulations are complemented by two implementing documents specifying the rules for reporting transactions involving large sums and suspicious payments and for reporting payment transactions in the Chinese currency as well as foreign currencies (ZXS 2003–01–15; BQB 2003–01–16).

59. Richard McGregor, "China Brings In New Rules to Stem Capital Flight," FT 2003–01–14. See also article by Huang Yuanxiang on how these regulations are touching the "nerves of the real name system" in GJJRB 2003–02–10.

60. For an overview of the myriad documents and regulations on party discipline, see Zheng Hongfan and Wang Leiming, "Official Discusses Anticorruption Tasks," Xinhua 1999–04–14, FBIS-CHI-1999–0422.

61. CD 1999–01–27.

62. Xinhua 1998–12–02; FBIS-CHI-98–336.

63. CD 1999–01–16.

64. CD 1999–03–11.

65. HKS 1999–03–13.

66. For details of Chongqing, which emphasized safety, see NFZM 2001–04–12.

67. CD 1999–04–05; AFP 1999–12–23. Records of the trial are in CCTV 1999. The high profile of the case raises the question of whether the defendants received a fair trial, but that is beyond the scope of the present study.

68. "Circular on Investigating Irregularities in Construction," Xinhua 1999–04–13, FBIS-CHI-1999–0419.

69. Numerous directors of construction bureaus or committees have been sentenced to jail time in recent years, often for cases involving huge sums. For example, Zhang Kexiao, the former head of the municipal construction committee of Wuhan, was put on trial for taking bribes or embezzling nearly 10 million yuan (ZXS 2001–10–23).

70. "Lessons Learned from Hongqiao Bridge Case," ZXS 1999–04–07.

71. This collapse occurred in February 1998, but the trial took place in late May 1999; RMRB 1999–06–03.

72. RMRB 2000–01–10.

73. "Lessons Learned from Hongqiao Bridge Case," ZXS 1999–04–07.

74. RMRBO 2001–03–21.

75. Xinhua 2000–09–28; 2000–12–25; 2001–03–20.

76. RMRB 2000–08–21.

77. CDBW 1999–08–01; QB 1999–12–24.

78. Interview with Li Jinhua, auditor general of the National Audit Office (RMRB 2000–08–21).

79. *Hubei ribao* 2001–06–14.

80. NFDSB 2003–03–25.

81. RMRBO 2001–02–23.

82. JFJB 2001–12–05.

83. CD 2000–08–21; ZXS 2002–01–16. Of the 19,000 local officials audited over January–September 2001, 152 were dismissed or demoted, 43 were given party and administrative disciplinary reprimands, and 261 were turned over to judicial authorities for judicial proceedings.

84. It should be noted that there are major variations even among developed countries. In the United States, the budget of the federal government is subjected to much congressional scrutiny and modification. In contrast, the government budget in Great Britain is presented in different documents at different times and is rarely changed.

85. QB 2000–10–18.

86. XKB 2002–12–01. In 2003, 80 percent of these incomes were included in the budget (Xinhua 2004–04–01).

87. ZXS 2001–01–06.

88. CJSB 2003–08–30.

89. JJRB 2000–10–18.

90. Fu Xu 2000.

91. ZXS 2000–03–06.

92. Lou Jiwei, quoted in Huang Peijian and Li Yan 2002.

93. Xinhua 2001–03–22.

94. JJRB 2000–03–28.

95. ZXS 2001–03–15. Jiangsu province, for instance, included 99.5 percent of the extra-budget funds in designated finance bureau accounts (*caizheng zhuanhu*) in the first three quarters of 2000 (YZWB 2000–11–11).

96. HQBD 2003–01–20; RMRBS 2003–01–20.

97. ZGB 2001–07–10.

98. CYD 1999–04–12.

99. JJRB 1998–06–30.

100. Text of the regulations can be found in "Methods Outlined for Collecting

Fines," Xinhua 1997–11–26, FBIS-CHI-97–337. Soon after this set of regulations, the Ministry of Finance also standardized the accounting system for administrative units. Some localities adopted the *shouzhi liangtiao xian* before 1998.

101. Finance bureaus in many localities can now check on the activities in the different bank accounts on the computer.

102. Yang Mei 2003.

103. See, for example, TJRB 1998–07–29; XHRB 1998–07–29.

104. Wei Jianxing 1999; see also ZGB 1998–07–13 for an example of the drive to promote the separation of income and expenditure.

105. RMRBO 1999–07–21; "Wei Jianxing on Revenue-Expenditure Rules," Xinhua 1999–07–20, FBIS-CHI-1999–0805.

106. The regulations can be found in RMRB 2000–02–18.

107. For example, Ma and Ortolano (2000: 23) report strong resistance among environmental protection bureaus.

108. ZGB 2000–04–05.

109. Hessler 2003: 33.

110. GMRB 2001–02–26.

111. FZRB 2000–12–21.

112. Xinhua 2000–08–21.

113. YCWB 2000–12–25. However, the Sun Zhigang case did occur in Guangdong and it prompted new reforms in 2003.

114. Yang Mei 2003.

115. ZHGSSB 1999–04–12.

116. JJRB 2000–10–01.

117. Xinhua 2000–01–03.

118. Huang Peijian and Li Yan 2002.

119. *Wenzhai bao* 1999–05–23; Xinhua 2000–08–10.

120. Huang Peijian and Li Yan 2002. Savings of tens of millions of yuan were also reported in Fujian (CJSH 2002–12–06).

121. ZXS 2002–11–28.

122. CJSB 2002–12–06.

123. BJCB 2002–10–07.

124. JJRB 2000–08–29.

125. RMRB 2000–05–23.

126. XDT 2000–02–02.

127. For more comprehensive treatment of this topic, see Wang Dianlong 2001.

128. ZGB 1999–06–11.

129. RMRBE 2000–06–28.

130. HSB 2000–10–01; XDT 2000–05–26.

131. JJRB 2000–12–27.

132. Xinhua 2000–11–14.

133. For the sake of space, I have eliminated discussion of this development here.

134. This was found to be true in Shaanxi, but the dynamics elsewhere are essentially the same (Xinhua 2000–08–10).

135. Zhang Jingping, "The Fall of Provincial-ministerial Ranked Officials Accelerates," Chinesenewsnet.com 2001–11–14.

136. Fewsmith 2001: 231.

137. See, for example, Fewsmith 2001: 165–167; cf. Gilley 1998b. Ironically, many residents in Beijing remain nostalgic about Chen's ability to get things done. The same is true in Xiamen, where arch-smuggler Lai Changxing bought off practically the entire local leadership but also helped the city economy along the way (FT 2001–11–03).

138. For these and more, see, for example, the article by Zhang Jing (pseudonym) in *Qianshao* (Outpost) no. 3 (2002).

139. See, e.g., Jeremy Hainsworth, "Canadian Lawyer Raises Death Penalty in Chinese Case," Reuters 2001–11–06.

140. WSJ 2000–08–24.

141. Bao Tong, "Admit the Injustice of the Tiananmen Crackdown," AWSJ 1999–06–04.

142. In 2001, *www.tehelka.com* used a sting operation to reveal the pervasiveness of corruption in India and precipitated a major political crisis there.

143. See, e.g., Xinhua 2001–08–07; JNSB 2001–10–31; FZRB 2001–10–20; RMRB 2001–10–17.

144. Treisman 2002.

145. YCWB 2000–02–20.

146. Auditor General Li Jinhua's speech to the National Audit Work Conference of July 2001 (ZGB 2001–07–25).

147. Quoted in Liu Jianfeng 2001.

148. Quoted in Mure Dickie and Richard McGregor, "Xiamen's Red Mansion Lifts the Lid on China's Underworld," FT 2001–11–03.

149. JCRB 2000–11–12.

150. RMRBO 2000–06–16; ZXS 2000–11–12; homeway.com.cn 2000–07–08.

151. This draws on Wei's talk at the Heilongjiang provincial group meeting at the NPC; Xinhua 2002–03–09.

152. Jia Shu, "Fubai yu youxi guize youguan" (Corruption is related to the rules of the game), CYD 2002–04–22. The press report that revealed the figures cited here does not provide details on how the figures were derived. Hence these figures must be taken with a grain of salt.

153. For the dissection of the case of Yang Xiuzhu, a deputy director of the Zhejiang provincial construction bureau, see Chen Dongseng, "Nü tingzhang shizong zhimi" (The mystery of the disappearing female bureau director), FZRB 2003–05–24. Space limitations have made it impossible for me to discuss China's efforts to capture corruption fugitives in any detail.

154. This draws on Wei's talk at the Heilongjiang provincial group meeting at the NPC (Xinhua 2002–03–09). See also the interview with Zhao Dengju, deputy procurator general of the Supreme People's Procuratorate (CCTV-4 2002–03–11); and Lam 2002.

155. For a brief overview of insights from cognitive psychology, see Yang 1996a: 11–14.

156. These results are cited in http://www.horizonkey.com/first/first_jb/ 401.htm. Accessed on November 4, 2001.

157. The survey results are available from http://www.horizonkey.com/first/ first_jb/518.htm. Accessed on November 17, 2002.

158. Full details of these surveys, based on randomly chosen samples, have not been released (Sun Chengbin and Zhang Jingyong 2002; Sun Chengbin 2004).

159. I have only presented the more conservative numbers in the text. In fact, when the questions are framed to ask only aspects of the anticorruption work, the results tend to be more favorable. Of the interviewees in a 2002 survey (N = 14,897) conducted by the urban survey teams of the State Statistical Bureau, 73.5 percent indicated approval of the government's anticorruption work; 69.1 percent believed that corruption had been curbed in certain spheres, and a surprising 78.8 percent of the interviewees expressed confidence in the anticorruption struggle (Sun Chengbin and Zhang Jingyong 2002).

160. The data from Transparency International are available from http://www. transparency.org and http://www.gwdg.de/uwvw/. Details of the time series of China's Corruption Perceptions Index are as follows: 1980–1985: 5.13; 1988–1992: 4.73; 1995: 2.16; 1996: 2.43; 1997: 2.88; 1998: 3.5; 1999: 3.4; 2000: 3.1; 2001: 3.5; 2002: 3.5; 2003: 3.4. Note that the 1980s score was based on fewer surveys and are thus not as comparable as later figures. For a discussion of utility and problems with the Corruption Perceptions Index, see Lambsdorff 2001.

161. It should be noted that, because of big changes in the number of countries included, a country's relative ranking from the TI surveys should not be compared across time.

162. In fact, in surveys since the mid-1990s India started out ahead of China but has fallen behind in recent years. "India Is More Corrupt than China, Says Transparency International Survey," *Times of India* 2001–03–31.

163. China's Corruption Score (10 = most corrupt)

Year	1995	1996	1997	1998	1999	2000	2001	2002
Score	7.3	8.0	8.1	7.0	9.0	9.1	7.9	7.0

The scores are based on surveys conducted in January–February each year of about 1,000 expatriates working in Asia by Political and Economic Risk Consultancy, Ltd. The data are reported in "Corruption in Asia in 2001," available at http://www.asiarisk.com/lib10.html, last accessed 2002–12–01; and *Ming Pao* 2002–03–06.

164. Needless to say, Western human rights organizations have protested the death sentences given to some corrupt officials.

165. "More on Zhu Rongji's Comments on Corruption," Xinhua 2000–03–15.

166. Xinhua 2002–01–15.

167. See, e.g., reports on two recent CDIC meetings in RMRBO 1999–01–16; and Xinhua 2000–01–14.

168. Jiang Zemin 2002.

169. "Communiqué of the Second Plenum of the CCP Central Discipline Inspection Commission," Xinhua 2002–02–19.

170. For evidence of such a commitment, see, e.g., reports of talks by top leaders of the Central Discipline Inspection Commission and the Ministry of Supervision (FZRB 2001–08–11).

171. For the vicissitudes of a whistleblower in Hebei's Tangshan, see Chen Jieren, "Yige shuming jubao ren de mingyun" (The fate of a signed whistleblower), CYD 2002–12–13.

CHAPTER 8

1. O'Donnell 2000. Schmitter 1999 argues for broadening the coverage of horizontal accountability beyond intrastate relations to include the relations between state and civil society.

2. A convenient collection of essays on this topic is Schedler, Diamond, and Plattner 1999.

3. It should be noted that there is also recognition of the limits of an institutional approach to curbing abuse of power. As O'Donnell notes: "History and comparative politics teach us that, even with the barriers that liberalism erected in modern times, there are no ultimate guarantees against the abuse of power—although of course some countries have been more prone to this risk than others" (O'Donnell 2000).

4. Scholars are divided over whether China has adopted constitutionalism, defined as the exercise of government power in accordance with law, with the constitution being the supreme law. For different views on this issue, see the symposium on China and constitutionalism in *Journal of Chinese Law*, various issues. For discussion of constitutionalism and its limits, see Brandon 1998. Note, however, that Brandon sees China meeting his definition of constitutionalism but is nonetheless unwilling to apply that appellation to China.

5. The current version of the PRC constitution has been amended four times, most recently in March 2004.

6. Scholars of constitutional law in China are divided over whether the preamble is legally binding. For a discussion of this issue, see, e.g., Zheng Lu et al. 1999: chapter 1.

7. Interview with the confidant of a former NPC leader, 1997.

8. Shirk 1993.

9. There is a growing literature on congressional oversight in the United States. See, for example, McCubbins and Schwartz 1984.

10. Cai Dingjian 1998: 514.

11. On Peng Zhen, see Potter 2003; on Qiao Shi, see Gao Xin 1995.

12. SCMP 1998–04–30.

13. RMRB 1998–07–15.

14. RMRBO 1998–09–28.

15. Hu Jintao 2002.

16. RMRBO 1998–09–28.

17. Li Peng 2001.

18. Scott Tanner 1999. Chinese publications have given prominence to law-making; see Cao Siyuan 1995, 1996; Cai Dingjian 1998.

19. Hu Jinguang and Tan Liming 1998; Tanner 1994.

20. With 125 of the 154 Standing Committee members present, the votes were 77 for, 6 against, and 42 abstentions, just one short of the number of votes needed to pass the amendments (CD 1999–04–30). An amended version was resubmitted and approved subsequently.

21. Ironically various former government officials opted to go to the toothless CPPCC rather than join Li Peng at the NPC in 1998.

22. However, the Legislation Law provides that amendments to existing laws may be put to a final vote if there are no serious disagreements.

23. RMRB 1998–04–30.

24. ZGB 1998–10–14.

25. On the recommendation of the premier, the NPC Standing Committee in November 1998 formally removed Niu Maosheng, minister of Water Resources, after a summer of costly floods. Niu was transferred to Hebei province. Local people's congresses have removed various officials from office. For example, in May 1989 deputies of the provincial people's congress in Hunan removed a deputy provincial governor from office for having done an inadequate job in cleaning up the financial system. For this and other cases from local people's congresses, see Cao Qirui, Huang Shixiao, and Guo Dacai 1996: 71–79.

26. Tanner and Chen 1998: 41.

27. Guo Donglai 1998: 28.

28. The titles of the documents are: "Circular on Strengthening Contacts with the NPC Deputies and Accepting Supervision of the NPC Deputies" and "Management Measures for the Supreme People's Procuratorate to Maintain Contacts with the NPC Deputies."

29. CD 1998–06–11.

30. CD 1998–12–25; 1999–02–26.

31. RMRB 2000–02–28.

32. SCMP 1999–03–16. The upward trend was not sustained, however. In 2001, the SPP report received 68 percent "yes" votes, with the rest voting "no" or abstaining (SCMP 2001–03–16). Han was retired in 2003. In contrast, the more reformist Xiao Yang was reappointed to a second term as Supreme People's Court president with a resounding 95 percent of the votes cast in spring 2003.

33. The first head of the Budgetary Work Committee was Guo Zhenqian, vice

chairman of the NPC Financial and Economic Committee and former auditor general of the National Audit Office.

34. ZXS 2000–08–25.

35. SCMP 1999–10–22; Xinhua 1999–12–21.

36. CD 1999–12–22; RMRBO 2000–01–17.

37. For an overview of the provincial people's congresses, see MacFarquhar 1998.

38. For an interesting discussion of the trade-off between autonomy and capacity, see O'Brien and Luehrmann 1998.

39. S. Lin 1992–93; M. Xia 1997.

40. In Shandong, 80 percent of all provincial-level legislation is drafted by the government (MacFarquhar 1998: 660).

41. CET 1998–03–12.

42. ZXS 2000–01–28.

43. *Ming Pao* 1999–02–01. For developments in the early 1990s, see Lam 1995: 317–319.

44. Lu did receive a majority of the votes at a MPC plenary session hastily arranged two days later (ZXS 2003–01–03).

45. Wei Naibin 1994: 144.

46. RMRB 1998–05–20.

47. LW 1998–03–30; QB 1998–07–17.

48. For evidence of such tests becoming perfunctory in certain localities, see RMRB 2000–05–10.

49. XDT 1998–08–03.

50. FZRB 1999–11–04.

51. CD 1999–03–13.

52. GZRB 1998–12–18.

53. CET 2001–03–02.

54. CET 2001–03–02.

55. This and the following three paragraphs on Beijing rely on Hu Jian and Yang Zhen 1999.

56. FZRB 1999–06–08.

57. RMRBO 2001–12–14.

58. Huang Zhimin and Yan Shigui 1998: 12.

59. NFRB 2000–01–28.

60. SCMP 1999–02–01; 1999–02–03.

61. Michael Kramer, "China Guangdong MPs seek accountability on GITIC," Reuters 1999–01–28.

62. SCMP 2000–02–22. The two nominees voted down were for the heads of the Provincial Land and Natural Resources Bureau and the Foreign Trade and Economic Co-Operation Bureau.

63. CYD 2000–01–29; CD 2000–01–29.

64. Of eight hearings, three were kept secret and not reported in the media.

65. Zhen Xi, "Weile pingdeng duihua" (For dialog on the basis of equality), NFZM, 2000–04–21.

66. YCWB 2000–07–29.

67. ZGB 2001–03–01.

68. HQBD 2003–01–20; RMRBS 2003–01–20.

69. Xinhua 2001–12–12.

70. XMWB 2000–01–04.

71. NFDSB 2002–12–04.

72. RMRBE 2000–07–06.

73. Jia Yongxiang, president of the Shenyang Intermediate Court, was put under investigation for personal corruption on the court report day. Jiang had sat on the podium in the morning. Two vice presidents were also taken into custody. Du Minghua, "SMPC Oks Court Report on Second Deliberation in Shenyang," *People's Daily* in English, available at http://fpeng.peopledaily.com.cn/200108/15/eng20010815_77372.html (accessed September 20, 2001).

74. JJRB 1998–05–02; 1998–05–06; GZRB 1998–05–03.

75. QB 1999–02–13.

76. In my interviews with several officials who went through evaluations at the local people's congress, some criticized the process as being too harsh while others saw this as the trend to be reckoned with.

77. XDT 1998–03–13.

78. Wang Kun, "Yizheng zhitong kuaiche de qishi" (Inspiration from the opinion and advice express trains), RMRB 1999–04–28; NFRB 1999–01–18.

79. ZXS 2000–07–29.

80. ZGJJNJ 1986: V-279–280; 1990: III-262–263.

81. Wu Jianghong 1993.

82. ZGJJNJ 1990: III-263.

83. ZGJJNJ 1991: III-278; interviews.

84. ZGJJNJ 1990: III-262.

85. At this time Premier Li Peng oversaw the National Audit Office, generally through his ally State Councilor Li Guixian, while Vice Premier Zhu Rongji was taking over the reins of the financial system.

86. ZGSJNJ 1999: 764.

87. ZGSJNJ 1999: 769.

88. The State Council gave its approval in June 1995 to the "Trial Methods for Auditing and Supervising Central Government Budget Implementation," which went into effect in July 1995.

89. ZGSJNJ 1999: 767.

90. Similar rituals are also performed in the provinces, though with less publicity.

91. ZGSJNJ 1999: 771.

92. ZZB 1999–05–18.

93. RMRB 1999–08–30.

94. Xinhua 2003–01–13.

95. These details are obtained from the Web site of the National Audit Office at www.audit.gov.cn.

96. See, for example, Auditor General Li Jinhua's article on fully implementing the Audit Law and promoting governance according to law (RMRB 1999–08–30). Meanwhile, retiring Auditor General Guo Zhenqian became vice chairman of the NPC Finance and Economic Committee.

97. "NPC Criticizes Misuse of Funds," *Beijing Review* 1999–07–19.

98. CD 1999–06–29.

99. ZXS 1999–12–17.

100. ZXS 2002–01–15; 2002–01–16.

101. ZXS 2002–01–15; 2002–01–16.

102. JJRB 2000–08–15.

103. CD 2000–08–16.

104. ZGB 2000–09–07; CYD 2000–09–02.

105. JNSB 2001–12–04.

106. SCMP 2000–08–25.

107. NYT 2000–10–01.

108. Li Jinhua 2003.

109. On constitutional faith, see Levinson 1988.

110. Data based on LW no. 23 (1998–06–08): 5–6; XWZK, NPC special supplement 2003.

111. For discussion of such confrontations at the county level, see Cho 2002.

CHAPTER 9

1. North Korea set up the Sinuiju Special Administrative Region in 2002. For India, see, e.g., Joanna Slater, "India's High Hopes for 'Special' Zones," WSJ 2003–05–01.

2. See, e.g., Zhu Rongji 2000.

3. For a brief review of such developments, see Yang 2003.

4. Polanyi 1957: 250.

5. Jiang Zemin 1992: 810–811.

6. Xinshiqi 1998: 1000–1030.

7. Hellman 1998; Schamis 1999.

8. I provide an update of this development in Yang 2003.

9. See, especially, Pei 1994.

10. For a summary of this literature, see Naughton and Yang 2004.

11. Fairbanks 1999: 53.

12. Needless to say, these nominal GDP figures can mean only so much. In fact, Russia's life expectancy has slipped while Chinese life expectancy continues to improve.

13. Stoner-Weiss 2000.

14. Braguinsky 1999.

15. Richard Pipes, "Russia Faces a Crisis in the Caucasus—and in the Kremlin," WSJ 1999–08–13. Solnick 1998 discusses the roots of the Soviet breakdown and traces them back to the years before Gorbachev.

16. Russia has an electoral though not liberal democracy. See McFaul 1999 on this point.

17. This is not to deny that Deng played to the provinces vis-à-vis the central bureaucrats: Shirk 1993.

18. Treisman 1999: 2.

19. Treisman 1999.

20. Wines 2000.

21. Kotkin 2000.

22. Lukin 1999: 39.

23. See, esp., Holmes 1997.

24. Until the Seventeenth Amendment to the U.S. Constitution, U.S. senators were picked by state legislatures rather than directly elected.

25. Wines 2000; "Russia Is Split on Putin's Reform Ideas for Legislature, Regional Governments," AP 2000–05–18.

26. It might be remembered that concerns about a weak central government were a major driving force for the Constitutional Convention of 1787 in the United States.

27. Michael Wines, "Some Russians Are Alarmed at Tighter Grip under Putin," NYT 2001–06–14; Homes 2001.

28. Leaving aside differences in political system, China at the start of the twenty-first century has a per capita income level comparable to the United States at the beginning of the twentieth (adjusted for factors of inflation and purchasing power).

29. Kahn 1997.

30. Hofstadter 1955 used "the age of reform" to refer to the period from 1890 to 1940.

31. Smith 1985: 345–347.

32. Chandler 1954: 1462–1465; Cheng Li 2001.

33. For a brief survey of this development, see Yang 2003.

34. Zhu Rongji 2003.

35. Friedrich 1974: 6; for Mao's reluctance to proceed with constitution making in the early 1950s, see Hua-yu Li 2001.

36. North and Weingast 1989; Weingast 1997b.

37. Montinola, Qian, and Weingast 1995; Yang 1996b.

38. Yang and Su 2000.

39. See, e.g., Tanner 2000. The Sun Zhigang case of 2003 pointed to the limits of these initiatives but has provided fresh impetus for further reforms. In September 2003, the Ministry of Public Security promulgated an important set of regulations on procedures to be adhered to in administrative cases (www.mps.gov.cn).

40. By early 2001, the NPC had enacted 390 laws and resolutions, and the

State Council had issued more than 800 administrative regulations to form a basic legal system (ZXS 2001–03–04). See also Peerenboom 2002.

41. Ying Songnian 1999.

42. As Friedrich (1974: 124) put it: "Freedom—or liberty—as the key value is closely linked to constitutionalism."

43. CET 1999–06–07.

44. Owen Brown, "China Takes Seat at WTO on Side of Free Traders," WSJ 2002–12–17.

45. "Supreme Court Overhauls 2,600 Judicial Explanations to Meet WTO Conditions," Xinhua 2002–03–11.

46. ZXS 2001–10–23.

47. Liu Gangxi, vice chairman of the Shanghai WTO Research Center, quoted in Wonacott 2001.

48. CD 2003–12–11.

49. See, e.g., Foot 2000; Pei 2000.

50. In economic governance, a saying that became widespread in the late 1990s was that the government should "do some things [well], and refrain from doing certain things" (*you suowei, yousuo bu wei*).

51. ZGB 2001–01–08.

52. BJCB 2001–03–10.

53. Wen Dao, "Zhengfu chengxin wujia" (The government's trustworthiness is priceless), CYD 2001–08–20.

54. Tong Zhiwei, "Xianfa shishi xu zhongdian guanzhu de sanda wenti" (Three major issues in implementing the constitution), CYD 2001–12–10.

55. Zhao Guodu, "Shimin liyi shequhua" (People's interests become embodied in communities), NFRB 2000–06–26.

56. NFRB 2002–01–07.

57. RMRB 2001–11–06; Xinhua 2001–11–03.

58. For a profile of Xi, see Zong Hairen 2002: chapter 8.

59. TKP 2002–02–27.

60. For comparison of Chinese and global attitudes, see Pew Research Center for the People and the Press 2002.

61. See, e.g., Wu Guoguang 2001. Interestingly, the more conservative journal *Zhanlue yu guanli* (Strategy and management) based in Beijing also published essays, including one by Hu Angang and Wang Shaoguang in the March 2002 issue, that are quite close to this view.

62. On the rhetoric of reform and reaction, see Hirschman 1991.

63. The search for "crisis" alone yielded 7.8 million items. The search was done on August 28, 2002.

64. For a recent volume predicting China's collapse, see Chang 2001.

65. Jiang Zemin (2002)'s political report to the sixteenth Communist Party National Congress in late 2002, is a comprehensive statement of the governing principles espoused by the ruling elite. There is a significant literature on the

trade-off between rapid economic growth and increased political participation. A classic statement is Huntington and Nelson 1976. For a contrasting perspective, see Przeworski, Alvarez, Cheibub, and Limongi 2000: chapter 3.

66. Gray 1998: 134.

67. There is growing attention to state failure and state weakness. See, e.g., Wright 2000; Rotberg 2002.

68. For a scholarly attempt, see Gregor 2000. Criticism of Gregor can be found in Joseph 2001. See also Bernstein and Munro 1997; statement of Richard Perle, former assistant secretary of defense, in *Washington Post* 1997–05–18; Harry Wu, "Labor Camps Reinforce China's Totalitarian Rule," CNN at www.cnn.com/SPECIALS/1999/china.50/; Ledeen (2002) compares China to Mussolini's Italy.

69. Kaplan 1999 made a similar point.

70. While admitting that history is not linear, it can be argued that, as China becomes wealthier and the Chinese government becomes more adept at dealing with the pressures of industrialization, urbanization, and globalization, and as employment pressures ease over time in line with China's changing population structure, the Chinese ruling elite in possession of improved institutional resources—including an efficient state apparatus that can collect taxes and better enforce justice—might be more willing to broaden political participation beyond the current confines. Some may even suggest that the metamorphosis of the Chinese Communist Party rule may provide the foundation for party-led political reforms, as was the case in Taiwan. More likely, the opening for political democratization will be precipitated by some sort of crisis; for a regime that relies on rapid economic growth for performance legitimacy, a major economic setback amid rising expectations can be a very significant challenge and lead to a realignment of the political forces in favor of greater democratic participation. There is a huge literature on the relationship between development and democratization (see, esp., Przeworski et al. 2000). There is also a growing literature on whether China will become democratic and how soon. Ogden 2002 provides a comprehensive review. Rowen 1996 offers an optimistic prediction that China would become democratic by 2020, but James Lilley disagrees in a face-off in *The American Enterprise* 9, no. 4 (1998). Bruce Dickson (1997) suggested that the CCP would not go down the road traversed by the KMT.

71. Nathan 2003 makes a similar point.

72. Huntington 1968: 461.

SELECTED BIBLIOGRAPHY

Alesina, Alberto, and Lawrence H. Summers. 1993. "Central Bank Independence and Macroeconomic Performance: Some Comparative Evidence." *Journal of Money, Credit, and Banking* 25 (May): 151–162.

Almond, Gabriel A., Scott Flanagan, and Robert Mundt, eds. 1973. *Crisis, Choice, and Change: Historial Studies of Political Development.* Boston: Little, Brown.

Amsden, Alice. 2001. *The Rise of "The Rest": Challenges to the West from Late-Industrializing Economies.* New York: Oxford University Press.

Aslund, Anders. 2002. *Building Capitalism: The Transformation of the Former Soviet Bloc.* Cambridge: Cambridge University Press.

Bahl, Roy. 1999. *Fiscal Policy in China: Taxation and Intergovernmental Fiscal Relations.* San Francisco: The 1990 Institute.

Bai, Chong-en, David Li, Yingyi Qian, and Yijiang Wang. 1999. "Limiting Government Predation through Anonymous Banking: A Theory with Evidence from China." Working Paper.

Baum, Richard. 1994. *Burying Mao: Chinese Politics in the Age of Deng Xiaoping.* Princeton: Princeton University Press.

Beech, Hannah. 2002. "Smuggler's Blues." *Time* (Asia), 160, no. 14 (October 14).

Bensel, Richard. 2001. *The Political Economy of American Industrialization, 1877–1900.* Cambridge: Cambridge University Press.

———.1990. *Yankee Leviathan: The Origins of Central State Authority in America, 1859–1877.* Cambridge: Cambridge University Press.

Bernstein, Richard, and Ross Munro. 1997. *The Coming Conflict with China.* New York: Knopf.

Bernstein, Thomas, and Xiaobo Lü. 2003. *Taxation without Representation in Contemporary Rural China.* Cambridge: Cambridge University Press.

Bickford, Thomas. 1995. "The Chinese Military and Its Business Operations: The PLA as Entrepreneur." *Asian Survey* 35, no. 5 (May): 460–474.

Bird, Richard, and Oliver Oldman, eds. 1990. *Taxation in Developing Countries.* Baltimore: Johns Hopkins University Press.

Blecher, Marc J., and Vivienne Shue. 1996. *Tethered Deer: Government and Economy in a Chinese County*. Stanford, Calif.: Stanford University Press.

Bo, Zhiyue. 2004. "The Institutionalization of Elite Management in China." In Naughton and Yang, eds.

Braguinsky, Serguey. 1999. "Enforcement of Property Rights During the Russian Transition: Problems and Some Approaches to a New Liberal Solution," *Journal of Legal Studies* 28, no. 2 (June).

Brandon, Mark. 1998. *Free in the World: American Slavery and Constitutional Failure*. Princeton: Princeton University Press.

Cai Dingjian. 1998. *Zhongguo renmin daibiao dahui zhidu* (The Chinese people's congress system). Beijing: Falü chubanshe.

Cao Qirui, Huang Shixiao, and Guo Dacai, eds. 1996. *Difang renda daibiao shi zenyang kaizhan gongzuo de* (How local people's deputies conduct their work). Beijing: Zhongguo minzhu fazhi chubanshe.

Cao Siyuan. 1996. *Pochan fengyun* (The vicissitudes of the bankruptcy law). Beijing: Zhongyang bianyi chubanshe.

———. 1995. *Bujuan de qiusuo: Siyuan wenxuan* (Tireless pursuit: Siyuan's selected works). Beijing: Jingji ribao chubanshe.

Cao, Yuan Zheng, Gang Fan, and Wing Thye Woo. 1997. "Chinese Economic Reforms: Past Successes and Future Challenges." In Woo, Parker, and Sachs 1997.

Carpenter, Daniel. 2001. *The Forging of Bureaucratic Autonomy: Reputations, Networks, and Policy Innovation in Executive Agencies, 1862–1928*. Princeton: Princeton University Press.

Central Discipline Inspection Commission. 2002. Zhongyang Jiwei Jijian Jiancha Yanjiusuo, ed. *Zhongguo Gongchandang fanfu changlian wenxian xuanbian* (Selected CCP documents on fighting corruption and promoting cleanness). Beijing: Zhongyang wenxian chubanshe.

Chan, Che-po, and Gavin Drewry. 2001. "The 1998 State Council Organizational Streamlining: Personnel Reduction and Change of Government Function." *Journal of Contemporary China* 10, no. 29 (November).

Chandler, Alfred, Jr. 1954. "The Origins of Progressive Leadership." In Elting Morison, ed., *The Letters of Theodore Roosevelt*, vol. VIII (Cambridge, 1954).

Chang, Gordon. 2001. *The Coming Collapse of China*. New York: Random House.

———. 1999. "China Rediscovers Mao." FEER (October 7).

Chao, Chien-min, and Bruce J. Dickson, eds. 2001. *Remaking the Chinese State: Strategies, Society, and Security*. London and New York: Routledge.

Che, Jiahua, and Yingyi Qian. 1998. "Insecure Property Rights and Government Ownership of Firms." *Quarterly Journal of Economics* 113, no. 2 (May).

Chen, Feng. 2000. "Subsistence Crises, Managerial Corruption and Labor Protests in China." *China Journal* no. 44 (July).

Chen Ruisheng, Pang Yuanzheng, and Zhu Manliang, eds. 1992. *Zhongguo gaige quanshu: zhengzhi tizhi gaige juan* (The complete Chinese reforms: political system reform volume). Dalian: Dalian chubanshe.

Chen Yuan. 1991. "Woguo jingji de shenceng wenti he xuanze (gangyao)" (The deep problems and choices of our country's economy [outline]). *Jingji yanjiu* (Economic research) no. 1.

Chen Zhiqiang. 2002. "Chuangzao bijiao youshi (Creating competitive advantage)." JJRB 2001–06–06.

Cheung, Tai-Ming. 2001. *China's Entrepreneurial Army.* Oxford: Oxford University Press.

———. 1997. "The Chinese Army's New Marching Orders: Winning on the Economic Battlefield." In Brommelhorster and Frankenstein, pp. 181–204.

China Reform Foundation (Zhongguo Jingji Gaige Yanjiu Jijin Hui). 1998. *Zhongguo jingji de 'ruan zhaolu'* (The soft landing of the Chinese economy). Shanghai: Shanghai Yuandong chubanshe.

Cho, Young Nam. 2002. "From 'Rubber Stamps' to 'Iron Stamps': The Emergence of Chinese Local People's Congresses as Supervisory Powerhouses." *China Quarterly* no. 171.

Chung, Jae Ho. 1995. "Beijing Confronting the Provinces: The 1994 Tax-Sharing Reform and Its Implications for Central-Provincial Relations in China." *China Information* 9, nos. 2–3 (winter): 1–23.

Clifford, Mark. 2002. "Banks under a Cloud." *Business Week* 2002–01–28; "Are China's Banks Caught in Quicksand?" *Business Week* 2002–11–25.

Collier, Ruth Berins, and David Collier. 1991. *Shaping the Political Arena: Critical Junctures, the Labor Movement, and Regime Dynamics in Latin America.* Princeton: Princeton University Press.

Cong Yaping. 1998. "A Heavy Blow to Smuggling." Xinhua Domestic Service, 1998–12–08. Trans. FBIS-CHI-98–351, 1998–12–17.

Delfs, Robert. "Saying No to Peking." FEER, 1991–04–04.

Deng Xiaoping. 1993. *Deng Xiaoping wenxuan* (Selected works of Deng Xiaoping). Vol. 3. Beijing: Renmin chubanshe.

———. 1984. *Selected Works of Deng Xiaoping (1975–1982).* Beijing: Foreign Languages Press.

———. 1982. "Streamling Organizations Constitutes a Revolution." In Deng Xiaoping 1984: 374–379.

Dickson, Bruce. 1997. *Democratization in China and Taiwan: The Adaptability of Leninist Parties.* Oxford: Oxford University Press.

Dodds, Robert F. 1995. "Offsets in Chinese Government Procurement: The Partially Open Door." *Law and Policy in International Business*, June 1.

Duckett, Jane. 1998. *The Entrepreneurial State in China: Real Estate and Commerce Departments in Reform Era Tianjin.* London and New York: Routledge.

Eckholm, Erik. 2002. "Corruption Protest in China Leads to Charges, Top and Bottom." NYT 2002–09–13.

Fairbanks, Charles H., Jr. 1999. "The Feudalization of the State." *Journal of Democracy* 10, no. 2 (April): 47–53.

Fang Zhengjun, Fu Gang, and Wang Shiqiang. 2000. "Xingzheng shenpi quan de loudong" (The loopholes of administrative approval). Xinhua, November 27.

Fewsmith, Joseph. 2001. *China since Tiananmen: The Politics of Transition.* Cambridge: Cambridge University Press.

Fligstein, Neil. 2001. *The Architecture of Markets.* Princeton: Princeton University Press.

Floyd, Sigmund. 2002. "China's Investment Environment Continues to Improve." Chinaonline.com (January 9).

Foot, Rosemary. 2000. *Rights Beyond Borders: The Global Community and the Struggle Over Human Rights.* New York: Oxford University Press.

Friedrich, Carl J. 1974. *Limited Government: A Comparison.* Englewood Cliffs, N.J.: Prentice-Hall.

Fu, Jian. 1999. "Report on Research in China." *China and the WTO: An Australian Perspective*, no. 3 (November).

Fu Xu. 2000. "Licai zoushang fazhi guidao" (Fiscal management goes on to a legal orbit). RMRB 2000–07–12.

Fu Wei, ed. 1998. *Ruan zhaolu* (Soft landing). Beijing: Zhongguo jingji chubanshe.

Fu, Zhengyuan. 1994. *Autocratic Tradition and Chinese Politics.* Cambridge: Cambridge University Press.

Gao Xin. 1999. *Xiangfu Guangdong bang* (Taming the Guangdong gang). Carle Place, N.Y.: Mingjing chubanshe.

———. 1995. *Zhonggong jutou Qiao Shi* (Communist giant Qiao Shi). Taipei: Shijie shuju.

Geddes, Barbara. 1994. *Politician's Dilemma: Building State Capacity in Latin America.* Berkeley: University of California Press.

Gershenkron, Alexander. 1962. *Economic Backwardness in Historical Perspective.* Cambridge, Mass.: Harvard University Press.

Gilley, Bruce. 1998a. "Stand-Down Order." FEER, September 10.

———. 1998b. *Tiger on the Brink: Jiang Zemin and China's New Elite.* Berkeley: University of California Press.

Global Business Policy Council. 2002. *FDI Confidence Index 2002.* Vol. 5 (September 2002). Accessed at http://www.atkearney.com/main.taf?a=5&b=3 &c=1&d=51.

Goldman, Merle. 1994. *Sowing the Seeds of Democracy in China: Political Reform in the Deng Xiaoping Decade.* Cambridge, Mass.: Harvard University Press.

Goldstone, Jack. 1995. "The Coming Chinese Collapse." *Foreign Policy* no. 99 (summer).

Gong Ting. 1994. *The Politics of Corruption in Contemporary China.* Westport, Conn.: Praeger.

Gong Yuzhi. 2002. "Shehuizhuyi shichang jingji xiejin 'shisi da' de neiqing" (The inside story of how the socialist market economy was written into the 'fourteenth Party Congress' [report]). NFRB, February 1.

Goode, Richard. 1990. "Obstacles to Tax Reform in Developing Countries." In Bird and Oldman, eds.

Goodman, David S. G., and Gerald Segal, eds. 1994. *China Deconstructs: Politics, Trade and Regionalism.* London: Routledge.

Gore, Lance. 1999. *Market Communism: The Institutional Foundation of China's Post-Mao Hyper-Growth.* Oxford: Oxford University Press.

Gourevitch, Peter. 1989. *Politics in Hard Times: Comparative Responses to International Economic Crises.* Ithaca, N.Y.: Cornell University Press.

Gray, John. 1998. *False Dawn: The Delusions of Global Capitalism.* New York: The New Press.

Gregor, A. James. 2000. *A Place in the Sun: Marxism and Fascism in China's Long Revolution.* Boulder, Colo.: Westview Press.

Grew, Raymond. 1978. *Crises of Political Development in Europe and the United States.* Princeton: Princeton University Press.

Guo Donglai. 1998. "Zhongguo zongli Zhu Rongji chuanqi" (The story of Chinese premier Zhong Rongji), *Zuopin* (Literary works) (special issue).

Gurtov, Mel. 1993. "Swords into Market Shares: China's Conversion of Military Industry to Civilian Production." *China Quarterly,* no. 134 (June): 231–241.

Gurtov, Mel, and Byong-Moo Hwang. 1998. *China's Security: The New Roles of the Military.* Boulder and London: Lynne Rienner.

Hao, Yufan. 1999. "From Rule of Man to Rule of Law: An Unintended Consequence of Corruption in China in the 1990s." *Journal of Contemporary China* 8, no. 22 (November): 405–424.

Hao, Yufan, and Michael Johnston. 1995. "Reform at the Crossroads: An Analysis of Chinese Corruption." *Asian Perspective* 19, no. 1 (spring–summer): 117–149.

He Guanghui. 1996. *Yige gaigezhe de zuji* (Footsteps of a reformer). Beijing: Gaige chubanshe.

He Qinglian. 1998. *Xiandaihua de xianjing* (The pitfalls of modernization). Beijing: Dangdai Zhongguo chubanshe.

He, Zengke. 2000. "Corruption and Anti-corruption in Reform China." *Communist and Post-Communist Studies* 33, no. 2 (June).

Hellman, Joel. 1998. "Winners Take All: The Politics of Partial Reform in Postcommunist Transitions." *World Politics* 50, no. 2: 203–234.

Hennessy, Peter. 1989. *Whitehall.* Fontana.

Hessler, Peter. 2003. "Chasing the Wall." *National Geographic* (January).

Higgs, Robert. 1987. *Crisis and Leviathan: Critical Episodes in the Growth of American Government.* New York and Oxford: Oxford University Press.

Hirschman, Albert. 1991. *The Rhetoric of Reaction: Perversity, Futility, Jeopardy.* Cambridge, Mass.: Harvard University Press.

Hofstadter, Richard. 1955. *The Age of Reform: From Bryan to F.D.R.* New York: Vintage Books.

Holmes, Stephen. 2001. "Simulations of Power in Putin's Russia." *Current History* (October).

———. 1997. "What Russia Teaches Us Now: How Weak States Threaten Freedom." *The American Prospect* 8, no. 33 (July–August).

Holz, Carsten. 1992. *The Role of Central Banking in China's Economic Reforms.* Ithaca, N.Y.: Cornell University East Asia Program.

Horizon Survey Group. 2003. "Zhongguo shizhang zaihuo minyi gao zhichi lü" (Mayors in China again win high support ratings). Accessed at www.horizonkey.com/first/first_jb/618.htm.

———. 2002. "Zhongguo ge da chengshi shizhang pubian huode gao zhichi lü" (Mayors of major cities in China generally garner high popularity ratings). Accessed at http://www.horizonkey.com/c-firsthand.html.

Hu Haiyan. 2002. "Shuishou zhengguan xinxihua tuijin shuigai, zhongyang zhengfu zhengzai shouquan" (The informationization of tax administration promotes tax reforms the central government is centralizing power); CJSB 2002–12–13.

Hu Hongjun. 2003. "1500 yiyuan renminbi de zhengfu caigou guimo yiwei zhe shenmo" (What does government procurement on a scale of 150 billion yuan mean). JJRB 2003–05–30.

Hu Jian and Yang Zhen. 1999. "Weile buzai chuxian Wang Baosen" (So that Wang Baosen will not reappear). RMRB 1999–07–21.

Hu Jinguang and Tan Liming. 1998. "Shichang jingji: yinglai fazhi shidai" (Market economy welcomes the era of the rule of law). CET 1998–04–07.

Hu Jintao. 2002. "Zai jinian xianfa shixing ershi zhounian dahui shang de jianghua" (Speech at the meeting commemorating the twentieth anniversary of the adoption of the constitution) Xinhua 2002–12–04.

Huang Hengxue. 1998. *Zhongguo shiye guanli tizhi gaige yanjiu* (The reform of China's *shiye* management system). Beijing: Qinghua daxue chubanshe.

Huang Liaoyuan. 2003. "'Yangguang faan' weihu shimin zhiqingquan" (Sunshine act protects citizens' right to information). XKB 2003–03–24.

Huang Peijian and Li Yan. 2002. "Caizheng zijin liucheng zaizao" (Remaking the fiscal flow of funds). *Caijing* (Finance and economy), no. 12.

Huang Weiting. 1998. *Shiluo de zunyan: cheng fu beiwanglu* (The lost dignity: memorandum on combating corruption). Beijing: Zuojia chubanshe.

Huang, Yasheng. 1996a. "Central-Local Relations in China During the Reform Era: The Economic and Institutional Dimensions." *World Development* 24, no. 4.

———. 1996b. *Inflation and Investment Controls in China.* Cambridge: Cambridge University Press.

Huang Zhimin and Yan Shigui. 1998. "Jiandu, zheng zhai daowei" (Supervision is being implemented). RMRBE 1998–07–07.

Huang Zhiying, ed. 2000. *Zhongguo fazhi zhi lu* (The road to the rule of law in China). Beijing: Beijing daxue chubanshe.

Huntington, Samuel. 1968. *Political Order in Changing Societies.* New Haven: Yale University Press.

Huntington, Samuel, and Joan Nelson. 1976. *No Easy Choice: Political Participation in Developing Countries.* Cambridge, Mass.: Harvard University Press.

Jen, Hui-wen. 1998. "Inside Story of CPC's Anti-Smuggling Drive and Ban on Army Engaging in Business." *Hsin Pao*, 1998–08–05; FBIS-CHI-98–219, 1998–08–07.

Jenkins, Simon. 1995. *Accountable to None: The Tory Nationalization of Britain.* London: Hamish Hamilton.

Jenner, W. J. 1992. *The Tyranny of History: The Roots of China's Crisis.* London and New York: Penguin.

Ji Bin, ed. 1998. *Guowuyuan jigou gaige gailan* (The State Council organizational reforms). Beijing: Xinhua chubanshe.

Jiang Yong. 2002. "Sanzhi 'yanjing' kan xintuo" (Looking at the trust companies with a third eye). *Shidai caifu* (Time fortune). 2002–10–08; accessed at http://finance.sina.com.cn/g/20021008/0811262844.html.

Jiang Zemin. 2002. "Report at the 16th Party Congress." Xinhua 2002–11–17. Retrieved at http://www.china.org.cn.

———. 1997. "Hold High the Great Banner of Deng Xiaoping Theory for an All-round Advancement of the Cause of Building Socialism with Chinese Characteristics to the Twentieth-first Century." Xinhua in English, September 21, 1997.

————. 1992. "Jinkuai jianli shehui zhuyi de xin jingji tizhi" (Build a new social-
  ist economic system as soon as possible). In Xinshiqi 1998: 806–813.
Joffe, Ellis. 1993. "The PLA and the Chinese Economy." *Survival* 37, no. 2 (sum-
  mer): 24–43.
Johnson, Ronald, and Gary Libecap. 1994. *The Federal Civil Service System and the
  Problem of Bureaucracy: The Economics and Politics of Institutional Change.*
  Chicago: University of Chicago Press.
Johnson, Paul. 1995. *The Offshore Islanders: A History of the English People.* London:
  Phoenix Giants.
Joseph, William. 2001. "Review of A. James Gregor, *A Place in the Sun,*" *American
  Political Science Review* 95, no. 1 (March).
Kahn, Jonathan. 1997. *Budgeting Democracy: State Building and Citizenship in
  America, 1890–1928.* Ithaca, N.Y.: Cornell University Press.
Kahn, Joseph. 2003. "Made in China, Bought in China." NYT (January 5).
Kaplan, Robert. 1999. "China: A World Power Again." *Atlantic Monthly* 284, no.
  2 (August).
Kaufman, Joan. 2003. "Can China Cure Its Severe Acute Reluctance to Speak?"
  Washington Post, 2003-04-27.
Kettl, Donald. 2000. *The Global Public Management Revolution.* Washington,
  D.C.: Brookings Institution Press.
Kingdon, John. 1984. *Agendas, Alternatives, and Public Policies.* New York: Harper-
  Collins.
Kornai, Janos. 1992. *The Socialist System: The Political Economy of Communism.*
  Princeton: Princeton University Press.
Kotkin, Stephen. 2000. "Putin and Other Parasites," *New Republic*, June 5.
Kuan Chieh. 1998. "Chinese Mainland—Smuggling Kingdom." *Cheng Ming* no.
  250, 1998-08-01, FBIS-CHI-98-222, 1998-08-10.
Kwong, Julia. 1997. *The Political Economy of Corruption in China.* Armonk, N.Y.:
  M. E. Sharpe.
Lam, Willy Wo-Lap. 2002. "China Defends Corruption Claims," CNN
  2002-03-09.
————. 1999. *The Era of Jiang Zemin.* Singapore: Prentice Hall.
————. 1998. "PLA Cashes in Its Assets," SCMP 1998-07-29.
————. 1995. *China after Deng Xiaoping: The Power Struggle in Beijing Since
  Tiananmen.* Hong Kong: P A Professional Consultants.
Lambsdorff, Johann Graf. 2001. "How Precise Are Perceived Levels of Corruption?" Transparency International Background Paper. June. Available at
  http://www.transparency.org/cpi/2001/dnld/precreg2001.pdf. Accessed on October 2, 2001.

Lardy, Nicholas. 1998. *China's Unfinished Economic Revolution.* Washington, D.C.: Brookings Institution.

Lau, Lawrence, Yingyi Qian, and Gerard Roland. 2000. "Reform without Losers: An Interpretation of China's Dual-Track Approach to Transition." *Journal of Political Economy* 108, no. 1 (February): 120–143.

Lawrence, Susan. 2000. "A Model People's Army." FEER (July 13).

Lawrence, Susan, and Bruce Gilley. 1999. "Bitter Harvest: The Handover of the Military's Business Empire Has Stirred Up a Hornet's Nest." FEER (April 29).

Ledeen, Michael. 2002. "From Communism to Fascism?" WSJ (February 22).

Lee, Hong Yung. 1992. "China's New Bureaucracy?" In Arthur L. Rosenbaum, ed. *State and Society in China: The Consequences of Reform.* Boulder, Colo.: Westview Press.

Leggett, Karby. 2001. "In Land Where Bribes Are Common, Mr. Lai Pushed the Envelope." WSJ November 23.

Levinson, Sanford. 1988. *Constitutional Faith.* Princeton: Princeton University Press.

Li Buyun, Zhang Zhiming, and Wang Shiqiang, eds. 2002. *Xinxi gongkai zhidu yanjiu* (Studies on information disclosure). Changsha: Hunan daxue chubanshe.

Li Changhong and Qi Xiaoping. 2000. "Zhengfu caigou" (Government procurement). RMRB 2000–08–03.

Li, Cheng. 2004. "Political Localism Versus Institutional Restraints: Elite Recruitment in the Jiang Era." In Naughton and Yang, eds.

———. 2001. *China's Leaders: The New Generation.* Lanham, Md.: Rowman & Littlefield.

Li, Cheng, and David Bachman. 1989. "Localism, Elitism, and Immobilism: Elite Formation and Social Change in Post-Mao China." *World Politics* 42 (October): 64–94.

Li, David. 1996. "A Theory of Ambiguous Property Rights in Transition Economics: The Case of the Chinese Non-State Sector." *Journal of Comparative Economics* 23, no. 1 (August).

Li, David, and Shan Li. 2000. "Growth vs. Graft: Beating China's Corruption." AWSJ 2000–05–30.

Li, Hua-yu. 2001. "The Political Stalinization of China: The Establishment of One-Party Constitutionalism, 1948–1954." *Journal of Cold War Studies* 3, no. 2 (spring).

Li Jinhua. 2003. "Shenji gongzuo baogao" (Audit work report). Mimeo. Delivered to the NPC Standing Committee on June 25, 2003.

Li Junling. 2002. "Yinjianhui zhenglun shengji" (The debate over bank supervisory commission intensifies). JJBD February 4.

Li Lanqing. 2003. "Zai quanguo caizheng, shuiwu gongzuo huiyi shang de jianghua" (Talk at the national conference on finance and taxation). RMRB 2003–02–22.

———. 2002. "Queshi tuijin xingzheng shenpi zhidu gaige" (Truly push forward the reform of the system of administrative approvals), Xinhua 2002–06–25.

Li Peng. 2001. "Work Report of the NPC Standing Committee." RMRB 2001–03–20.

Li Yinyan. 2000. "Zhengfu gongcheng caigou weihe nanyi tuixing" (Why it has been hard to introduce competitive bidding into government construction projects). CET 2000–07–27.

Lieberthal, Kenneth G., and David M. Lampton, eds. 1992. *Bureaucracy, Politics, and Decision Making in Post-Mao China.* Berkeley: University of California Press.

Lieberthal, Kenneth, and Michel Oksenberg. 1988. *Policy Making in China: Leaders, Structures, and Processes.* Princeton: Princeton University Press.

Lin, Nan. 1995. "Local Market Socialism: Local Corporatism in Action in Rural China." *Theory and Society* 24: 301–354.

Lin, Sen. 1992–1993. "A New Pattern of Decentralization in China: The Increase of Provincial Powers in Economic Legislation." *China Information* 7, no. 3 (1992–1993).

Lin Shiyu. 2002. "Tingzheng: dakai baixing zhiqing canzheng zhi men" (Hearings: open the doors of public information and participation). JCRB 2002–09–16.

Lin Yifu, Cai Fang, and Li Zhou. 2001. *Development Strategy and Economic Reform.* Hong Kong: The Chinese University Press.

Ling Zhijun. 2003. *Bianhua: 1990 nian–2002 nian Zhongguo shilu* (Change: A chronicle of China 1990–2002). Beijing: Zhongguo shehui kexue chubanshe.

———. 1998. *Chenfu: Zhongguo jingji gaige beiwang lu* (Vicissitudes: memoranda on China's economic reform). Shanghai: Dongfang chuban zhongxin.

Linz, Juan, and Alfred Stepan. 1996. *Problems of Democratic Transition and Consolidation: Southern Europe, South America, and Eastern Europe.* Baltimore: Johns Hopkins University Press.

Liu, Binyan. 1990. *China's Crisis, China's Hope.* Cambridge, Mass.: Harvard University Press.

Liu Jianfeng. 2001. "Shenji fanfu: sannian da pandian (Using audits to fight corruption: a three-year assessment." ZGB (August 22).

Liu Renwen and Xiao Junyong. 2003. "Sifa gaige de huigu yu zhanwang" (Judicial reforms: review and prospect). In *Zhongguo shehui xingshi fenxi yu yuce: 2003 nian* (Analyses and forecasts of China's social situation: 2003). Beijing: Shehui kexue chubanshe, 2003.

Liu Shijin. 1998. "Structural Change Leaves Gap: China's Economy Faces Problems, Choices." *Guanli Shijie* (Management world), November 24; translated in FBIS-CHI-1999–0303, March 4, 1999.

Liu Xirui. 2000. "Linian, zhineng, fangshi" (Concepts, functions, and ways). *Renmin luntan* (People's forum), July.

Lou Jiwei, ed. 1998. *Zhengfu caigou* (Government procurement). Beijing: Jingji kexue chubanshe.

Lu Dongtao and Xu Yan. 1993. *Gaige lilun fengyun lu* (Storms over reform theories). Beijing: Beijing yanshan chubanshe.

Lü, Xiaobo. 2000a. *Cadres and Corruption.* Stanford, Calif.:: Stanford University Press.

———. 2000b. "Booty Socialism, Bureau-preneurs, and the State in Transition: Organizational Corruption in China." *Comparative Politics* (April).

———. 1999. "From Ranking-seeking to Rent-seeking: Changing Administrative Ethos and Corruption in Reform China." *Crime, Law & Social Change* 32, no. 4.

Lukin, Alexander. 1999. "Forcing the Pace of Democratization." *Journal of Democracy* 10, no. 2 (April): 4–18.

Lyons, Thomas P. 1987. *Economic Integration and Planning in Maoist China,* New York: Columbia University Press.

Ma Hong and Sun Shangqing, eds. 1993. *Xiandai Zhongguo jingji dashidian* (Encyclopedia of the contemporary Chinese economy). Beijing: Zhongguo caizheng jingji chubanshe.

Ma Licheng and Ling Zhijun. 1998. *Jiaofeng: Dangdai Zhongguo sanci sixiang jiefang shilu* (Crossing swords: a chronicle of the three waves of thought liberation in contemporary China). Beijing: Dangdai Zhongguo chubanshe.

Ma, Xiaoying, and Leonard Ortolano. 2000. *Environmental Regulation in China: Institutions, Enforcement, and Compliance.* Lanman, Maryland: Rowman & Littlefield.

McCubbins, Matthew, and Thomas Schwartz. 1984. "Congressional Oversight Overlooked: Police Patrols versus Fire Alarms." *American Journal of Political Science* 28.

MacFarquhar, Roderick. 1998. "Provincial People's Congresses." *China Quarterly,* no. 155 (September 1998).

McFaul, Michael. 1999. "The Perils of a Protracted Transition." *Journal of Democracy* 10, no. 2 (April): 4–18.

McMillan, John. 1998. "Competition in Government Procurement." Mimeo.

McMillan, John, and Barry Naughton, eds. 1996. *Reforming Asian Socialism.* Ann Arbor: University of Michigan Press.

Manion, Melanie. 1998. "Issues in Corruption Control in Post-Mao China." *Issues and Studies* 34, no. 9 (September): 1–21.

Ministry of Finance. 2003. "2003 nian zhengfu caigou gongzuo jihua yaodian" (Key points of the 2003 plan for government procurement work). *Caibankuo* [2003] no. 27, 2003–03–07, accessed on May 27, 2003 at www.mof.gov.cn.

———. 2002. "2001 nian quanguo zhengfu caigou guimo 653 yi yuan" (The scale of government procurement in 2001 was 65.3 billion yuan). Available at http://www.ccgp.gov.cn/web/zxdt/tj-baogao-0527/qkbg-10.htm. Accessed on October 26, 2002.

Ministry of Land and Resources. 2000–2003. "Guotu ziyuan gongbao" (Communiqué on land and resources). Available at www.mlr.gov.cn/query/gtzygk/index.htm.

Montinola, Gabriella, Yingyi Qian, and Barry Weingast. 1995. "Federalism, Chinese Style: The Political Basis for Economic Success in China." *World Politics* 48, no. 1 (October).

Moore, Barrington. 1967. *The Social Origins of Dictatorship and Democracy: Lord and Peasant in the Making of the Modern World.* Boston: Beacon Press.

Mulvenon, James. 2001. *Soldiers of Fortune: The Rise of the Military-Business Complex in the Chinese People's Liberation Army, 1978–98.* Armonk, N.Y.: M. E. Sharpe.

Murphy, David. 2002. "Competition Is Heating Up in China's Property Market." FEER, June 27.

Murray, Geoffrey. 1998. "State-owned Enterprises for Sale at Bargain Prices." *China News Digest,* September 28.

Nathan, Andrew. 2003. "Authoritarian Resilience." *Journal of Democracy* 14, no. 1 (January).

Naughton, Barry. 1995. *Growing Out of the Plan: Chinese Economic Reforms 1978–1993.* Cambridge: Cambridge University Press.

———. 1992. "Hierarchy and the Bargaining Economy: Government and Enterprise in the Reform Process." In Lieberthal and Lampton, eds.: 245–279.

Naughton, Barry, and Dali Yang, eds. 2004. *Holding China Together.* Cambridge: Cambridge University Press.

Nee, Victor, and Sijin Su. 1996. "Institutions, Social Ties, and Commitment in China's Corporatist Transformation." In McMillan and Naughton: 111–134.

Nolan, Peter, and Xiaoqiang Wang. 1998. "The Chinese Army's Firm in Business: The Sanjiu Group." *Developing Economies* 36, no. 1 (March): 45–79.

North, Douglass. 1990. *Institutions, Institutional Change and Economic Performance.* Cambridge: Cambridge University Press.

North, Douglass C., and Barry Weingast. 1989. "Constitutions and Commitment:

The Evolution of Institutions Governing Public Choice in Seventeenth-Century England." *The Journal of Economic History* 49, no. 4 (December): 803–832.

Nye, John V.C., and John N. Drobak, eds. 1997. *Frontiers of the New Institutional Economics*. New York: Academic Press.

O'Brien, Kevin, and Laura Luehrmann. 1998. "Institutionalizing Chinese Legislatures: Trade-offs Between Autonomy and Capacity." *Legislative Studies Quarterly* 23, no. 1.

O'Donnell, Guillermo. 2000. "Further Thoughts on Horizontal Accountability." Paper presented at the Workshop "Political Institutions, Accountability, and Democratic Governance in Latin America," University of Notre Dame, Kellogg Institute, May 8–9, 2000.

Ogden, Suzanne. 2002. *Inklings of Democracy in China*. Cambridge, Mass.: Harvard University Press.

Oi, Jean. 1999. *Rural China Takes Off: Institutional Foundations of Economic Reform*. Berkeley: University of California Press.

———. 1992. "Fiscal Reform and the Economic Foundations of Local State Corporatism in China." *World Politics* 45, no. 1: 99–126.

———. 1989. *State and Peasant in Contemporary China: The Political Economy of Village Government*. Berkeley: University of California Press.

O'Neill, Mark. 1999. "Alimony Far from Settled Despite End to Military Liaison." SCMP 1999–01–18.

Ostergaard, Clemens Stubbe, and Christina Peterson. 1991. "Official Profiteering and the Tiananmen Square Demonstrations in China." *Corruption and Reform* 6.

Ostrov, Benjamin. 2000. "The Fight against Smuggling." *China Business Review* (July-August): 44–47.

Pearson, Margaret. 1994. "The Janus Face of Business Associations in China: Socialist Corporatism in Foreign Enterprises." *Australian Journal of Chinese Affairs*, no. 31 (January): 25–46.

Peerenboom, Randall. 2002. *China's Long March Toward Rule of Law*. Cambridge: Cambridge University Press.

Pei, Minxin. 2002. "The Long March against Graft," FT 2002–12–09.

———. 2000. "Rights and Resistance: The Changing Contexts of the Dissident Movement." In Perry and Selden 2000.

———. 1999. "Will China Become Another Indonesia?" *Foreign Policy* no. 116 (fall 1999): 94–109.

———. 1994. *From Reform to Revolution : The Demise of Communism in China and the Soviet Union*. Cambridge, Mass.: Harvard University Press.

People's Bank of China. 2003. *Zhongguo huobi zhengce zhixing baogao 2002* (Report on monetary policy implementation 2002). January. Retrieved from www.pbc.gov.cn 2003–02–21.

Perry, Elizabeth, and Mark Selden, eds. 2000. *Chinese Society: Change, Conflict and Resistance.* London and New York: Routledge.

Pew Research Center for the People and the Press. 2002. *What the World Thinks in 2002.* Washington, D.C.: Pew Research Center for the People and the Press.

Pierre, Jon, ed. 2000. *Debating Governance: Authority, Steering, and Democracy.* Oxford: Oxford University Press.

Polanyi, Karl. 1957 [1944]. *The Great Transformation: The Political and Economic Origins of Our Time.* Boston: Beacon Press.

Pomfret, John. 1998. "Chinese Army Out of Business?" *Washington Post* (November 23).

Potter, Pitman. 2003. *From Leninist Discipline to Socialist Legalism: Peng Zhen on Law and Political Authority in the PRC.* Stanford: Stanford University Press.

——. ed. 1994. *Domestic Law Reforms in Post-Mao China.* Armonk, N.Y.: M. E. Sharpe.

Pottinger, Matt. 2000. "China's Military Building Mobile Phone Empire." Reuters, February 15.

Pottinger, Matt, and Peter Wonacott. 2002. "Downfall of Chinese Banking Boss Highlights Nation's Poor Policing." WSJ (January 21).

Prakash, Aseem, and Jeffrey Hart, eds. 2000. *Coping with Globalization.* London: Routledge.

Przeworski, Adam, Michael Alvarez, Jose Antonio Cheibub, and Fernando Limongi. 2000. *Democracy and Development: Political Institutions and Well-Being in the World, 1950–1990.* Cambridge: Cambridge University Press.

Qian, Yingyi, and Chenggang Xu. 1993. "The M-form Hierarchy and China's Economic Reform." *European Economic Review* 37: 541–548.

Quade, Christopher. 2000. "Chinese Provincial Political Elites." Paper presented at the Annual Meeting of the Midwest Political Science Association, Chicago, Illinois, April 27, 2000.

Reform. 1984. "Zhonggong zhongyang guanyu jingji tizhi gaige de jueding" (Decision of the Central Committee on economic system reforms) (October 20, 1984), in ZGJJNJ 1985: Section I, 1–12.

Roemer, John, ed. 1997. *Property Relations, Incentives and Welfare.* New York: St. Martin's Press.

Root, Hilton. 1996. "Corruption in China: Has It Become Systemic?" *Asian Survey* 36, no. 8.

Rose-Ackerman, Susan. 1999. *Corruption and Government: Causes, Consequences, and Reform.* Cambridge: Cambridge University Press.

Rotberg, Robert, ed. 2002. *State Failure and State Weakness in a Time of Terror.* Washington, D.C.: Brookings Institution Press.

Rowen, Henry. 1996. "The Short March: China's Road to Democracy." *National Interest*, no. 45 (fall 1996).

Schamis, Hector. 1999. "Distributional Coalitions and the Politics of Economic Reform in Latin America." *World Politics* 51, no. 2: 236–268.

Schedler, Andreas, Larry Diamond, and Marc F. Plattner, eds. 1999. *The Self-restraining State: Power and Accountability in New Democracies.* Boulder, Colo.: Lynne Rienner.

Schmitter, Philippe C. 1999. "The Limits of Horizontal Accountability." In Schedler, Diamond, and Plattner, eds., 1999.

Schroeder, Gertrude. 1990. "Economic Reform of Socialism: The Soviet Record." *Annals of the American Academy of Political and Social Science* no. 507 (January): 35–43.

Schumpeter, Joseph. 1975 [1942]. *Capitalism, Socialism, and Democracy.* New York: Harper & Row.

Shen Liren and Dai Yuanchen. 1990. "Woguo 'zhuhou jingji' de xingcheng jiqi biduan he genyuan" (The formation, adverse consequences, and roots of "duke-style economies" in our country). JJYJ no. 3: 12–20.

Shi, Tianjian. 1997. *Political Participation in Beijing.* Cambridge, Mass.: Harvard University Press.

Shirk, Susan. 1993. *The Political Logic of Economic Reform in China.* Berkeley: University of California Press.

Shou Peipei, Wang Hua, and Chi Liwei. 1999. "Qiche dasi shiwu nian" (Fifteen years fighting vehicle smuggling). NFZM 1999–07–16.

Shue, Vivienne. 1988. *The Reach of the State: Sketches of the Chinese Body Politic.* Stanford, Calif.: Stanford University Press.

Silberman, Bernard. 1993. *Cages of Reason: The Rise of the Rational State in France, Japan, the United States, and Great Britain.* Chicago: University of Chicago Press.

Simon, Herbert. 2000. "Public Administration in Today's World of Organizations and Markets." *PS: Political Science & Politics* 33, no. 4 (December).

Sklar, Martin. 1988. *The Corporate Reconstruction of American Capitalism, 1890–1916: The Market, the Law, and Politics.* Cambridge: Cambridge University Press.

Skowronek, Stephen. 1982. *Building a New American State: The Expansion of National Administrative Capacities.* Cambridge: Cambridge University Press.

Smith, Page. 1985. *America Enters the World: A People's History of the Progressive Era and World War I.* New York: McGraw-Hill.

Solnick, Steven. 1998. *Stealing the State: Control and Collapse in Soviet Institutions.* Cambridge, Mass.: Harvard University Press.

Song Defu. 1999. "1998 nian Guowuyuan jigou gaige de shijian yu sikao" (The practice of and thoughts on the 1998 State Council organizational reforms). In Zhonggong Zhongyang Xuanchuanbu 1999, vol. 3: 1708–1720.

Song Yongjian. 2003. "Yinian shenchu shuifen 40 yi, Hunan xiang xujia caiwu baogao shuo 'Bu'" (Hunan says 'No' to fake financial reports, uncovers 4 billion yuan in accounting froth). *Xiaoxiang chenbao* (Hunan morning news), retrieved at http://news.xinhuanet.com/newscenter/2003–01/15/content_690505.htm.

Stoner-Weiss, Kathryn. 2000. "Wither the State? The Regional Sources of Russia's post-Soviet Governance Crisis." Paper presented at the Annual Meeting of the American Political Science Association, Washington, D.C., September 1–4, 2000.

Studwell, Joe. 2002. *The China Dream: The Quest for the Last Great Untapped Market on Earth.* New York: Atlantic Monthly Press.

Su, Fubing, and Dali Yang. 2001. "Elections, Governance, and Accountability in Rural China." Paper presented at the International Symposium on Villagers Self-Government and Rural Social Development in China, Beijing, China, September 2–5, 2001.

Suleiman, Ezra. 1999. "Bureaucracy and Democratic Consolidation: Lessons from Eastern Europe." In Anderson, ed., 1999.

Sun Chengbin. 2004. "Diaocha xianshi woguo minzhong dui fanfu changlian manyidu jinyibu tigao" (Survey indicates further improvement in public satisfaction with anticorruption). Xinhua 2004-01-25.

Sun Chengbin and Zhang Jingyong. 2002. "Duoge diaocha xianshi, da duoshu qunzhong dui fan fubai chengji biaoshi renke" (Several surveys indicate that the majority of the public approve of the anticorruption results). Xinhua 2002–10–17.

Sun Ding. 2002. "Zhongguo zhengfu wangzhan de zhenxiang" (The realities of China's government websites). *Jisuanji shijie* (Computer world) (September 10), accessed at http://www.ccw.com.cn/htm/news1/it/deep/02_9_10-5.asp.

Sun Wenxue, and Wang Yuwu. 1994. "A Discussion on Obstacles to All-Around Implementation of the Tax-Assignment System and Their Solutions." *Caijing wenti yanjiu* (Research on financial and economic problems), no. 10 (October 5): 43–46; FBIS-CHI-95–002.

Sun Yafei. 2002. "Zhengfu shoushen: xiaoguo ruhe?" (What is the outcome of the government downsizing?). XWZK no. 36 (November).

Sun, Yan. 1999. "Reform, State, and Corruption: Is Corruption Less Destructive in China Than in Russia?" *Comparative Politics* 32, no. 1: 1–20.

————. 1995. *The Chinese Reassessment of Socialism, 1976–1992*. Princeton: Princeton University Press.

————. 1991. "The Chinese Protests of 1989: The Issue of Corruption." *Asian Survey* 3.

Sun Yubo. 2002. "Zhengdun he guifan jianzhu shichang zongshu" (Overview of [measures to] rectify and regulate the construction markets). Xinhua 2002–12–29.

Suzhou Industrial Park Administrative Committee. 2001. *Exhibition on the Achievements of Adapting Singapore's Experience in SIP*. Suzhou: n.p., June.

Tan Shigui, ed. 2003. *Sifa fubai fangzhi lun* (On preventing and curbing judicial corruption). Beijing: Falü chubanshe.

Tang, Shenming. 1997. "From Social Control to Disorganization: Official Corruption in China." *Social and Economic Studies* 46, no. 1.

Tanner, Harold. 1999. *Strike Hard! Anti-Crime Campaigns and Chinese Criminal Justice, 1979–1985*. Ithaca, N.Y.: Cornell University, Cornell East Asia Series.

Tanner, Murray Scot. 2000. "Shackling the Coercive State: China's Ambivalent Struggle Against Torture." *Problems of Post-Communism* 47, no. 5 (September-October).

————. 1999. *The Politics of Lawmaking in Post-Mao China*. Oxford: Oxford University Press.

————. 1994. "Organizations and Politics in China's Post-Mao Law-Making System." In Potter 1994.

Tanner, Murray Scot, and Chen Ke. 1998. "Breaking the Vicious Cycle: The Emergence of China's National People's Congress." *Problems of Post-Communism*, no. 3 (May/June).

Tao Ran. 2003. "Jinrong yayi, niming chuxu yu jingji zhuangui" (Financial repression, anonymous banking, and economic transition). JJGCB 2003–02–17.

Teiwes, Frederick C. 1993. *Politics and Purges in China: Rectification and the Decline of Party Norms, 1950–1965*. 2d ed. Armonk, N.Y.: M. E. Sharpe.

Ter-Minassian, Teresa, ed. 1997. *Fiscal Federalism in Theory and Practice*. Washington, D.C.: International Monetary Fund.

Ter-Minassian, Teresa, and Jon Craig. 1997. "Control of Sub-national Government Borrowing." In Ter-Minassian, ed.

Thomas, Jeffrey. 2002. "The Role and Powers of the Chinese Insurance Regulatory Commission in the Administration of Insurance Law in China." *Geneva Papers on Risk and Insurance: Issue and Practice* 27, no. 3 (July): 413–434.

Treisman, Daniel. 2002. "Postcommunist Corruption." Paper presented at the Comparative Politics Workshop, University of Chicago, November 6, 2002.

————. 1999. *After the Deluge: Regional Crises and Political Consolidation in Russia*. Ann Arbor: University of Michigan Press.

Unger, Jonathan. 1987. "The Struggle to Dictate China's Administration: The Conflict of Branches vs Areas vs Reform." *Australian Journal of Chinese Affairs* no. 18 (July)

Unger, Jonathan, and Anita Chan. 1995. "China, Corporatism, and the East Asian Model." *Australian Journal of Chinese Affairs* no. 33 (January): 29–53.

Vogel, Steven. 1996. *Freer Markets, More Rules: Regulatory Reform in Advanced Industrial Countries*. Ithaca, N.Y.: Cornell University Press.

Wade, Robert. 1990. *Governing the Market: Economic Theory and the Role of Government in East Asian Industrialization*. Princeton: Princeton University Press.

Walder, Andrew. 1995. "Local Governments as Industrial Firms." *American Journal of Sociology* vol. 101: 263–301.

Wang Dianlong. 2001. *Kuaiji weipai zhi lilun yu shiwu* (The accountant assignment system: theories and practices). Beijing: Xinhua chubanshe.

Wang Hua and Zhuang Huining. 1998. "Latest Trends of Anti-smuggling Struggle in China." *Liaowang*, November 30, FBIS-CHI-98–364, December 30.

Wang Ke. 1998. "Building the Army Through Thrift and Hard Work Is a Long-Term Guiding Principle of Our Army." *Qiushi* (Seek truth) no. 2 (January 16); FBIS-CHI-98–028, 1998–01–28.

Wang Lianzhou and Li Cheng. 2000. *Fengfeng yuyu zhengquanfa* (The vicissitudes of the securities law). Shanghai: Shanghai sanlian shudian.

Wang Lingling. 1998. "Zhiluan jianfu weihe zheban nan?" (Why is it so difficult to rectify the rampant [collection of levies] and reduce burdens?). *Zhongguo jidian ribao* (China machinery and electronics daily), 1998–02–27

Wang Mengkui. 2000. *Zai jingji zhuanzhe zhong* (Amid economic transition). Beijing: Huawen Chubanshe.

Wang Shaoguang and Hu Angang. 1993. *Zhongguo guojia nengli baogao* (Report on China's state capacity). Shenyang: Liaoning renmin chubanshe.

Wang Xiaobing. 2001. "Jundui cheli shanghai de yubo" (Repercussions from the divestiture of the military businesses. QB 2001–02–11.

Wang Xu and Yin Hongdong. 2002. "Bukesiyi de ling bodong wending zengzhang" (Amazingly stable growth with zero fluctuations). Xinhua 2002–09–19. Accessed at http://www.xinhua.sd.cn/zt-5/sdms-918/sdms.htm.

Wang Yanjuan. 2003. "Buliang jinrong zichan guanli yu chuzhi de zhanlue xuanze" (The strategic choice in managing and disposing of bad financial assets), CET 2003–04–04.

Wang Yaping. 1999. *Feichang diaocha* (Unusual investigation). Beijing: Zhongguo xiju chubanshe.

Wang Zheng. 2001. "Weifa zhaotoubiao weihai gongcheng zhiliang" (Illegal tendering and bidding undermine project quality). RMRB 2001–12–17.

Wang Zhi 2002. "Guoyou shangye yinhang de kexi zhuanzhe" (A welcome turning point for the state-owned commercial banks). JJRB (January 15).

Wang Zhongyu. 2003. "Guanyu Guowuyuan jigou gaige fang'an de shuoming" (Explanation of the State Council administrative reform plan), available at http://www.npcnews.com.cn/gb/paper403/1/class040300002/hwz230787.ht m. Accessed on March 20, 2003.

Wank, David. 1995. "Private Business, Bureaucracy, and Political Alliance in a Chinese City." *Australian Journal of Chinese Affairs* no. 33 (January): 55–71.

Weber, Max. 1978. *Economy and Society.* Berkeley: University of California Press.

Wei, Jianxing 1999. "Step up Efforts To Tackle Both the Immediate and Root Causes of Problems and Deepen the Anticorruption Struggle." Xinhua 1999–01–13; FBIS-CHI-99–015, 1999–01–15.

Wei Naibin. 1994. *Zai renda zhuren gongzuo gangwei shang de sikao yu shijian* (Reflections and practices of a people's congress chairman). Beijing: Zhongguo minzhu fazhi chubanshe.

Weingast, Barry. 1997a. "The Political Foundations of Democracy and the Rule of the Law." *American Political Science Review* 91, no. 2 (June).

———. 1997b. "The Political Foundations of Limited Government: Parliament and Sovereign Debt in 17th and 18th-century England." In Nye and Drobak.

Weitzman, Martin, and Xu Chenggang. 1997. "Chinese Township-Village Enterprises as Vaguely Defined Cooperatives." In Roemer 1997.

Wen Siyong and Ren Zhichu. 2002. *Hu Jintao zhuan* (Biography of Hu Jintao). Carle Place, N.Y.: Mirror Books.

Wenxian Yanjiushi. 1996. Zhonggong Zhongyang Wenxian Yanjiushi, ed. *Shisida yi-lai zhongyao wenxian xuanbian: shang* (Selection of important documents since the fourteenth CCP Party Congress: part I). Beijing: Renmin chubanshe.

White, Gordon. 1996. "Corruption and Market Reform in China." *IDS Bulletin* 27, no. 2.

White, Lynn T III. 1989. *Policies of Chaos: The Organizational Causes of Violence in China's Cultural Revolution.* Princeton: Princeton University Press.

Wiebe, Robert. 1967. *The Search for Order 1877–1920.* New York: Hill and Wang.

Winckler, Edwin, ed. 1999. *Transition from Communism in China: Institutional and Comparative Analysis.* Boulder, Colo.: Lynn Rienner.

Wines, Michael. 2000. "Putin Aims to Weaken Region Chiefs and Bolster Central Control." NYT May 18.

Wonacott, Peter. 2001. "Chinese Lawyers, Judges Prepare for WTO Fallout," WSJ. November 9.

Wong, Christine. 1992. "Fiscal Reform and Local Industrialization: The Problematic Sequencing of Reform in Post-Mao China." *Modern China* 18 (April): 197–227.

———. 1991. "Central-Local Relations in an Era of Fiscal Decline: The Paradox of Fiscal Decentralization in Post-Mao China." *China Quarterly* no. 128 (December).

Woo, Wing Thye, Stephen Parker, and Jeffrey Sachs, eds. 1997. *Economies in Transition.* Cambridge, Mass.: M.I.T Press.

Woodall, Brian. 1996. *Japan under Construction: Corruption, Politics, and Public Works.* Berkeley: University of California Press.

The World Bank. 2001. *Building Institutions for Markets: World Development Report 2002.* New York: Oxford University Press.

———. 1997. *The State in a Changing World: World Development Report 1997.* New York: Oxford University Press.

———. 1990a. *China: Between Plan and Market.* Washington, D.C.: World Bank.

———. 1990b. *China: Macroeconomic Stability and Industrial Growth under Decentralized Socialism.* Washington, D.C.: World Bank.

———. 1990c. *China: Financial Sector Policies and Institutional Development.* Washington, D.C.: World Bank.

Wright, Robin. 2000. "Clinton Visits an Africa Whose 'Renaissance' Has Collapsed." *International Herald Tribune,* 2000–08–26.

Wu Bangguo. 1999. "Wu on Quality, Technical Supervision." Xinhua Domestic Service 1999–03–26; FBIS-CHI-1999–0405.

Wu, Guoguang. 2001. "Fear and Loathing: A Recipe for Chaos." *Asiaweek* 27, no. 2 (January 19).

———. 1997. *Zhao Ziyang yu zhengzhi gaige* (Political reform under Zhao Ziyang). Taibei: Yuanjing chuban shiye gongsi.

Wu Jianghong. 1993. "Shenji lifa" (Auditing legislation). In Ma Hong and Sun Shangqing 1993: 1311–1312.

Wu Jinglian and Liu Jirui. 1991. *Lun jingzhengxing shichang tizhi* (On competitive market system). Beijing: Zhongguo caizheng jingji chubanshe.

Xia Changyong. 2002. "Gongjian zhizhang—guanzhu quanguo xiangzhen jigou gaige" (Crucial battle—the reform of township and town institutions in the country). RMRB (April 18).

Xia, Ming. 1997. "Informational Efficiency, Organizational Development and the Institutional Linkages of the Provincial People's Congresses in China." *Journal of Legislative Studies* 3, no. 3 (autumn).

Xiang Huaicheng. 1997. "Socialist Market Economy and Building the Taxation System." RMRB July 10, FBIS-CHI-97–212.

Xiao Chong, ed. 1999. *Zhong Rongji dazhan zousi jituan* (Zhu Rongji fights smuggling gangs). Hong Kong: Xiaerfei Guoji chuban gongsi.

Xiao Jie. 2002. "Zai quanguo zhengfu caigou gongzuo huiyi shang de jianghua" (Talk at the National Government Procurement Work Conference), accessed on May 25, 2003 at www.ccgp.gov.cn/web/zywxdetail.asp?condition=00000000035.

Xinshiqi. 1998. Zhonggong Zhongyang Wenxian Yanjiushi, ed. *Xinshiqi jingji tizhi gaige zhongyao wenxian xuanbian* (Selections of important documents on economic system reform in the new era). Beijing: Zhongyang wenxian chubanshe.

Xue Muqiao. 1990. *Lun Zhongguo jingji tizhi gaige* (On reforming China's economic system). Tianjin: Tianjin renmin chubanshe.

Yan Zhenhua. 2001. "Xingzheng shenpi zhidu gaige xu jinyibu guifan" (The reform of the system of administrative examinations and approvals needs to be further standardized). CET (February 28).

Yang, Dali L. 2003. "Leadership Transition and the Political Economy of Governance." *Asian Survey* 43, no. 1 (January/February).

———. 2002a. "Can the Chinese State Meet Its WTO Obligations? Government Reforms, Regulatory Capacity, and WTO Membership." *American Asian Review* no. 2 (summer).

———. 2002b. "China in 2001: Economic Liberalization and Its Political Discontents." *Asian Survey* 42, no. 1 (January/February).

———. 2001a. "The Great Net of China: Information Technology and Governance." *Harvard International Review* (winter).

———. 2001b. "Rationalizing the Chinese State: The Political Economy of Government Reform." In Chao and Dickson, eds.: 19–45.

———. 1999. "Economic Crisis and Market Transition in the 1990s." In Winckler, ed.: 151–177.

———. 1996a. *Calamity and Reform in China: State, Rural Society, and Institutional Change Since the Great Leap Famine.* Stanford: Stanford University Press.

———. 1996b. "The Dynamics and Progress of Competitive Liberalization in China." *Issues & Studies* 32, no. 8 (August 1996): 1–27.

———. 1994. "Reform and the Restructuring of Central-Local Relations." In Goodman and Segal, eds.: 59–98.

———. 1990. "Patterns of China's Regional Development Strategy." *China Quarterly* no. 122 (June).

Yang, Dali, and Fubing Su. 2000. "Taming the Market: China and the Forces of Globalization." In Prakash and Hart 2000.

Yang Jingyu. 2002. "Guanyu 'Zhonghua Renmin Gongheguo xingzheng xuke fa (caoan)' de shuoming (Explanation of the PRC Administrative Licensing Law [draft]).” *Zhongguo renda xinwen* (NPC news), 2002–08–26, retrieved at http://www.npcnews.com.cn/gb/paper6/20/class000600004/hwz217152.htm.

Yang Mei. 2003. “Shoufei fakuan jinnian qi tong jiao guoku” (Levies and fines must all be turned over to the state treasury this year). CJSB 2003–01–04.

Yang Peixin. 1990. *Chengbao zhi: qiye fada biyou zhilu* (The contracting system: The only road to enterprise prosperity). Beijing: Zhongguo jingji chubanshe.

Yang Yang, Fu Aiping, and Zhao Guilin. 1999. “Qibu zou—chu shanghai” (Walk out of business in unison). *Shidaichao* (Tide of the times) no. 3.

Ye Xiaoping. 2000. “Tiaotiao shei lai jiandu” (Who supervises the vertical administrations?). CYD 2000–12–18.

Yeh Tan. 1998a. “Zhongnanhai Angered at Army, Police Involvement in, Protecting Smuggling Activities.” *Ching Pao* 1998–09–04, FBIS-CHI-98–247, 1998–09–04.

———. 1998b. “Secrets of Zhu Rongji’s Southern Trip to Fight Corruption.” *Ching Pao* 1998–12–01: 26–29, FBIS-CHI-98–348, 1998–12–14.

Ying Songnian. 1999. “Xingzheng susong zai Zhongguo” (Administrative litigation in China). RMRBO 1999–12–24.

Yu Bin. 2003. “Zhongyang qianghua xunshi zhidu” (The party center strengthens the roving inspection system). LW no. 33 (August 18).

Yuan Shang and Han Zhu 1992. *Deng Xiaoping nanxun hou de Zhongguo* (China after Deng Xiaoping’s southern tour). Beijing: Gaige chubanshe.

ZGJJNJ. 1981–. *Zhongguo jingji nianjian* (Almanac of China’s economy). Beijing: Jingji guanli chubanshe,

ZGSJNJ. 1999. *Zhongguo shenji nianjian (1994–1998)* (China auditing yearbook 1994–1998). Beijing: Zhongguo shenji chubanshe.

ZGTJNJ. 1990–2002. *Zhongguo tongji nianjian* (China statistical yearbook). Beijing: Zhongguo tongji chubanshe.

ZGTJZY. 1998–2003. *Zhongguo tongji zhaiyao* (China statistical abstract). Beijing: Zhongguo tongji chubanshe.

Zhang Dingmin and Li Wenfang. 1998. “Regulation Urgently Required to Curb Corruption and Cut Waste in Government Spending.” CDBW November 15.

Zhang Hong. 1998. “How Will China Open Up Government Procurement Market to the Outside World?” ZXS 1998–07–14, FBIS-CHI-98–197.

Zhang Liang [pseudonym], compiler. 2001. *The Tiananmen Papers*. New York: Public Affairs.

Zhao Zhiwen and Wang Hua. 1998. “Soul Stirring—First Commentary on Launching in Depth the Struggle Against Smuggling.” RMRB 1998–08–04; FBIS-CHI-98–223, 1998–08–11; “Why Does it Occur Again and Again Despite Repeated Crackdowns—Second Commentary on Launching in

Depth the Struggle Against Smuggling." RMRB 1998–08–06; FBIS-CHI-98–222, 1998–08–10; "Third Commentary on Launching in Depth the Struggle Against Smuggling." RMRB 1998–08–09; FBIS-CHI-98–225, 1998–08–13.

Zheng Hongfan. 1999. "To Fight Against Corruption, It Is Necessary To Get At the Root and Strike at the Source." RMRB 1999–01–12; FBIS-CHI-99–020, 1999–01–20.

Zheng Lu et al., eds. 1999. *Zhonghua Renmin Gongheguo Xianfa zuixin shiyi duben* (The constitution of the People's Republic of China: latest explanatory reader). Changsha: Hunan renmin chubanshe.

Zhong Guoxing. 1998. "Shichang jingji jia fubai daoxiang shenmo" (What does the combination of market economy and corruption lead to?). ZGB (October 28).

Zhonggong Zhongyang Wenxian Yanjiushi. 1998. *Deng Xiaoping sixiang nianpu (1975–1997)* (The genealogy of Deng Xiaoping's thought, 1975–1997). Beijing: Zhongyang wenxian chubanshe.

Zhonggong Zhongyang Xuanchuanbu Lilunju, ed. 1999. *Jinian dang de 11 jie san zhong quanhui ershi zhounian lilun yantaohui wenji* (Compendium of papers from the symposium in commemoration of the twentieth anniversary of the third plenum of the eleventh central committee). Beijing: Xuexi chubanshe.

Zhongyang Jiwei Jijian Jiancha Yanjiusuo, ed. 2002. *Zhongguo gongchandang fanfu changlian wenxian xuanbian* (Selected Chinese Communist Party documents on fighting corruption and promoting clean [behavior]). Beijing: Zhongyang wenxian chubanshe.

Zhou Faming. 2000. "Gongshi shigi xuyao tiqian" (The timing of public comments needs to be advanced). *Shidaichao* (Tide of the times) no. 7.

Zhou Hanhua. 2002. "Women wei shenmo xuyao zhengfu xinxi gongkai zhidu" (Why we need a system for government information transparency). NFZM 2002–11–21.

Zhou Wanyun. 2002. "Woguo fan fubai douzheng chengjiu huigu yu zhanlue sikao" (The achievements of and strategic reflections on the anticorruption struggle of our country). FZRB 2002–11–18.

Zhu Renxian. 2002. "Gengxin xingzheng guannian tanxi" (Renewing the concepts of administration). RMRB (April 11).

Zhu Rongji. 2003. *Zhengfu gongzuo baogao* (Government work report). Beijing: Remin chubanshe.

———. 2000. "Congyan zhizheng, quanmian jiaqiang guanli" (Rigorously and comprehensively strengthen governance). RMRB 2000–03–10.

———. 1998. "Tongyi sixiang, jiaqiang lingdao, xunsu er yanli de daji zousi fanzui huodong" (Unify thinking, strengthen leadership, swiftly and sternly crack down on criminal smuggling activities). JJRB (September 1).

Zhu Shaoping. 1999. "Qianyi zhengfu caigou fa yu zhaobiao toubiao fa" (Preliminary comments on the government procurement law and tendering and bidding law). CET 1999–08–31.

Zong Hairen. 2002. *Disidai* (The fourth generation). Carle Place, N.Y.: Mirror Books.

INDEX

1911 Revolution, 299

Abuse of power, 202, 208, 222, 269, 301, 363
Accountability, 23, 148, 157, 173, 175, 187–192 *passim*, 196, 215, 218, 224, 230ff, 251, 282f, 289, 291, 308; system, 230ff. *See also* Horizontal accountability
Accountant secondment system, 247
Accounting, 23, 88, 93, 147f, 166, 235, 246f, 252; Law, 147f, 281
Accounting Management Bureau, 247
Administration, vertical, 47, 66, 74ff, 93, 97–101, 108, 241, 279, 281, 308, 336. *See also* Vertical control
Administration in accordance with law, 150, 154, 305
Administrative agencies, 156, 163f, 176, 310
Administrative approval and licensing, 2, 23, 54, 103, 151–165 *passim*, 172–178 *passim*, 184–185, 214, 217, 231, 237–241 *passim*, 252, 271, 290, 301, 305f, 310
Administrative (service) center, 151, 172, 174
Administrative charges, fees, and levies, 237, 241f. *See also* Fees
Administrative discretion, 153, 198, 207, 216
Administrative expenses, 30, 54, 123, 247f, 275
Administrative innovation, 177, 186
Administrative Licensing Law, 162ff, 263, 307
Administrative Litigation Law, 306
Administrative penalties, 164, 241, 286, 306
Administrative rationalization program, 20, 152. *See also* Rationalization
Administrative reforms, 20, 45f, 152, 241
Administrative state, 1, 2, 10, 152, 155, 164, 183–186 *passim*, 216, 291, 306, 309, 314;
Agricultural Bank of China, 87f
Agriculture, 49, 58, 63, 237, 261, 272, 280
Aircraft manufacturing, 29
Airline, 58f, 149, 302

Air quality, 302
AJPG businesses, 110f, 116, 125–133 *passim*, 136, 141–149 *passim*
All China Federation of Trade Unions, 37
All China Women's Federation, 37, 238
Allocation, 207f, 212, 215, 275, 310. *See also* Land; Resources; Stocks.
Anhui, 48, 174, 199, 246–249 *passim*
Anonymous banking, 228
Anti-competitive practices, 196. *See also* Competition
Anticorruption, 200, 208, 210, 217–225 *passim*, 248–258 *passim*, 308; agencies, 172, 183, 195, 222–225 *passim*, 253f, 259; bureau, 6; establishment, 195, 216, 222, 226f, 237, 254, 258; laws, 224, 227, 251; strategies, 23, 199. *See also* Corruption
Anticrime campaign, 104
Antimonopoly, 300
Antiriot units, 6
Antismuggling, 112, 114, 118–124 *passim*, 133, 135, 201. *See also* Smuggling
Antismuggling Bureau, 122–123
Antismuggling police, 113, 123, 339
Appointive power, 4, 261
Appointment, 226, 233, 260, 263, 269, 294, 306; ratification, 288
Appraisal services, 147
Approval and licensing system, *see* Administrative approval and licensing
Aquatic safety, 99
Arbitrage, 218
Armed forces, 217, 296. *See also* Military; People's Liberation Army
Armed police, 6, 133, 294
Arms trading, 130, 139
Arrest, 223, 276
Asia, 115, 185, 251
Asian Development Bank, 198

Asian financial crisis, 1, 10, 20f, 36, 44, 63, 66,
     81, 84, 91f, 107, 110–114 *passim*, 132, 188,
     199, 221ff, 266, 273, 294, 313
Aslund, Anders 14f
Asset, 35, 67, 91, 128, 135, 137, 140ff, 149, 227,
     236f; management, 35, 144, 146
Asset Management Companies (AMCs), 60,
     87, 212
Association, industrial, 49, 163
Auctions, 151, 155, 208–216 *passim*, 286. *See
     also* Land; Procurement; Resources
Audit, 123, 147, 166, 182, 224, 234f, 244, 252f,
     259, 272, 278–286 *passim*; end-of-term,
     233f, 251, 287; financial, 23, 218, 233;
     institutionalized, 287; internal, 281; Law,
     279–282 *passim*; price, 195
Auditing Regulations, 128
Audit office, 206, 242, 279–284 *passim*, 287.
     See also National Audit Office
Auditors, 214, 257, 280, 284, 287
Audit Work Report, 264, 281–288 *passim*
Austerity program, 67, 70
Authoritarianism, 6, 299, 311
Autocracy, 3
Auto industry, 57, 62, 111, 114, 124
Avoidance policy, 5

Badong County, 231
Balance of power, 20
Bank, 12, 68, 86–91 *passim*, 213, 219, 222, 228f,
     234, 240, 286, 294, 300, 302; accounts, 218,
     228, 239–242 *passim*, 246, 284; credits and
     grants, 10, 68; deposits, 69, 228, 245; loans,
     219f
Banking industry, 90, 222
Banking Laws, 91, 281, 302
Banking regulation, 88f
Banking system 36, 60, 66, 84–88 *passim*,
     220, 244f, 252, 294
Bank of China (BOC), 86–89 *passim*, 120,
     144, 234, 286
Bankruptcy, 33, 222, 273
Bank supervisory bureau, 89
Bao Tong, 250
Baoshan district legislature, 276
Baotou city, 173
Barriers to entry, 153
Basic construction, 235. *See also* Capital
     construction
Beijing, 3, 6, 16, 29, 42, 44, 48, 77f, 98, 100,

105, 107, 116, 118, 138, 152–158 *passim*, 167,
     170, 174, 178, 181, 188, 196–206 *passim*, 210,
     232, 238, 243, 249f, 255, 264, 270–273, 277,
     308, 313, 361
Beijing Currency Printing Plant, 207
Beijing Land Trading Market, 210
Beijing Military Region, 203
Beijing Municipal Construction Committee,
     197
Beijing Shoujian Zhaobiao company, 195
Beijing Subway Group, 195
Bidding, 187–206 *passim*, 210–216 *passim*, 231,
     232, 252, 257f, 287
Bid rigging, 176, 195
Black market, 111
Bonds, 8, 68f, 78, 86, 160, 188, 190, 197, 229,
     266, 286, 304, 309
Bonuses, 239, 243
Bourgeois liberalization, 4
Brazil, 194
Bribery, 77, 158, 163, 187, 191–198 *passim*,
     208–215 *passim*, 227, 230f, 253; giving, 227f
Bridges, 197, 219
Britain, 215
Brokerage accounts, 219, 229
Budget 19, 57, 74, 124–129 *passim*, 134, 140,
     206, 235ff, 266f, 271, 276, 283, 285, 296,
     305f, 359; deficits, 34, 70, 78, 211, 266, 304,
     309; funds, 247, 284; implementation, 238,
     267, 272; reforms, 236, 238f, 301f;
     supervision, 267, 271–276 *passim*, 288. *See
     also* Budget management; Budgeting;
     Revenue
Budget and Accounting Act of 1921, 301
Budgetary funding, 239f, 243, 246
Budgetary purchases, 204
Budgetary Work Committee, *see under*
     National People's Congress
Budget Implementation Law, 78
Budgeting, 23, 235–239 *passim*, 248, 251, 258,
     266–271 *passim*, 276, 305; departmental
     (*bumen yusuan*), 236ff; Zero-base, 237f
Budget Law, 235, 281
Budget management, 206, 236, 267, 284, 286,
     305
Buildings, 219
Burden of proof, 227
Bureaucracy, 2, 8–13 *passim*, 20–24 *passim*, 29,
     37, 41–44 *passim*, 54, 56, 63, 77, 101, 153,
     161f, 172–183 *passim*, 187, 190, 198, 217,

244, 251, 277–282 *passim*, 310–314 *passim*; discretion, 151, 157, 161, 222; efficiency, 156, 174; fragmentation, 38, 58; and Latin America, 323; subterfuge, 155
Bureaucratic entrepreneurialism, 12
Bureaucrats, 151f, 166, 169, 176f, 187, 207, 215f, 277, 280
Bureau for Anticorruption and Bribery, 225
Bureau of Industry and Commerce, 103.
Bureau of Internal Trade, 42
Bureau of Supervision, 179
Bureau of the Budget, 301
Bureau of Water Affairs (*shuiwu ju*), 40
Bush, George, 4
Business disengagement, *see* Divesture
Businesses, 149, 208, 217, 220, 232, 240, 256, 291–296 *passim*, 301–305 *passim*, 310
Business practices, unfair, 146
Butterfield, Fox, 3
Buyer's market, 21, 31, 292

Cadre, 4f, 13, 47, 129, 179, 182, 187, 189, 220, 226, 233, 257
Campaign, 208, 220, 257
Canada, 121, 194, 249
Cao Zhi, 283
Capital, 10, 20, 27, 75, 305
Capital construction, 190, 237. *See also* Basic construction
Capitalism, 4, 7, 297
Capitalism, Socialism, and Democracy, 2
Cash flows, 230
CCP (Chinese Communist Party), 220, 290, 296, 312. *See also* Communist Party
CCTV (China Central Television), 168, 302
CDMA system, 138
CD-ROMS, 119
Centers for land-use transactions, 209
Central Bank, *see* People's Bank of China
Central Commission on Organizations and Staff Size, 36f
Central Committee, 71, 84, 86, 98, 117, 131–138 *passim*, 143, 159, 166, 200, 214, 230, 233, 293
Central Comprehensive Governance and Control Committee, 6
Central control, 5, 302
Central coordination, 156, 225
Central decree/directive, 116, 168, 246
Central Discipline Inspection Commission

(CDIC), 69, 118, 120, 135, 166, 182, 191, 193, 210, 220–227 *passim*, 232f, 241, 254–257 *passim*, 278, 305; CDIC Party Style and Clean Administration Office, 226
Central Enterprise Work Committee, 59, 61
Central Financial Security Leading Small Group, 90
Central Financial Work Commission, 90, 144
Central government, 115, 242–246 *passim*, 267, 281–285 *passim*, 296, 299, 304
Centralization, 66, 92f, 202, 204, 243–248 *passim*
Central Large Enterprise Work Committee, 144
Central-local relations, 69, 107
Central Military Commission (CMC), 52, 118, 125–138 *passim*, 260
Central Party School, 7, 8, 221, 223
Central planning, 22, 37, 68, 152, 183
Central Politics and Law Commission, 135
Changjiang Dongli, 35
Chang Jiang River, 99
Changzhi, 348
Changzhou, 30
Chechnya, 298
Checks and balances, 124, 203, 207, 259f, 289, 291, 304, 306
Chemicals State Asset Management Corporation, 35
Chen Guorong, 120
Chen Liangyu, 310
Chen Xitong, 6, 199, 220, 222, 249, 270, 350
Chen Youwu, 113
Chen Yuan, 71
Chen Yun, 71
Chen Yuqiang, 120
Cheng Kejie, 192, 208, 219, 222, 228
Cheng Weigao, 249
Chengdu, 85, 155, 195, 255, 269, 277
Chernobyl nuclear accident, 171
Cheung, Tai-Ming, 126, 140
Chief judges, 270
Chief procurator, 275
Child labor, 301
China Aerospace Industry Corporation, 38
China Agricultural Development Bank, 234
China Banking Regulatory Commission (CBRC), 90f, 108
China Central Television, *see* CCTV

China Certified Accountants Association, 148, 344

China Certified Auditors Association, 344

China Compulsory Certification (CCC), 102

China Construction Bank, 86, 88, 144, 188, 286

China Construction News, 192

China Daily, 128, 192

China Economic Herald, 192

China Everbright (Group), 86, 138

China Insurance Regulatory Commission (CIRC), 49f, 84

China Meteorological Administration, 51

China Mobile, 56

China National Audit Office, *see* National Audit Office

China Netcom, 56

China Petrochemical Corporation, 115, 121

China Petroleum and Chemical Corporation, 61

China Petroleum and Natural Gas Corporation, 38

China Railcom, 56

China Reform News, 12

China Securities Regulatory Commission (CSRC), 49, 84, 92f, 147, 160, 167, 213ff, 234

China-Singapore Industrial Park (Suzhou), 153, 172f

China Telecom, 33, 38, 56, 138

China Unicom, 56, 138

China United Airlines, 137, 139

China Venture Capital, 94

Chinese Academy of Sciences, 50f, 244

Chinese Consumers' Association, 95, 106

Chinese People's Political Consultative Conference, 143, 214, 245

Chongqing, 77, 101, 155, 158, 165, 188, 190, 199, 231, 244, 246, 268f

Circular Concerning Military, People's Armed Police, Judicial, Procuratorial, and Public Security Organs Disengaging from Business Activities, 135

CITIC, 15

Citizens, 171, 248, 269, 299

City commercial banks, 89

Civil affairs bureau, 177

Civil-military relations, 139

Civil servants, 64, 159, 172f, 176, 181, 218

Civil service, 181, 183, 252, 301, 305; reforms, 9, 43, 54, 151, 175–183 *passim*, 305

Civil War, 9, 301

Clean administration, 224

Clean Administration Complaint Center, 176

Coal, 22, 99, 105, 141

Coast (regions, cities), 151, 156, 165, 198, 204

Coast guard, 110, 130

Collective enterprise, 166

Collectivization, 9f

Colonialism, 304

Command Center for Corruption Investigation, 225

Command economy, 26, 29, 296

Commercial businesses, 126–141 *passim*, 149, 234

Commission of Science, Technology, and Industry for National Defense (Costind), 40, 140, 203, 214

Committee on Government Procurement, 199

Communism, 292

Communist countries, 295, 313

Communist Party, 2–7 *passim*, 16–20 *passim*, 35, 37, 66, 84, 169, 226, 230–233 *passim*, 245, 261, 289, 293, 295, 301, 303, 308, 314, 370. *See also* Central Committee; National Party Congress

Communist Youth League, 37, 106

Community administrative centers, 174

Community services, 174

Company Law, 61

Competition, 13, 27, 88, 95f, 116, 127–131 *passim*, 140, 145–151 *passim*, 156f, 161, 167, 174f, 179–182 *passim*, 186f, 198, 202, 251, 264, 302, 305; unfair, 105, 125f, 130f

Competitive bidding, *see* Bidding

Competitive mechanisms, 216, 290

Competitive tendering, *see* Tendering

Complaints, 176, 206, 265, 276, 310. *See also* Public complaints

Compliance, 75, 212, 215, 226–232 *passim*, 268, 278, 306

Comprehensive management, 121, 223

Computer networks, 193

Conflict-of-interest, 224, 232, 251, 305

Confucius, 313

Constitution, 107, 149, 260–262, 267, 275–284 *passim*, 288f, 298, 304–309 *passim*

Constitutional convention of 1787, 368
Constitutional faith, 288
Constitutionalism, 259, 306, 363
Construction bureau/committee, 39, 155, 196, 228
Construction industry, 191–198 *passim*, 216, 231, 252, 302
Construction markets, 189, 193
Construction projects, *see* Projects
Consumer Right Day, 302
Consumers, 86, 300ff
Contract Law, 351
Contractor, 195, 231, 244
Coordination Center for Complaints by Overseas Investors, 175
Copyright Law, 106
Corporate governance, 62, 214
Corporate income tax, 75–80 *passim*, 107
Corporations, 36, 77
Corporatism, 11, 125, 127, 139
Corruption, 2, 5f, 12–17 *passim*, 21, 23, 34–36, 63, 84, 86, 111–118 *passim*, 122f, 126, 130–133, 149, 153–156 *passim*, 161, 178–183 *passim*, 186–204 *passim*, 207–242 *passim*, 247–265 *passim*, 270, 276f, 281–294 *passim*, 297–302 *passim*, 357, 361; fighters, 192
Corruption Perceptions Index (CPI), 256
Cotton, 311
Counterfeit (products), 94, 97, 102, 106
County, 75, 78, 178, 228, 268
Courts, 12, 47, 120, 129, 149, 230, 236, 241, 245, 262, 268
Crackdown, 119–125 *passim*, 208, 220, 222, 232, 243, 253–257 *passim*, 280, 294
Crime, 221, 230ff, 255, 265, 276f; economic, 221, 229; securities, 92
Criminal, 90, 105, 228, 233, 281, 286; Law, 92, 227, 357
Cultural Revolution, 9, 301
Culture Bureau, 155
Currency, 20, 68, 111, 114, 121
Customs Administration, 13, 21, 39, 75, 94, 100, 110–115 *passim*, 119–125 *passim*, 130, 201, 229f, 234, 236, 252f, 294, 306
Customs duties, 111–115 *passim*, 120
Customs Law, 122, 124

Dai Xianglong, 85, 90
Dams, 219
Danwei system, 312

Daqing, 222
Death penalty, 222, 227
Debt, 78, 84–87 *passim*, 142
Decentralization, 22, 26, 65, 74, 97, 102, 107, 116, 187, 239f, 278, 296, 298
Decertification, 230
Decision on Various Issues Concerning the Building of a Socialist Market Economic System, 293
Defense factories, 203
Defense spending, 125, 139f
Deflation, 115
Delinking, 144. *See also* Divestiture
Demand, 27, 68, 115, 188, 281
Democracy, 2, 218, 239, 250f, 259, 261, 273, 297–300, 311–314 *passim*, 368
Democratic evaluations, 270
Democratization, 217, 259, 313f, 370
Demotion, 178, 233
Deng Xiaoping, 3–7 *passim*, 15–21 *passim*, 66–72 *passim*, 84, 107, 117, 125ff, 131, 133, 220f, 293f; Theory, 261
Departmental interests, 224, 227
Departmentalism, 116
Department of Land and Resources, 176
Deposits, 88, 90, 219, 229; direct 245. *See also under* Bank
Deregulatory reforms, 161
Dereliction of duty, 222, 231f
Development plan/program, 167, 170, 273
Development zones, 67
Digital Guangdong, 203
Disbursement reforms, 206, 244ff
Discipline, 210, 216, 220, 233f, 251, 260, 281f, 291, 304ff
Discipline and inspection system, 224ff
Discipline Inspection Committee, 45, 144, 176, 197, 224, 276. *See also* Central Discipline Inspection Commission
Discontent, 221, 265
Discretion, 207f, 215f, 238, 270, 298
Discretionary accounts, 238
Discretionary power, 74, 187, 305
Discretionary spending power, 273
Disillusionment, 311
Disintegration, 71, 297f, 312
Dismissal, 233f, 269
Dissidents, 311, 313
Divestiture, 2, 21ff, 33, 35, 52, 58f, 110, 127f,

132–150 *passim*, 156, 186, 193, 216, 240–243
passim, 290–296 *passim*, 305
Divestiture Order, 134, 137, 140, 142
Divide-and-rule strategy, 72, 296
Divorce, 184
Dongguan, 112
Dongjiang-Shenzhen water project, 195
Downsizing, 45, 150f, 296
Drugs, 203, 302. *See also* State Food and
Drug Administration
Dual prices, 15, 31, 126, 214, 292
Dual-tracked reforms, 9
Due process of legislative deliberation, 205
Duma, 299
Dunhuang, 195

Eastern Europe, 1, 14f, 71, 293
Eastern Industrial Trading Company, 113
East India Company, 116
Economic development, 6, 7, 125, 221, 268,
290, 295, 303
Economic environment, 143, 145, 156, 221
Economic governance, 2, 25, 149, 164, 171,
218, 257. *See also* Governance
Economic growth, 221, 228, 303, 311
Economic legislation, 266, 301
Economic performance, 160, 233f
Economic stabilization, 4, 20, 66–69 *passim*.
Education, 48ff, 220, 235–240 *passim*, 266,
272, 274, 303, 313
Efficiency, 65, 124, 153, 172, 184, 203, 244, 291,
314
E-government, 175, 203. *See also* Internet
Elections, 251, 259f, 299–314 *passim*
Electric Power Regulatory Commission, 64
Electronic convenience stations, 175
Elevators, 204
Elite, 72, 150, 164, 169, 292, 306, 309
Embezzlement, 121, 173, 206, 222, 228,
242–245 *passim*, 285
Employment, 10, 34, 44, 96, 126, 145, 162,
277; government, 42, 46, 53f, 153
End-of-term audit, *see* Audit
Energy, 10, 29, 64, 239
Enforcement, 10, 89f, 103, 106, 203, 229, 232,
240, 251, 297, 306f; local, 97. *See also* Law
enforcement
England, 304
Enron, 9, 88, 145–148 *passim*
Enterprises, 18, 25, 27, 37, 47, 51, 56f, 74f,

139f, 144, 147, 185, 237, 279, 293, 296, 302;
army-run, 132
Enterprise Work Committee, 144
Entertainment, 208, 247
Environment, 22, 236, 243, 255, 274, 276,
302, 311
Environment, soft, 151, 156, 176
Environmental (Protection) Bureau, 39, 274.
See also under State Administrations
Environmental protection, 22, 236, 243, 255
Equipment, 198, 201
Ethnic extermination, 313
Europe, 304
Examinations, 237, 242, 288
Exchequer system, 237, 244. *See also* State
exchequer
Executive discretion, 236
Exit-entry administration, 39
Expenditure, 10, 83, 236–242 *passim*, 246,
279f, 284; defense, 139
Expenditure management, 243, 251
Expert panels, 205, 214
Extra-budget funds/revenue, 26, 236–243
passim, 247, 271, 284
Extradition, 249
Extralegal privileges, 142

Fairbanks, Charles, 297
Fair Deal, 300
Fairness, 182, 187f, 192–195 *passim*, 201,
209–212 *passim*, 262, 291. *See also*
Competition
Fake names, 228
Falungong, 164, 290
Family planning, 236
Fang Kuanrong, 120
Far Eastern Economic Review, 221
Farmers, 4, 46, 167, 284, 301, 312, 330
Farmland, 167
Federal government, 80, 359
Federalism, 107, 296, 298
Federal Reserve Act of 1913, 300
Federal Reserve System of the United States,
40, 295, 300, 302
Federal Trade Commission Act of 1914, 301
Federation Council, 66, 298, 299
Fees, 142, 152, 154, 172ff, 209, 212, 235f, 241,
247f, 252, 263. *See also* Administrative
charges, fees, and levies
Fewsmith, Joseph, 249

Fiduciary operations, 59, 144
Film, 115
Finance, 128, 218, 266, 302
Finance Bureau/Department, 203–207
    passim, 228, 235–246 *passim*, 272, 280;
    municipal, 207, 246, 271f
Financial and Economic Committee, 266,
    272, 275, 283, 286
Financial and fund management rules, 188,
    280
Financial discipline, 85, 247f
Financial fiefdom, 243
Financial fraud/irregularities, 94, 217–220
    passim, 229, 233, 235, 242f, 260, 283. *See
    also* Fraud
Financial instability, 228
Financial institutions, 76, 91, 147, 229, 234,
    273, 280, 285, 294
Financial laws and regulations, 88, 300
Financial management, 2, 23, 176, 189,
    235–241 *passim*, 248, 253, 258, 271, 278,
    283–291 *passim*, 305; centralization, 244,
    248
Financial reforms, 218, 243, 258
Financial regulation, 94, 98
Financial Regulations on Administrative
    Units, 240
Financial security, 294
Financial services, 224, 258
Financial system, 20, 36, 64, 66, 84, 220
Financial Times, 3, 230
Fines, 152, 235–243 *passim*, 247f.
Fire safety department, 130
Fireworks industry, 105
Fiscal, 18–21 *passim*, 45, 47, 70ff, 79, 110, 116,
    142, 187, 198, 200, 208–212 *passim*, 215,
    245, 266, 270–275 *passim*, 293, 298f, 303,
    309; contracting, 26, 70, 72;
    decentralization, 26, 298; Particularism,
    72; reform, 5, 27, 70–73 *passim*, 78, 107,
    294, 296; system, 70, 72, 295–298 *passim*
Fishing administration, 38
Five Do's, Six No's, 136
Five-tier loan classification, 89
Flood control, 285
Focus, 223
Food, 22, 171, 247, 302
Foreign debt, 70
Foreign exchange, 84, 88, 111f, 124, 165; fraud,
    117–121 *passim*

Foreign (direct) investment, 7, 54, 58, 84, 156,
    165, 174, 185, 303
Foreign securities firm, 160
Forestry Police, 136
Four-category classification, 87
Fraud, 76, 86–89 *passim*, 104, 124, 148, 192,
    235, 287. *See also* Funds; Tax; Financial
    fraud/irregularities; Foreign exchange
Free speech, 250
Freedom, 217, 300, 304, 313
Fujian, 43, 85, 111, 117, 120f, 155, 176, 181, 194,
    204, 222, 246, 250, 253, 310
Fujian provincial marine police headquarters,
    120
Fujian Yuanhua Group, 112
Funds, 133, 187–191 *passim*, 214, 233, 237–245
    passim, 248, 274–288 *passim*; diversion,
    206, 245, 267, 272; hidden, 247, 284;
    misused, 246, 248, 252f, 284ff; off-budget,
    236. *See also* Fraud
Futures, 147
Fuzhou, 155

Gansu, 44, 85, 182, 195, 226
Gansu Administrative Management
    Association, 44
GATT, 205, 303
GDP (per capita), 18, 73, 207, 256, 293, 297,
    367
Gehua, 35
General Administration of Customs, *see*
    Customs Administration
General Armament Department, 132, 203
General Logistics Department, 133, 135, 141
General Political Department, 117
General Staff Department Equipment Office,
    117
Germany, 313
GITIC, *see* Guangdong International Trust
    and Investment Corporation
Glass Stegall Act, 89, 302
Global 1,000 companies, 185
Global Business Policy Council, 185
Global economy, 305, 307
Global learning, 295
GMP, 70, 103
Goldstone, Jack, 15
Golden Tax Project, 77f
Gongshi zhi, 181f
Goods, 165, 186, 201, 203

Google, 312
Governability, 311
Governance, 8, 20, 24, 207, 247, 258f, 285, 288, 290–296 *passim*, 312f; defined, 323; reforms, 297, 299, 303, 314
Government Acceleration Project, 159
Government accounting, 244–247. *See also* Accounting
Government administration, 132, 178, 238, 283, 307
Government agencies/bureaus/departments, 144–147 *passim*, 152, 159, 167–177 *passim*, 192–195, 201f, 205, 219f, 226–230 *passim*, 236–243 *passim*, 284f, 305
Governmental power, 216, 292, 303f
Government approval, *see* Administrative approval and licensing
Government budget, 50, 79, 139, 164, 201, 206, 240, 245, 266, 272, 275, 283, 285. *See also* Budget
Government-business relations, 111, 149, 292
Government downsizing, 34, 56, 225
Government Efficacy Complaints Centers, 176, 310
Government exchequer/treasury, 122, 236, 242, 243, 246, 281–286 *passim*
Government expansion, 10, 29
Government expenditure, 267, 283
Government finances, 27, 195, 282f, 287,
Government functions, 151, 153, 161–166 *passim*, 173
Government funds, 231, 235, 252. *See also* Funds
Government ministries, 156, 160, 172, 201, 237, 307. *See also individual ministries and administrations by name*
Government Offices Administration, 201
Government procurement, 23, 154, 157, 173, 175, 186ff, 198–207 *passim*, 217, 232, 252, 257, 290, 305, 307; contract suppliers, 200; Law, 205ff, 307
Government projects, 215, 219, 244, 276, 285, 305. *See also* Construction; Projects
Government reform, 25f, 36f, 41, 97 285, 305, 309, 310; 2003 plan, 90
Government revenue, 70f, 123, 211, 215, 239f, 284. *See also* Revenue
Government service, 151, 174, 305
Government Work Report, 304
Graft, *see* Corruption

Grain, 139, 281, 311
Grass-roots, 237, 311
Gray, John, 313
Great Britain, 85, 107, 359
Great Leap Forward, 9, 67
Great Wall, 241
Great Wall Telecom (GWT), 137, 138
Gresham's Law, 145, 196
Guangdong, 39, 41, 51, 66f, 85, 101, 111, 117, 119, 124, 142ff, 154, 160, 168ff, 174f, 179–183 *passim*, 187, 193, 197–204 *passim*, 208f, 222, 233, 238, 242–245 *passim*, 251f, 270–278 *passim*, 287, 310, 343
Guangdong Construction Committee, 209
Guandong Huilai Country Armed Police Unit, 113
Guangdong International Trust and Investment Corporation (GITIC), 84, 86, 222, 273
Guangdong People's Congress, 273–278 *passim*
Guangdong Phenomenon, 273
Guangdong Provincial CCP Party Committee, 278
Guangdong State Tax Bureau, 78
Guangxi, 35, 46, 85, 119, 182, 192, 219, 251, 276
Guangxi Yinxing Industrial Development Company, 228
Guangzhou, 85, 167–170 *passim*, 187, 221, 243, 255, 269, 287
Guangzhou Metro, 351
Guangzhou Municipal People's Congress, 274
Guangzhou Subway Corporation, 195
Guizhou, 46, 85, 198, 226
Guo Zhenqian, 282f, 364
Guomindang, 309

Haicheng, 35, 63
Hainan, 30, 45, 85, 150, 172, 203, 207, 244f, 305
Hainan Health Bureau, 203
Han Zhubin, 230, 265
Hangzhou, 36, 119, 210
Hao Gang, 243
Harding, Warren, 301
Hayekian experimentalism, 7
He Ping, 117
He Qinglian, 12, 219
He Yong, 216

He, Zengke, 217
Health care, 49f, 202ff, 255, 273, 275, 303, 313
Health Quarantine Bureau (HQB), 241ff
Hearings, 151, 168, 264, 270–273, 277
Hebei, 85, 142, 176, 182, 190, 199, 204, 224, 238, 242–251 *passim*, 286, 343, 364
Hebei Provincial Economic and Trade Committee, 142
Hefei, 199
Heilongjiang, 85, 158, 181, 190, 244–249 *passim*
Heilongjiang River, 99
Hellman, Joel, 14f
Henan, 46, 66, 77, 85, 96, 168, 190, 198, 203, 207, 228, 269
Henan Provincial Transportation Bureau, 197
Heze prefecture, 233
Hierarchy, 5, 98–101 *passim*, 108, 224, 227, 260, 296
Higgs, Robert, 20
Highway Law, 263
Highways, 168, 188f
Hitler, Adolf, 313
Hobbes, Thomas, 313
Holmes, Stephen, 14f
Hong Kong, 94, 113, 184f, 210, 249, 251, 256, 310, 341, 355
Horizon Survey (Group), 178, 184, 254f
Horizontal accountability, 2, 24, 259f, 277f, 289, 291, 305, 363
Hospitals, 49f, 202ff, 241
Household registration, 184
Housing, 210, 248, 255, 275
Housing and Municipal Appearance, 177
Hu Angang, 15
Hu Changqing, 222, 228
Hu Jintao, 19, 45, 66, 90, 131–138 *passim*, 149, 248, 262, 342
Hu Yaobang, 65
Huang Longyun, 176
Huang Ningguo, 155
Huang Zhong, 41
Huangshi Garment Factory, 213
Hubei, 35, 44–47 *passim*, 77, 85, 187, 213, 231, 233, 244, 246, 268, 276
Huizhou, 119
Human rights, 308, 361
Hunan, 85, 148, 226, 246, 269
Huntington, Samuel, 9, 313f

Ideology, 69, 311
Imperialism, 304
Implementation, 170, 183, 207f, 224, 226, 237, 241, 243, 251, 258, 268, 273, 276, 282f, 306f
Implementing Rules for Auditing and Supervising Government Fiscal Revenue and Expenditure, 282
Imports, 115, 122
Incentives, 141, 151, 204, 218, 223–232 *passim*, 239, 243, 251, 264, 277, 292, 295, 301, 304; institutional, 27, 177, 223, 291
Income, 128, 153, 227f, 236, 241, 296, 313; illegitimate, 227
Incrementalism, 237
Independent planning status, 75, 175
India, 13, 85, 251, 256, 291, 361
Individual business, 296
Indonesia, 13, 20, 84, 294
Industrial and Commercial Bank of China (ICBC), 87, 120
Industrialism, 9
Industrialization, 8f, 300, 379
Industrial policy, 40, 62
Industry and Commerce Administration/Bureau, 30, 35, 58, 101, 239, 241, 270. *See also under* State Administrations
Infectious diseases, 99, 171
Inflation, 8, 15, 41, 67–70, 107, 127, 139, 293, 309
Informant, 254
Information, 8, 38, 145, 165, 170f, 192f, 197, 203, 205, 212–215, 253f; false, 248. *See also* Internet
Infrastructure, 8, 52, 57, 176, 178, 188f, 219, 233, 286, 305, 345
Initial public offerings (IPOs), 213ff, 229
Inner Mongolia, 39, 85, 173
Inspection, 39, 113, 124, 189, 206, 225, 227, 231f, 242, 273; accounting, 278
Inspectors, 194,
Inspectors' Office for Major Construction Projects, 196
Institutional changes, 60, 114, 292, 308, 314
Institutional development, 306, 308, 312f
Institutional improvement, 124, 235, 238
Institutional innovations, 17, 153, 172, 186, 294

Institutional integrity, 123, 141, 149
Institutionalization, 200, 207, 211, 268, 275, 284
Institutional reforms, 19, 108, 122, 148, 155, 207f, 215f, 222, 248–258 *passim*, 284, 295ff, 303–309 *passim*
Institutions, 22, 106, 240f, 295
Insurance, 22, 89f, 108, 199, 229, 294
Intellectual Property Bureaus, 45
Interagency office, 146
Interdepartmental working groups, 143
Interest rate, 68, 85
Interests, parochial 57, 117, 157, 263, 299
Interim CCP Regulations on Internal Supervision, 227
Interim Methods for the Administration of Government Procurement, 200
Interim Provisions on Managing Material Purchasing in State-Owned Industrial Enterprises, 201
Interim Regulations on Strengthening Audit Work, 280
Interior, 173, 246
Intermediaries, 51, 144ff, 163, 204, 207
International Covenant on Civil and Political Rights, 308
International Covenant on Social, Economic, and Cultural Rights, 308
International engagements, 307ff
Internet, 165–170 *passim*, 174f, 180, 197, 203, 212, 309, 312. *See also* E-government *and individual web sites*
Inter-party competition, 250
Inter-regional trade, 162
Interstate Commerce commission, 300
Intra-governmental discipline, 305
Intrastate relations, 259
Investigation, 209, 225, 263, 274, 284, 286
Investigation Bureau (Xiamen Customs), 120
Investment, 2, 10, 13, 18, 27, 32, 39f, 53, 62, 67f, 74–79 *passim*, 84, 152f, 158, 161, 167, 173, 175, 219, 294, 296, 305, 307, 311; fixed asset, 68; projects, 176. *See also* Capital construction
Investment companies, 86
Investors, 12, 93, 151, 156, 172f, 185, 213ff, 229, 248, 253
Irregularities, 208, 210, 222, 236, 281. *See also* Fraud

IRS, 234
ISO 9000, 98
Italy, 313

Japan, 19, 85, 191, 291, 303
Ji Shengde, 113, 121
Jia Qinglin, 250, 339
Jia Yongxiang, 366
Jiang Chunyun, 264
Jiang Zemin, 4–8 *passim*, 15, 19–21 *passim*, 27, 36, 45, 58, 65–72 *passim*, 84, 92, 108, 111, 116ff, 125–135 *passim*, 139, 220ff, 248f, 257, 293, 313, 327, 369
Jiangning district, 178
Jiangsu, 30, 47f, 52f, 67, 85, 113f, 172–176 *passim*, 180, 190, 195, 201–206 *passim*, 211, 226, 244, 246, 253, 276, 345, 359
Jiangsu Drug Administration, 101
Jiangxi, 46, 85, 105, 173, 190, 198, 212f, 228
Jiangyin, 52
Jilin, 51, 85, 132, 190, 203, 226, 251, 306
Jinan, 85, 165, 255
Jingmen municipality, 246
Jinhua municipality, 246
Joint venture, 33, 35
Journal of Chinese Law, 363
Judges, 230
Judicial institutions, 27, 47, 118, 125, 127, 133–138 *passim*, 227–230 *passim*, 240, 259–265 *passim*, 288f, 294, 306–309 *passim*,
Jurisdiction, 130, 230ff

Kaili Group, 117
Kangsai Group, 213f
Kleptocracy, 13
Kodak, 115
Kotkin, Stephen, 299
Kunming, 173

Labor, 8, 301, 312
Labor and Social Security, 237
Labor Bureau, 54, 153
Labor unions, 301
Lai Changxing, 113, 120f, 249
Lake Tai, 276
Lan Pu, 120
Land, 19, 23, 187, 151–157 *passim*, 161, 186f, 207–215 *passim*, 218, 258, 274, 290, 305; and corruption, 208, 210, 221; auctions,

208–212 *passim*, 252, 257f, 291; banks, 210f, 258; Hong Kong, 355; revenue, 210f. *See also* Allocation; Resources

Lanzhou, 195

Latin America, 295

Law(s), 66, 99f, 108, 144, 150, 165, 173, 184, 216f, 230–235 *passim*, 250, 252, 262, 266, 268, 276–279 *passim*, 285, 287, 297f, 306f; exam, 146, 269; firms, 129, 147f, 160, 214

Law enforcement, 22, 38f, 50, 77, 97, 102, 112f, 118, 130–135, 153, 173, 189, 243, 257, 262, 265; agencies, 121, 258, departments, 125

Lawmaking, 262f, 268, 273, 280, 288

Law on Certified Accountants, 148

Law on Fisheries, 38

Law on Land Management, 208

Law on Public Tendering and Bidding, 191–196 *passim*, 354

Lawsuit, 93, 206

Leader accountability system, 230

Leasing, 33, 219

Legal entities/persons, 114, 130, 149, 269

Legal information, 166

Legal reforms, 306, 308

Legislation Law, 166, 263

Legislative activism, 273–276 *passim*

Legislative activities, 268

Legislative Affairs Bureau, 262

Legislative oversight, 236, 259–267 *passim*, 272, 278, 288

Legislative process, 263

Legislative-executive relations, 260–276 *passim*

Legislature, 239, 262, 265–268 *passim*, 282–289 *passim*, 299, 306, 308; local, 167, 268, 276, 287, 299; municipal, 272, 276. *See also* People's Congress

Legitimacy, 6, 65, 198, 215, 220, 311

Leizhou, 222

Leninism, 261

Leninist organizational structure, 20

Levies, 152, 173, 176, 209, 235–242 *passim*, 248, 252, 263. *See also* Fees

Li Xiaoyong, 249

Li Changchun, 66, 117, 208, 222, 273, 278

Li Jiating, 219

Li Jinhua, 234, 253, 283–288 *passim*

Li Jizhou, 112, 114, 120

Li Lanqing, 106, 156f

Li Peng, 4, 19, 65–70 *passim*, 108, 249, 261ff, 282–286 *passim*

Li Rongrong, 61

Li Tieying, 35

Li Xiong, 213

Li Yizhong, 61

Li Yuanchao, 177

Liability, 21, 148

Liability insurance, 148

Lianyungang, 113, 172

Liaoning, 35, 85, 117, 202, 209, 246

Liberalization, 108, 218, 220

Liberties, 311, 314

Licenses, 152, 173, 218, 305, 310; marriage, 174. *See also* Administrative approval and licensing

Light Industry, 37

Liming Group, 56

Limited government, 304, 209ff, 326

Lin Shiyuan, 231

Ling Zhijun, 4

Liu Binyan, 15, 120

Liu Huaqing, 131

Liu Jibin, 140

Liu Liying, 225

Liu Mingkang, 90

Liu Weiliu, 242

Liu Zhongli, 72

Local authorities, 143, 151, 156–161 *passim*, 166, 171, 175, 181, 193, 197, 201, 203, 207, 210–215 *passim*, 224, 238–244 *passim*, 280f. *See also* Local governments

Local embededness, 224

Local governments, 11, 142, 192, 195, 204, 214, 231f, 293, 296f, 305f. *See also* Local authorities

Local initiatives, 210, 296, 298

Local interests, 96, 116, 224–227 *passim*, 295

Localism, 5, 9, 278, 324

Localities, 116, 150f, 174, 178, 187–190 *passim*, 204, 222–225 *passim*, 233f, 242–247 *passim*, 258, 268f, 276, 296f, 348, 360

Local officials, 188, 198, 224, 231, 273, 287, 359

Local protectionism, 12, 96, 107f, 163, 225, 281, 292

Local tax bureau, 74ff

London, 107, 230

Long Yongtu, 310

Lottery, 236
Lu Ruihua, 273, 348
Lü, Xiabo, 12–15
Lungang, 46
Luo Bisheng, 269
Luo Gan, 40f, 116
Luo Yicheng, 113

Macroeconomic control, 8, 62, 67–70 *passim*,
    84, 113f, 157, 163, 281
Madison, James, 304
Malfeasance, 202–206 *passim*, 238–241, 247,
    284f
Malpractice, 189, 230
Management, 187, 201f, 213, 215, 226, 230,
    238, 241, 287
Managerial state, 302, 312
Manufacturers, 242
Manufacturing, 96, 232
Mao Zedong, 261, 287; rule of, 9, 117, 313
Maoism, 304
Maoming, 119
Market, 7–15 *passim*, 19, 39, 41, 105ff, 115,
    139ff, 153, 161, 163 183, 193, 203, 208, 214,
    218; designated, 209; failure, 183
Market economy, 2f, 11–15 *passim*, 21, 29, 37,
    42, 126–129 *passim*, 149, 281, 290–295
    passim, 309. *See also* Order, market
Marriage Law, 167
Marxism, 261
Meat Inspection Act, 300
Media, 49, 104, 116, 121, 138, 150–155 *passim*,
    167–173 *passim*, 180, 186, 192, 216, 219, 223,
    249, 265, 274, 277, 288, 313. *See also*
    Internet; Press
Meng Jianzhu, 173
Merger, 46–50 *passim*, 61, 80, 86, 144, 146f
Methods for Hearings on Government Price
    Decisions, 169
Mexico, 85, 256
Mianyang, 156, 305
Microsoft, 106, 336
Military, 5, 12, 16, 22, 27, 36, 52f, 65f, 110–117
    passim, 125–144 *passim*, 202f, 234, 240; and
    Deng, 323; expenditures, 125, 132, 140. *See
    also* People's Liberation Army
Military businesses, 127f, 139–143 *passim*;
    earnings, 134, 290. *See also* AJPG
    businesses

Military intelligence agency, 113
Mining rights, 212
Ministries, 40, 226, 235, 288; industrial, 37f,
    64, 143, 154, 161, 185, 296. *See also*
    individual ministries
Ministry of Agriculture, 38ff, 51, 58, 206
Ministry of Broadcast, Film, and Television,
    38
Ministry of Civil Affairs, 55, 236
Ministry of Commerce, 62, 212
Ministry of Communications, 40, 99, 118,
    188, 195, 196
Ministry of Construction, 40, 51, 104, 106,
    154, 172, 193–198 *passim*, 201, 208
Ministry of Culture, 104
Ministry of Education, 40
Ministry of Electric Power, 42
Ministry of Electronics Industry, 38, 42, 56
Ministry of Finance, 40, 59, 61, 68–72 *passim*,
    75, 79, 86, 93, 100, 144–148 *passim*, 181,
    188–207 *passim*, 232–247 *passim*, 266f,
    284–287 *passim*, 360
Ministry of Foreign Affairs, 40
Ministry of Foreign Trade and Economic
    Cooperation, 39f, 57, 62f, 111, 121, 165, 212
Ministry of Health, 39, 50, 59, 171, 202, 226,
    232, 241f
Ministry of Information Industry (MII), 38,
    42, 56, 58, 167f
Ministry of Justice, 136, 166
Ministry of Labor, 98
Ministry of Labor and Social Security, 40
Ministry of Land and Resources, 40, 51, 99,
    166f, 172, 208–212 *passim*, 232
Ministry of Materials Supply, 29
Ministry of Metallurgical Industry, 154
Ministry of Personnel, 40, 179ff, 233
Ministry of Posts and Telecommunications,
    38, 56
Ministry of Public Security, 77, 118, 128, 134ff,
    169, 180, 184, 229–232 *passim*, 248
Ministry of Railways, 40, 58, 118, 168
Ministry of Science and Technology, 39, 244
Ministry of State Security, 6, 134, 136
Ministry of Supervision, 69, 118, 156, 193–198
    passim, 201f, 208, 210, 225, 232f, 241f, 254,
    278, 284–289 *passim*, 305
Ministry of Water Resources, 39f, 51, 118, 166,
    244f, 285f

MITI (METI), 62
Mobilization capacity, 9
Modernization, 9, 108, 149, 313
Monetary policy, 22, 83, 89f
Money laundering, 228f, 252
Monitoring, 108, 194, 203–206 *passim*,
    226–229 *passim*, 239–247 *passim*, 272, 277,
    281, 288f, 309
Monopolies, 9, 168, 300f, 314
Moscow, 298
Mu Suixin, 208f, 225
Multinational corporations, 106, 175, 255
Municipal Administrative Efficiency
    Supervisory Center, 176
Municipal Complaints Center for
    Administrative Efficiency, 177
Municipal Economic and Trade Bureau, 54
Municipal government, 60, 135, 167–177
    passim, 199, 211, 246, 277; Procurement
    Center, 207
Mussolini, Benito, 313

Nanchang, 173
Nanjing, 85, 167, 176ff, 196f, 212, 253, 255;
    Construction Bureau, 153; Land and
    Resources Bureau, 212
Nanning Intermediate Court, 228
Nanning, 35, 192, 224
Nanping, 194
National Antismuggling Leading Group, 112
National Antismuggling Office, 119
National Audit Office, 24, 94, 195, 202, 208,
    233f, 242, 252, 260, 278–289, 305f, 309. *See
    also* Audit Office
National Conference on Auditing Work, 257;
    on Financial Work, 92; on Quality Work,
    96
National Council of Textile Industry, 213
National Financial Work Commission, 84
National Geographic, 241
National industries, 116
National Party Congress, 5, 7, 19, 35, 61, 66,
    90, 92, 183, 225, 249, 257, 290
National People's Congress (NPC), 24, 36f,
    40f, 60, 64, 78, 101–105 *passim*, 131, 143,
    162, 166, 191f, 200, 205, 208, 219–222
    passim, 231, 235, 237, 256–271 *passim*,
    275–289 *passim*, 306; Budgetary Work
    Committee, 235–239 *passim*, 266f, 364;

delegates, 264–267; Standing Committee,
    101, 191, 262f, 266, 281–289 *passim*, 364
National Receiving Office, 136
Nepotism, 5, 130
Network-based industries, 167
New Deal, 301
New Freedom, 300
Newspapers, 180, 212, 287, 302, 309
New York City, 301
New York Times, 3, 287
Ningbo, 155, 158, 176, 222
Ningxia, 85
Niu Maosheng, 286
Nomenklatura system, 4f
Nomination, 260, 264, 269
Nongovernmental organizations, 95, 245
Nonperforming loans (NPLs), 86–91 *passim*
Nonprofit institutions/organizations, 26, 95,
    157, 233, 241, 280
North America, 205
North Korea, 291
Notaries public, 194, 206

Office equipment, 202f
Office for the Hand-over of Enterprises, *see*
    National Receiving Office
Office of Special Inspectors for Major
    Projects, 188, 195, 197
Oi, Jean, 27
Oil, 62, 111, 115, 119, 297
Olympics, Summer (2008), 196
One-stop service, 153, 172–178 *passim*
Open-market operations, 85
Opinions on Implementing the Reform of
    the Administrative Approval System, 157
Order, economic, 8, 119, 121, 149, 281
Order, market, 41, 65, 94, 95, 100–104 *passim*,
    193
Order, political, 303, 312
Organization Department, 144, 179–182,
    224–227 *passim*, 233
Organizations, 6, 30f, 45, 74, 225f, 285, 295,
    305, 312. *See also* Hierarchy
Oriental Horizon, 354
Overseas investments, 74, 77, 151, 174, 176
Oversight, 264–273 *passim*, 277, 284, 305;
    congressional, 262, 268, 273
Ownership, 74–80 *passim*, 140f, 149, 193

Palace Hotel, 126, 137, 138
Passports, 184
Patronage, 9f, 45, 145, 182f
Payments, 203, 285
Payment Transaction Monitoring
    Department, 229
Payroll, 145, 237, 243, 245
Penalty, 222, 227, 234
Pendleton Act, 183
Peng Zhen, 261
Pension, 34, 245
People's Armed Police, *see* Armed police
People's Bank of China (PBOC), 20, 40–42
    passim, 68, 71, 81–93 *passim*, 108, 143f, 147,
    228f, 242, 244, 281, 284, 294f, 297, 302
People's Congress, 124, 245, 260f, 267–278,
    289, 298f, 301, 308; municipal, 269–273,
    277, 287; provincial, 269, 273f, 289. *See
    also* National People's Congress
People's Daily, 4, 100, 112–116 *passim*, 309
People's Liberation Army (PLA), 5, 16, 21, 118,
    125–142 *passim*, 149, 294. *See also* Military
People's Procuratorate, 245, 261.
Performance, 115, 214, 224, 226, 231–234
    passim, 248, 263, 268f, 283
Personnel, 4f, 66, 153, 179, 182, 226, 230, 243,
    264, 274, 279, 286, 289
Petrochemicals, 115, 122
PetroChina, 33
Pharmaceutical Administration Law, 102f
Pharmaceutical regulation, 55
Philippines, 13, 251
Ping'an Insurance, 199
Pinggu County, 181
Polanyi, Karl, 7, 16, 94, 290, 292
Police, 6, 12, 21f, 27, 47, 52, 110–114 *passim*,
    118–121, 127–138 *passim*, 142, 149, 155, 230,
    232, 236–241 *passim*, 297, 306. *See also*
    Armed police
Political and Economic Risk Consultancy,
    185, 256, 361
Political Bureau, 29, 117, 132f, 220–227
    passim, 250, 270, 282
Political crisis, 273, 292
Political development, 3, 292, 300
Political participation, 301, 311–314 *passim*
Political reform, 250f, 312
Pollution, 274
Poly (Technologies) Group, 59, 126, 140

Port management reforms, 39
Postal savings institutions, 89
Poverty relief funds, 287
Power industry, 59f, 249, 302
Preferential policies/treatment, 10, 79, 132
Press, 171, 196, 217f, 269, 287, 302, 313. *See
    also* Media
Price, 8, 152, 168f, 203, 206–210 *passim*, 215,
    275, 292f, 304; Law, 167
Princeling, 117, 130
Principal-agent relationship, 170, 260, 267
Privatization, de facto, 33, 108
Procurator-general, 221, 266
Procuratorates, 47, 133, 149, 254, 262, 268,
    278; local, 129, 224f, 230, 241, 265
Procuratorial Cadres' School, 129
Procurement, 140, 161, 186, 195–207 *passim*,
    215, 219, 245, 252; weapons, 129
Product Quality Law, 102f
Production safety, 104
Professionalism, 5, 124, 128, 141, 148, 151;
    military, 131
Professional services, 144–149 *passim*
Profits, 87, 111, 122, 127ff, 140, 218, 236
Progressive Era, 9, 104, 292, 299–303
Projects, 23, 153–157 *passim*, 161, 173, 186–198
    passim, 203–207 *passim*, 211, 217, 219, 231,
    237, 239, 252, 254, 280, 287. *See also*
    Bidding; Tendering
Promotion, 208, 219, 226, 230, 234, 247
Propaganda department, 27, 50, 170f
Property rights, 8, 11, 27, 60, 172, 296
Provincial authorities/governments, 34, 44,
    51, 53, 60, 67, 70, 72, 76, 80f, 135f, 146,
    154–158 *passim*, 168–176 *passim*, 184, 190,
    197, 201–204 *passim*, 209, 212, 238, 242,
    273, 275, 306f
Provincial planning commission, 168
Provincial units, 80, 118, 142, 180, 189, 193,
    204, 225, 238, 246, 247, 248; defined, 324
Provisions on Implementing the
    Responsibility System for Improving Party
    Style and Building a Clean Government,
    230
Public auctions, *see* Auctions
Public bidding, *see* Bidding
Public complaints/discontent, 168, 221, 239,
    255, 265, 294. *See also* Complaints
Public confidence, 221, 253, 255

Public evaluations, 269
Public finance, 173, 178
Public goods, 9, 14, 22, 168, 297, 310, 313
Public health, 36, 171, 272, 291, 302f, 311. *See also* Health care
Public notices, 165, 212, 349
Public projects, 48, 186, 212, 252. *See also* Projects
Public hearing, *see* Hearings
Public Security, *see* Police
Public utilities, 39, 300
Publishing houses, 49
Pudong, 159, 305
Punishment, 210, 220, 227–234 *passim*, 242, 269
Purchases, government, *see* Procurement
Pure Food and Drug Act, 300
Putin, Vladimir, 298f

Qianshao, 249
Qian Shi, 261
Qijiang County (Chongqing), 231
Qin Chaozheng, 142
Qingdao, 154, 167, 176, 185, 207
Qinghai, 85
Qinghua, 93
Qu Xulu, 242
Quality, 96, 187ff, 231, 247, 265, 302, 305
Quality Administration, 98–104. *See also* Quality; State Administration of Quality
Quality and Technical Supervision Bureau, 22, 153
Quality brands Protection Committee, 336
Quotas, 69, 76, 187, 212f, 218, 239f, 243

Railway projects, 195
Rainbow Bridge, 187, 188, 191, 231
Rationalization, 20, 25, 35, 42, 60, 65, 70, 97, 144–152 *passim*, 185f, 259, 290
Raw materials, 10, 29, 62, 201
Real estate, 8, 68f, 152–155, 159, 208f, 219, 232, 236, 286
Real names, 228f,
Rear services, 52f
Recruitment, 180ff
Red tape, 184, 305
Redistributive policy, 69
Reform Commission/Office, 62, 213, 226
Reformers, 4, 14, 169f, 192, 307

Reforms, 14, 20f, 33–37 *passim*, 51, 69, 86f, 100, 202; partial, 3, 8, 10, 14, 21, 29ff, 126. *See also* Reconstructuring
Regional disparities/differences, 184, 310
Regional protectionism, 97
Regulation, 146f, 159, 165, 182–185 *passim*, 194, 201–213 *passim*, 217, 227–241 *passim*, 246, 252, 268, 274ff, 284, 287, 291, 300, 302, 306f
Regulations for Selecting and Appointing Leading Party and Government Cadres, 182
Regulations for the Discussion, Approval, and Supervision of Budgets in Guangdong, 275
Regulations on Countering Money Laundering by Financial Institutions, 229
Regulations on Discussing and Deciding on Major Issues, 274
Regulations on Emergency Public Health Cases, 171
Regulations on Government Information Disclosure, 169
Regulations on Managing the Stock Exchanges, 91f
Regulators, 143, 148, 154, 167, 208, 211
Regulatory agencies/institutions, 64, 66, 94, 109, 239, 291–296 *passim*, 308
Regulatory authority, 50, 92, 96ff, 130, 183, 259, 305; fragmentation, 63
Regulatory state, 9, 22, 41, 58, 106–111 *passim*, 129, 139, 142, 296, 300
Rent-seeking, 27, 43, 152, 154, 161, 172f, 184, 199, 211, 218, 243f, 297
Reorganization, 77, 144, 219, 246, 305
Research and Development, 50, 129
Research institutes, 49, 254
Reserves, 210
Resettlement, 244, 285, 287
Resignation, 231, 234, 276
Resolution on Strengthening the Examination and Supervision of the Central Government Budget, 267
Resources, 161, 258, 274
Responsibility, 189, 199, 230, 232, 250. *See also* Accountability
Restructuring, 58, 61, 66, 85, 225, 294. *See also* Reforms
Retirement, 42, 233, 234, 275
Revenue, 10, 15, 31, 43, 63, 72f, 78, 80, 87, 94,

115f, 139, 141, 145, 208–211 *passim*, 215, 235–244 *passim*, 271, 279f, 293, 296; customs, 112f, 122. *See also* Extra-budget funds/revenue; Tax revenue
Ring Road project, 195
Rip van Winkle, 290
Roosevelt, Franklin D., 301
Roosevelt, Theodore, 300
Root, Hilton, 13ff
Roving inspection team, 357
Rule of law, 250, 261, 306, 310
Rule of minimalism, 163
Rules of Procedure, 273
Rural credit cooperatives, 89, 91
Rural tax and fees, 48
Russia, 5, 15, 24, 65, 256, 291f, 295, 298f, 303, 367f

Safety, 54, 99, 104, 231; maritime, 22
Salary, 226, 245, 275
Sanjiu (999) Group, 126, 140f
Sarbanes-Oxley Act, 148
SARS, 1f, 20, 36, 105, 164, 169–171 *passim*, 232, 290f, 302f, 308
Scandal, 201–204 *passim*, 208, 214, 222, 233, 244, 248, 253, 270
School teachers, 245
Schools, 47–55 *passim*, 202
Schumpeter, Joseph, 2
Securities, 89–92 *passim*, 108, 147, 186f, 207, 213, 218, 229, 294, 303, 233; Law, 92f, 160, 214, 262. *See also* Stocks.
Service-orientated government, 172, 184
Services, 126, 145, 150, 165–168, 172–178 *passim*, 184, 200–203 *passim*, 297
Shaanxi, 85, 182, 190, 245f, 270; Huanglong county, 31, 41
Shandong, 46f, 51, 75, 77, 85, 99, 101, 117, 154, 159, 195, 204, 211, 233, 246f
Shanghai, 30, 35, 39f, 44, 67, 77, 85, 92, 124, 158f, 165, 173–178 *passim*, 185, 191, 199–204 *passim*, 209–212 *passim*, 221, 255f, 270, 276, 310
Shanghai Municipal People's Congress, 270
Shanghai Stock Exchange, 214, 335
Shanghai Tangible Construction Market, 191
Shantou, 155, 224
Shanxi, 50, 85, 128, 190, 244, 251, 348
Shao Ning, 202

Shareholders, 214
Shenyang, 13, 85, 155, 178, 202, 208f, 219, 222, 234, 248, 255, 269, 276f
Shenyang Intermediate People's Court, 276, 366
Shenzhen, 30, 54, 60, 77, 92, 119, 152f, 159, 165, 172–175 *passim*, 195–199 *passim*, 207–211 *passim*, 215, 224f, 239, 253, 256, 268, 276, 305
Shenzhen Bureau for Production Safety, 54
Shenzhen Chengjian Group, 120
Shenzhen Construction Investment Holdings Company, 60
Shenzhen Customs, 119
Shenzhen Donghu Water Plant, 351
Shenzhen Investment Management Corporation, 60
Shenzhen Municipal People's Congress, 194, 225, 276
Shenzhen Party Committee, 225
Shenzhen SEZ Regulations on Tendering and Bidding for Construction Projects, 194
Shenzhen State Asset Committee, 60
Shenzhen Trade and Commerce Investment Company, 60
Sherman Anti-Trust Act of 1890, 300
Shi Zhaobin, 121, 222
Shijiazhuang, 176
Shirk, Susan, 11, 261
Shishi, 31
Shiye danwei, 22, 26, 49–54 *passim*, 64, 157, 230, 238, 245
Shock therapy, 297f
Shouzhi liangtiao xian, 240–243
Shue, Vivienne, 13
Shunde, 35, 185
Shuyang County, 180
Sichuan, 45f, 53, 85, 156, 195, 198, 203, 213, 246, 305
Sichuan Provincial People's Procuratorate, 129
Sihui, 274
Simon, Herbert, 22
Sinclair, Upton, 97, 302
Singapore, 6, 153, 185, 251, 256
Smuggling, 2, 19–23 *passim*, 110–125 *passim*, 129–133 *passim*, 139, 141, 148ff, 217, 222, 231, 249, 253, 294
Smuggling Investigation Bureau, 122
Socialism, 7, 293

Social organizations, 49, 83, 200, 312
Social protests, 220ff, 301
Social security, 64, 236, 242, 272
Social welfare, 248, 255, 272
Song Defu, 37, 53, 172, 310
South China Morning Post, 287
South China Sea Fleet, 113
Southeast Asia, 34
Southern Weekend, 171
South Korea, 6, 20, 84, 256, 294, 356
Soviet Union, 1, 14, 20, 65, 71f, 171, 293, 297f, 312
Special development zones, 153
Special economic zones (SEZs), 153, 176f, 291, 305
Spending, 236, 239, 271f, 296
Spring Festival, 168
Stability, 4, 6, 67, 149, 296, 311f
Staff, 74, 230, 285
Standardized receipts, 241
Standard Oil Company, 300
Standards, 102f, 158, 241
State, 63, 116, 133, 218, 220, 290
State Administrations: Coal Industry, 99; Coal Mine Safety Supervision, 55, 99, 105; Environmental Protection, 95, 98, 100, 166, 302; Exit-entry Inspection and Quarantine; (Food and) Drug, 55, 60, 95, 98, 102f, 226, 302; Industry and Commerce (SAIC), 59, 95, 121, 128f, 152, 155, 226, 241; Light industry, 118; Metallurgical Industry, 118; Petroleum and Chemical Industry, 38; Press and Publications, 95, 207; Quality and Technical Supervision, 39, 95, 97, 302; Radio, Film, and Television (SARFT), 118; Sport, 236; Taxation, 74–79 *passim*, 146, 232, 244; Textile Industry, 42; Workplace Safety Supervision, 55, 95, 99, 105
State assets, 59ff, 107, 212, 219, 242, 248
State Bureau of Surveying and Mapping, 51
State-business relations, 18, 29, 186, 291
State Commission for National Defense Science, Technology, and Industry, 136
State Council, 17–22 *passim*, 26, 39, 43, 48, 52–62 *passim*, 68f, 79, 84, 92–98 *passim*, 105, 117, 124, 127, 133–138 *passim*, 143–146 *passim*, 156ff, 162, 166, 171, 189, 191, 201,

205, 210, 228–236 *passim*, 241–244 *passim*, 252, 265ff, 271, 279–288 *passim*, 294, 306
State Council Development Research Center, 89, 96
State Council General Office, 42f, 236
State Council Informatization Office, 175
State Council Leadership Small Group on the Reform of the System of Administrative Approvals, 156
State Council Leading Group on Improving and Rectifying Social Intermediary Organizations, 146
State Council Office of Legal Affairs, 162, 169, 244
State Council Regulations on Information Transparency, 171
State Council Securities Committee, 91
State Council Three Gorges Construction Committee, 194
State Development and Reform Commission (SDRC), 62, 64, 95, 152, 208
State Development Bank, 180
State Development Planning Commission (SDPC), 37, 40ff, 56ff, 62f, 152, 158, 167ff, 188–202 *passim*, 232; Special Inspector's Office, 189
State Economic and Trade Commission (SETC), 37–42 *passim*, 49, 51, 55–60 *passim*, 201f, 213, 248; Department of Enterprise Reforms, 202
State Economic System Reform Commission, 62
State entrepreneurship, 11
State enterprises, *see* State-owned Enterprises
State Ethnic Affairs Commission, 40
State exchequer, 244f
State expenditure, 30
State Family Planning Commission, 40
State Food and Drug Administration, *see under* State administrations
State Grain Bureau, 244
State granaries, 244
State Information Center, 49
State institutions, 47, 112, 129ff, 139, 141, 148, 217, 227, 289–296 *passim*
State Intellectual Property Office, 95
State Natural Science Foundation, 244
State-owned Assets Supervision and

Administration Commission (SASAC), 60ff, 95, 144
State-owned (or controlled) enterprises (SOEs), 4, 8, 10, 21, 25–34 *passim*, 41, 52–65 *passim*, 80, 115, 140–143 *passim*, 148, 166, 201f, 213f, 219, 230, 233, 248, 278, 280, 285; sale of, 157. *See also* Privatization
State Planning Commission, *see* State Development Planning Commission
State Power Corporation, 33, 37, 42, 249, 286
State Secrets Bureau, 169
State sector, 18, 21, 32, 34, 62, 67, 296
State Seismological Bureau, 51
State-society relations, 43, 45, 185, 291, 312
State Statistical Bureau, 31, 68, 94, 361
State Tax Administration Information System, 77
State Taxation Bureau, 75, 80, 100
Steel, 57, 231
Stocks, 8, 23, 33, 69, 79, 88–92 *passim*, 154, 161, 186, 207, 213ff, 229, 252, 285, 305
Student demonstrations, 7, 220, 311
Subcontracting, 190
Sub-provincial governments, 47, 51, 81, 176, 211, 310
Substandard products, 106
Suggestions for Using Competition for Positions in Party and Government Agencies, 179
Suharto, 12, 84
Sun, Yan, 223
Sun Zhigang, 368
Sunshine Group, 195
Supervision, 108, 201–204, 224–230 *passim*, 238–241 *passim*, 247f, 257, 262–266 *passim*, 270f, 288, 306–310 *passim*; financial, 19, 84, 196, 242, 278, 284; legislative, 262, 276f
Supervision Bureau, 45, 177, 226
Supreme People's Court, 93, 129, 134, 136, 221, 227, 230, 257–267 *passim*, 307
Supreme People's Procuratorate, 129, 134, 136, 180, 221–227 *passim*, 231, 257, 264ff
Suqian municipality, 180, 349
Suzhou, 77, 153, 172f, 185, 256, 305

Taft, William Howard, 300
Taiwan, 6, 253
Tang Bingquan, 274
Tanner, Murray Scot, 262, 264

Tatarstan, 298
Tax, 59, 72–81 *passim*, 87, 92, 107, 113, 115, 129, 142, 146, 151, 228, 231, 244, 266, 286, 293–298 *passim*; assignment system, 70–74 *passim*, 296; collection, 19, 74–77 *passim*, 105, 127; evasion 19, 76f, 228; payer, 76, 77, 172; reforms, 20, 22, 34, 75–83 *passim*, 140
Tax administration (bureaus), 47, 74–78 *passim*, 107, 146, 154, 229
Tax Collection and Administration Law, 76
Tax incentives (exemptions, privileges, rebates, reductions), 10, 51, 69, 73f, 78f, 130, 151, 298, 305
Tax revenue, 70, 76, 92, 96, 115, 127. *See also* Revenue
Technology, 122, 245, 258, 300
Telecommunications, 58f, 130, 138, 149, 165–168 *passim* 302; Law, 56
Telephone hotline, 168
Televised trials, 231
Tendering, 191–196 *passim*, 200f, 208–215 *passim*, 231, 252. *See also* Bidding
Terrorism, 229, 313
Textiles, 35, 37
Thailand, 84
Thatcher, Margaret, 107, 215
The Economist, 302
The Great Transformation, 292
The Reach of the State, 13
Third Front Program, 141
Three Gorges Dam, 194, 196, 244, 285, 287
Tian Fengshan, 249
Tian Jiyun, 101
Tiananmen, 1–6 *passim*, 20, 65f, 71, 107, 127, 220, 250, 261, 280, 311f
Tiandu Realty Company, 129
Tianjin, 44, 77, 85, 90, 124
Tibet, 85, 172
Totalistic government, 309f
Township and village enterprises (TVEs), 11, 15, 47
Townships, 48, 242, 267
Toyota Land Cruisers, 114
Trade, 8, 112, 141, 165; foreign, 62, 130, 151, 165f
Trading companies, 116, 121
Transactions, 209, 214, 228f, 252
Transfer, 49, 116, 234
Transfer payments, 73, 81, 115, 238, 298

Transition, 27f, 54ff, 127, 225, 292, 306, 312

Transparency, 23, 55, 77ff, 93, 124, 150, 163–174 *passim*, 178–187 *passim*, 192–196 *passim*, 201, 203, 209–217 *passim*, 238f, 244, 252, 267, 273, 285, 291, 302–308 *passim*, 314.

Transparency International, 251, 255f

Transport/Transportation, 64, 79, 123, 128, 168, 239, 196f, 244, 275; bureau, 231, 273

Treisman, Daniel, 298

Trust and investment sector, 84, 86

Twenty-first Century Global Report, 171

Underdevelopment, 36, 44, 307

Underwood Tariff Act of 1913, 300

Underwriters, 214

Unemployment, 18, 34, 221, 255, 275, 277, 296, 303, 312; insurance, 275; payment, 34; system, 303

Unilever, 106

United Front Department, 118

UN Convention against Corruption, 308

United States, 9, 24, 58, 80, 85, 97, 104, 145, 152, 185, 205, 229, 250, 292, 297–303 *passim*, 308, 359

U.S. Constitution, 299; Seventeenth Amendment, 368

U.S. Securities and Exchange Commission, 94

U.S. Senate, 299

Universities, 41f, 49–52 *passim*

Unlimited government, 309

Urban management, 50, 240, 243

Urban neighborhood, 166, 274

Urban planning, 209

Urbanization, 8, 300, 311, 370

Utilities, 167, 223

Value-added tax, 73, 76–79 *passim*, 115. *See also* Tax

Vehicle, 79, 184, 212, 244, 263

Vertical administration, *see* Administration, Vertical

Vertical control, 99

Veteran Cadres' Group, 129

Veto, 100

Viability, 297

Vice presidency, 260, 264

Village elections, 301

Village enterprise, *see* TVEs

Vogel, Steven, 161

Votes, negative, 264

Walder, Andrew, 27

Wall Street Journal, 250f

Wan Li, 261

Wang Baosen, 270

Wang Hai, 302

Wang Hongming, 56

Wang Huaizhong, 249

Wang Ju, 209, 225

Wang Ke, 129, 133ff

Wang Leyi, 119

Wang Mengkui, 127

Wang Qishan, 66, 117, 222

Wang Shaoguang, 15

Wang Xuebing, 86f, 144, 249, 287

Wang Yuanhua, 144

Wang Zhongyu, 43

Wang Zikui, 274

Water works, 39, 189f, 195, 197, 285f

Weber, Max, 13

Web sites, *see* Internet

Wei Jianxing, 191, 225, 254

Welfare, 66, 82, 142

Wen Jiabo, 19, 25, 60, 90, 171, 194, 307

Western Railway Station, 188, 350

Whistleblowers, 253

Wiebe, Robert H., 8

Wilson, Woodrow, 301

Wire transfer, 245

Women, 301, 312. *See also* All China Women's Federation

Wong, Christine, 27

Woodrow Wilson, 300

Workplace safety, 60

Work style, 220, 226

World Bank, 10f, 188, 198

Worldcom, 9

World Health Organization, 308

World Trade Organization (WTO), 18, 23, 39, 56–58 *passim*, 62f, 88, 103f, 145, 149, 151, 156, 158, 161–165 *passim*, 169, 185, 205, 252, 297, 303, 307–310 *passim*; Accession Protocol, 165

World War I, 301

Wu Bangguo, 97, 98

Wu, Harry, 313

Wu Wenying, 213, 214
Wu Yi, 119
Wu Yubo, 120
Wuhan, 35f, 85, 195, 255, 276f
Wuhan Guolu, 35
Wuhan Municipal People's Congress, 269, 276
Wuxi, 196
www.ccgp.gov.cn, 203
www.chinabidding.com.cn, 192, 203
www.jdzfcg.com, 203

Xi Jinping, 310
Xiaguan District (Nanjing), 174
Xiamen, 13, 112f, 119–122 *passim*, 178, 196, 207, 222, 224, 234, 248, 253, 361
Xiamen Customs Office, 120
Xiamen municipal party committee, 120
Xi'an, 255
Xiang Huaicheng, 146, 200
Xiangfan, 187
Xiao Yang, 265
Xicheng District, 181
Xihua County, 269
Xinguoda Futures, 249
Xinjiang, 85, 156, 244
Xu Guanhua, 51
Xu Penghang, 213f
Xue Muqiao, 70

Yang Fan, 12
Yang Jingyu, 283
Yang Qianxian, 120
Yang Shangjin, 120
Yangtze Bridge project, 197
Yao Yilin, 70
Ye Jianying, 117
Ye Jichen, 120
Ye Xuanning, 117
Yeltsin, Boris, 14, 65, 223, 298f
Yichun city, 173
Yinchuan Guangxia Company, 147
Youth Reference, 171
Yu Fei, 222
Yuanhua Group, 120, 122f, 339
Yueyang, 269
Yugoslavia, 297

Yunnan, 85, 173, 219, 244, 248

Zaozhuang municipality, 247
Zhan Shuangding, 178
Zhang Aiping, 126
Zhang Gaoli, 159, 211
Zhang Kaike, 231
Zhang Kexiao, 358
Zhang Kuntong, 228
Zhang Wannian, 134
Zhang Wenkang, 202
Zhang Yongding, 120
Zhang Youcai, 145
Zhang Yuren, 213
Zhang Zhijian, 36
Zhangping city, 253
Zhangzhou Hospital, 195
Zhanjiang, 111, 119, 222
Zhanjiang Customs, 112f, 119
Zhao Xiangzhong, 231
Zhao Yucun, 119
Zhao Ziyang, 3f, 6, 65, 250
Zhejiang, 47, 77, 85, 101, 155, 175, 183f, 196, 203f, 206, 210f, 246, 310
Zhengming, 249
Zhengwu gongkai, 124, 166, 174
Zhengzhou Baiwen, 94, 148
Zhengzhou, 255
Zhiqing quan, 169
Zhishu jigou, 46, 95
Zhong Guoxing, 12
Zhongguancun Science and Technology Park, 155
Zhongshan Hotel Group, 52
Zhongtianqin, 147
Zhou Enlai, 287
Zhou Xiaochuan, 93f
Zhou Xuehua, 228
Zhou Zhengyi, 209
Zhu Rongji, 17–20 *passim*, 25, 36f, 45, 53, 58ff, 66, 68, 72, 79, 83, 96, 105, 108, 111, 114, 117ff, 125, 128, 132ff, 138, 150, 194, 199, 205, 235, 249, 256f, 263f, 281–284, 294, 303
Zhu Xiaohua, 86
Zhuang Rushun, 120
Zhuhai, 176–181 *passim*